# CRISIS OF STATE AND NATION

## SOUTH ASIAN STATES BETWEEN NATION-BUILDING AND FRAGMENTATION

# CRISIS OF STATE AND NATION

*South Asian States Between*
*Nation-Building and Fragmentation*

*Edited by*

JOHN P. NEELSEN AND DIPAK MALIK

MANOHAR
2007

First published 2007

© Individual contributors, 2007

ISBN 81-7304-731-6

The publication has been partly financed
by Indian Association for Canadian Studies

*Published by*

Ajay Kumar Jain for
Manohar Publishers & Distributors
4753/23 Ansari Road, Daryaganj
New Delhi 110 002

*Typeset at*

Digigrafics
New Delhi 110 049

*Printed at*

Lordson Publishers Pvt. Ltd.
Delhi 110 007

*Distributed in South Asia by*
**FOUNDATION**
**B ● ● K S**

4381/4, Ansari Road
Daryaganj, New Delhi 110 002
and its branches at Mumbai, Hyderabad,
Bangalore, Chennai, Kolkata

# Contents

6                                    *Contents*

# Contributors

GIL DARYN, British Academy Post-doctoral Fellow, Dept. of Anthropology, School of Oriental and African Studies, London/ UK

SIRI GAMAGE, Senior Lecturer, School of Professional Development, University of New England, Armitage/Australia

BJÖRN HETTNE, Professor, Dept. of Peace and Development Research, Göteborg University/Sweden

RAJESH KHARAT, Reader, Dept. of Politics, University of Mumbai/ India

NANI GOPAL MAHANTA, Rotary World Peace Scholar Lecturer, Dept. of Political Science, Gauhati University/India

DIPAK MALIK, Professor, Dept. of Commerce, Banaras Hindu University, and Director, Gandhian Institute of Studies, Varanasi/ India

B.V. MURALIDHAR, Associate Professor of Political Science and Public Administration, Srivenkateswara University, Tirupati/India

JOHN P. NEELSEN, Professor, Dept. of Sociology, Tuebingen University/Germany

DIETMAR ROTHERMUND, Professor (Emeritus), South Asia Institute, Heidelberg University/Germany

REHMAN SOBHAN, Professor, Chairman, Centre for Policy Dialogue, and Director, South Asia Centre for Policy Studies, Dhaka/Bangladesh

DIETHELM WEIDEMANN, Professor (Emeritus), Humboldt University, Berlin/Germany

HIROICHI YAMAGUCHI, Professor (Emeritus), Bunkyo University/ Japan

CHAPTER 1

# Introduction: South Asia— Social Fragmentation and Political Crisis in the Periphery

*John P. Neelsen and Dipak Malik*

## AN OVERVIEW

The post-Independence period, aimed at building a modern industrial society with a strong centralized state as its pivot has obviously come to an end. The task of creating a common national identity around the core values of democracy, secularism, economic development and social justice superseding the multitude of primordial, rather localized, groups based on caste, ethnicity, language or religion, has failed. If not the paradigm as a whole, at least the state in its intended functions, its role and legitimacy has been put into question. The future seems to hold not only growing inequalities and conflicts, the geo-political map of South Asia may even be redrawn.

The challenge of Maoist guerrillas in Nepal, the rise of Islamic fundamentalism accompanied by a military dictatorship in Pakistan, the civil war in Sri Lanka threatening to split the country apart, the Hindu-Muslim confrontation in India together with government sponsored 'cultural nationalism' are—in spite of all the divergencies—the manifest symptoms of a general turning point in the history and the polities of the societies in the sub-continent.

South Asia is limping back to a phase of reconstruction particularly after the hustings of 2004 in India. A new polity is being crafted ushering in the formation of broad-based coalition governments. The trajectory adopted in the post-colonial, post-World War II period seems to have reached an exhaustion point.

If not addressed, it may lead the merely looming crisis to burst out into the open. The scaffold on which the state, economy and society were made to stand until now has come to be vigorously contested. The crisis lurks behind the superstructural arrangements with its heady mix of organic and inorganic processes in the society. The institutional architecture that was essentially put in place six decades ago and comprised the economy, the polity and society, has largely failed to achieve the major goal of nation-building. Yet, it remains an open question whether it failed because it was an exogenous process as claimed by post-colonial historiography or whether it failed due to deficits in management and in socio-political engineering.

In varying degrees, coalition politics has come to stay in the parliamentary as much as in the extra-parliamentary realm of South Asian politics. At face value, this augurs well for the subcontinent since coalition politics in the classical sense of the term means a mutually agreed upon political line represented by a united movement that has been forged out of diversity. In practice, however, the countries of South Asia present a heterogeneous profile of coalition politics. In fact, many do not fit into a democratic representational mode offering different permutations and combinations amongst the treasury benches as well as among the opposition. Thus, in India a United Progressive Alliance (UPA) has been cobbled together with the left supporting the government from the outside. This backing is, moreover, conditional on progress in implementing a 'common minimum programme'—whose significance and content is detailed by Yamaguchi—and otherwise guided by the merit of the issues involved. It is a new mode of loose coalition based on a modus operandi where the actors have the freedom to influence and back as much as to differ and oppose government policies. Similarly in Nepal, where a seven party alliance that includes apart from the two Congress parties and the Marxist left even the revolutionary outfit of the Maoists, has entered into negotiations for eventually instituting a democratic system. It is good news that the global movement for democracy should take note of. For, it gives the lie to cherished cold war formulas and hostilities on which conservative forces of feudalism and reaction have prospered at the expense of the division and the woes of the people. As to Pakistan, its state and society stand on precarious grounds with its traditional religious foundation having been transformed into a major bastion of religious fundamentalism and terrorism during Gen. Zia-ul-Haq's regime backed by the US. At present an important movement aiming at a realignment in the military and the political quarters has been launched trying to cleanse the state, if not the society of the heavy tag of fundamentalism. Even in Bhutan, as the contribution by Kharat details, steps towards democratization of society and state have recently been initiated. The only exception in the subcontinent's landscape is Sri Lanka with its blend of coalitional politics, intermittent warfare and ceasefire, and outside interventions. These few illustrations indicate that nation-building is anything but a linear movement, but rather a process that has to go through a maze of cross-currents before reaching some conscious conclusions. Coalitional politics play an essential role in this process once the momentum of the early independence phase is lost. For, coalition-building and nation-building based on the integration and growing participation of erstwhile marginalized forces in formal representative democracy are important destinations and go hand in hand in the search of a new consensus.

The present volume analyses various dimensions of the problems involved. Regional systematic overviews followed by empirical case studies of particular groups, of countries, of manifestations of crisis, form the basis for theoretical conclusions. The book assembles twelve individual papers covering altogether six countries of the region, i.e. Nepal and Bhutan, Pakistan and Bangladesh, India and Sri Lanka. The authors approach their subject from the vantage point of different disciplines, i.e. history, economics, political science, anthropology, and sociology. The same diversity holds for the political inclinations of the individual contributions inevitable in studies on on-going struggles that include armed confrontations, even civil wars, and demands for secession.

The common focus is on crisis, of which very different forms are identified: of the nation, of the state, of the regime, of the society, of the system as a whole. Crises vary in depth and seriousness, from temporary to prolonged, from the crisis of a particular political regime to a systemic or structural one. Certain crises are remediable within the existing socio-political system, others result from a failure of a whole development model because of general inadequacies and/or of unintended consequences unleashing forces that eventually cannot be accommodated within the system. In either case, easy short-term solutions may not be in sight.

Crisis as point of reference demands a historical perspective taking into account, where necessary, the colonial legacy to understand the forces that moulded society.

The subsequent remarks attempt first to isolate major concepts employed in the different contributions, followed by an identification of principal tendencies concerning the social and political developments in the region. General conclusions together with theoretical concepts and explanatory theses on the origin of the crises are formulated, embedded and based as it were on a summary of the individual contributions.

## COMMON TRAITS

The subcontinent is characterized by an extreme diversity in practically every respect. The countries covered vary in terms of population from 1 million to 1.1 billion; in per capita income from one of the poorest in the world (Nepal $260) to one which has crossed the line to middle income countries (Sri Lanka $1100); from a mini-state of the Fourth World (Bhutan) to the emerging global power and future's most populous state in the world, India. The same holds as to ethnic and cultural aspects: from rather homogeneous Bangladesh to the very heterogeneous India, Nepal, or Sri Lanka. A similar variety is observed as to the nature or ideological foundation of the state ranging as it were from Buddhist Bhutan, Islamic Pakistan and Hinduist Nepal over semi-secular Sri Lanka to secular India. And, while multi-ethnicity is the norm, the constitutional arrangements differ greatly: from centralized unitary states to federal systems, from kingdoms with substantial royal power (Nepal, Bhutan) over military regimes (Pakistan) to multi-party democracies (Bangladesh, India, Sri Lanka).[1]

However different, the countries share some common traits impacting on politico-economic developments:

- A growing population putting great pressure on the labour market.
- Growing socio-economic inequality combined with rising aspirations among the ever higher educated people, an expanding middle class and emerging neo-bourgeoisie.
- A growing assertiveness and clamour for equal social and economic participation by the traditionally underprivileged, and by ethnic groups.
- A rise of ethno-nationalism frequently in conjunction with majority politics.

The nations that were formally part of British India, all started their road into independence on the premise of secularism, democracy, and social justice. Led by elites groomed in the spirit of European enlightenment, of liberalism and parliamentarianism, they wanted to modernize their societies, rid them of feudal traits in social structure, values and belief systems while simultaneously industrializing them with the objective to catch up as quickly as possible with the West. The West defined progress and provided at the same time the model to be followed to escape from underdevelopment. The colonial state with its administrative and security apparatus, including most of its personnel, endured. The political institutions were typically modelled after the British system. The same holds for the constitutions some of which had even been drawn up during colonial days. Within this institutional framework, the government, having changed into the hands of an indigenous leadership, was typically charged with building the state and the nation, and steer the drive for rapid economic development.

## TENSIONS AND AREAS OF CONFLICT

The decades since Independence have, however, witnessed developments quite different from what had been envisaged by the fathers of independence.

The case studies identify various forms of crises and areas of profound and lasting conflict. They concern in particular the nature of the state (secular, religious), the question of an inclusive national identity in the face of ethno-cultural heterogeneity (Bhutan, Sri Lanka), they arise from the pressure of modernization (indigenous peoples in north-east India). Other problems relate to the political regime and its legitimacy (Nepal, Pakistan), and to the functioning of democratic political institutions (Bangladesh, Sri Lanka, India). Finally, the stability, if not the survival of the state, is called into doubt faced as it were with growing internal conflicts (Sri Lanka, Pakistan, India, Nepal). Confronted with a deep-seated socio-economic and political crisis, a few contributions eventually wonder at least indirectly as to the appropriateness of the basic concepts and strategies of development that have been pursued since Independence (Nepal, India, Pakistan, Sri Lanka).

According to our case studies, problems have arisen particularly in the following areas:

- *The nature and ideological foundation of the state:* with the exception of the two Himalayan kingdoms which had from the very beginning a specific cultural-religious basis, and Pakistan faced with the task of creating a state and forging a national identity based on Islam, all others were originally conceived as secular democratic republics. The general consensus on these principles has in the course of time been eroded. Communalism, or an exclusive cultural nationalism has been on the rise. The neutrality of the state as enshrined in the principle of secularism has been denounced as operating objectively in favour of minority communities. Typically, demands for a re-foundation of the state in line with the identity of the majority have been raised.
- *Majority minority relations:* all South Asian countries are multi-ethnic, multi-cultural societies. The individual ethnic groups have often had quite distinct histories and were formally moulded together only in modern times. United from above essentially for the purpose of governance (typically first under British colonial rule), common administrative measures and legal regulations remained superficial and had little impact on the configuration of

society. With a nation-wide division of labour and a national identity emerging only partially and slowly, the exigencies of the central state were considered by quite a few sub-national communities as imposed and rejected as alien. Where, furthermore, the post-Independence ruling elite essentially originated from the same ethnic group, primary collective identities were strengthened as were traditional value systems and social relations. Majority rule compounded by a unitary state frequently added to the feeling of foreign rule, of belonging for ever to a marginalized and discriminated minority.

- *Democratic rule and democratization:* more than a question of type of government, ranging from royal power over military rule to multi-party parliamentary democracy, questions have been raised as to the political system in its entirety, i.e. the division and independence of powers, the question of federalism *vs* unitary state, the role of civil society, including trade unions, the media, NGOs, etc., and the role of the state.
- *Conflict constellation and conflict management:* different types of social conflict have emerged ranging from regional-ethnic over religious to class conflicts.

The following general long-term tendencies have been observed:

- Despite the domination of bourgeois institutions and a market economy, a class configuration along the line of classical (metropolitan) capitalism superseding traditional primary group identities, such as caste, region, ethnicity, culture or religious affiliation, has not emerged. The latter have not disappeared, but have been reconstituted in new forms as major pressure groups.
- Universal franchise and regular elections have not led to democratic, transparent and responsive representative government. On the contrary, the ruling elite has become ever more entrenched and alienated from the general population.
- Political power and the state have become more and more

appropriated for particularistic ends, i.e. privatized for the benefit of the political elite, and/or instrumentalized by the majority. The state is less an instrument of the bourgeoisie to realize societal goals but a business venture to acquire booty.

- Everywhere there is a trend towards majoritarian rule in conjunction with authoritarian government, most explicit in long lasting periods of emergency and military regimes.
- Communalism or ethno-nationalism has come to dominate 'nation-building'. In contrast to an all-encompassing, socially inclusive ideology, ethno-nationalism values the organic or ascribed membership in a primordial group; because of this principal exclusivity it carries racist overtones. Being the opposite of a democratic nationalism that by necessity is secular and leaves space for diversity, it bears the seeds of communal conflict.
- The state—increasingly less able to fulfil its basic functions of security—loses its overall legitimacy. In addition, violence is no longer a prerogative of the state, but is privatized and has become a wide-spread means of conflict regulation whether in politics, in business or in private affairs. Political parties use it as favourite means of political mobilization and competition.

## ETHNIC HETEROGENEITY AND CONSTITUTIONS

Before entering into a debate over how to avoid or minimize ethno-cultural conflicts, a sociological distinction carrying important legal implications is in order:

- *Migrant populations:* In Bhutan the question of the citizenship of former Tibetan refugees and earlier Nepalese migrants has been raised manifestly in the context of the cultural identity of the state, implicitly for reasons of political participation and allegiance and eventually also for reasons of economic competition. Backed up by weak administrations, and insufficient birth and residency records, the government of Bhutan—as independent Ceylon in 1948[2]—questions the citizenship rights of certain groups of its inhabitants treating them as foreign nationals or stateless persons who may even be expelled. An internationalization of the issue at least in terms of bilateral negotiations between the states directly concerned, here Bhutan and Nepal, then India and Sri Lanka, is almost inevitable.

- The Indian or estate Tamils in Sri Lanka reveal another specific trait: they represent an ethnically distinct *underclass* of immigrant workers who have been discriminated against for a long time. After decades of statelessness and without any social and civic rights, a few hundred thousand have become citizens of Sri Lanka (the others obtained Indian passports). Meanwhile, quite a number have left the estates: some in search of employment, some because of fear of ethnic violence directed against them. With increased mobility, a process of internal differentiation in terms of greater socio-economic stratification is taking place. Proof of these developments is the emergence of a collective consciousness in the form of a political party of their own, the Up-Country People's Party. Having risen from a (stateless) underclass to a minority, it cannot be excluded that one day the Indian Tamils will claim recognition as a distinct nationality and, consequently, greater autonomy for those areas where they have been historically concentrated.

- The subcontinent counts many ethnic groups which either qualify as *minorities* or as nations/nationalities. Their common feature is their status as a social group distinct from the majority population by language, religion, ethnic origin, etc., on the one hand and their numerical inferiority on the other. People belonging to a minority community, typically live more or less dispersed over a wider area, physically intermixed or in close proximity with other ethnic groups. Once recognized as such by their respective state, they enjoy specific rights according to international law which include the free association with other members of their group, the cultivation of their own language (in education), of their religion (places of worship), etc.

Occasionally, constitutions entitle them to practice their specific jurisprudence in matters of marriage, inheritance, etc. But, it is essential to note that minority rights are fundamentally *individual* rights.

- *Nations or nationalities* are minorities with the difference that their members share a common history and conscious identity; most importantly, they can refer to a particular territory as their traditional settlement area where they constitute the majority community. They have collective rights as 'peoples', i.e. enjoy in principle the right to self-determination, either in the form of administrative autonomy within the boundaries of an existing state or in the form of a state of their own. Under international law the right to independence, if necessary by force of arms, has automatically been accorded to nations newly liberated from European colonialism, while in other cases only a peaceful and mutually agreed upon break-up of an existing state is generally accepted as legitimate and legal[3] in view of the sacrosanct principle of territorial integrity and inviolability of boundaries of an existing state. As a result, the entry of a new state into the international comity of nations created as a result of a war of secession is a very rare occurrence indeed. The violent fragmentation of Pakistan and the creation of Bangladesh as an internationally recognized state presents such an early example. But this may change since internal 'ethnic' wars have become more frequent (than wars between states) and more violent. Moreover, because of typical regional, if not global repercussions they affect the security situation of several states which international law will sooner or later have to take cognisance of including their specific causes and potential solutions. In reverse, the principle of 'non-intervention in internal affairs' giving effectively carte blanche to governments while ignoring, if not criminalizing insurgent 'ethnic' movements will have to give way to a more differentiated approach. The papers on Sri Lanka, the conflict over Khalistan or Kashmir in India referred to by Rothermund and Hettne are cases in point.

- The Nagas, an '*indigenous people*', represent a totally different matter. As the contribution by Mahanta details the Nagas suffer especially from large-scale internal migration and encroachments of their lands and resources. Apparently less politically discriminated against, they rather fear for 'the Naga way of life', for their survival as a people with a distinct culture and tradition. They are primarily the victims of the modern state with its all-encompassing socio-political and administrative structures and institutions characterized by a uniform legal code with equal civil and political rights, including the freedom of movement and residence for all citizens. It means also the establishment of an integrated economy based on private property and the free flow of capital, goods, services and labour. The implicit notions of nation-building, modernization, and progress run not only counter to the traditional economy and society of indigenous peoples who stress the primacy of the collective, and its special relation to a sanctified territory, they threaten the material existence of the group. The exigencies and the impact of modern society were frequently instrumental in the formation of a collective identity of formerly often mutually antagonistic tribes. To better preserve their identity, demands for political unification in a territorial entity of their own is raised. As the Nagas again demonstrate, the demand for self-determination may not only run counter to existing administrative, even international boundaries. If implemented, they in turn would be confronted with an ethnic heterogeneity, replicating on the micro-level so to speak the same 'ethnic' conflicts only with new masters at the helm. While international instruments recognize the specificity of 'indigenous peoples', that include their socio-economic orders, their culture and belief systems, their knowledge of nature and their special relation to the land, few internationally binding charters have so far been agreed upon. Still, while such indigenous communities unequivocally qualify as 'peoples', they have not been accorded the right to *external* self-determination.

South Asian societies, as the individual case studies show, reveal the whole range of social groups ranging from ethnic underclass to religious or ethnic minorities, from indigenous peoples to nations. They also illustrate the evolution from statistical to social groups, from underclass to political minority to a 'people' respectively with claims ranging from participatory rights over autonomy to secession. The 'two-nation theory' first propounded by Jinnah in the 1940s eventually providing the ideological foundation for the break-up of British India and the creation of Pakistan is being referred to in the analyses by Hettne, Rothermund and Weidemann as not only historically the first to pose the problem of nation-building in a heterogeneous social context, but also as being at the root of major conflicts and crises in the post-colonial period. The insurgent movements of the Nagas and even more so of the Sri Lankan Tamils, of Sikhs and Kashmiris, of Bengalis and Baluchis indicate, however, an underlying structural and lasting problem.

To deal adequately with the double challenges of nation- and state-building in societies composed of different minorities, indigenous peoples, and nations, more than a state sponsored overarching nationalist ideology over and above particularistic identities is obviously required. The studies demonstrate that certain constitutional devices even though not sufficient by themselves are more conducive to create social harmony than others. Thus (a) an authoritarian repressive regime potentially contributes more to ethnic conflict than a democratic system, that is at least in principle more responsive to the electorate; (b) a constitutional guarantee of human rights enforceable in a court of law would provide a basic reassurance for minorities against discrimination and allow their specificities to be cultivated; (c) far-reaching internal autonomy in a federal, even confederal system, would go far indeed to permit indigenous peoples and nationalities to govern themselves. In fact, only a very small number of countries are homogeneous in terms of ethnic-cultural composition rendering the narrow definition of 'nation-state' a simple myth; this holds even for the classical 'nation-states', France and Great Britain. Quite a number of them, in the North as in the South, having taken account of this fact are constitutionally federations. While no panacea against ethnic strife, this leaves, nevertheless, in principle more room for accommodation than a unitary centralized state.[4]

This does not necessarily mean neither a fragile state nor a weak centre unable to shoulder the task of economic development, as is feared in Sri Lanka. Thus, Nehru, convinced of the need for a strong centralized state in conjunction with a democratic political system, was no friend of federalism in general and originally deeply opposed the redrawing of linguistic boundaries in the Indian Union. However, the creation of ever new states even along linguistic lines has served the unity of the country rather than fomented the threat of fragmentation. By contrast, political conflicts between the centre and the states may be accentuated, the regionalization of politics favoured. In practice, federalism signifies only the principle of power sharing. The way it operates depends decisively on the modalities; rather then being a zero-sum game, a plurality of institutional arrangements to join forces in a cooperative effort to advance the fortunes of the state in everyone's interest can be envisaged. India demonstrates that a second chamber, minority rights, that extend to family and inheritance law, including linguistically defined states, are such possible devices. Still, they are guarantees neither against communal conflict nor against a strong, even authoritarian central state. India with its administrative service (IAS), the extensive powers over state governments concentrated in the hands of the president, the planning commission and not least the all-India security forces which have unhesitatingly been employed in the suppression of ethnic movements, can serve once more as illustration. Between India, Canada and Yugoslavia (the latter's) liberal federal constitution eventually served to break-up the country are many possibilities. Suffice it to say, that constitutional provisions taking into account the multi-cultural, multi-national character of a society can go far in alleviating potential conflicts, giving every group a real chance to participate in government.

## THE STATE

All contributions underline the central role of the state making it the object of a fierce struggle for political power. A variety of

structural reasons are responsible for the importance attached
to the state even under conditions of neoliberal globalization
with its primary emphasis on the market.

- There is first of all the underdevelopment and fragmentation of the economy in general, of the private sector,
  not least of private capital, in particular. The concentration
  of material resources in the hands of the government made
  it objectively the primary agency of development in the
  early years of Independence even independently of the
  ideological foundation of the 'statist' development strategy.
- A closely-related argument concerns the role of the state
  in social matters. Given the widespread poverty in combination with the underdevelopment of private social institutions, the state is called upon to install a system of
  universally accessible modern services in health, education,
  etc. Through the welfare state indirectly, through the policy
  of positive discrimination in conjunction with the penal-
  ization of violations of the principle of equality directly,
  the state is the motor of the transformation of the traditional, hierarchical (feudal, caste, gender, etc.) order. The
  state is similarly thought of as a model for private enterprise
  in his role as an employer: he is to set high standards in
  terms of employment and working conditions.
- As Malik in line with early Communist Party thinking
  points out, more than a mere economic actor, and contrary
  to materialist theory, the state in the Third World is not
  just a superstructure reflecting the underlying state of the
  material forces of production and the related social
  relations, but is itself the principal actor in the transformation of the social and economic basis of society. An
  agent of modernization both in terms of social and
  industrial policy it exercises a decisive influence on the
  evolution of the economy as well as the social configuration, including the balance of forces. It plays this role—
  independently of its political form—through economic
  planning, resource allocation, its educational and industrial
  policies which imply new economic opportunities impacting
  on the labour market, social mobility, and through it on
  class formation, and value systems.

The plethora of central functions, the access to material resources and their distribution, the influence on legislation, employment and investment render the question of 'who governs', in whose interest, for which purpose as one of utmost importance. It concerns the political system as much as the class configuration and power equation apart from the availability of resources and the state of the economy. The thesis of the developmental state being the natural driving force of development rather independently of particularistic interests has proved true for only a short period at best. The evolution of economy and society turned out to be different from what had been originally envisaged impacting in the course of time on the use to which political power was put. In this context, the question of class formation and eventually democracy occupies centre stage.

## PERIPHERAL CAPITALISM AND A FRAGMENTED SOCIAL CONFIGURATION

Marx had expected that spurred on by colonialism, capitalism would penetrate and transform the South as it had the North some hundred years earlier. The notion of the South essentially developing as the mirror image of the North was basically shared by the modernization school of development which dominated the 1950s and 1960s. History has proved them wrong. The developed industrialized countries did not provide the model for the latecomers. It was not for lack of trying. But the globalization of capital spreading from the centre into the south naturally did so in the form and based on the conditions prevailing in the metropolitan countries: Its major characteristics are multinational companies representing a massive concentration of capital and huge productive capacity (economies of scale), high labour costs and a mode of production that is capital not labour intensive, incorporating a high content in technology and research. The factors of production in the south are rather different given a huge, in large parts un- and semi-qualified labour force, and a lack of capital. Under such conditions the capital from the industrialized economies came not only to dominate the world market, but universalized by the same token its methods and organization of production. This acted just like a gene transplanted into an alien organism (Vandana Shiva). It produced a special type of capitalist development in the south quite unlike the bourgeois socio-economic order that developed over time in today's leading market economies. A *peripheral* capitalism emerged characterized by a dominance of the market but a permanently insufficient capacity to absorb the available manpower in formal capitalist employment relations. As a result, less than one out of four of the economically active population lives in the formal sector. The remaining three quarter majority carves out a meagre existence in the informal economy as unemployed or underemployed at best or—for want of gainful alternatives—as self-employed in agriculture, trade and commerce.

Capitalist production relations do not supplant and eliminate successively all earlier modes of production. This translates into a *structural heterogeneity* characterized by a formal juxtaposition of capitalist, semi-capitalist and pre-capitalist modes of production. Different from the social history of the metropolitan countries this is not a transitional phase but one to last because the demographic development together with the capital intensive modernization process imposed from the outside causes an ever greater problem of marginalization, insecurity and impoverishment for the vast majority of the population. At the same time, these different modes of production interact under conditions of dominant market mechanisms. As a result, the older modes are formally reproduced while emptied of their social content. Traditional socio-economic relations as a network of services and duties between members of different groups are stripped of their mutual obligations. Reduced to economic exchanges between individuals, they are guided by purely market rationality for maximum profit. In the process and given the drastic inequality, the older modes provide the human and material resources for the better accumulation of capital while at the same time serving as social security system for the unemployed, the young, the sick and the old. With the informal sector showing no sign of retreating despite continued impoverishment, many flock to the cities in the vain hope for better opportunities and greater security. But in a situation of urbanization without industrialization, of growth without jobs, of increasing inequality, the gap between the expectations and the aspirations not least of a formally better educated youth continues to widen. This creates a potentially explosive environment of heightened tensions, of violence and political unrest. Thus, young educated people have been in the fore front of often violent political movements, as reported in the case-studies on north-east India by Mahanta, on the insurgencies of the JVP in Sri Lanka by Gamage or on the Maoists today in Nepal by Daryn.

## FRAGMENTED CLASS STRUCTURE AND INTEREST ARTICULATION

The modern representative state, independently of the institutional form of government, is based on universal franchise, i.e. presupposes the existence of the universal citizen endowed with equal rights and acting in his capacity as a free individual. What today is rightly considered an inalienable birthright has, however, socio-historical roots. Thus, the emergence of the citizen and his political participatory rights resulted from the development of capitalist society, not least in the period of industrialization, and were spurred on by social struggles. In other words, a representative state, more so a functioning democracy, presupposes a modern class society, not a configuration based on collectively ascribed inequality and hierarchy such as caste.

In the Third World by contrast, representative institutions were introduced not only without social struggle, but also without the relevant social substratum of modern social classes. The earlier stated condition of peripheral capitalism as a state of perennial transition to an exclusive capitalist mode of production is reflected in the social configuration in as much as modern social classes come to structure society only imperfectly. In fact, every social class and stratum is fragmented as manifest in the collective consciousness where caste, class, religious and regional identities remain over time. Where the vast majority of the population continues to subsist in the informal sector a modern working class with a related consciousness cannot blossom.

Correspondingly, class organizations evolve only alongside other, often more important group formations. They are often highly fragmented, with a typically low and unstable membership, comparatively strong only in the public sector. The classical relationship between social class, trade union and political party is reversed. The party becomes the decisive institution to advance the interests of its members with the trade union reduced to being the transmission belt for party politics. Under such conditions it is not surprising that trade union membership changes dramatically along with changes in government. Only those trade unions whose party affiliation promises access to power and privilege can count on a seizable and mobilizable membership.

By contrast, with class formation and class organizations remaining weak, seemingly traditional forms of group identity, such as caste, clan, ethnic community, religious or linguistic community emerge to advance collective interests. They provide a fertile ground for the 'ethnicization', including the casteism, of politics, for the instrumentalization of the state, for the clientelism and alienation of the ruling class. The societal configuration does not correspond with the modern forms of the economy and the institutions of the state which however provide the mould and the channels through which power and privilege are accessed and distributed.

In the end, it is the political process based on universal franchise which essentially accounts for the emergence of interest groups. In view of the major role of the state in the accumulation and distribution of resources it is only natural that the struggle for power and control over the state apparatus is very fierce. Access mediated through the competitive politics of numbers is a powerful mechanism to weld together different groups to form a lobby able to command enough votes to influence government decisions, to obtain favours from the administration.

The fact that they take the form of traditional identities has led a number of authors to see them as proof of their primordial character. But this is only the outer appearance; in reality and in substance they have nothing in common with the primary groups of old. These are but the typical vehicles for the advancement of group interests in transitional semi-feudal semi-capitalist societies.

Today's emergence of the Other Backward Classes as powerful lobby in India which challenges the traditional twiceborn caste privileges is a case in point: (a) they illustrate the modern democratic phenomenon of mass politics; (b) they testify to the process of empowerment of traditionally backward and suppressed social groups; (c) they illustrate the switch in societal goals and the methods to achieve them: from purity and prestige via collective status to individual wealth and influence. Most importantly, while in the traditional order they were compartmentalized closed sub-groups which, if not mutually antogonistic, at any rate made a virtue out of their separate, jealously guarded, identity, have now joined forces in a collective front for common goals.

## DEMOCRACY *VERSUS* DEMOCRATIZATION

Advocated by its proponents as a panacea for all social and economic ills, democracy is promoted as a bulwark against war (because wars are said to be harmful for business), as an institutional device and accompaniment of a free market system, as a protection against corruption, inefficiency and authoritarianism. Finally, it is proclaimed to guarantee human rights. In international politics, Western governments and political foundations have even turned the call for democracy into a tool to destabililize, if not overthrow, regimes they consider hostile to their interests; examples from Eastern Europe (Ukraine), Latin America (Cuba, the Sandinistas in Nicaragua) and, currently, the 'Greater Middle East' (Iraq to begin with) readily come to mind.

However, too much has been made of democracy as an institutional device to form governments. Too little has been said about the modern representative state, including democracy, as an institutional device for the exercise of power in bourgeois society.

- As such democracy—like other socio-political system—is not only borne out of social antagonisms manifesting and recreating for ever the distinction between rulers and ruled but defends, cements, advances a particular social order based on exploitation. Democracy, in other words, forms an integral part of a societal system in the sense of representing primarily the interests of a particular class and advancing a particular socio-economic order (mode of production). Manifestly representing the common weal and being answerable to the people as ultimate sovereign, it nevertheless incarnates a system of government charged with the task to balance countervailing contradictory forces not only in order to prevent system-threatening open class conflict but also to further the process of accumulation and to enlarge the rule of the market. In this sense, democracy is the recognition of the rule of the minority over the majority.

- Apart from the rule of a minority over the majority in terms of social class, it implies also the reverse, i.e. the rule of the electoral majority in quantitative terms. In a multi-ethnic society it often enough means, however, the rule of the majority over the minority communities. As already Tocqueville in his study of American democracy in the early nineteenth century remarked, in a given context democracy becomes an instrument of the majority to permanently triumph over the interests of the minorities, even to discriminate against them. Democracy turns into outright tyranny if power is concentrated in the hands of the executive, as Tocqueville further observes.[5] Finally, without adequate checks the basic attribute of democracy, i.e. to regulate conflict by peaceful means, becomes not only illusory; the system itself becomes a mechanism to enflame political conflict. The studies assembled here, particularly those on Bhutan, Pakistan, and Sri Lanka, prove the correctness of Tocqueville's analysis concerning the monopolization, if not the appropriation of state power by and for the benefit of an ethnically defined majority. Together with the rise of the Hindutva or the OBC movements they provide further evidence that this is not an aberration or passing phenomenon but a form of collective interest articulation typical for the heterogeneous social configuration of peripheral societies.

Democracy—as the events in Pakistan, Nepal, Bangladesh or Bhutan—demonstrate are considered the antithesis to authoritarian rule whether in the form of extended periods of emergency, of military rule or rather unlimited royal power. The latter symbolize the repressive character of government, and are thought to be easy prey to corruption, to arbitrariness, to violation of civil and political rights. By contrast, democracy is assumed to systemically imply a plurality of interests in conjunction with the settlement of disputes by dialogue and negotiation rather than by violent means. Government is thought to reflect the general rather than particularistic interests, dependent as it were on the regular approval of the sovereign people. But, as the contribution on Bangladesh shows in detail and the ones on Sri Lanka and Nepal also indicate there is a growing alienation of the political class from the citizenry. The state is treated as their property, as a means to wield power and gain wealth. In its final avatar there is collusion, if not merger between the highest echelons of the administration, the ruling class, and business. In the struggle for power every means is considered appropriate, even the employment of violence. Democracy as a formal mechanism to allocate power to a restricted number of persons and parties in regularly held competitive elections based on universal franchise is manifestly neither sufficient to guarantee popular participation nor transparency and accountability of the rulers. It is not even an antidote to violence in politics or in conflict management. Democracy without large-scale *democratization* of society leading to a broad based and articulate civil society remains apparently a hollow shell.

## CRISIS OF THE STATE

This prime importance of the state allows better to understand the struggle for power that many of the case studies refer to. Still, when taking a long-term view it has also been noticed that the monopoly of violence attributed to the state as one of its foremost prerogatives has decisively been eroded. It manifests itself in various forms and is all the more serious since the legitimacy of the state rests on its capacity to provide security to its subjects. A situation of crisis is easily associated with challenges to the state by armed secessionist movements such as the Nagas or the Tamil Tigers or by insurgents trying to overthrow the existing social order as the then JVP in Sri Lanka or the Maoists in Nepal (and India). But these are challenges of existing orders, they do not question the institution of the state as such. A much more profound crisis is described in a number of studies which go even beyond an absence of due process of law often in connection with states of emergency or military rule. Even under formally democratic governments, a privatization of violence, the instrumentalization of the coercive powers of the state to arbitrarily and violently suppress opponents of the ruling party to persecute minorities or to consciously instigate violence for short-term electoral gains has been of regular occurrence. It Proves that the South Asian states have retained, if not directly in their constitutions, at least in spirit, the legacy of exploitation and repression of the colonial state. It indicates that a systemic crisis has developed, that the state is losing its legitimacy, and altogether its *raison d'être*. Neoliberal globalization accompanied by a general diminution of the role of the state, prioritizing instead the market forces in the form of privatization, deregulation, and world market opening can only augment this tendency. More than mere policy imperatives, it changes also the parameters of the economic and the socio-political space. While the struggle between classes and for democracy remains confined within the national boundaries, the ruling classes and the political elites are operating in the international arena. In the end, the observed tendencies of growing inequalities within countries and between regions, the divorce of the political elite from the masses, and the marginalization of civil society will be reinforced.

## TOWARDS AN ALTERNATIVE VISION

In his analysis of Pakistan Weidemann questions the appropriateness of Western economic and political development models; Malik in his study of the socio-political origin of the RSS and the emergence of a Third World type of fascism argues that the initial Nehruvian concept of nation-building has run its course, that a more radical platform is needed to face the crisis of nation and state. The contribution by Yamaguchi, finally, makes an outright plea for the modernity of Gandhian thoughts. There is a convergence in all case studies concerning the diagnosis of multiple crises everywhere in South Asia as more than mere passing symptoms. A comparative view reveals, moreover, that the crises observed are eventually independent of the existing political systems or the respective political regimes. While these obviously do play a role in the form and depth of a crisis and in the degree of violence of the related conflicts, their roots manifestly go deeper and concern the development path as a whole. It lends credence to the hypothesis that the post-Independence concepts of a state centred market based development model in a secular democratic political framework has not only failed, but that the tendency towards a systemic crisis, not least in the direction of ethnicized authoritarian government, is permanent, if not irreversible. The path ahead appears tortuous, the state of flux for the long haul.

The modernization project of state, society and economy seems to have run out of steam. But before we come to this conclusion, the historical antecedents and 'the add on' thereof have to be objectively evaluated. As a matter of fact, South Asia is going through a process of massive societal churning. At times seemingly quite unpalatable, they may well represent late post-colonial movements aiming to correct the in-built imbalances and inequities bequeathed by history. Unrecognizable in the modern lexicon of political science, they emerged wherever democratic space has been opened up. This was not the case at the time of the Independence movement, as the focus then was on the removal of the colonial rule. Already for tactical reasons and as an encountering device of resistance, it required the formation of the widest possible coalitions and a minimum of internal contradictions. Today's social churning is not unilinear. It appears in quite different forms ranging from religious fundamentalism to various manifestations of identity politics, giving the impression of chaotic change tilted towards a specific sort of primordialism. It depends on historical antecedents of a variously and differently matured anti-colonial struggle whether they take the path of either a reactionary regression or of a further deepening of democracy and the empowerment of weaker sections of the population. The dialectical fulcrum inherent in an iniquitous and semi-feudal society could not altogether bypass this very fragile and vulnerable, yet natural outburst after direct colonial rule had ended. Yet, it has been a fundamental miss in the nation-building effort not to build and empower civil society without which all add-ons would be considered mere inadequate grafting and ultimately be dysfunctional. It was Mahatma Gandhi who developed a two-pronged strategy of fighting colonialism as well as building and empowering civil society because he understood that without the latter all attempts at nation-building engineering would go to waste.

In the early phase of decolonization, all governments, including the bureaucratic-military and even dwindling monarchical regimes, took to nation-building in a rather uniform pattern. All these developmental societies were 'statist', i.e. state-centred, and while they did not last long, they left an indelible mark on the exercise of nation-building in South Asia. As a matter of fact, the basic structures for the evolution of an independent national economy were put in place. Policies of industrialization and agrarian reforms laid the basis for an independent and 'sustainable nation-state'. By the same token, they helped in the formation and expansion of a more cogent modern class structure that included an industrial bourgeoisie in the urban areas and kulaks in the countryside. However fragile and weak, this seemingly modern state provided the instruments and the structures that—without presenting any kind of historical or institutional antecedent—allowed the later-day neo-liberal shift. In fact, the phase of state centred development was exhausted by the early 1980s, not only in India but all over the globe. Often it had degenerated into a one party monopoly rule with a corrupt elite at the top. In India, democratic representative institutions survived and evolved with some indigenous colours. The Nehruvian state, which was the main motor of nation-building in post-colonial India, had no cogent social base but represented some sort of popular voice of the long subjugated people. It was, furthermore, built on the post-World War II consensus of the welfare state as ideational fulcrum. Handicapped by an overall conservative state cadre and a Congress party that consisted of an uncomfortable alliances of different classes, under-classes and social identity groups, the capacity for truly radical transformation at the essential delivery points was limited.

Efforts to form left blocs were short lived, eventually giving leeway to a creeping neo-liberal political economy that re-fashioned the Indian state in the 1990s. Already weakened, the post-colonial concept of the nation-building trajectory by the state failed, giving lee-way to the proliferation of communally divisive politics, as well as caste conflicts, and the assertion of regional forces.

These findings and observations enlarge the scope of future research beyond further thematic case studies (into the hypothe-sized deepening crises and conflicts) and open a perspective towards alternative socio-economic models, the conditions and the potential groups for their realization. While the neoliberal paradigm will certainly not present a solution, the role of the state in development and the related question of the classes, the social and political forces able to carry out such an alternative historic mission will have to be posed. The answer may well go beyond the narrow confines of the individual state (as Hettne indicates by referring to 'regionness'), that the Nehruvian vision of a national-bourgeois revolution under the leadership of the state as a progressive, historically necessary intermediate stage in a long-term process towards a post-capitalist social order is no longer on the agenda. While concrete answers may only emerge in the process of socio-economic struggles for an end to alienation, to underdevelopment, and exploitation, the subjects of such changes may have to be looked for not only in the countries of the South. If globalization is an irreversible process which touches everyone, then all are called upon to participate to make a difference!

## NOTES

1. Concerning the level of development, South Asian countries vary markedly whether measured in terms of income per capita, of success and rank on the human development index (HDI) or of the stage of

societal evolution. Bhutan and Nepal have remained largely rural societies with strong pre-modern pre-capitalist socio-economic relations and forms of production. While they are faced with the task of developing an infrastructure taking the first steps out of an informal economy towards an industrial society, India at the other extreme is competing on a global level and counting in decades only the period until it emerges as an economic super-power.

| Country | Pop. (mio) | Density pop./km² | GNP (bio.$) | GNI p.c.$* | Life exp. men/women | Literacy %>15 |
|---|---|---|---|---|---|---|
| Bangladesh | 141 | 1079 | 61 | 440 (2000) | 61/62 | 41 |
| Bhutan | 1 | 19 | <1 | 760 | 62/65 | – |
| India | 1080 | 363 | 675 | 620 (3100) | 63/64 | 61 |
| Nepal | 25 | 176 | 7 | 260 (1160) | 60/60 | 49 |
| Pakistan | 150 | 179 | 91 | 600 (2160) | 63/65 | 49 |
| Sri Lanka | 20 | 301 | 20 | 1010 | 72/76 | 90 |

*Note:*    * Numbers in brackets refer to per capita income expressed in terms of PPP (purchasing power parity).

*Source:*   World Bank, World Development Report 2005, Washington 2005, Appendix Table 1.

2. The Indian Tamils who had migrated to Ceylon in the nineteenth century were disenfranchized soon after Sri Lanka constituted itself as an independent state in 1948 with its own distinct citizenship rights in place of the earlier common status as subjects of British India.

3. Eritrea's separation from Ethiopia is such an example.

4. Examples are Canada, Finland, Germany, Russia, Switzerland, the USA or Brazil, India, Nigeria, South Africa.

5. Tocqueville, A. de, 1945, *Democracy in America*, New York: Random House.

6. C.Y. Thomas, 1984 *The Rise of the Authoritarian State in Peripheral Societies*, New York: Monthly Review Press.

# CHAPTER 2

# State and Nation in South Asia: Historical Perspectives

## Dietmar Rothermund

## INDIA AND PAKISTAN

In current usage, the terms 'state' and 'nation' are often inter-changeable. We speak of 'new nations' and mean the states that have emerged from the process of decolonization after the Second World War. They are all members of the United Nations which are actually an association of states. Using 'state' and 'nation' as synonyms has its origins in the experience of West European nation states such as Great Britain and France where royal power had consolidated 'national' territories at an early stage and nationalism was rooted in a well-defined nation state. But there were other nations in Europe whose experience was rather different from that of the British and the French. The most drastic example is that of the Polish nation whose state had been eradicated by its neighbours who distributed the Polish territory among themselves. Polish nationalism was denial-driven, it was aimed at restoring the state of which the Polish nation had been deprived. The nationalism of the 'new nations' was similar to the Polish one. Self-determination had been denied to them under European colonial rule and this rule influenced their denial-driven nationalism in a special way. The rulers confronted them with a strong sense of national solidarity which made them act in a corporate spirit. None of the colonial proconsuls ever rebelled against his nation and carved out an empire of his own. African and Asian nationalists perceived this and acutely felt the lack of national solidarity in their own 'nation'. Without this solidarity they could never hope to achieve self-determination. Mahatma

Gandhi's manifesto *Hind Swaraj* provides an eloquent testimony to this feeling.

South Asia was a region which by its very nature did not lend itself easily to an experiment of creating national solidarity. Its British colonial rulers used to call it 'a congeries of nations' implying thereby that it would never be able to produce a nation state. For a long time they even doubted whether there had been any tradition of genuine state-formation in this region. 'Oriental despotism' based on the 'Asiatic mode of production' seemed to be all that mattered here. This prejudice was not confined to the colonial rulers, it was widely prevalent in Europe. In Germany Friedrich Schlegel and Georg Friedrich Hegel had a long debate on the lack of state-formation in India. To Hegel, the state was the highest form of human solidarity and since he did not recognize any trace of this in India, he held that India had no value in world history. Schlegel, who was fascinated by his study of Sanskrit and who saw in a highly developed language rather than in the state the proof of human value, could not convince Hegel, who argued that even people with an impressive language who did not create a state were not worth taking note of. Later historical research and the discovery of the *Arthashastra* have shown that there was a high degree of political sophistication in ancient India and that there was a great deal of evidence of elaborate state-formation. In fact, the model of the Indian state was even exported to South-East Asia. Indian nationalists used this as evidence for the existence of a 'Greater India'. This contributed to national pride and was used as an argument against the colonial rulers who denied self-determination to India because of its alleged political ineptness. But pride in the glory of ancient India might have fired the imagination of intellectuals, it did not necessarily promote the national solidarity in the people. Since India is rich in religious symbolism, it was tempting to use this as a means of communication. Mahatma Gandhi did this to good effect. He was not at all a religious revivalist or a Hindu communalist, but he found that people would understand his message more easily if he used popular imagery. Instead of lecturing to the people on ideas of justice and solidarity in abstract terms, he referred to Ram Rajya, the rule of the legendary King Rama whose conduct signified these ideas in an exemplary fashion. Jawaharlal Nehru who was a rational secularist was aghast when he heard Gandhi talk about Ram Rajya, because he felt that it would appeal to reactionary and traditionalist feelings among the people. Of course, Gandhi did not want to restore a Hindu monarchy. To him Ram Rajya was an evocative allegory. Nehru was not only concerned about the meaning that this kind of allegory would have for Hindus, he also knew that it would offend Muslims. Gandhi was eager to reach the Muslims and compensated for his use of Hindu symbolism by propagating the song *Ishwara Allah tere naam* at his prayer meetings. But equating the name of a Hindu god with that of Allah did not at all please the Muslims, the orthodox among them might even have found it blasphemous.

Gandhi's great adversary, Mohammed Ali Jinnah, witnessed Gandhi's rise to political prominence with envy and disdain. He had wanted to be an ambassador of Hindu-Muslim unity, but in constitutional terms and not on the basis of religious equations. He became a Muslim communalist only because he was left with no alternative. In pursuing this path he finally articulated his two-nation Theory according to which Hindus and Muslims were separate nations—'by any definition of the term', as he hastened to add so as to preclude any further questions. Jinnah had been a representative of the Muslim diaspora so far, i.e. he had led the Muslims in the Muslim minority provinces in which the Congress party had formed governments under the new scheme of 'provincial autonomy' in 1937. He thus knew that claiming a nation-state for Indian Muslims would go against the interests of the Muslim diaspora. No exchange of populations would be able to solve the problem of the huge diaspora. Nevertheless, he proclaimed his theory in 1940 for very specific reasons and actually betrayed the Muslim diaspora knowing fully well what he was doing.

By introducing 'provincial autonomy' the British had designed a new political arena for Indian nationalists which would absorb their political energies while the central Government of India was kept under undiluted imperial control. But in 1939 'provincial autonomy' had to be partly suspended when the Congress ministers resigned at the beginning of the Second World War. The British governors once more resumed full control of those provinces. This also closed the political arena in which Jinnah had operated so far. The remaining political arena consisted of the two Muslim majority provinces, Bengal and the Punjab, in which regional parties had formed governments which did not resign in 1939. Jinnah had not taken much interest in those two provinces earlier and he had no hold on their governments whose leaders were not at all his obedient followers. They had made their careers on their own and would not tolerate Jinnah's interference in their provincial politics. At the most, they would accept him as a spokesman on the 'national' level. In order to justify this role, Jinnah proclaimed the two-nation theory. It was a 'virtual' nation which he projected in this way.

When Jinnah proclaimed his theory at the Lahore conference of the Muslim League, the name 'Pakistan' was not yet mentioned, but it soon gained currency as a designation of the territory claimed by Jinnah's nation. The borders of this territory were not yet clearly delineated and Jinnah deliberately kept his claims vague so as not to alienate Muslims who would not be encompassed by Pakistan. The demand for Pakistan for the first time introduced the problem of territoriality in the debates of Indian nationalists. So far they had given hardly any thought to the limits of the national territory. The borders determined by the British were taken for granted. There had also been no discussion of the future defence of the national territory. The further existence of the British-Indian army was not doubted. Gandhi's views were typical for this state of mind. He initially opposed the idea of Pakistan and said that partition would amount to a 'vivisection of India'. When he finally accepted the plan of partition, he was surprised to hear that this would also imply the division of the army. He had not thought of this at all, but when he saw that this would be inevitable he prophetically stated that the two armies would fight each other.

Gandhi's acceptance of the plan of partition for which he was criticized by many of his followers was due to the British 'Plan Balkan' whose implementation Nehru had prevented at the very last moment. Initially this plan referred only to the partition of India and the creation of Pakistan. Nehru had seen it before it was sent to London by the Viceroy, Lord Mountbatten. But then it was changed in London. To Mountbatten these changes appeared to be technical details, but Nehru exploded when he saw the new draft. Those who worked on the plan in London had taken the idea of self-determination literally and had vested it in the provinces of British India which would attain independence separately and could then decide by themselves how they would get together again. This seemed to be an elegant solution. It would absolve the British from partitioning India. The British would not bequeath any central government to India and Pakistan. This is what alarmed Nehru who preferred partition as a last administrative act of the British to the actual Balkanization of India which could prove to be irreversible. In addition to the British-Indian provinces, there were also the princely states which would become independent due to the 'lapse of paramountcy'. If the princes were not faced with a strong central government, those who ruled large territories could dream of remaining independent and the smaller ones could join a neighbouring province, preserving their internal autonomy. Mountbatten, who was at first surprised at Nehru's reaction, quickly saw his point and the plan was redrafted once more. Mountbatten got it accepted in London, but he also managed to get Gandhi's endorsement of the plan. Jinnah then suggested the name of the British judge who was commissioned to determine the actual boundary based on census data. Jinnah, who had initially hoped to get the whole of Bengal and the Punjab, had to accept what he called a 'moth-eaten Pakistan'. His own two-nation theory could be quoted against him if he insisted on including the Hindu majority districts of these two provinces in his new state.

Jinnah faced a difficult task because the central Government of India was bequeathed to India whereas he had to build a central government of Pakistan from scratch. Nevertheless, he had reasons to be grateful to Nehru for preventing the implementation of 'Plan Balkan' as revised in London. If a united Punjab and a united Bengal had attained independence by themselves, they might have decided to remain independent and refused to form Pakistan. There was a striking paradox: enthusiasm for Pakistan was greater in the Muslim minority provinces which could not join it than in the majority provinces which had maintained their provincial autonomy throughout the war. They had accepted Jinnah as a spokesman at the national level. If this level disappeared due to 'Plan Balkan', the spokesman could very well have been left speechless. When the 'transfer of power' was finally consumated, Nehru and Jinnah could settle down to the task of governing India and Pakistan respectively. But there was still the problematic task of the integration of the princely states. The terms of reference of the judge who partitioned India did not extend to the princely states whose rulers recovered their full sovereignty after the lapse of paramountcy. Most of these states were landlocked in India and had to come to terms with its central government. Pakistan had hardly any such states to deal with, but it bordered on Kashmir and claimed this Muslim majority state by applying the two-nation Theory. India had accepted partition as a secession but it did not and could not accept the two-nation theory, because a large Muslim minority had remained in India. Jinnah himself, when leaving Mumbai for Karachi, had admonished the diaspora Muslims whom he left behind that they should become good citizens of India. But he did not apply this advice to the Kashmiris. He wished to annex Kashmir by force. India defended Kashmir after the Maharaja of Kashmir declared his accession to India. Nehru appealed to the United Nations against the advice of Gandhi who felt that this would not help at all. This proved to be true. Nehru's plea was that the United Nations should ask Pakistan to vacate the territory which it had seized by force. After this a plebiscite could be held to determine the wishes of the people of Kashmir. Instead of insisting on the withdrawal of Pakistan from Kashmir, the United Nations tried to find a 'political solution' based on a plebiscite. Since there was no withdrawal there was never a plebiscite. Pakistan has continued to challenge India in Kashmir. In 1999, General Musharraf even performed the feat of conducting a conventional war against India in Kashmir although by now both powers possessed the atom bomb. The doctrine of mutual deterrence derived from the experience of the Cold War did not work here.

A deeper problem which hides behind this facade of regional conflict is that India and Pakistan are locked in an embrace of state and counter-state. Jinnah's two-nation theory presupposes that the Muslim nation is seen in contrast to the Hindu nation.

The solidarity of the Muslim nation is derived from this contrast. In the meantime the national solidarity of the Muslim nation as envisioned in Jinnah's theory has been destroyed by the secession of Bangladesh from Pakistan. But this has not freed Pakistan from its fixation on India. In fact, the Pakistani army needs the perception of being threatened by India. Its size and expenditure is disproportionate to the normal requirements of the Pakistani nation. In order to maintain itself, the Pakistani army requires, again and again, American military aid which it can only get for purposes other than arming itself against India. To the Americans, Pakistan was a 'frontstate' facing West, whereas Pakistan was always facing India.

India as a nation-state was less concerned with Pakistan. The undeclared wars which Pakistan had imposed on India had always been won. The more serious' problem for India was its own internal solidarity. Nehru was a nation-builder who saw in the living practice of parliamentary democracy the best guarantee of national solidarity. He was not a federalist but he had preserved the federal structure bequeathed by the British colonial rulers to India. When the provinces of southern India insisted on linguistic principles for the reorganization of Indian federal states, Nehru first resisted this as he saw the spectre of Balkanization raise its ugly head again. Finally he yielded to the quest for linguistic self-determination and could see that it strengthened India rather than tearing it apart.

At the time of Nehru's death in 1964 the territorial cohesion of the Indian nation state was no longer a problem. But under his successors the synchronization of parliamentary democracy at the centre and in the federal states became more and more of a problem. As long as the Congress party was in-charge, both at the centre and in the states, this problem did not exist. But when regional parties asserted their influence in the federal states, tensions between the centre and the states emerged with increasing intensity. The Bharatiya Janata Party then tried to counteract this development by stressing Hindu solidarity. Since about 83 per cent of Indians are Hindus, this seemed to be a passport to political success. But Hinduism is a many-splendoured thing which does not lend itself to ideological streamlining. The concept of 'Hindutva' created by V.D. Savarkar in the 1920s was therefore initially regarded by Indians who knew about it as a rather extravagant construct. To Savarkar, 'Hindutva' was not a religious concept but an idea of national solidarity with a territorial base indicated by the term 'Hindu', meaning the people living to the east of the river Indus. But even Savarkar's own arguments were not free from religious connotations and among his followers Hindutva and Hinduism became practically synonymous. They were also tempted to articulate Hindu solidarity by turning against the Muslims, thus providing a belated justification for Jinnah's two-nation theory. This 'Hindu'-ideology was strengthened by a threat perception and unfortunately Pakistan provided grist to this ideological mill by attacking India. The attempt of Muslim terrorists to capture the Indian parliament in December 2001 confirmed the threat perception in a dramatic way, although these terrorists obviously did not act on behalf of Pakistan's government but wanted to sabotage the 'Alliance against Terror' which both India and Pakistan had joined. The terrorists were shot before they could enter the parliament, but in the short run they had succeeded in upsetting the 'Alliance against Terror'. Indian troops were deployed on the border of Pakistan, and in the summer of 2002 a war seemed to be imminent. American mediation helped to prevent this war. Since then peace has prevailed once more, but there is no guarantee that this peace would be permanent. The history of South Asia's two most important nation states is rich in terms of sources of conflict which may re-emerge at any time.

## SRI LANKA

The island of Sri Lanka is at first sight ideally suited for the development of a well-defined nation state. Its compact territoriality was not determined by the colonial rulers. But its population is not homogeneous. It consists of immigrants who came to the island centuries ago and have since preserved a strong sense of separate ethnic, religious and linguistic identity. In earlier times the island was sparsely populated and the Sinhalese who settled in the highlands and along the southern coast were isolated by the buffer zones of inhospitable intermediate regions from the Tamils of the north. Increasing interaction was fostered by the introduction of democratic representation under British rule. Adult suffrage, which other colonies obtained only very much later, was introduced in Sri Lanka in 1931. Political interest aggregation or the articulation of conflicts could have resulted from this. But the constitutional arrangements made by the British at that time were of a peculiar kind. They did not follow the Westminster model but that of the London County Council. The government consisted of seven committees which elected their chairmen who functioned jointly as a kind of Cabinet. Whether these committees elected Sinhalese or Tamils as their chairmen was not regulated.

In the first round, the Tamils were represented in the 'Cabinet', but in the second Cabinet they were no longer represented as all committees had elected Sinhalese chairmen. This was resented by the Tamils, but it did not lead to a major conflict. Politics was still conducted by a small educated elite deliberating in English in a gentlemanly fashion. This continued even after the attainment of independence under Don Stephen Senanayake and his United National Party (UNP). There had been no freedom struggle in Sri Lanka and nobody had rocked the boat. Turbulence was created only when Salomon Bandaranaike and his Sri Lanka Freedom Party (SLFP) wished to unseat the UNP by appealing to broader strata of the society. They found an enthusiastic following among the 'swabasha educated' Sinhalese who had been educated in Buddhist monasteries where Sinhalese was the only medium of instruction. This excluded them from civil service jobs which required a knowledge of English. Most of these jobs had been captured by the Tamils who had been to English medium schools. After only three years in office, Bandaranaike was shot by a Buddhist monk who felt that the prime minister's measures were not sufficient to ensure Sinhalese ascendancy. To the Tamils, however, these measures had been alarming. They now saw themselves as a threatened minority. Paradoxically, the Sinhalese also regarded themselves as a threatened minority. They added the Tamils on the continent to those living on the island. When Tamil terrorism flared up in Sri Lanka and the terrorists used the Indian state of Tamil Nadu as a safe haven from which they could operate with impunity, the Sinhalese threat perception seemed to be justified. A spiral of violence engulfed the island nation and the ill-advised intervention of the 'Indian Peace-Keeping Force' did not help to solve the problem. Rajiv Gandhi, who had got involved in this intervention, lost his political reputation and finally his life due to it. He was assassinated by Tamil terrorists during the election campaign of 1991, because they feared he would intervene again if he returned to power.

Federalism of the Indian type could have helped to settle the problems of Sri Lanka. But among the Sinhalese, federalism had become a 'dirty' word. To them it implied the disintegration of their nation state, which had to be prevented by all means. The political competition of UNP and SLFP complicated matters. Federal concessions could easily be represented as a betrayal of the nation. Actually, the Sinhalese idea of the unitary nation state fostered the claim for 'Tamil Eelam'. The phenomenon of state and counter-state, which has been mentioned earlier with regard to India and Pakistan, manifested itself in Sri Lanka in a similar way. In spite of frequent attempts at peace-making and mediation, the conflict still exists. It shows that the equation of state and nation remains a problem in South Asia.

## NEPAL

State and nation in the only Hindu monarchy of the world pose a problem of a peculiar kind. Actually, the rise of the present ruling dynasty in the eighteenth century could have paved the way for the rise of a nation-state just as the ascendancy of royal power had done in earlier times for Great Britain and France. But the impact of Nepalese royal power was more ephemeral. Rana autocracy, which rivalled royal power, prevailed for a long time. British influence was also very important and after 1947 the powerful Indian neighbour emerged as determining factor in Nepal's political life. India helped to restore the power of the dynasty under King Tribhuvan and also favoured the steps taken towards democracy under his rule. But then King Mahendra terminated the democratic experiment and played a successful game of balancing India and China so as to enhance his own political role. Under King Birendra there seemed to be a successful return to democracy, but then two obviously unrelated events upset Nepal's positive development. Almost the whole royal family was wiped out by the Crown Prince in an orgy of violence which has not yet been fully explained. At about the same time the Maoist rebels made headway in most parts of Nepal and challenged the Government of Kathmandu which has anyhow been always somewhat remote from the realities on the ground in the countryside. This countryside is not at all homogeneous but segmented in many isolated valleys inhabited by various ethnic groups for whom the Nepali 'nation' is a distant phenomenon. The present king has gone back to square one, emulating the practice of King Mahendra in suspending democracy and reasserting royal power. But this may only increase social conflicts. State and nation are not at all well settled in this troubled mountain kingdom.

## CONCLUSION

The modern concepts of state and nation have been adopted by the people of South Asia in the course of a denial-driven struggle for self-determination. This struggle was not carried on by feudal forces interested in the restoration of an ancien regime. It was led by educated men for whom self-determination also meant an equal status in the comity of nations. This status could only be achieved if their own state and nation matched the international standard. This was not a harmonious development because it often accentuated latent conflicts. Jinnah's two-nation theory is a case in point; it translated the difference of religious communities into the modern discourse of nationality. It also derived the claim for a separate state from this discourse. The problems arising from this kind of 'translation' are still with us today.

## SELECT BIBLIOGRAPHY

Benner, E., 1995, *Really Existing Nationalisms: A Post-Communist View from Marx and Engels,* Oxford: Clarendon Press.

Brecher, M., 1959, *Nehru. A Political Biography,* London: Oxford University Press.

De Silva, K., 1986, *Managing Ethnic Tensions in Multi-Ethnic Societies. Sri Lanka, 1880-1985,* Lanham, MD: University Press of America.

Jalal, A., 1985, *The Sole Spokesman. Jinnah, the Muslim League and the Demand for Pakistan,* Cambridge: Cambridge University Press.

Kulke, H. and D. Rothermund, 2004, *A History of India* (4th edn.), London: Routledge.

Rothermund, D., 1986, *The German Intellectual Quest for India*, New Delhi: Manohar (Chapter 3: Friedrich Schlegel and the Wisdom of India).

———, 1991, *Mahatma Gandhi: An Essay in Political Biography*, New Delhi: Manohar.

———, 2000, *The Role of the State in South Asia and Other Essays*, New Delhi: Manohar.

Wolpert, S., 1984, *Jinnah of Pakistan*, New York: Oxford University Press.

# Conflict Dynamics and Conflict Management in South Asia: Comparative Perspectives

*Björn Hettne*

## INTRODUCTION: A NOTE ON REGIONAL CONFLICT MANAGEMENT

This chapter compares conflict dynamics and conflict management in and between different countries in the South Asian region, historically as well as in the more recent context of the war against terrorism. The pattern of conflict has been shaped by the nation-building processes, in turn marked by the pre-colonial legacy, the structures built by British empire, and the trauma of partition. Over time the external world has exercised increasing influence, but for a long period political dynamics has been remarkably intra-regional. This introverted security strategy also forms part of the imperial legacy carried over from the British to the succeeding regional hegemon. The various national political centres had a lot of domestic conflicts to manage, and in the process new conflicts were created. Thus the nature of these centres and their obsession with stability were equally important as the original conflicts, whatever their nature and causes.

Due to its extreme heterogeneity, the region provides an interesting base for comparative analysis of conflict, as do some of the individual countries, which are almost as complex as the region as a whole. However, because of the many cross-country interconnections and the trend towards regionalization of conflict, a regional perspective is needed. Furthermore, as suggested earlier, the conflict pattern to a large extent emerged through the break-up of British India at independence, the partition, the forceful integration of some of the princely states and tribal peoples, the division of some peoples through new political borders, and the non-coincidence of languages and state borders within the countries. The creation of Pakistan to become the largest Muslim nation in the world, and the subsequent formation of Bangladesh (which in turn must be understood against the artificial creation of Pakistan) were of course the most important products of partition, a fate that also later was to threaten Sri Lanka.

Sri Lanka was (literally) given its freedom in 1948, as part of the winding up of the British empire, together with a liberal, Westminster-type constitution. Later constitutions (1972, 1978) strengthened the Sinhala-Buddhist character of the polity. As far as the other nations are concerned, Nepal and Bhutan were independent traditional kingdoms, Hindu and Buddhist respectively. Both have seen rising conflicts between dominant groups and minorities. The Maldives, in contrast, is a homogeneous Muslim mini-state, an autocracy with a growing democratic opposition.

In most of the cases any lasting conflict resolution must be linked to a healing of the wounds from partition, i.e. deeper regional integration towards a regional security community, which at the same time provides a reasonable degree of autonomy for local groups asserting their own identity. The region, to the extent that it is politically organized, can also be an instrument for management of, including interventions in, conflicts.

Regionalism and conflict can be related in many different ways. One has to do with the choice of unit for investigation (e.g., a regional security complex), another with the regional implications of a local conflict, which depends on the nature of the security complex and a third has to do with the conflict-management role of the organized region for internal regional security for the immediate environment of the region, and for world order. By *security regionalism* is meant attempts by states and other actors in a particular geographical area—a region in the making—to transform a security complex with conflict-generating inter-state and intra-state relations towards a security community with cooperative external (inter-regional) relations and domestic (intra-regional) peace. The concept also includes more acute interventions in crises, but the long-term implications should always be kept in mind. By *regionalization of conflict*, the reference is to both the outward spread or spillover of a local conflict into neighbouring countries, and the inward impact from the region in the form of more or less diplomatic interference, military intervention and, preferably, conflict resolution carried out by some kind of regional body.

In discussing regional crisis management in the longer perspective beyond intervention, it is important to link security regionalism and development regionalism. The two aspects of regionalism, security and development, are complementary and mutually supportive. By *development regionalism* is thus meant concerted efforts from a group of countries within a geographical region to enhance the economic complementarity of the constituent political units and capacity of the total regional economy. This can be through trade agreements or through more comprehensive regional development strategies.

Provention (in terms of development) and prevention (in terms of diplomatic action) are early forms of civil intervention, but by intervention is mostly meant military intervention in order to put an end to a violent conflict.[1] Distinctions can be made between different modes of military intervention in acute regional security crises: unilateral, bilateral, plurilateral, regional, and multilateral. Unilateral and most plurilateral interventions lack legality in terms of international law but may on some occasions appear legitimate. The record in South Asia is unfortunately more characterized by hegemonic, unilateral intervention in conflicts than regional, or for that matter multilateral conflict prevention or resolution. Kashmir is the only case of multilateral UN peacekeeping, but this was long ago. Sri Lanka, an unusual case of bilateral intervention (1987), has more recently sought third-party (Norwegian) facilitation. A recent crisis, rebellion and *coup d'état* in Nepal, has raised a lot of international concern, but international involvement is resisted by India.

The regional dimension has become also increasingly important in South Asia, if for no other reason than that it constitutes an explosive security complex—according to some 'the most dangerous place in the world'. A regional security complex is defined as security interdependence which implies the risk of a local conflict spilling over into neighbouring areas, throughout the region. On a higher level of 'regionness', or convergence across countries of views and policies in different fields, the security complex is transformed into a 'security community', defined as a stage in political development where positive interdependencies among a group of states make it inconceivable that violence may be used as a method to solve conflicts. Regional integration is traditionally seen as inherently peace-promoting. Regionalization of conflicts may also stimulate regional cooperation with the purpose of preventing spillovers between countries.

Regional cooperation has more recently been motivated by global and regional terrorism, since terrorist networks move between countries, in particular to those where the law and order situation is deficient. Regions could thus be important actors in crises. A regional organization can better assume the role of mediator in ethnic conflicts than the immediately concerned states, and in terms of culture and values still be closer to the parties than international, extra-regional mediators, which under all circumstances are excluded in this case due to Indian resistance (Sri Lanka being an exception).

A peace settlement may include principles of conflict resolution to be applied, or simply be confined to conditions of ceasefire. In any case the way out of the conflict goes through political restructuring of some kind, i.e. a new political relationship between the contending groups, typically ethnic groups. Ethno-national mobilization may have the historical function of modifying the nation state project, and the pattern of development inherent in it. The question is how? If we exclude coercive assimilation of ethnic or other minorities in the mainstream nation-building project, a method which usually forms part of the problem rather than of the solution, there are in principle three political ways out of such domestic crises. First, *constitutional change*, modifying the skewed ethnic power structure and establishing a power-sharing arrangement within a particular state formation. A political constitution can itself be seen as an instrument of conflict resolution in a multi-ethnic state. This is why ethnic demands, at least in an early stage, often include constitutional reform, for instance, decentralization of political power to ethnically more or less distinct provinces, internal self-determination referring to social groups rather than to administrative territorial units, and 'consociational democracy' where democracy functions as a human rights regime rather than as a formal political model of transfer of political power. Second, *the dismemberment of the state*, sometimes accompanied by an organized 'ethnic cleansing', is an option that remains open when the preferred solution—constitutional reform—has failed. Partition is rarely a good solution, since the old inter-ethnic conflict is simply redefined as an interstate conflict—pathological Westphalianism—but in some cases it may nevertheless be necessary in order to prevent massacres and massive human rights violations by the drawing of frontier lines. Third, a completely reversed process is the *integration* of neighbouring states into a regional formation, a process providing solutions to ethnic tensions simply by downplaying the role of borders, so central to the old Westphalian order based on national sovereignty. Ethnic conflicts often spill over into nearby countries where they are perceived as threats to national security. Conflicts among states are therefore more easily solved within an appropriate regional framework.

It is reasonable to expect that increasing 'regionness' will be a response to the stronger presence of the external world, manifested in different ways. The security problems of the region are seen as disruptive by the international community, putting pressure on the parties to find more realistic solutions. Regionalism, or more particularly 'the new regionalism', could in a certain sense be seen as a re-creation of empire in a new and more benevolent form as an alternative to a conflict-prone nation state system. Since the 1980s globalization has *de facto* integrated the region in economic terms and removed the resistance to Indian dominance thus, in a way, unmaking partition. Regionalism is also a possible remedy for some problems related to globalization. The catastrophic consequences of the tsunami made it very clear that there was a fatal lack of preparedness at the level of the region. Recently a more constructive regionalist option seems to have been more widely recognized in South Asia with the rising interest in SAARC. This trend was unfortunately broken by the postponement of the planned summit meeting in Dhaka, an incident we shall return to.

## I. THE PATTERN OF REGIONAL CONFLICT
## IN SOUTH ASIA

The regional pattern of conflict is analysed as a series of inter-connected levels: conflict events, particular conflict structures, and types of conflict, together shaping the general conflict pattern. The pattern of conflict is thus formed by different types of conflict (ideal types), which are manifested in concrete conflicts (normally mixed) and, finally, conflict events. The conflicts and hence ultimately the pattern of conflict is transformed over time under the impact of globalization and now latterly the war against terrorism. It is obvious that a large number of different types of conflicts are being collapsed into the overall category of terrorism, a new discourse which seems to replace, as far as India is concerned, the old discourse focused on communalism, but with little change in substance.

The pattern of conflict in the South Asian region during the last five decades can be described as pathological in the sense that the image of 'the other' is based on a distorted perception of reality, coupled with suspicion and fear. The artificial and only lately established nation state structure has further contributed to this. Pakistan was created on the basis of the 'two-nation theory', which, in wording reminiscent of 'Huntington's thesis', asserted that coexistence between the two civilizations was impossible.[2] After Pakistan was split up (disproving the theory), there are more Muslims in India than in Pakistan (and Bangladesh), namely, 130 million. The Hindus in India see themselves, in their quality as Hindus, as alone in the world and surrounded by Islam. The same subjective experience of latent threat is to be found in the Buddhist Sinhalese 'majority' in Sri Lanka in relation to the more than 50 million Tamils who live in Sri Lanka and in southern India (as well as in parts of South-East Asia). The Tamils in southern India, on the other hand, have built their identity on opposition to what is described as a north Indian oppression of Dravidian south India going far back in history. The small states in the region, Nepal and Bhutan, are concerned about their larger neighbours; and in all states immigrant groups (whether they are refugees or in search of livelihood) from neighbouring countries are persecuted.

To this suspicion among peoples must be added the suspicion between states, nurtured by several wars between India and Pakistan as well as repeated interventions by India in neighbouring states. The interrelationship between the two types of hostilities, inter-state and inter-people, may be said to define the South Asian security complex where most security threats emerge from within the states only to poison relations between the states.

The traditional security policy in South Asia has been characterized by the efforts of the regional great power, that is to say India, to avoid external interference (Kodikara 1983), while the smaller countries occasionally have attempted to escape India's hegemony by the contrary means of establishing relations external to the region (Muni 2000). Sri Lanka thus once tried to achieve a rapprochement with the regional organization ASEAN. Pakistan has conducted an energetic West Asian policy in the search for national identity, and by trying to control Afghanistan it acquired 'strategic depth' *vis-à-vis* India. The Soviet invasion of Afghanistan in 1979 gave Pakistan an important extra-regional role in the anti-communist counter-offensive that ultimately resulted in the 'Talibanization' of Afghanistan. Two decades later, paradoxically enough, the country again acquired a key international role, this time in the war efforts against the Taliban regime and the al-Qaeda network's bases in Afghanistan. By this drastic move Pakistan lost control over Afghanistan, except in the Pathan inhabited areas.

## 1. LEGACY OF POLITICAL VIOLENCE

In a historical perspective, South Asia has got its fair deal of political violence in spite of being the birthplace of a number of non-violent doctrines. The major event was of course the Partition in which context the father of the Indian nation, Mahatma Gandhi, in complete disagreement with the idea of dividing the former British India, was killed. A remarkably long series of heads of state and government have since been assassinated in most countries of South Asia: Indira Gandhi (1984) and Rajiv Gandhi (1991) in India; Liaquat Ali Khan (1951) and Zia ul-Haq (1988) in Pakistan; Sheikh Mujibur Rahman (1975) and

Ziaur Rahman (1981) in Bangladesh; S.W.R.D. Bandaranaike (1959) and Ranasinghe Premadasa (1993) in Sri Lanka. The majority of these assassinations, in so far as it has been possible to establish the motives, were linked with religious or ethno-national conflicts. In the classical political assassination the target is one single carefully selected individual. Often moderate leaders within a particular movement (sometimes even chief ministers) are killed by militants in order to prevent a certain political outcome. Rajiv Gandhi was killed by a suicide bomb attack, a method associated with the Tamil struggle.[3]

## 2. A TYPOLOGY OF CONFLICTS

The following nine variants of conflict more or less associated with violence can be distinguished in South Asia. They are derived from many different sources, and have been distinguished with respect to horizontality/verticality of conflictual relations. I do not include 'religious conflict' as such in this typology, since the conflict normally is created by politicized segments of a particular religion rather than being derived from the religion as such. Notwithstanding, religion plays a role as an ingredient in many types of conflict.

HORIZONTAL CONFLICTS

1. More or less spontaneous, locally limited, *riots* between two social, often ethnic/religious groups. Motivated by a struggle for power, status and scarce resources, they are as a rule sparked off by a provocative religious ritual or neighbourhood conflict of a more material or personal nature. In connection with a liberation movement, this relatively old and recurrent pheno-menon, rarely associated with large scale violence, acquired, as it took national dimensions, the designation of 'communalism' and then referred primarily to the (politicized) relation between Hindus and Muslims. This is a horizontal conflict in the sense that there are two distinct groups with limited interaction living side by side.

2. *Sectarian clashes* within the same religion, for instance Shia and Sunni Muslims in Pakistan or rival sects within Sikhism

in Punjab, e.g. the conflict between the Nirankaris and the more
orthodox Khalsa Sikhs. This conflict is also horizontal since we
are dealing with two groups unilaterally claiming to have the
correct interpretation of a particular religion. As mentioned
above, the major religions of India cannot as such be seen as
being in conflict. They constitute ingredients in ethnic and
communal conflicts.

3. *Inter-ethnic struggle* between 'sons of the soil' and immigrants from poor neighbourhoods looking for jobs (Weiner
1978). 'South Indians' in Mumbai, Bengalis in Assam and other
parts of the Indian north-east, Baluchis in Karachi, Nepalis in
Bhutan are cases in point. This conflict is also horizontal: two
groups competing for the same scarce resources.

4. *Gang wars*, normally ethnically organized, purely criminal
clashes which may use a religious or political cover but essentially
fight for criminal space, control over smuggling routes, production of drugs, services of 'protection' or simply dominance.
They thus have a horizontal character. It has been suggested
that the Karachi gang wars are instigated by the intelligence
agencies to keep a check on them. For these reasons many such
killings go unreported and unsolved (Wilson 2003: 33).

5. *Ethno-national* political violence, aimed at political independence or some other form of autonomy for a specific ethnic
group having national aspirations, for example, the liberation
movement in Kashmir, the Sikh movement for Khalistan in
Punjab, the Tamil struggle for Eelam in Sri Lanka and the Naga
people (or rather the Naga peoples) fighting for their independence in north-east India. This type of conflict is horizontal
since the purpose is separation or autonomy (statehood) on the
basis of a linguistic and territorially defined group.

VERTICAL CONFLICTS

6. Socio-economically motivated actions of violence, or *class
struggle*, carried out by extremist left-wing movements, often
directed against the local symbols and representatives of the
state, for example, police stations and administrative buildings.
Annihilation of class enemies is a major goal. Examples of this
are the Naxalite movement in some of the states in India; the

People's Liberation Front (JVP), a guerrilla movement formed in
Sri Lanka by radical students in 1971; and the Maoists in Nepal
who began their revolt in 1996. This is a vertical type conflict,
since it is characterized by the class dimension. Naxalism was
founded on revolutionary theory.[4] Today it is generally referred
to as 'terrorism', which certainly makes the making of revolution
(whatever its potential) even more difficult. Revolutionary theory
has some status, less so terrorism.

7.  *Caste violence*, typically from upper castes directed at the
Dalits' and Other Backward Classes' (OBC) attempts at emanci-
pation and liberation from feudal bonds and the discrimination
implied in the caste system. Here acts of terror, such as burning
Dalit quarters in rural villages, are used in a very conscious way
to threaten people into passivity. Violence rarely comes from
below in this case of vertical conflict characterized by caste or
hierarchy, but may of course be part of a socio-economic struggle
(see point 6).

8.  *Social banditry* refers to outlaws in non-accessible areas,
where they establish a local popular hero cult and lead a more
or less institutionalized struggle against the state surviving on
various criminal activities. One example is Veerappan, who for
a long time operated in the forest border area between Tamil
Nadu and Karnataka. In this case there were connections both
to ethno-national and socio-economic conflicts.

9.  Politically motivated *pogroms*, which are more organized,
politicized and nationwide communal riots than the traditional
type (point 2). Examples are the July 1983 massacre in Colombo,
and the 1984 killings of Sikhs in Delhi. The most prominent
example of the political fallout is the Hindu nationalist movement
which seized power partly by means of political violence.[5]
Typically the criminal acts carried out in the context of such
pogroms are rarely taken to court, and when they are the
criminals are often acquitted. Vandalism can be targeted against
artefacts, cultural events, films, and books which are said to
defame certain (now mostly Hindu) values.[6] This can be described
as a verticalization of horizontal relations, in the sense that it
aims at political subordination of a specific group, dividing the
population into majority and minorities.

These conflict types can be seen as 'ideal types' which in real life are mixed to create what the author calls distinct concrete conflicts in the framework developed above, that is, ongoing tensions and hostilities which form particular histories, which can be identified in space and time, and which are manifested in conflict events such as (before 2001) the Black July massacre of Tamils in Colombo in 1983, the killing of Sikhs in Delhi in 1984, the December 1986 riots in Karachi, the destruction of Babri Masjid in Ayodhya on 6 December 1992, and the consequent Bombay blasts on 2 March 1993. On the level of the actual conflict there is a mixture of motives and identities. For instance, the sectarian violence in Karachi where it is difficult to distinguish between sectarian terrorists and members of criminal syndicates (Wilson 2003: 24). To create an atmosphere of fear, which essentially is what terrorism is about, also gives a reason to provide income-generating protection. Religious zeal is often a cover for criminal activities. Obviously such links are hard to research, and we therefore mostly rely on journalists who are risking their lives in the process.

## II. CONFLICT STRUCTURES: AN HISTORICAL OVERVIEW

These different types of conflicts can in different combinations be found in most countries in the region in the form of historical conflict structures. By 'historical' I mean in this case that every conflict is a process that must be understood historically. Regional diversity is, as mentioned earlier, also reflected within the individual states. This has implications for external as well as internal conflicts. In fact, both are intimately related, which can be exemplified from all over the region. This overview departs from the trauma of Partition and then goes on to discuss (more or less) resolved and unresolved conflicts. Conflicts in other parts of the region are discussed for the purpose of comparison and in order to better grasp the regional dimension.

### 1. THE PARADIGM

The Partition in 1947, and the religious mobilization behind it back in the 1920s, marks the most important starting point for communal clashes between Hindus and Muslims as well as for the Sikh problem. The importance of this event can hardly be exaggerated (Ahmed 2002). In the Lahore-declaration 1940, the by then only one-decade-old two-nation theory was most clearly stated: 'Hindus and Musulmans belong to two different religious philosophies, social customs and literatures. They neither inter-marry or interdine together and indeed they belong to two dif-ferent civilizations which are based mainly on conflicting ideas and conceptions.' The idea that the two categories at that time constituted distinct, homogeneous groups is of course nonsense. This Muslim declaration, which had its counterpart in Hindu radical nationalism, nevertheless opened the gate for communal politics, destroying the framework of a pluralist inclusive nationalism. Normal politics became pathological politics. In Punjab, the system of organized political power collapsed, which enabled extremists to take over by ruling the streets. Private armies turned from self-defence to genocidal violence (Hansen 2002). The Hobbesian catastrophy was to mark the formation of post-colonial India, thereafter always extremely sensitive to threats against the state. Jawaharlal Nehru later (in his letter to chief ministers 1961) made a strong normative distinction between what he saw as nationalism and what later became known as 'communalism' in India: 'Communalism is one of the obvious examples of backward-looking people trying to hold on to something that is wholly out of place in the modern world and is essentially opposed to the concept of nationalism. In fact, it splits up nationalism into a number of narrower nationalisms.' Nehru's position on the correct meaning of nationalism—inclusive pluralism—represents what in India is generally referred to as 'secularism', now questioned particularly by the Hindu nationalist movement (Panikkar 2001). Communalism now constitutes a hegemonic discourse in India. This 'narrativization' of history (Chadda 1997: 50) was systematized by the BJP regime, through influencing both research councils and textbooks for the secondary school system. The two-nation theory born in British India thus became 'communalism' in Independent India, a concept normally referring to the continued tension between Hindus and Muslims, which did not disappear on account of the Partition. The Sikhs who suffered most from it and lost their homeland

later developed their own 'two (or three) nation theory', the
need for Khalistan. We shall come back to this.

## 2. EXPERIENCES OF CONFLICT MANAGEMENT

Another potentially equally serious conflict at the birth of the
Indian nation state was the simultaneous Dravidian resistance
to the Aryan-North Indian-Hindi domination. Separatism was a
major option in this case as well. The early Dravidian (south
Indian) movement, dominated by Tamil intellectuals, wanted a
separate Dravida nation, consisting of four linguistic groups:
Kannadigas, Telugus, Malayalis, and Tamilians. Only the Tamils
subsequently pursued this through the DMK and other party
formations gradually dominating the Madras state, later renamed
Tamil Nadu. The later Tamil struggle in Sri Lanka was supported
in and by Tamil Nadu, but nevertheless failed to revive the
nationalist fervour of the 1960s (particularly the language
agitation of 1964-5). The democratic transition in 1967 from
Congress to DMK rule (a very dramatic event at the time) is
significant here. Secondly, the secessionist demands were soon
played down. Thirdly, the factionalism and corruption within
the Tamil political movement had a sobering effect on exaggerated populist expectations. In this case a more accommodating
conflict resolution model within the framework of the Indian
state was used. In later conflicts elsewhere in the country, the
centre was to turn to more confrontational methods (Chadda
1997; Cohen 1988).

The Punjab crisis that erupted in the 1980s also goes back to
Partition which was a disaster for the Sikh community in Punjab.
Without going into details one could say that the crisis resulted
from repeated frustrations in the effort to restore the homeland
of the Sikhs (who have a legacy of political independence since
the decline of Mughal power up to the annexation of the Punjab
by the British in 1849). These frustrations were intensified by
divisive policies orchestrated from the political centre with the
purpose of consolidating its power with little regard for the
local consequences. The Akali demands on the centre were
initially quite modest and of a rather practical nature. They had
little to do with identity and nothing to do with secession. The

demonization of the Sikhs was the work of the Congress, and it was successful, much too successful. The demonization was particularly effective among Punjabi Hindus fearing the horrors of a new partition. A radicalization also took place among the Sikh unemployed youth (Bhindranwale) and polarization became a fact.

The unrest ultimately resulted in the armed intervention and partial destruction of the Golden Temple in Amritsar, the assassination of Indira Gandhi, and the massacre of Sikhs in Delhi and other places in 1984.[7] The state of Punjab was drawn into anarchy and terror by militants (demanding an independent Sikh state—Khalistan). The crisis in the words of Paul Brass was a crisis for the federal system and for the Indian state (Brass 1994). The agitation met with a very rough response from the central government. The suspicion that Pakistan was behind it contributed to this. There had been no such suspicion in the case of the Tamil agitation. In Tamil Nadu the solution, a radical devolution in political-practical rather than constitutional terms, was found in the 1960s. In Punjab the moderates were eliminated and President's Rule established from 1987 to 1993. The 'solution' was based on rigid suppression, isolation of the militants, and a general wish for normalization among the exhausted Sikh population.

## 3. UNRESOLVED CONFLICTS

The ethno-national conflicts in Tamil Nadu and Punjab are two now (as it seems) resolved crises.[8] Both go back to the 1920s and the early phase of the (Congress-dominated) nationalist movement, but the peaks of the respective conflicts were different. The Kashmir problem stems from the same time but this conflict has reappeared in different forms and is still unresolved. Like Palestine it is a big conflict in a very small area, and with early futile UN involvement. The Kashmir conflict is often seen as the probable cause of an eventual major war (perhaps even nuclear war) in the region. For this reason international attention has increased, particularly after 9/11.

The Kashmir conflict also goes back to Partition, and the history of how it really happened is still controversial. The conflict, which has led to two major wars (1947 and 1965) between India and Pakistan and 30,000 dead in terrorist related clashes, refers to a problem unsolved at the time of independence, namely, what status should be accorded to the predominantly Muslim but Hindu governed princely state of Kashmir. Together with Hyderabad, Kashmir was the only example of enforced integration of the princely states, otherwise a remarkably peaceful process (Menon 1961).[9]

The question was seen as a matter between the two emerging nation-states (Kashmir independence was thus not on the agenda), and India in particular has therefore opposed all involvement from outside. Kashmir represented different national projects: *Kashmiriyat* negated the two-nation principle and was therefore of great significance for civic nationalism in India, as well as the idea of a secularized Pakistan, if that should turn out to be a possibility. As a country with a majority of Muslims, Kashmir automatically belonged, on the same principle, to Pakistan. According to the Hindu view of history, Kashmir was Indian and its Muslim population therefore a 'minority', like the remaining 130 million Muslims in India. The people of Kashmir were never consulted but a majority would probably have preferred independent status of some sort. The major political figure pursuing this aim was Sheikh Abdullah, leader of the National Conference, the Kashmir movement that later emerged as the dominant party in the first free and fair elections in 1977, similar to the DMK in the 1960s.

According to journalist Tavleen Singh who covered the 1983 elections in Kashmir, the issue of separatism was not raised when Farooq Abdullah (Sheikh Abdullah's son) led the National Conference to victory (Singh 1966). As had been the case in Punjab this victory provoked manipulative power politics from Delhi, destabilizing the state (the 'cricket test'). The government had low legitimacy. The conflict thus erupted again in 1989. At that time there was a new political generation, largely un-employed, as well as new political issues (Ganguly 1997; Schofield, 2003). Incompetence in the state and political machination from the national capital in the context of a countrywide Muslim awakening triggered an *intifadah*, in which fundamentalist parties were increasingly dominant. Pluralist

Kashmir (*Kashmiriyat*) was on the losing side. A civil-war like situation followed, and throughout the 1990s the regime can only be described as state terrorism (Quraishi 2004).

The Indian north-east emerged as another yet unresolved (or partly resolved) problem after independence because many peoples (Naga, Mizo, etc.) here did not consider themselves as Indians (Brass 1994: 202).[10] New federal states were created after negotiations with the moderates, but the militants continued their struggle. In addition, this area (with its tea plantations) is an area of immigration, resulting in growing tensions between immigrants and the indigenous population. Assam was already an internal colony under the Bengalis in British India. After 1971, many more immigrants came as refugees from Bangladesh. The complexity of the situation was underlined by a number of insurrectionist movements. The crisis was met with state terrorism sanctioned by anti-terrorist legislation (TADA). This had repercussions in neighbouring Bhutan where the insurgents set up camps. A hundred thousand Bhutanese citizens of Nepali origin in southern Bhutan were in turn forced to flee to Nepal. This exemplifies the regionalization of conflict.

Among the unresolved conflicts must be counted the Naxalite struggle (or People's War), which refuses to go away due to resilient tribal poverty (the not so shining India) and police suppression (false encounters) throughout the forest belt stretching from Andhra Pradesh to Nepal.[11]

## III. INDIA'S NEIGHBOURS

Let us now turn to the conflicts in the other South Asian countries, most of which can compete with India in terms of social and cultural complexity. Pakistan can also compete with India as far as internal conflicts are concerned in spite of having been founded on the principle of a unified religion. Pakistan is seen by many as the most explosive state in the region, close to being a 'failed state' with many no-go areas. Ethnic identities have shown to be stronger than religious bonds, first in the separatism of the Bengalis (and Baluchis and Pathans), then the transformation of the Mohajirs (Muslim immigrants from India) from a nation-building class to the 'fifth nation' fighting with the Sindhis and the Baluchis in the territory of Karachi. Apart from this there is sectarianism of a militant kind within Islam between the Sunni majority and the Shia minority, and between these two and the Ahmediyas. The problem is that further Islamization leads to deeper sectarianism, the root cause of political violence in Pakistan. The military has all along been the major political factor keeping the country together, and in the initially very professional military organization, fundamentalism, and therefore sectarianism, has grown stronger.

Religion has not shown to be an integrating principle. East Pakistan revolted on the basis of Bengali identity, and Bangladesh was created after a civil war in which India intervened. This was a clear case of unilateral intervention, and it met with international protests. Bangladesh is now a reasonably homogeneous country since most of the Hindus there have fled to India. The main ethnic conflict in Bangladesh is between the small group of Hill People and the dominant Bengali population.

Sri Lanka has one long-standing conflict, which for decades has taken the form of a civil war. Here, interestingly, we have a case of bilateral intervention, that of the IPKF mission (Indian Peace Keeping Forces) in northern Sri Lanka from 1987 to 1990. This is a controversial episode in the history of South Asian conflicts (Dissanayake 2004: 107). It can be compared to the Dayton agreement on Bosnia in the sense that it was imposed by a strong external hand against the predominant mood of large parts of the population, Sinhalese as well as Tamils (who initially were more positive). This exemplifies what has been called 'the Indian model of conflict resolution': a relatively generous reform programme unilaterally decided and with the purpose of marginalizing the militants (Perera 2000: 82). It may have worked in Punjab, but it misfired in Sri Lanka. This in spite of the fact that the political formula was basically sound. Political changes in both countries undermined the arrangement (Muni 1993). India pursued several not fully compatible objectives in intervening in the Sri Lankan conflict. It wanted to support the Tamils, to put pressure on the Sri Lankan government for geopolitical reasons (the Trincomalee harbour), and to prevent the formation of Eelam as it could have provoked renewed separatist sentiments in Tamil Nadu.

Since 1996, Nepal, after a rather unsuccessful democratic experiment which started in 1990, is in the midst of a violent rebellion by Maoist guerrillas inspired by the Chinese Cultural Revolution and the Sendero Luminoso in Peru. The socio-economic background is abject poverty in combination with elite corruption. There are caste and ethnic dimensions involved as well similar to the Naxalite uprisings in India. Professionals who are active are mainly teachers and students. Women too are active, as well as Nepalese living and working in India.

Bhutan is not free from conflicts either. One major tension is between the majority population and a minority of Nepalese origin. A second problem is Indian insurgents from the north-east establishing camps on the Bhutanese side of the border.

The Maldives is a homogeneous but authoritarian Muslim country. Political conflict led to another unilateral intervention by India in 1988. There are no signs of democratization. On the contrary, Amnesty International has stated: 'By repeatedly dismissing reports of human rights violations in the country, the government of President Gayoom has allowed perpetrators to continue to act with impunity. This has effectively perpetuated a cycle of repression, eroding people's confidence in the state's institutions to protect their fundamental rights. It is high time that government authorities accept their own responsibility and failure to protect and promote human rights.'

The traumatic India-Pakistan conflict, which so far has exploded in three wars (not counting minor skirmishes), has prevented all more organized efforts towards regionalism. This conflict has been fuelled by later national, religious, and ethnic struggles: the problem of Kashmir, the Bengali uprising against West Pakistan, and Sikh aspirations for Khalistan. Bangladesh's initial warm relations with India soon turned sour because of Indian arrogance, refugee problems, and conflicts related to water management problems. Relations between India and Sri Lanka became increasingly tense as the Sinhalese–Tamil conflict erupted and Tamils fled to Tamil Nadu where they also received covert military training. The northern mountain kingdoms of South Asia were more or less absorbed into the Indian Union through processes of democratization and anti-monarchy agitations, discretely encouraged from India. Bilateral conflicts in the region invariably involve India. The prospect of a multilateral intervention in a conflict is distant, the regional power would not even permit regional conflict management. However, this attitude seems to be changing.

## IV. CONFLICT TRANSFORMATION?

After 11 September, South Asia found itself at the centre of the war against terrorism. The international Jihad continued, now against India; this occurred more precisely in Kashmir where many war veterans from Afghanistan (Arabs and Afghans, but also Bosnians and Chechens) were gathered to establish a second front. Pakistan was requested by the USA to make a choice between joining the war against terrorism or be regarded as a rogue state. A large number of conflict events followed one another.[12] The state assembly in Kashmir was the target of a bloody action on 1 October 2001. Subsequently on 13 December, there was an attack on the Indian Parliament House in New Delhi, when terrorists shot dead a number of security guards (and a gardener), but failed in their objective of killing MPs who were in the building. India immediately accused Pakistan of being responsible and staged along the border with Pakistan the biggest mobilization since the war of 1971.[13] The conflict was sharpened further after an attack on the USA Information Centre in Calcutta when five policemen were shot dead. In Pakistan a journalist from the *Wall Street Journal* was kidnapped in Karachi and later brutally executed. The arrest of a variety of more or less suspected individuals revealed much about the terrorist network in South Asia; for example, on the one hand the link between religious and political militants, and criminal organizations. The latter did much of the dirty work: murdering, kidnapping, and collecting ransoms; in return they were protected by militant political organizations and their contacts with the rest of the political world, the security service, and so on. This protection consisted of supplying false passports (the most prominent terrorists had a number of different identities) and houses in different countries in the region, as in the Middle East. A political analysis that only considers the overt part of politics will obviously not get far. The darker side cannot be penetrated until much later, or through successful but dangerous investigative journalism. Thus many of what I call here conflict events are never fully investigated, which makes it hard to relate them to specific conflicts and categorize them in terms of types of conflicts.

In other cases the connection is more obvious. An alleged Muslim attack against a train of pilgrims/activists (*kar sevaks*) who had been on a visit to Ayodhya, the scene of the temple conflict ten years earlier, initiated a large-scale conflict between Hindus and Muslims. Some sixty men, women, and children were burnt to death when the train made a stop in the city of Godhra in Gujarat. In the subsequent revenge actions against Muslim areas of the city of Ahmedabad and other places, 1,000–2,000 people died, while more than 100,000 were driven out to live in refugee camps. On 24 September, two Muslims entered the Akshardham temple in Gandhinagar, Gujarat, and shot dead thirty-seven people and injured eighty-one. There is much to suggest that this was an act of revenge. The same has been suggested about the Mumbai blasts in August 2003, which killed fifty people, although no organization has claimed responsibility. This anonymous terrorism seems to be a general pattern.

Let us now examine what has happened as regards the different types of political violence mentioned earlier. Attempts at political assassination continue but tend to form a part of terrorist attacks in which many lives are lost, the 2 December 2003 attempts to kill Musharraf being the most obvious examples. Hindu-Muslim communalism is on the increase. The rapidly growing Hindu movement of the last decade is, however, a totally different phenomenon from the elite conflict between the Indian National Congress and the Muslim League before 1947. While Islam is a universal religion, not rooted theologically in any specific culture or territory, Hinduism is a 'territorial' religion which, after having been a fundamental part of an Indian (Indic) civilization, has evolved towards religious nationalism: Hindutva. The inclusive characteristic, a capacity to absorb other cultures, which many see as central to Hinduism, is being replaced by a monolithic, masculine arrogance. The traditional cultural capacity for absorption is now associated with weak feminity which in this context is thus given a decidedly negative meaning.

The Hindutva movement distinguishes between religions which are regarded as internal and hence more acceptable, such as Buddhism, Jainism and Sikhism, and religions that have come from outside such as Christianity and Islam. In recent years there have been a number of attacks against Christians also, and several churches have been burnt down. But as Hinduism's historic enemy, Islam is in a class of its own. After 9/11, Indian Muslims are seen as terrorists at its worst, and as a minority at its best.

A polarization between Hindus and Muslims, like that now taking place in India, can have unforeseeable consequences for the whole region. Up to now large-scale violence of the pogrom type has been concentrated in the state of Gujarat, which has an exceptionally bad record as regards what we have called 'power political terrorism'. This is the worst communalist political crisis since Partition in 1947. The state government in Gujarat trivialized the preceding events by speaking of 'communal riots', while the train attack against Hindus was immediately described as 'terrorism'. The government, moreover, has been implicated by various human rights organizations as being directly responsible, and party-politics is openly suggested as the motive. It is thus a matter of a form of state terrorism. The pattern can be recognized from the massacres in Colombo in 1983 of the Tamils, and in Delhi in 1984 of the Sikhs. It can, however, be noted that in the case of Gujarat there was a larger element of the middle class among those responsible for the violence and that sexualized violence played a more prominent role. Several witness reports describe an unimaginable bestiality. The political objective is, however, obvious. The trend is towards power-policy motivated by the political struggle for power and directed terrorism linked to state power. It also happens that state power links up with 'local sovereignties' embodied in mobilized communities and 'strong men', as also that such local power is transformed to state power.

Since 11 September 2001, terrorism in South Asia has acquired greater significance on the global scale, given that Hinduism together with Christianity ('the West') and Judaism (Israel) have become targets for Islamic terrorism. All these religions have their own form of fundamentalism, which gives the cultural

conflicts of today, or what Huntington called 'clash of civilizations', an apocalyptic character. One may think what one
will about Huntington's terminology but not unexpectedly it
seems to become more and more popular with the self-appointed
representatives of civilization among both Muslims and Hindus.
It is, however, quite misleading to see the Hindutva phenomenon
as a civilizing renaissance. It is rather a 'new-minted chauvinism'
which arises from the frustrations of globalization and has little
to do with Hinduism as a civilization. As such it has formed
part of a pluralistic Indian (or Indic) civilization.

The major conflict is thus once again the original communalism in a new international context. The state election in
Gujarat took place in an atmosphere of recurrent attacks by
Hindus on Muslims and vice versa. The chief minister of the
state, Narendra Modi, went into the election on an anti-terrorist
platform in which he identified Pakistan as responsible for the
Muslim attacks. The militant Hindus saw Gujarat as a 'Hindutva
Laboratory'. If the tactic worked there, which unfortunately it
did, it can be expected to be applied on a national basis and the
wholly decisive dialogue will be made the more difficult, perhaps
irreparably. In the State Assembly elections that followed, the
BJP emerged as the clear victor which encouraged the government
to plan for early elections in 2004. At the same time, a militant
Islam based in Kashmir has become a pan-Indian phenomenon
with attacks that are more and more coordinated. Although
militant Muslims constitute a very small minority, Islamic
terrorism is described as a major threat by nationalist Hindu
leaders. The increasing number of unsuccessful terrorist attempts
may indicate that polarization stimulates a less professional but
more desperate youth to violent action. As in Israel, the hardening
attitude towards supposed terrorists leads to ever more terrorist
actions. 'Terrorism', whatever that may mean, has become an
integral part of politics.

Today the uprising in Kashmir despite its complex historical
background is regarded more as international terrorism organized
by Pakistan, which of course is not the whole truth but which
cannot be entirely denied. There are more than a hundred
revolutionary movements in the state. The struggle for independence in Kashmir has more and more been subordinated to

International Jihad. On the occasion of his visit to the region, US Secretary of State Colin Powell described the conflict as 'international'. This caused great consternation in India which decisively rejected the idea of international electoral observers during the elections in October 2002. It is, however, not only a matter of internationalization; behind the change lies a more profound ideological difference: from the focus on territory to the principle of a non-territorial Islamic community. Opposed to a territorial project in which religion was part of an ethno-national identity—*Kashmiriyat*—is a theological, non-territorial project, namely, the global Islamic community, which observes no political boundaries. There are still internal forces that strive for some form of autonomy. But the assassination of the moderate leader, Abdul Ghani Lone, before the elections diminished the possibility of a Kashmiri solution based on some form of autonomy, a solution which now, after a series of round table conferences, begins to be discerned in Sri Lanka. It was a sign of progress, though, that the elections could be held, to a considerable degree as a result of pressure from the USA, which in turn was motivated by the war against terrorism.[14] After the Islamabad SAARC summit in 2004, serious negotiations were at least started. These may marginalize the jihadis but provoke the old Kashmiri sentiment of a legitimate right to autonomy.

Let us now turn to the other countries in the region, starting with Pakistan. Islam has many faces. On 12 January 2002, the Pakistani general and dictator, Musharraf, delivered an important speech in which he assumed a role similar to that played in an earlier time by Kemal Ataturk in Turkey. His speech implied a break with fundamentalist forms of Islam and signalled the modernization of Pakistan, which has long been in a state of anarchy, criminality, and general social dissolution and decay. The two most prominent radical Islamist organizations were banned. Also, sectarian violence was defined as terrorism. This was followed by the arrest of activists and a tighter control over the Koranic schools (*madrassas*) with a total foreign student population of 36,000. The majority of the 2,000 activists arrested were later released (*Financial Times*, 29 April 2,002). However, many 'freedom fighters' were now renamed 'terrorists'. The reaction in India was cautiously sceptical but some individual voices called on the government to facilitate in every way this extremely difficult modernization project. The paradox in the situation is that the once secularist India is at the same time evolving in a fundamentalist direction and thereby confirming *a posteriori* the two-nation Theory, which was the original motivation for the creation of Pakistan. The 2004 elections put a break to this, but we do not know what Hindutva's next step will be.

In the case of Sri Lanka, the conflict between Tamils and Sinhalese, which has resulted in 65,000 deaths, has come closer to a solution in that the international war against terrorism has reduced the freedom of movement of the Tamil Tigers branded as a terrorist organization by several countries including India. Interestingly enough, before the negotiations opened the movement was legalized in Sri Lanka. It does not suffice to define terrorism as criminal since that excludes the possibility of negotiations. A peace process was started after international involvement (Norway), and international support for the Tigers diminished.

In Nepal the opposite path has been chosen, denying the Maoists any legitimacy. The Maoist insurgence that has been going on since 1996 is directed against police stations in remote and extremely poor corners of the country. Eventually the army, under imperial control, was brought into the fighting and so reinforced the character of civil war. After a guerrilla attack in February 2002, when 130 police and soldiers were killed, representatives of the government emphasized the criminal aspect of terrorism.[15] This was obviously influenced by 9/11. In October 2002, there was a 'Musharraf' solution when King Gyanendra dismissed the government and put an end to a twelve-year democratic experiment. It had not, however, been particularly successful, and the coup therefore did not lead to any extensive protests at the beginning. In February 2005, the king (and the army) took complete control. The justification was the government's incompetence in combating the Maoist uprising, i.e. what was called terrorism.

The Maoists are extremely anxious not to be dubbed as 'terrorists' for the simple reason of being able to consolidate their position after an eventual take over of the country instead of risking an Indian intervention (to the BJP Nepal was particularly important as the only existing Hindu kingdom). The king has used this labelling game as a negotiation card, playing off the Maoists against the democratic opposition. In contrast with India, the USA has not formally designated the Maoists as terrorists (Muni 2003). Certainly there is nothing whatsoever in common between Marxist revolutionaries of the Maoist/Naxalite type and religious fundamentalists. India, which for decades has had problems with similar uprisings by the Naxalite movement in Bihar, Jharkhand, and Andhra Pradesh, will, however, give Nepal discreet support in this objective, since these movements more and more coordinate their training in distant and unruly districts which cannot be reached by the arm of the law. There is thus a regionalization of the socio-economically motivated left-wing terrorism in different countries.[16] There are terrorist networks, increasingly integrated with criminal networks, which embrace the whole region and build on no-go zones, open frontiers (between India and Nepal), frontiers that cannot be policed (between India and Bangladesh), and false passports. Bangladesh is increasingly polarized between fundamentalists and secularist forces. The former are on the offensive and are believed to receive support from al-Qaeda and Pakistan's security service.[17]

If we look at the South Asian region, what is completely clear is that internationally organized terrorism demands internationally organized counter-measures and systematic cooperation, in the first instance regionally. The old-time military and security policy actions are insufficient and in many cases counter-productive. We can also note that even within a specific region the concept of terrorism can be used to designate radically different political conflicts, and that branding something as terrorism therefore does not always facilitate the search for political solutions.[18]

## V. REGIONAL COOPERATION: UPS AND DOWNS

The other side of conflict is lack of cooperation. South Asia is one of the last regions to wake up to the challenge of the new regionalism, although a breakthrough may be on its way (Muni

2005). It has been a region of distrust and conflict, penetrated by external powers, which, as a matter of fact, sometimes have been invited by the individual states in the region as part of their managing of internal hostilities. Until the mid-1980s, there was no formal regional cooperation whatsoever. To the extent that one can say that South Asia had reached a certain level of 'regionness', its network of relations was mainly conflictive, creating a violent security complex (high level of regionness in terms of criminal activities), security and development regionalism (Buzan and Rizvi 1986).

The early evolution of the South Asian Association for Regional Cooperation (SAARC) coincided with serious internal conflicts (Sri Lankan Tamil and Sikh separatism), and is proof of the inherent soundness and logic of the idea of regional cooperation that a number of important meetings, including the summit in Dhaka 1985, took place in spite of these disturbances, which also had serious inter-state (Pakistan-India, Sri Lanka-India) implications. The crucial inter-state conflict is, of course, that between India and Pakistan. It is a conflict that defines the regional security complex and provides a key to its transformation into a regional security community. Its elimination would make all the difference as far as further regionalization is concerned. Summits of SAARC have emphasized regionalism as the most appropriate way to relate to current changes in the world order, but at the same time nationalist suspicions linger on as nationalist and fundamentalist movements gain strength. It is, however, both a strength and a weakness that SAARC contains all the South Asian states. It is a weakness because the conflicts in the region have paralysed SAARC, confining its scope to non-controversial and marginal issues such as tourism and meteorology. It is a strength, however, precisely because controversial problems can be handled within one organization, providing at least a framework for regional conflict management. Put differently, the regional organization coincides with the regional security complex and can therefore be seen as an embryo to a security community. Conflict resolution, however, is so far not considered a task for SAARC. There have therefore been cases of unilateral and bilateral interventions, the most traumatic after the emergence of Bangladesh being the IPKF mission in northern Sri Lanka.

Obviously South Asia has a long way to go before a regional approach to economic development, security and conflict resolution can be adopted. Regional cooperation in the economic field, or development regionalism, is (similar to the issue of security regionalism) at best embryonic. In the field of resource management, there are due to the shared river systems strong interdependencies (environmental security complexes) which so far have been a source of conflict rather than cooperation. They may also, however, be turned into imperatives for regional cooperation, as shown by the agreement between India and Bangladesh on the sharing of Ganga waters. This treaty may change the political climate between the two neighbours and pave the way for a broader regional agreement (including Bhutan and Nepal).

The reason why it is important to search for regional solutions is that bilateral suspicions make any other solution fragile. The overall trend in the region is towards occasionally crisis-ridden muddling-through democracies, where the threats from intra-state heterogeneity are more problematic than inter-state conflicts. However, to an increasing degree internal and external issues become interwoven, re-inforcing the arguments for regional development and security, but unfortunately not necessarily the political will to implement them. But surprises do occur. Before the January 2004 SAARC summit in Islamabad (after two postponements due to inter-state tensions), a number of prominent politicians expressed what seemed to be a more serious and sincere opinion beyond the usual rhetoric about the need for regional cooperation. Former prime minister Atal Behari Vajpayee at a conference envisaged mutual security cooperation, open borders, and even a single currency in the region in the long run. He called for promotion of peace and banishing of hostility in South Asia and cited the increased people-to-people contacts between India and Pakistan as a reflection of the 'intense desire for amity and goodwill'. He said the demands of globalization and the aspirations of the people provided the objective basis for the energetic pursuit of a 'harmoniously integrated' South Asia. People have waited for over half a century for the fulfilment of the 'unexploited potential in their own neighbourhood', and were now impatient to move ahead, Vajpayee said.[19] The former minister of foreign affairs in Sri Lanka similarly asserted in a newspaper article: 'Today, any serious instability in a country will necessarily affect the stability of neighbouring countries. In the South Asian context, the very essence of regional security and cooperation is, first, the political will to forge a cohesive and concerted association amongst ourselves.'[20] These expectations were fulfilled when India and Pakistan towards the end of the summit in Islamabad declared that formal peace negotiations would start in the near future. It is, however, problematic that the regional summit was completely bilateralized, while regional integration, which is the long-term solution to the crisis, may receive a backseat. However, there were significant regional agreements as well: SAFTA, an additional clause to the 1988 declaration on terrorism, and a Social Charter. On the other hand, the Dhaka summit that was to take place in February 2005 (after already having been postponed due to the tsunami) was postponed after a request from India with reference to the *coup d'état* in Kathmandu and the security situation in Bangladesh. The need for regional cooperation had been dramatically demonstrated by the tsunami disaster striking the region in December 2004. The impact of this disaster on the conflict in Sri Lanka is still unclear, although both parties to the conflict have expressed hopes that the joint emergency activities could provide a model for further cooperation.

## VI. PROSPECTS

South Asia is a region of conflicts in terms of multitude and dimensions as well as complexity. The security policy in this region has been determined by internal conflicts with repercussions in neighbouring countries and beyond. It is therefore logical that the interest of the surrounding world should increasingly be directed towards these conflicts and their resolution. The external factor has thus become very strong. In the USA South Asia has got a new neighbour at the same time as India is emerging as a great power. This contradicts India's traditional policy of maintaining regional hegemony and avoiding outside involvement. This policy has also characterized the pattern of conflict resolution, both within India and in India's involvement in neighbouring countries. The Indian approach has been accommodative up to a point, and suppressive beyond that point. This, however, has left a number of conflicts unresolved, particularly conflicts that have become regionalized and internationalized. Kashmir, for instance, is an ethno-national conflict that has become an international jihad. It seems that a new approach is called for. The new bus service (between Srinagar and Muzaffarabad) linking the two parts of Kashmir could be the first sign, soon after confirmed by the statement of the two governments that the peace process was 'irreversible' and that 'terrorism' would not be allowed to impede it (*The Hindu*, 19 April 2005).

What are South Asia's prospects for stability and peace in the light of the geopolitical change following the Cold War? There are both bright spots and darker elements. In all the states of the region a distinct brutalization of politics is taking place (in the case of Gujarat on an unimaginable scale). That can, naturally, not be traced back to 9/11, but it is clear that repressive violence is held to be justified by the danger of terrorism and is facilitated by more extreme anti-terrorist legislation. In addition to the degeneration of internal politics, which is bad enough, the continuing risk of war between Islamic Pakistan and Hindu India must be mentioned. The current peace process has only started and could easily be derailed. It is difficult to imagine a stable Pakistan in which Islam is severely restrained. After the 2004 election, India returned to secularism with the new Congress-based government led by the non-traditional politician, Manmohan Singh. The new prime minister follows the principle of 'positive unilateralism' first suggested by Inder Kumar Gujral (the Gujral doctrine), who served as minister for external affairs during 1996–7. According to this principle or doctrine it is for the stronger party to show good faith by going more than halfway towards a solution (Mohan 2004).

In Sri Lanka, fresh elections were also carried out, which, as earlier in its history, has complicated the peace process. In Nepal the Maoist insurgency continues; in Bangladesh there is a polarization between secularist and fundamentalist forces, and the relationship with India is also becoming worse. Recently Bhutan closed a number of militant camps and prevented the entry of militants from the Indian north-east. In the Maldives, the media continue to face rough times.

The regionalization and internationalization of terrorism also affects the forms of the struggle against it. The regional co-operation organization of South Asia, SAARC, might be able to play an important part as a regional means of solving conflicts, but so far the rock-hard Indian bilateralism has prevented it. The atmosphere of suspicion between the states in the region is thus itself a partial cause of terrorism (destabilization), and also facilitates terrorist activity through the existence of bases on the other side of the frontier. The relations between the countries are, however, so strained that they have been unable to create a common security organization for combating terrorism, despite the fact that in 1987 SAARC adopted a resolution against terrorism.[21]

We have noted that internal conflicts which include violence, nowadays increasingly frequently described as 'terrorism', have become a transnational phenomenon in South Asia as in other regions of the world. Certain conflicts are regionalized, others internationalized. The geopolitical landscape is changing. At its extreme, the whole of the future world order is affected. Central Asia has come into focus geopolitically at the same time as the instability in South Asia is becoming a security threat beyond the region itself. The boundary between South Asia and Central Asia was never rigid. In Afghanistan the new Great Game,[22] relating to geopolitics and control over energy resources (oil and gas) in Central Asia, is shaping up. Academic interest in Central Asian studies has increased considerably in Indian universities, which is an indication of India's strategic ambitions.[23] In the struggle for Afghanistan, Pakistan has lost its 'strategic depth' *vis-à-vis* India, while India has increased its influence through its cooperation with the Northern Alliance. Thus Pakistan feels surrounded by enemies. The war against terrorism therefore embraces something more than the struggle against terrorism. It changes the geopolitical map. Afghanistan is no longer a far away corner where nodes of terrorist networks can be hidden. It is a strategically situated route for the transport of Central Asian oil.

International terrorism constitutes part of a global security complex in which security must be defined in ways differing radically from the nation state idea of security, with its emphasis on national security and military defence. The war against terrorism, as manifested in Afghanistan and Iraq, has, as is usually the result of war, reinforced the power of the state and the military apparatus, and for that reason a neo-Westphalian type of world order appears, at any rate in the relatively short term, to be more likely than a post-Westphalian experiment. That applies particularly to the unilateral superpower which ever more explicitly disdains multilateral forms of global governance. The prospect for regionalism is a complex issue, however. In the longer term it may see its great opportunity in the fact that so many other options are failing. Thus the process of regional co-operation must go on regardless of temporary setbacks since the geopolitical transformation of the subcontinent is irreversible.

## NOTES

1. Burton (1990) coined the concept 'provention', meaning preventing conflict by promoting balanced economic development and social peace.
2. This theory declared civilizations as the new geopolitical rivals. For Huntington (1997) Islam and Hinduism constitute civilizations. For Chinese civilization he prefers the more encompassing concept Sinic rather than Confucian, but he does not apply the same logic to Indian civilization, calling it Indic rather than Hindu. The culture of the subcontinent is incomprehensible without taking Hindu-Muslim interaction into consideration. The same can be said about Buddhist-Hindu interaction in Sri Lanka.
3. The massacre of the royal family in Nepal has so far not been proven to have any political connections. However, what people believe is not without political importance.
4. The original uprising in the north Bengal countryside near Naxalbari took place in early 1967. The formation of the CPI(ML), the supportive party, took place in mid-1969 (Ray 2002).
5. Its terror, in the sense of creating fear, was first aimed at the destruction of 'the other's' cultural symbols, for example, the Babri Masjid in Ayodhya, demolished in 1992. However, the terror was not limited to

physical structures. Thousands of Muslims died in the subsequent riots, and the response to this came with large-scale bombings in Mumbai at the beginning of 1993. History repeated itself ten years later in the state of Gujarat, to be discussed later.

6. A significant event happened in January 2004. A mob entered the famous Institute for Oriental Studies in Pune, vandalizing the place and destroying invaluable documents. The reason was a book about Shivaji, questioning the parenthood of the hero/king. The book had been written by an American professor who had used the institute for archive studies. Later the Maharashtra goverment banned the book, which by then had already been withdrawn by the publisher.

7. The nature of the state changed in 1984 when the Hindu card was played.

8. The spectacular escape from the Chandigarh prison of three militants in January 2004 seems to have created some enthusiasm among Sikhs who still feel that the suppression by the military and the police had been unreasonably severe. *The Tribune*, 28 January 2004.

9. In her pioneering study (1968) Urmila Phadnis noted: 'In the consolidation of the political unity in India after Independence the relatively peaceful integration of the princely states has generally been regarded as a noteworthy achievement.'

10. More problematic cases: Assam, Nagaland, Manipur, Tripura; less problematic: Meghalaya, Mizoram, Arunachal Pradesh.

11. In a comparative analysis of conflict it is important not to forget cases where no conflicts occurred, although there were similar preconditions as in the other cases. In India, the southern state of Kerala is very often referred to as a Third World welfare state (compare Sri Lanka). It is a successful case of conflict 'provention'. In fact, this has been described as a paradox, since it is not a situation one would expect in a poor country, which, furthermore, has not been a great performer in economic growth. This raises doubts as to the sustainability of the Kerala model, particularly in the current context of globalization and erosion of state capacity as far as redistribution and social policy is concerned. However, it is hard to deny the importance of the fact that the dominant regime has had a redistributive orientation. We shall here use Kerala as an example of successful provention, i.e. a pattern of development inducive to ethnic and religious peace. 'Kerala is a unique instance of large numbers of three major world religions living peaceably in one territory.' Kerala shows that a reasonably equal society can be created by a responsive government and a highly mobilized population, although it may be wrong to speak of the Kerala Model, since some of the preconditions were created long ago. What is of particular interest here is that the relative social welfare also has

implied social peace. This argument has also been made with regard to Sri Lanka.

12. From September 2001 to December 2002 there were 3,940 terrorism related acts of violence; 604 persons from the security forces, 1,197 civilians and 2,412 terrorists were killed (*Frontline*, 17 January 2002). Though there is no proof, some major railway accidents have also been linked to terrorist-related sabotage.

13. Three accused terrorists, all Indians, were condemned to death in December 2002 under the Prevention of Terrorism Act (POTA). There was a lynch atmosphere at the trial and Amnesty has questioned whether it was properly conducted (*Frontline*, 17 January 2003).

14. In Kashmir a new regional party, the People's Democratic Party (PDP), came in third place (with 16 seats) after the Congress party (in second place, with 28 seats) and formed the government with support from Congress. The National Conference remained the largest party but was severely weakened.

15. 'There is no question of sitting for a dialogue, rather we are moving ahead with a full strength and massive strength to crush the terrorists completely,' said the Minister of Interior, Khum Bahadur Khadka, quoted from the *Herald* (Panjim), 19 February 2002.

16. The Maoists of South Asia have since 2001 organized themselves in the Co-ordination Committee of Maoist Parties and Organisations of South Asia (CCOMPOSA), see Muni 2003.

17. According to the Indian journal *Frontline*, 3 January 2003.

18. In March 2002 the Indian Parliament passed a controversial anti-terrorist law, the POTO, on the basis of which suspected terrorists (both Indian citizens and foreigners) can be held in custody for ninety days without trial. On the basis of this law, twelve LTTE sympathisers were arrested in Tamil Nadu. The new regime took measures to repeal this law. The President made the following declaration: 'My government is concerned about the misuse of POTA in the recent past. While there can be no compromise on the fight against terrorism, the government is of the view that the existing laws could adequately handle the menace of terrorism. The government, therefore, proposes to repeal POTA'.

19. Conference on 'Peace Dividend—Progress for India and South Asia', organized by *Hindustan Times*, *The Hindu*, 12 December 2003. Also, Benazir Bhutto participated in this conference and expressed similar views.

20. Lakshman Kadirgamar, 'Securing South Asia', *The Hindu*, 29 December 2003. The Pakistan Foreign Office spokesman told newspersons that the summit provided a 'rare and historic' opportunity for Pakistan and India to move towards a dialogue process.

21. At the first SAARC summit meeting terrorism was identified as a threat to the region's political and economic stability, which justified regional cooperation. A Regional Convention on Suppression of Terrorism was signed in Kathmandu in November 1987. However, terrorism was never defined. This issue was raised again at the Islamabad summit in January 2004.
22. The Great Game is a reference to the geopolitical struggle in the region during the nineteenth century between Great Britain and Russia.
23. Wheras the BJP regime approached the USA, the Congress regime is expected to favour a multipolar world.

## SELECT BIBLIOGRAPHY

Ahmed, I., 1996, *State, Nation and Ethnicity in Contemporary South Asia*, London and New York: Pinter.

Ahmed, Ishtiaq, 2002, 'The 1947 Partition of India: A Paradigm for Pathological Politics in India and Pakistan', *Asian Ethnicity*, vol. 3, no. 1, March 2002, pp. 9–28.

Brass, Paul, 1994, *The Politics of India Since Independence* (New Cambridge History of India), New Delhi: Cambridge University Press.

Burton, J., 1990, *Conflict: Resolution and Provention*, London: MacMillan.

Buzan, B. and G. Rizvi (eds.), 1986, *South Asian Insecurity and the Great Powers*, New York: St Martins.

Chadda, M., 1997, *Ethnicity, Security and Separatism in India*, Delhi: Oxford University Press.

Cohen, S.P., 1998, 'Causes of Conflict and Conditions for Peace in South Asia', in Kanet, 1998.

Ganguly, Sumit, 1997, *The Crisis in Kashmir*, New Delhi: Cambridge University Press.

Grewal, J.S., 1994, *The Sikhs of Punjab*, New Delhi: Cambridge University Press.

Hansen, Anders Björn, 2002, *Partition and Genocide: Manifestation of Violence in Punjab 1937-1947*, New Delhi: India Research Press.

Hettne, B., 1993, 'Ethnicity and Development: An Elusive Relationship', *Contemporary South Asia*, vol. 2, no. 2, pp. 123-49.

Hettige, S.T. and M. Mayer (eds.), 2000, *Sri Lanka at Crossroads: Dilemmas and Prospects After 50 Years of Independence*, New Delhi: Macmillan.

Huntington, Samuel, 1997, *The Clash of Civilizations and the Remaking of World Order*, London: Simon & Schuster.

Kaldor, M., 1999, *New & Old Wars: Organized Violence in a Global Era*, Cambridge: Polity Press.

Kanet, R.E. (ed.), 1998, *Resolving Regional Conflicts*, University of Illinois Press.

Kodikara, Shelton, 1983, *Strategic Factors in Interstate Relations in South Asia*, New Delhi: Heritage Publishers.

Menon, V.P., 1961, *The Story of the Integration of the Indian States*, New Delhi: Orient Longman.

McLeod, W.H., 2000, *Exploring Sikhism: Aspects of Sikh Identity, Culture and Thought*, New Delhi: Oxford University Press.

Mohan, C. Raja, 2004, 'Cooperative Security in South Asia', *South Asian Journal*, October–December 2004, pp. 34–48.

Morris, J. and H. McCoubrey, 1999, 'Regional Peacekeeping in the Post-Cold War Era', *International Peacekeeping*, vol. 6, no. 2, pp. 129-51.

Muni, S.D., 1993, *Pangs of Proximity: India and Sri Lanka's Crisis*, New Delhi: Sage.

Muni, S.D., 2000, 'India in SAARC: A Reluctant Policy-Maker', in Björn Hettne, et al., *National Perspectives on the New Regionalism in the South*, London: Macmillan.

Muni, S.D., 2003, 'Maoist Insurgency in Nepal: The Challenge and the Response', Paper prepared for the Observer Research Foundation, New Delhi, April 2003.

Panikkar, K.N. (ed.), 2001, *The Concerned Indian's Guide to Communalism*, Delhi: Viking.

Perera, J., 2000, 'The Inevitability of Violence: The Centralized State in a Plural Society', in Hettige and Mayer.

Phadnis, Urmila, 1968, *Towards the Integration of the Indian States, 1919–1947*, London: Asia Publishing House.

Quraishi, Humra, 2004, *Kashmir: The Untold Story, New* Delhi: Penguin Books Judia.

Rai, Mridu, 2004, *Hindu Rulers, Muslim Subjects: Islam, Rights and the History of Kashmir*, New Delhi: Permanent Black.

Ray, Rabindra, 2002, *The Naxalites and their Ideology*, New Delhi: Oxford University Press.

Singh, Kushwant, 1992, *My Bleeding Punjab*, New Delhi: UBSPD.

Singh, Tavleen, 1996, *Kashmir, A Tragedy of Errors*, New Delhi: Penguin Books India.

Schofield, Victoria, 2003, *Kashmir in Conflict: India, Pakistan and the Unending War*, London: I.B.Tauris.

Varadarajan, Siddarth (ed.), 2002, *Gujarat: The Making of a Tragedy*, New Delhi: Penguin Books India.

Weiner, Myron, 1978, *Sons of the Soil: Migration and Ethnic Conflict*, Princeton, N.J.: Princeton University Press.

Wilson, John, 2003, *Karachi: The Terror Capital in the Making*, New Delhi: Rupa & Co. In association with Observer Research Foundation.

# CHAPTER 4

# Crisis of the State in Pakistan: Roots and Evolution

## Diethelm Weidemann

In August 1947, the jewel of the crown, British India, became a part of the past, and India and Pakistan as new independent subjects entered the political map of the world. This, indeed, left a deep mark on the history of South Asia and was the beginning of political, economic and social processes which drastically changed the face of the subcontinent. The specific conditions under which the new states achieved their independence, have proved to be till today a grave burden, a potential conflict zone. So, the crisis of the post-colonial state in nearly all South Asian countries is a long time consequence of the development of colonial rule.[1]

This chapter concentrates on the internal factors of the crisis of the state in Pakistan and its incorporation in the general crisis of the post-colonial state in South Asia.[2]

## I. THE EMERGENCE OF PAKISTAN— HISTORICAL CONDITIONS AND PERCEPTION OF THE NEW STATE

The multi-ethnic, multicultural and poly-confessional structure of British India imperatively required a federal organization of a post-colonial India. The provinces were not historical or ethnic entities but the result of a long process of conquest, lasting from the eighteenth century to the beginning of the twentieth century. The territorial situation was additionally complicated by the scattered 562 princely states. The anti-colonial question in India, therefore, also had a considerable intra-national component, the struggle of major ethnic and confessional groups to live free on the basis of their own culture, language and value systems. But the strong regional driving force of the national movement in the last decades of British rule was paralysed by the interplay of a pronounced anti-Indian wing within the Raj's establishment with communal forces and representatives of particular interests in the Indian society. All basic documents on constitutional questions between the Government of India Act, 1935, and the statements and bills of the Labour Government from 1945 till 1947, give evidence of the controversies over federalism and minority rights.

Thus, in the final phase of colonial rule, the different currents within the national movement could not overcome the existing internal contradictions and conflicts in India. The core problem was the rivalry between the leading political parties, the Indian National Congress (INC) and the All-India Muslim League (AIML), which in the public and in the media figured as 'Hindu Muslim conflict'. But, contrary to common perception, it was not a religious antagonism but a political struggle for power and economic interests, for which the acting middle classes needed mass support—which on the Muslim side could only be achieved by religious mobilization. This was the background for the formulation of the 'two-nation theory', and for the emergence of the Pakistan Movement. Under the banner of the struggle for the preservation of the religious identity of the Indian Muslims that theory postulated that the major religious communities constitute different nations, and that their cultural distinctions would make their existence on the territory of a single state impossible.[3] This construct, linked with the demand for a separate Muslim state called Pakistan, in 1940 became the sole political programme of the AIML.[4] In 1941, its president, Mohammed Ali Jinnah, unmistakably declared that Muslim India would never accept an all-Indian Constitution and a central government, and would resist any attempt to assimilate their national and political identity.[5] The course was set for the partition of India, and the Indian Independence Act, 1947,[6] was only the formal execution of decisions which had been passed between 1937 and 1945. But the developments since 1947, too, demonstrated that the partition of India was no solution of the famous 'Indian question'.

The core problems continued to exist in the successor states and the inability of the now ruling elites to master them created a whole bunch of conflict potentials, and an enormous fragility concerning the internal security.

## 1. AN OWN STATE AND NATIONAL HOMELAND
## FOR INDIA'S MUSLIMS

Pakistan's elites in power, despite the differences in their particular political positions, had the same basic perception of Pakistan, the same enemy images, and in their majority defined Pakistan as an ideological state. The occasional times intense clashes over the nature of the state mainly centred around the question of how much ideology and which particular expression of Islam were viewed to be indispensable for a Pakistani state. Only in the third generation after the partition of British India, the alternative ideological or democratic state seems to have gained in significance. At the same time, it must be stressed that *one* commonly accepted concept of the state does not exist in Pakistan.

The Muslims in British India had spiritualized the historical glamour of the Mughal Empire and derived their self-image from it. But they had no idea in which state they themselves would like to live after colonial rule. Consequently, the only chance for Jinnah to get the desired Pakistan was to fall back on the Islamic card. Only religious or communal mobilization could force the British to divide India. Finally he got Pakistan in 1947, not the country he had envisaged with the undivided provinces of Punjab and Bengal, but, in his own words, a 'moth-eaten' Pakistan with borders like open wounds. On the other side, the orthodox current in the Indian Muslim community strongly opposed the very idea of Pakistan out of a principled universalistic Islamist creed. Favouring the Ummah concept they rejected any projects for national Muslim states. Even after its foundation and having lived in Pakistan, they rejected it and its legitimation for many years after 1947. And their spiritual respectively ideological successors today are again on the warpath against the present Pakistani state which in their assessment is 'un-Islamic'. But Jinnah's vision and the foundations laid down by him were the

only clearly formulated state idea and, at least formally, accepted
by a majority in the society. A few basic points shall, therefore,
be considered in this section.

In the perception of the founders of the state, Pakistan was to
be a national homeland for the Indian Muslims. Safeguarded by
the constitution equal rights were to be extended to all segments
of the population living in the provinces of the new state. Jinnah
was convinced that the core values of the Muslim population,
the Pakistan idea and the pride in the country for which they
struggled hard, would create favourable conditions for the
Muslims' identification with Pakistan and the emergence of a
national bond between the major components of the people.[7]
For Jinnah, the decisive criterion was the loyalty of all citizens
*vis-à-vis* the state and respect for the law. He fought for an own
state for the Indian Muslims but he never had in mind the creation
of an Islamic state. In the first session of the Pakistan Constituent
Assembly he said: 'Now, I think we should keep that in front of
us as our ideal (equal rights for all citizens—D.W.) and you will
find that in course of time Hindus would cease to be Hindus
and Muslims would cease to be Muslims not in the religious
sense, because that is the personal faith of each individual, but
in the political sense as citizens of the state.'[8] In view of the
embittered relations between the AIML and the INC in the last
phase of colonial rule, these words were rather heretical and
made for the practical burial of the two-nation theory.

It is not by chance that the people have not been told of these
positions of the 'father of the nation' for decades. And it is also
not accidental that for many years now a resentful struggle
against the basic pillars of Jinnah's concept of the state can be
observed. That is not surprising because of their direct relevance
for Pakistan's self-perception and the identity of its citizens.
Immediately after the demise of Jinnah on 11 September 1948,
the process of turning away from his concept started. Very soon
his national homeland for the Muslims was replaced by a vague
concept of an Islamic state, and Jinnah's call for the rule of the
constitution and the law was substituted by the priority of the
Koran. The *de facto* replacement of the nationalist Pakistan idea
by the postulate of the Islamic nature of state and society, and

later General Zia-ul-Haq's enforced Islamization of the country, produced an interaction and linkage of elementary deficits of the political system, of military rule, and mass perception. It signalled the elimination of Jinnah's concept of the state.

But there is still a further reason that Pakistan has not become the state of Indian Muslims as originally conceived. When India was divided, the Muslim upper strata and middle classes, who had been the proponents of the Pakistan idea, migrated to the new state. About ten million Muslims, mainly from East Punjab, Greater Delhi, and Bihar, involuntarily went to Pakistan, driven out of their homes by a fanaticized, merciless, and irrational mob. The same number of non-Muslims in the now Pakistani provinces suffered that fate and fled to India. However, despite this mass-exodus the majority of the Indian Muslims remained in their homeplaces and today we have about the same number of Muslims in Pakistan and India. In other words, on the very day of the proclamation of Pakistan one pillar of the Pakistan idea—the national homeland for all Indian Muslims—clashed with the reality.

Misuse of political and economic power over decades, enormous corruption, reckless nepotism, and, not least, the repeated usurpation of power by the military have discredited the structures and institutions of the Pakistani state and caused a dramatic loss of authority and legitimacy. They have paralysed the Pakistan idea, blocked the process of national formation in major parts of the territory, and fostered the emergence of a new regionalism and the revitalization of ethno-nationalism. *In toto,* these developments have been the mainspring of a deep-seated identity crisis. The present struggle between civil society and military rule, between liberal and enlightened sections of the people and the growing anti-democratic Islamist forces is the unavoidable result of the failure of the very idea of a national state in Pakistan.

## 2. THE QUESTION OF IDENTITY—A COMPLEX LEGACY

A rather specific self-image and enemy-image in Pakistan *ab ovo* led to a definitely ideological *raison d'être,* and via its feedback in the education system as well as in the country's internal and external policies produced striking pre-formations of the collective political behaviour. The Pakistani self-perception is a very complex problem. The self-image, in its individual and collective expressions, was strongly shaped by historical and ideological factors, and more or less deliberately produced by the elites since the colonial era. It is constituted mainly by three major components: the collective self-assessment of Pakistan, images of their own history in line with this self-assessment, and the ideological foundation together with the perception of the state itself.[9] The understanding and the concepts of the state, can only be grasped in their interaction with the other two elements, because they exist only within this context. In the following paragraphs the essential elements of Pakistan's self-perception with special reference to their relevance for the complex crisis of the country are outlined.

The question of the Pakistani self-perception is an inquiry into the Pakistani identity, which till today is shaped by the historical heritage.[10] The self-image of the Indian Muslims during the colonial era resulted from their picture of the past as the rulers of the subcontinent from the first millennium to the eighteenth century. British foreign rule and politics during the territorial expansion of the East India Company, and especially the period after the great insurrection of 1857–9, left deep mental wounds. As the Pakistani historian Khursheed Kalam Aziz wrote, their problems with identity started when the Mughal imperial rule ended.[11] In his opinion the Muslims had perceived themselves as 'rulers', it constituted their psyche, kept the society together and compensated for the age-old fear of the Hindu majority. With the suppression of the 1857–9 uprising, all of that suddenly ended. The feelings of humiliation and degradation further increased by the fact that Hindus, Sikhs and Parsis adapted much easier to the British colonial-capitalist regime, with some strata rising to the top within the limits of the colonial society. At the dawn of the twentieth century, a depressive perception of their status was the major reason that certain sections of the Muslim upper classes organized themselves in the All-India Muslim League, which became a conservative counterpart to the Indian

National Congress which dominated the Indian political scene.

The Muslim League's refusal to live in one state with the other Indians, irrespective of their being Hindus, Sikhs, Parsis, Christians or tribal animists, was, in plain words, the definition of the Indian Muslims as non-Indians. Ayesha Ayal has stated that the Indian Muslims always insisted on having an identity different from that of the Hindus, and they have finally got that Pakistan, but not the state they have struggled for.[12] Nevertheless, this theory and the campaign for Pakistan in a comparatively short time produced the initial forms of a Muslim consciousness which had been absent during the preceding hundred years and which was to fade again from the 1970s onward.[13]

Yet even the constitution of an own state for the Indian Muslims in August 1947 was not the starting point for the emergence of a stable national identity in Pakistan. There are many reasons for this situation. Beyond the historical deficits in the Muslim self-perception, the major causes responsible for the difficulties with the national identity rest in the social and political structures of the new state, in its political system, and not least in the politics and power struggles of the ruling groupings in Pakistan, or, as Saeed Malik states, the concentration of power in the hands of a small oligarchy.[14] As a consequence, Pakistan today is confronted with a tangle of different identities and loyalties, partly overlapping or directly clashing with each other, with remarkable political and ideological effects. Some essential elements of this tangle or of the hierarchy of identities can be characterized as follows:

- Local and tribal identities and loyalties in the Northern Territories, in the North-West Frontier Province, in Baluchistan, and in Sindh are still playing an important role.
- In all segments of the Pakistani population, ethnic identity is a strong factor which even can lead to the refusal of defining themselves as Pakistanis (Pakhtoon tribal areas, Sindhi nationalists), and to the rejection of the central government.[15]
- Religious affiliation still is a central mark of identity. In

the whole Islamist section of Pakistani society this aspect definitely has priority ahead of national identity. Following the philosopher and theologian, Ghulam Ahmed Parvez, belief in the Koran is the only binding force in Pakistan.[16] That means, the first line of demarcation in identity is between Muslims and non-Muslims, whereby non-Muslims should be granted human rights but no political rights.[17] A second line is drawn between the Pakistani Muslims themselves, resulting in the bloody schism between Sunnis and Shias, and the outlawing of groups like Ahmadiyas and Ismaelites. So, *one* Islamic identity even in Pakistan is out of the question.

- In consequence of these different identities and loyalties, even after nearly sixty years of independence the national identity in Pakistan is still rather fragile. One must not forget that the officially declared Pakistani identity was the result of a process of multiple negation. The anti-colonial/anti-British thrust of the Pakistan movement left as much its mark as the struggle for Pakistan against the INC. Stressing again and again the distinctiveness of the Muslim community, this aimed to present the Indian Muslims as non-Indians. Not a few of the specifics of Pakistan's state- and nation-building as well as the shape of the elite consciousness are rooted in this background. For a long time, it was not seriously taken into consideration that the attempt to create a Pakistani identity out of a *de facto* anti-identity by political, ideological, and even administrative means was one of the most momentous legacies of India's partition. An anti-identity, the self-perception of being not Indians, was not suited to producing a constructive Pakistani self-image. Even today it is rather difficult to define what in fact is unmistakably Pakistani in the present society and the existing state.

The last decades produced a lot of evidence that none of the basic concepts of state, which have been engineered by the administrations, the army or the media, resulted in a commonly accepted national identity. By contrast, there is a very close connection between the problems of identity and the crisis of the state and the society.

## II. PAKISTAN: FROM A TRADITIONAL REGIME CRISIS TO A SYSTEMIC CRISIS OF STATE AND SOCIETY

### 1. ROOTS AND DEVELOPMENT OF THE CRISIS

With the foundation of Pakistan, the postulate of a separate Muslim nation in South Asia was elevated to a state doctrine. Islam as a unifying religion and common denominator for the existence and the activities of the community as well as for the individual; Islamization of the state, of its institutions, and of the social life in accordance with religion, became the dominant myth, with the purpose to legitimate the takeover of power of the Muslim League and the politics of its leadership.[18]

In contrast to the real multi-ethnicity of society, compounded by a gradient of civilization between the east and the west of the country, and between Punjab and the rest of West Pakistan, the ruling elites for a long time seemed to be relatively homogeneous. It resulted from the fact that, for several decades, they exclusively consisted of representatives from the Muslim upper and middle classes that had immigrated from India, and of West Punjabis. Only because of the power requirements of the later military regimes, the upper strata in the North-West Frontier Province, in Baluchistan, and in Sindh were step by step included. To the nexus of the social upper classes with the high echelons of the army, which is a specific feature of Pakistan, the ethnic component has to be added as an additional dimension. The Punjabis are dominating the economy, the political structures, the armed forces and services, higher education, and to a great extent the media also. Next to them, especially in the wake of the war in Afghanistan, the upper strata of the Pakhtoons have acquired a new status in the establishment, and enormous wealth from arms trade and drug traffic.

From the very beginning, the basic problem for the legitimacy of the state was the contradiction between constitutional structure and political practice, which became evident in 1949 with the Objectives Resolution. The nucleus of the problem was and is the role of Islam; and the relations between the centre and the periphery, as the relationship between Islamabad and the so-called smaller provinces demonstrates. Since the 1960s, Pakistan's place in the regional strategy of the United States has resulted in extensive military and economic aid from Washington to the power elites. That led not only to a massive rise of the prestige and influence of the military establishment in Pakistan but also to a key position of the military even in some sectors of the economic sphere. During the Afghan War, the public could observe, that this situation reached a new, unprecedented level through the diversion of American arms and funds, meant for the Afghan Mujahedeen by the army and the ISI, and their entanglement in the drug trade.

It is not without interest that, especially during the periods of military rule, Islam, on the one hand, was used as an instrument of politics for the consolidation of its power position by the respective ruling group and, at the same time, it also served as an external link between the different factions of the power elites. This process, staged in the course of several decades, and the use of the state's institutions for Islamization, left a deep impression on society and the mass consciousness, and strengthened the role of religion in public life.

Today the legitimation of Pakistan's ruling elites is challenged from three different angles and with different motives.

- No government since 1958 has enjoyed national legitimation because they withdrew from the foundation consensus of the Pakistani state, or because they have broken it consciously and deliberately.
- The military has no right to rule Pakistan in times of peace. It is not legitimized to exert influence on the installation of governments or to overthrow elected administrations.
- The whole political system of Pakistan is without legitimacy because it is un-Islamic. Instead the state, the party system, the judiciary, and nationalism should correspond with the basic reqirements of Islam.

That means the challenge to the legitimacy of the present

state and political system is motivated either by demands for a consequent parliamentary democracy or by the claims of orthodox Islamic and radical Islamist forces.

Some further essential aspects in the context of the legitimacy question can be outlined briefly:

- The state of Pakistan was founded by an elite who was extraneous to the autochthonous population of West and East Pakistan, and who enforced Urdu as the national language, which caused bitter resentment in East Bengal. The bulk of the new rulers came from provinces which remained with India; many of them had served in the Indian Civil Service.
- The basic concept for a Pakistani identity, the Pakistan ideology, was deduced from the two-nation Theory. As such it directly collided with the history based ethnic, cultural, and linguistic identities, and with the legitimate interests of the population in the provinces.
- The deficits in the legitimacy of the ruling groups have been implicit since 1947. During the whole existence of Pakistan its elites have tried again and again to contain the increasing loss of authority and loyalty by calling any resistance against the centralistic power politics 'anti-national' and later even 'un-Islamic'. It is an irony of history that the former rhetorics of the ruling elites are nowadays used by the Islamist currents against the establishment and against the state.

## 2. FROM A REGIME CRISIS TO A CRISIS OF THE STATE

Between the death of General Zia-ul-Haq (1988) and the seizure of power by General Musharraf (1999), the international public in general was rather indifferent or even ignorant with regard to the economic, social, and political processes in Pakistan notwithstanding the fact that the country during this decade passed through four acute phases of the crisis of the state. They signalled the degree of political instability, the strength of the looming crisis, and the depth of societal dissent.

The overthrow of the elected governments of Benazir Bhutto

(1990 and 1996) and Nawaz Sharif (1993 and 1999) by a presidential order and a military *coup d'etat* respectively were not a chain of separate events. They must be analysed in the context of the general development of Pakistan, of the formation of its political system, and of the problem of legitimacy, discussed earlier. The enduring crisis situation of Pakistan is characterized by three phases of evolution: regime crisis, crisis of the state, crisis of the society. Since the end of the Zia-ul-Haq regime, these have evolved more and more simultaneously. The Pakistani crisis, therefore, is complex and cannot be reduced to the immediate sphere of the state.

Since the assassination of the first Prime Minister Liaqat Ali Khan (1951), Pakistan has been confronted with a continuing and open regime crisis. It started, as has been said earlier, with the departure from the liberal and democratic state-perception of Mohammed Ali Jinnah, and the course towards an Islamic state. The Objectives Resolution of the Constituent Assembly of 12 March 1949 was a compromise between liberals and Islamists, and very vaguely formulated, so that it later could be interpreted in different directions.[19] In the view of the Islamists, the inclusion of this resolution as preamble in the constitution justified the definition of Pakistan as an Islamic state, because the inaugural formula states the absolute sovereignty of Allah and the limited authority of the state of Pakistan.[20] In 1985 Zia-ul-Haq made it a constitutional requirement for all laws and legal acts in Pakistan to be in concordance with the Koran and the Sunnah.[21] The general causes of the political and regime crisis have been discussed earlier: some of its more specific features have been

- the very heterogeneous structure of the political class in Pakistan, including the non-existence of an indigenous urban middle class and intelligentsia outside of West Punjab and East Bengal;
- the subsequent dominance of bureaucratic, semi-feudal, and military elements in the spheres of decision-making from the very first days of Pakistan onward;
- the direct claim for power, which is characteristic for political forces, socially and culturally still rooted in a feudal milieu, and for military establishments stemming

from the ruling social strata, and their view of the state and of the national resources as the corporate property of the ruling groups;

- and not least the consequences of the interplay of the said moments, like the political immaturity of great parts of the power elite, a striking voluntarism in politics, the extremely selective application of constitutional principles, and of parliamentary democracy.

Under such social, political, and governmental conditions, the tendency for political crises to end in regime crises is immanent. In fact, Pakistan had to face veritable regime crises in 1954, 1957/8, 1969–71, 1977/8, 1989/90, 1993, 1996 and 1999. The crisis of 1969–71, beginning with the fall of General Yahya Khan and climaxing with the declaration of an independent Bangladesh, was the first regime crisis which turned into a crisis of the state and of the very fabric of Pakistan. Since then, all regime crises have been first of all crises of the state and the political system.

## 3. CHARACTERISTICS OF THE SYSTEMIC CRISIS OF THE STATE

Considering the development of Pakistan since the death of Zia-ul-Haq in its entirety the diagnosis of the societal situation has to move beyond the level of regime crisis. It has been stated that Jinnah's state-perception had no chance of a lasting realization, and the national homeland for the Indian Muslims came into existence only in a very limited form as the post-Independence development was dominated by the basic dichotomy of a national versus an Islamic state. But beyond this contradiction, the state-building even in the starting phase was subject to still other compulsions.

State-building had priority over nation-building because its purpose was mainly to secure the power of succeeding elite factions. Immediately after August 1947, these were the groups of well-off, well-educated immigrants from the past centres of Muslim rule in India, as for instance, the United Provinces, not a few of them with experiences in governance, administration, and services. Pakistan had been their claim since 1940, and in

1947/8 they took over *de facto* the new, emerging state and occupied the professions, while businessmen coming from Bombay slipped into economic key positions. Later, and for a long time, the dominant faction was the military elite, purporting to be the real representative of the nation. After Zia-ul-Haq, the ruling circles consisted of a non-transparent net of party politicians, higher echelons of bureaucrats, influential semi-feudal landlords, entrepreneurs with political ambitions (mainly from Punjab), and the army command as final arbiter in decision-making. The coup by General Musharraf in October 1999 only changed the hierarchy within this net, but not the system as such.

Stephen P. Cohen, a leading US specialist in South Asian affairs, states that when the internal stability of a state is definitely lost, neither the instruments of the state nor the rule of the military are able to restore it. A long-term occupation or usurpation of the functions of the state by the armed forces, or the self-perception of the military establishment to be the state, will, on the contrary, not only throw discredit upon the army but also on the state *per se*, as an institution.[22] Besides the general characteristics and consequences of military rule, the political incompetence of Pakistan's presidents in uniform and martial law administrators was an additional and specific factor. For a long time they refused a legitimate balance of interests within the political system, and made the repressive component of state power an end in itself. In the final analysis one can only conclude that the power ambitions of the armed forces have been the root cause for the chronic instability that led to the crisis of the state blocking a sound political development in Pakistan.

Akmal Hussain defines four major characteristics of the crisis of the state:

1. The differences between the political and the repressive apparatus of the state are diminishing. The political and social mediation is not performed by people's parties but by organizations with a narrow social basis and rather specific interests. The inevitable result is a growing tension between the social strata.
2. The state, dominated by the repressive apparatus, is highly

centralized and does not recognize the legitimate rights of the smaller nationalities. The pre-eminence of Punjabis in all spheres lies at the root of separatist tendencies (Sindh, Baluchistan).

3. Some segments of the population consider the official interpretation of religion by the elites in power as a smokescreen to pursue their specific class interests and to justify the repression of anybody questioning their legitimacy. So, in the course of the crisis of the state, the ruling elites have lost the capacity to stay in power without use of force. And that again is the point where the army comes in.

4. The long periods of military rule have destroyed the balance between the different institutions of the state, namely, between the army, the bureaucracy, and the judiciary. That is the central cause of the institutional crisis of the state, and of its authority.[23]

After fifteen years of studying the emergence and evolution of South Asian internal and inter-state conflicts, crises and conflict potentials the research group 'Militant Conflicts in South Asia' arrived at the conclusion that the crisis of the state in Pakistan was neither the result of an unlucky coincidence of factors, nor of bad government alone. It is, as in Sri Lanka, Bangladesh, Nepal, and India, of a systemic nature, and has many facets and expressions. From the author's point of view, some of the most important aspects can be outlined as follows:

- The drastically reduced authority of the state in consequence of its inability to resolve the vital problems in the economy, in the social sector, in the political and national sphere;
- The dysfunctionality of major parts of the inflated state apparatus, and the direct involvement of politicians and bureaucrats of all ranks in the looting of the country;
- The self-isolation of the higher administrative establishment from the real life in the country, and from the conditions of daily life of the population;
- The discredit of the major political parties, resulting from the uninhibited breach of their election programmes, from

their open nepotism, and the unlawful enrichment of many
party leaders;

- The insignificance of real political differences between the
  parties which, with the exception of the Islamists, are more
  or less nuances in a demagogic vocabulary; and
- The degeneration of the political parties, which has
  seriously undermined the credibility of the public institutions, not least the democratic system.

The crisis of the state as an institution and of the political
system have raised again the question of the legitimacy of these
pillars of statehood. That is for a country with fragile social and
political structures a matter of existential dimension as the rise
of anxious statements on the future of democracy in Pakistan
testifies. It is not by chance that the legitimacy of the present
system is challenged most aggressively by the Islamist forces,
especially the different formations of Jihadis. Both tendencies
are indicators for the indeed critical situation in the country.

## 4. ON THE CRISIS OF SOCIETY—
### THE PROBLEM OF IDENTITY

In the final analysis, the crisis of the state in Pakistan is a crisis
of the system which was brought about after 1947, of its sense
and meaning. Destabilization, delegitimation, acute contradictions and conflicts in the social, political and ethnic spheres
are its pronounced characteristics. The obvious links between
them and the interaction of these features are raising the question
of whether they are different elements and manifestations of a
crisis of the society as a whole.

An adequate answer requires still more detailed research, but
it can be said that this is not exclusively a Pakistani problem. In
a number of countries which achieved independence after 1945,
similar processes can be observed.[24] But it is especially evident
in Pakistan because state and society have been deformed by
three long phases of military rule. In the nearly sixty years after
achieving independence, the models installed in the economic
sphere, in the political system, and in the structures and functions
of the state have reached their limits, have exhausted their

capability to resolve structural problems and, therefore, have entered into a stage of chronic instability. It suffices to enumerate
but a few evident features of the societal crisis.

- The continuing dichotomy of traditional and modern social
  structures during the last decades caused several social,
  political and ethnic eruptions, not to speak of religious
  confrontations (Karachi, Baluchistan, Interior Sindh, South
  Punjab, Malakand).
- The painful collision of the Pakistani self-image with the
  realities of the twentieth and the beginning of the twenty-
  first century have led to a growing political and ideological
  uprooting of increasing parts of the population. This
  process finds its expression in the rising jeopardizing of
  the basic principles and pillars of the present society, but
  also in the alarming tension between Islamization and
  national consciousness, followed by a crisis of identity
  looming not only in some provinces but even in the centres
  of power.
- The growing discord in the perceptions and concepts of
  society has a tendency towards an open conflict (for
  instance, civil society vs. Islamism), which could have grave
  consequences for the internal security and may even
  endanger the survival of Pakistan in its present form.[25]

Besides the loss of authority of the state, the deep and widespread distrust in the political class, and the growing social
cleavages, the evolving crisis of society is also closely connected
with the problem of identity.

Several decades after independence it is evident that in all
former colonial countries in the South Asian region the identity
problem is one of the key questions. That is not surprising in the
case of India with its multi-ethnic and poly-religious structure,
or for the sharp ethno-cultural confrontation in Sri Lanka. But
which specific factors are at work in ethnically homogeneous
Bangladesh? Concerning Pakistan, history has proved that Islam
alone, or Islamization, does not produce a common identity in
a country with different ethnic segments of the population.

The rising number of 'Us and Them' constellations (as a
quantitative moment), and the *de facto* ouster of the post-colonial

state from the 'Us' (qualitative moment), is, in the international discourse, mainly linked with the phenomenon of ethnicity, or with religious factors like militant Islam, Hindu chauvinism, and violent currents of Buddhism. But these explanations are not sufficient for providing satisfying answers. In any case, the political dimension, the experiences of the different components of the society with the post-colonial state must be taken into account. For evidently growing segments of the population do not recognize themselves in the structures and mechanisms of this state. Seeing their chances of participation either very limited or even non-existent, they have ceased to identify themselves with the present state. That is the main reason for their retreat to pre-national loyalties and identities, but not ethnicity and/or religion as such.

The past decades have demonstrated that none of the concepts of state that were propagated by the ruling elites and executed by state apparatus, army, and media have provided the 160 million Pakistanis an identity, which is commonly accepted in all provinces and by all segments of the population. The two-nation Theory, which was instrumental in the achievement of Pakistan, could not prevent the secession of Bangladesh (1971). It dealt a deadly blow to the self-perception of Pakistanis, and their world-view. It was of lasting negative consequence that they refused to recognize and to accept that the two-nation theory was a historical phenomenon and, therefore, only temporarily valid—if at all. Its offspring, the Pakistan Ideology, made, outside of the big cities and the Punjab, an impact only on the surface. The intense regional contradictions and conflicts (Baluchistan, Sindh) speak for themselves. The Pakistan Ideology nevertheless possesses a remarkable mobilization potential. If rationally handled, it could be instrumental in the development of a true Pakistani nation state. After all, in this context, the Islamic definition of Pakistan, enforced by Zia-ul-Haq and since then even violently demanded by the Islamist forces of different shades, has to be named. The real content of this concept is that religion has to be the ferment for the emergence of the nation state, that confession and nationality are identical, and that the Ummah has priority over the nation. Bangladesh has proved the failure of such a concept, because the cultural nationalism of the Bengalis was much stronger than the common religion with West Pakistan. It is striking that under the conditions of the twenty-first century, major parts of the Pakistani elites still adhere to theoretical constructs which in many other Muslim countries are of no real relevance. It is all the more striking as Islamization in Pakistan is directly linked with blatant anti-democratic currents, with the militarization of radical Islamist groups, with the drastic deterioration of the relationship between Sunnis and Shias, and not least with bloody sectarian strife. That means that even as a Muslim country Pakistan is torn, and to speak of an Islamic identity would be adventurous.[26]

*In summa*, Pakistan is faced with a crisis of the post-colonial state, a crisis of its political system, and an evident crisis of identity. Under such circumstances, it is not exaggerated to speak also of a crisis of the present society, may it be named post-colonial or otherwise.

## 5. The Unending Crisis: Pakistan's Path Towards New Military Rule

Herbert Feldman titled one of his books on Pakistan, *From Crisis to Crisis*.[27] This title could serve also as a symbol for the development between 1988 and 2001. Without going into the details of the successive phases of the crisis of the state in Pakistan, in the following the characteristic features, which once more encouraged the army command to takeover power, and to set up a military regime are highlighted.

After the dismissal of prime minister Benazir Bhutto by president Farooq Ahmad Khan Leghari on 4 November 1996, the installation of a caretaker government under Malik Meraj Khalid, and the announcement of elections within ninety days,[28] Syed I.H. Gilani wrote sarcastically that the cycle 'elections–constitutional coup–elections–constitutional coup' had now reached a soothing frequency of three years.[29] The elections took place on 3 February 1997 and, as expected, the Muslim League (N) under Nawaz Sharif achieved a clear victory, interpreted by the new prime minister as a 'massive mandate'. But the electorate was convinced that with the old faces the old problems would also continue to exist; more than half of those who went to the polls did not believe in a change.[30]

The course taken by Nawaz Sharif since March 1997 made it quite plain that his priorities were the consolidation and expansion of his own power and personal rule while eliminating all potential competitors. His power strategy surfaced mainly in eight elements:

1. The deprivation of the president of his exclusive powers, the enforced resignation of president Leghari, and his substitution on 1 January 1998 by the so far unknown Justice Tarar who was nothing but a client of the Sharif clan;[31]

2. The transformation of Parliament into an institution of acclamation, the limitation of the rights of the MPs, and the mobilization of an Islamist mob against the Senate in autumn 1998;[32]

3. The abolition of the independence of the judiciary and its massive political manipulation, including the dismissal of the Chief Justice who had refused to close some pending corruption cases against the Sharif clan;[33]

4. The long-term exclusion from power of all potential enemies by a combination of political repression, legal tricks, and denunciation through the media;

5. The attempt to domesticate the armed forces that included the direct intervention in the elevation of officers close to him. An especially blatant example was the enforced resignation of COAS General Jehangir Karamat, a man of integrity, and the appointment of General Pervez Musharraf as COAS instead of the selected successor, Lt. Gen. Ali Quli Khan.

6. The denial of the rights of the smaller provinces, and the accelerated process of Punjabization. In late 1998, all top civil and military positions in Pakistan were occupied by Punjabis.

7. The streamlining of the media was an important aspect of Nawaz Sharif's power game. His clan exerted massive pressure on papers that did not fall in line with his politics,

like the Jang group, the editors of *Frontier Post* and *Muslim.*

8. In view of the widespread opposition to Nawaz Sharif's politics, it was a risky attempt to consolidate his power with the assistance of the Islamists. He lauded radical groups, declared his sympathy for the Taliban, and introduced on 29 August 1998, a bill for the adoption of the *Shariah* justice in Pakistan.[34]

It was not surprising that the media started to call the regime a 'mandated autocracy'.[35] Despite its firm hold on power, the second cabinet of Nawaz Sharif failed in all important sectors. The economy was chronically on the brink of bankruptcy, the social situation worsened, the education and health systems were in a shambles, and internal security declined to such an extent that the helpless government was forced to call for military courts in Sindh.[36] Since the end of 1998, it had become evident that a new acute phase of the systemic crisis was impending. In view of the record of the government, the international public should not have been surprised by the events in October 1999.

After 1990, and the active role of the then COAS, General Mirza Aslam Beg, in the dismissal of the first cabinet of Benazir Bhutto, the army, despite the turbulent political development, did not intervene openly. But no prime minister since then has passed an important political or economic decision without the consent of the army command, not to speak of any decision against the interests of the military. Between 1990 and 1999, the forces formally remained in the background, but they always were the real power factor. For the COAS, the chief of staff, and the corps commanders, the general course of events since 1996 was disturbing and alarming. The focus of their discussions were mainly four aspects:

1. The decline of the economy and the growing scarcity of funds limited the growth of the military budget, and especially the availability of foreign currency for new weapons systems. When the financial consequences of the sanctions imposed by the West after the nuclear tests of May 1998 surfaced and the real costs of participation in the nuclear arms race became clear, the economic and

financial crisis, in the view of the generals, became a strategic problem.

2. The Pakistan Armed Forces undoubtedly count in their ranks a remarkable number of not only well-trained, but also well-educated and intelligent officers. For the respective groups in the higher echelons, the total corruption of the political class, the incompetence of the ruling factions, and the dysfunctionality of the political system had been no secret. They also registered the deficits in real democracy and the fact that the opposition was no alternative, coming as it were from the same corrupt and incompetent milieu. The military, of course, did not care for the fate of democracy in Pakistan, but for the stability and security of the country, which, in their perception, were increasingly endangered. That was the reason for their growing dissatisfaction with Nawaz Sharif, the former darling and political instrument of the brass, and their strong opposition to his playing the Islamic card. They also viewed his struggle for personal rule as an affront to the central position of the army in the power structures of Pakistan.

3. The Karamat affair, and the prime minister's attempt to exert a direct influence on the army, was the final turning point for the increasing conviction of the military that Nawaz Sharif had to be dismissed.

4. In 1999, relations between Nawaz Sharif and the army deteriorated further and the point of no return was reached with the events around the Kargil Operation.[37] Nawaz Sharif and his government, though they had full knowledge of the operation, tried to escape the political consequences of this military and international disaster by putting the blame on the army leadership and denying knowledge of the adventure. General Musharraf and his colleagues were outraged and convinced that the honour of the army had to be restored. In early summer of 1999, it became obvious that the army was not ready to tolerate the situation any longer; the *Herald* called the state of affairs a 'creeping coup'.[38]

So, the takeover of power by the army in no way was a spontaneous counter-coup. The army had decided to seize power at the next possible opportunity, and the likewise power-hungry and incompetent Nawaz Sharif provided this opportunity on 12 October 1999 on a silver platter when he tried to prevent Musharraf's plane from landing at Karachi Airport. General Musharraf, already before his departure from Colombo, was aware of Nawaz Sharif's measures against him and had ordered the army to take action.

The army took action, and the government, including Sharif and his family and many top bureaucrats, found themselves in jail. General Musharraf in a sweeping action dismissed all elected bodies and set up the third military regime in Pakistan.

However, the coup of October 1999, the following military rule, and its step-by-step transition into a guided democracy of the Kemalist type, or, in other words, into a semi-civil combination of Ayubian and Kemalist instruments of power, was not the end of the systemic crisis of the state in Pakistan. On the contrary, the coup itself and the military rule signified a new climax of this crisis. The regimes are changing, but the problems and the criteria of the crisis remain. The developments and disturbances in Pakistan in 2001–2 in the aftermath of Washington's war against the Taliban, the continuing political instability, and the unending bloody confrontations between armed Islamic sects prove that the crisis of the authority and legitimacy of the state has neither been contained nor has it been driven back.

## 6. Chances of Resolution of the Crisis of the State in Pakistan

Since 1988 the Pakistani media has called all the successive elections in the country as the most free and fair in Pakistan's history. But as a matter of fact none of the five elected governments in the course of ten years could complete their terms being overthrown either by interest-guided presidents or by the army. No election resolved the crisis of the state; the old faces and forces always turned up again. So any new government at best lessened the acute tensions for a certain time until the next climax knocked on the door. The change of regime was of only secondary importance. If Pakistan is to meet the requirements and challenges of the present century, the whole societal structure, the political system, and not least the existing state will have to be reformed fundamentally.

The systemic crisis in Pakistan continues unabated, and without the smokescreen of George W. Bush's 'war against terrorism' the international public would have taken notice long ago. The following remarks summarize the evidence in the form of preliminary theses.

- The Pakistani crisis is not a traditional policy or regime crisis but a complex and systemic crisis of the state with tendencies of transition into a general crisis of the society. No single party, and also not the army, has the capacity to institute and to enforce the necessary reforms. Such reforms must be in concordance with the national interests of Pakistan and the legitimate interests of the whole population, and not, as in the past, mainly a device to accommodate specific group interests. It requires a strategy which is accepted by the major political and social forces.

- In the political spectrum of Pakistan, there is no consensus on the basic national questions: neither on economic, social or home politics, nor on foreign policy, nor in the fields of education and science. Only a small segment of the ruling elites has a realistic perception of the not very encouraging situation of the country. The present political parties, their leaders and office-bearers lack the political maturity and the competence required today. So the starting conditions for a qualitative political change, for a necessary reversal of the course seem to be rather dim.

- An additional retarding factor is the political system which is weakened by the non-existence of real political competition. The democratic rules of the game are restricted in three ways: by the exclusive powers of the president (see the infamous Article 58.2, always used to topple elected governments), by the *de facto* power of the military, and by the media power of the respective ruling forces. All factions of the ruling elites and, therefore, the cadres of the political parties, the higher ranks of the army, and the top bureaucrats essentially come from the same social milieu. So, we cannot expect alternative policy concepts and a policy which is different in terms of quality.

- The composition of the leadership, their political social-ization, their regional and/or religious loyalties, and the uninhibited pursuit of their particular interests when being in power or in high positions, have favoured the emergence and escalation of a number of internal conflicts in Pakistan. In some cases the behaviour of the political class has even created such conflicts. These are primary factors for the inability of the political class to resolve existing internal conflicts in Pakistan.

- As far as the resolution of the crisis is concerned, we should not overlook some objective factors of retardation such as the general economic and social situation, the structural weakness of Pakistan's economy, its low level of diversi-fication, the fragile infrastructure, the striking scarcity of capital, and the dependence on foreign funds. On the other side, enormous resources are wasted in a hectic arms race, which, in perspective, anyway is useless.

- The military rule of General Musharraf, subsequently presented as a kind of guided democracy, and at present as an amalgamation of Field Marshal Mohammed Ayub's 'basic democracy' and of Kemal Pasha Atatürk's modern-ization dictatorship, has neither solved any of Pakistan's core problems nor ended the systemic crisis of the state. As long as the system, which produced the crisis, exists, a decisive change cannot be expected.

In sum, the prospects for a solution of the Pakistani crisis are not very bright: both Benazir Bhutto and Nawaz Sharif have twice failed to deliver; the military rule installed in October 1999 has not achieved its aims; and the semi-civic regime of today still has to pass the test of time.

## III. THE CRISIS OF THE STATE IN PAKISTAN AS A CRISIS OF THE POST-COLONIAL STATE AND SOCIETY IN SOUTH ASIA: CONCLUDING REMARKS

Since the 1970s, the institutions, structures, and mechanisms of mass mobilization in the former colonial countries of South Asia have obviously lost more and more of their dynamics, and their capacity for problem resolution. The progressive loss of legitimacy and authority on one side, and the diminishing loyalty *vis-à-vis* the state and its institutions on the other, have seriously reduced the capability of the state and the political system to govern and to ensure law and order.

In South Asia, between 1947 and the beginning of the 1970s, the crisis situations were mainly traditional conflicts of power and interests. Since then the countries have had to face qualitatively new conflict potentials: the challenge to the perceptions and concepts of the national state, as defined in the anti-colonial struggle; and a crisis of the political systems as installed after independence.

### 1. GENERAL AND SPECIFIC ASPECTS OF THE EMERGENCE OF THE CRISIS OF THE POST-COLONIAL STATE IN SOUTH ASIA

A first manifestation of the new and complex challenges was the Pakistani crisis of 1970–1 (the separation of East Pakistan as Bangladesh), which was followed by the crises in Bangladesh in 1975 (assassination of Sheikh Mujibur Rahman), 1976–7 in India (declaration of emergency and fall of Indira Gandhi), 1977 in Sri Lanka (fall of Sirimavo Bandaranaike), 1977–8 again in Pakistan (overthrow of Zulfikar Ali Bhutto, followed by the military regime of General Zia-ul-Haq), and the beginning of the civil war in Sri Lanka in 1983. The fact that no country till today has been able to return to the former state of internal stability and political normalcy demonstrates that these developments were not accidental but an indicator of the existence of a basic process of destabilization.

The political developments in Pakistan, India, Bangladesh, Sri Lanka, and several years later in Nepal too, reveal that the existing state, and the political system, together with the respective ideological superstructure as inherited from the first years of independence are confronted with a systemic crisis. It may be defined as a new type of crisis, since not only the respective regime but the very nature of the present state, if not the state *per se* as an institution are challenged, the given political system rejected.[39]

The complex crises of state and identity in all countries of South Asia are the result of the interplay of serious deficits in nation-building, insufficient economic models and economic politics, lack of dynamics in development coupled with growing social disparities, and polarization. The post-colonial state proves itself incapable to solve the recurring problems, contradictions, and conflicts in the interest of the whole nation, and with the participation of the main social, political, and ethnic components of society. These crises are complex and all-pervasive, affecting the very structure of society as well as the political system and the self-perception of the people. Research is confronted with a whole range of conflict potentials and manifest conflicts which raise serious questions in the field of authority, legitimacy, and identity in the post-colonial world.

Considering that the crises of the state and of identity in South are expressions of one general process, it must be underlined that they nevertheless

- have no identical internal structures;
- demonstrate remarkable differences in the interaction of specific conflict potentials;
- and, because of differences in the level of development, social stratification, state of political organization, and mass consciousness, vary greatly in terms of explosiveness as much as in the forms of articulation and struggle.

*In summa,* all crises of the state in South Asia have typological commonalities characteristic of post-colonial societies, while their individual features require a subtle analysis in the South Asian context in conjunction with a consideration of the general aspects of the systemic crisis of post-colonial states and societies.

As a specific feature, the question of legitimacy made itself felt in some South Asian states on the very day of independence, especially in Pakistan. It concerned the legitimacy of the new state, of the rule of the elites who were able to seize power from the Raj. The problem also included the acceptance of the respective constitutions and of the new state ideologies rooted as it were in the concrete circumstances under which the South Asian countries achieved independence:

- The colonial state apparatus more or less continued to exist in the power-relevant structures, but also in the bureaucracy, in the judiciary, and in the armed forces.
- Already in the last phase of colonial rule there started a fierce confrontation between the rival political groupings over the future exercise of power.
- Bitter battles took place concerning the objectives of the new state, the preservation of existing positions and privileges, and over the accommodation of diverging interests in the constitutions (the papers of the constituent assemblies provide rich evidence).
- Different ideologies of the new elites like state-nationalism, regional nationalisms, and communal ideologies based on religion, struggled for a dominance, and for their recognition as authentic 'voice of the people'.

In the formative phase of the newly independent states, the legitimacy of the ruling groups rested on national myths and symbols, which served as justification for the power monopoly and the drive towards a uniform national ideology.[40] The content was irrelevant as long as it fulfilled the purpose. It ranged from the anti-colonial struggle and state-nationalism, like the thesis of the unity of India;[41] over the construction of a set of values and legitimizing religion (Pakistan, Iran after the fall of the Shah regime); to a functional ideology (anticommunism in Indonesia after 1965, socialism in China and Vietnam). In any case, that process was connected with the dogmatization of the principles of legitimacy and with a tendency towards a supremacy of the state—both roots of the future crisis.

## 2. THE DEFICITS OF THE POST-COLONIAL STATE IN PROBLEM RESOLUTION AS A DECISIVE FACTOR FOR THE EMERGENCE OF A NEW TYPE OF STATE CRISIS

Besides the legitimacy complex, the existing state, and administration lacked the capability to cope with the vital problems of the post-colonial societies, which in South Asia has been proven during more than half a century. Together they gave rise to a new type of crisis of the state. Two aspects especially contributed to the failure of the post-colonial states in achieving their self-declared goals. First, the attempt to create a nation from above led on the contrary to the further fragmentation of society; and secondly, the adoption of extra-regional models and structures in state, politics, and economy without sufficient consideration of their long-time consequences proved inadequate.

- The key position of the bureaucracy strenghtened the structures of the state, but it also perpetuated the colonial legacy, blocking the organization of a true national state.
- The priority of state-building reduced nation-building more or less to a lip-service.
- The import of economic models without proven relevance to the concrete local conditions and to the real requirements of the people had grave economic and social consequences.

In general, these factors led to a deep-rooted split in the society and created an everlasting chain of struggles for power, interests, and resources causing new divisions in society. Even if one accepts that in South Asia the state is not yet fully 'nationalized', it cannot be considered still colonial, not even post-colonial. Whether any realistic alternative existed under the concrete conditions of the first years after 1947 is an open question. But regarding the present political structures—that means the existing political system and the state—they are in no better position to live up to the requirements of true nation-building. Real nation-building is a process aiming at voluntary and conscious integration, creating a sense of loyalty, and belonging to a nation-state without surrendering one's own values.

The conflict over the state was the central confrontation in the former colonial countries dominating not only the years immediately before independence but also the whole period after colonial rule. That was the case in India and Pakistan. The founding of Bangladesh was in addition a classical example for a struggle over the state ending in secession after all constitutional ways for power-sharing had been exhausted and after the

Pakistani army had started an open war against the people of East Bengal. Struggle over the state here means:

- The political and legal struggle over the contents of the respective state concept and over the shape of state power. In the case of Pakistan this meant the choice between a national state for the Muslims or an Islamic state, between equal status and participation of all social groups or absolute dominance of one component;
- The confrontation between different groups of the ruling elites for control over the state and the national resources;
- But also the lasting struggle of different social, ethnic, and religious groups and communities for participation in the national process of decision-making and for real democracy.

The transition from the struggle over the state with its traditional crises of policy and regimes to a crisis of the state and, finally, of the whole system is a cumulative and qualitative process, resulting from the aggregation of conflict potentials. It is in no way surprising that in many former colonial countries the deficits in nation-building, the non-performance of the national development strategies, the weakness of democratic structures, and the divergences between the aspirations of the people and the real possibilities of participation resulted in conflicts over the state and with the state. In practice nation-building, modernization, and economic politics have favoured certain groups and marginalized large segments of society in the South Asian countries. The basic deficits in the whole process of post-colonial societal, political, and state formation can be outlined as follows:

- After the achievement of independence, the new ruling elites had to face a very complicated situation—different value systems, loyalties and images of identity. Irrespective of the fact that the forces coming into power articulated themselves as either nationalist-secular or politico-religious, their *de facto* reaction was analogous with the enforced organization of state power along Western models, with the super-elevation of the idea of unity and the propagation of a mainstream nationalism (the Pakistan Ideology too was mainstream nationalism against the East Bengalies and the Pakhtoons).

- Despite its inability to amalgamate the different socio-economic formations, including the existing tribal societies, the post-colonial economic model in the first decades after 1947 produced some remarkable results. But, this model has exhausted its historical potential long ago, not to speak of its original economic and social target horizon. Gross disparities in the economic structure, in the development of the regions, and a growing social polarization are the main features of the crisis of the economy and of the economic policy. Without basic reforms instead of populist programmes there will be no way out. And some thousands of IT specialists are not going to cause a change in the system.

- In the political sector too, state-perception, nation-building from above, and the adopted political system have not met earlier expectations. Particularistic group interests, the tendency of all regimes towards centralization of power and decision-making, the institutionalized corruption in all spheres, and the arrogant behaviour of the elites have alienated the citizens. It not only impeded nation-building, and the capability of the state for real modernization, it dangerously lowered the trust in the state, in the authority and the legitimacy of the whole political system. The grave consequences for internal security became evident in Pakistan in 1977, 1990, 1993, 1996, 1999, and 2001; and in the civil wars in Sri Lanka and Nepal.

These factors are the reason for the emergence of numerous new conflict potentials and conflict areas in societal key sectors. They have made the deep-rooted alienation between society and state manifest and raised the question of whether the existing system of power and authority is legitimate. The societal dissent reaches a new and negative dimension when the structural violence radiating from any state, is rising to the level of open repression, and when the forces striving for a change of the existing system tend to militancy or direct use of force against the state. In the concrete case of South Asia, in the last thirty years the conditions for the interaction of state and society did not produce a consolidation of the states or a consensus in substantial national questions, or peaceful political solutions to divergent interests, contradictions, and conflicts. They produced an escalating helix of militant confrontations with the use of force and counter-force, including organized crime and terrorism even in political and social relations.

A crisis of the state becomes manifest when the bonds between the society and the state became untied to that extent that the different components of society—social, political, ethnic, and religious—fall back on themselves and on their respective group identities, challenging the national identity and the national state.

## NOTES

1. In the German language the term 'post-colonial' simply means after colonial rule, while in the UK and India, post-colonial has a specific connotation stemming from the theoretical positions of a certain school of historiography. To avoid any misunderstanding, in the frame of this text, 'post-colonial' only means the development after having achieved independence.

2. For a more detailed discussion, including the role of external factors, see Diethelm Weidemann, 'Die Krise des postkolonialen Staates als der Schlüsselkonflikt in der südasiatischen Konfliktkonstellation', in *Nachkoloniale Staats-, Identitäts- und Legitimationskrisen - die Kernkonflikte in Südasien,* ed. Eva-Maria Hexamer, René Hexamer and Diethelm Weidemann (Berlin: Humboldt-Universität zu Berlin, 1998), pp. 59–148; Diethelm Weidemann, 'Die Krise des Staates in Pakistan: Umrisse einer ersten Bestandsaufnahme', in ibid., pp. 235–305.

3. Presidential address of M.A. Jinnah to the All-India Muslim League at Lahore, 22 March 1940, in J. Ahmad (ed.), *Some Recent Speeches and Writings of Mr. Jinnah,* vol. 1, Lahore: Sheikh Mohammed Ashraf, 1952, pp. 159–81.

4. Resolution adopted by the All-India Muslim League at Lahore, 23 March, 1940, in *Jinnah-Gandhi Talks (September 1944),* ed. Central Office All-India Muslim League, Delhi, 1944, pp. 83–4.

5. *The Indian Year Book 1941/42,* vol. 27, Bombay and Calcutta, 1942, p. 921.

6. Text in K. Sarwar Hassan, *Documents on the Foreign Relations of Pakistan: The Transfer of Power,* Karachi: Pakistan Institute of International Affairs, 1966, pp. 263–76.

7. M.A. Jinnah, Message to the Nation on the Occasion of the Inauguration of the Pakistan Broadcasting Service, 15 August 1947, in Quaid-i-Azam Mohammed Ali Jinnah, *Speeches and Statements as Governor-General of Pakistan* (Islamabad: Government of Pakistan, Ministry of Information and Broadcasting, 1989), pp. 55–6; M.A. Jinnah, Address to Civic, Naval, Military and Air Force Officers of the Pakistan Government, Karachi, 11 October 1947, in ibid., pp. 74–8.

8. Mohammed Ali Jinnah, Presidential Address to the Pakistan Constituent Assembly, 11 August 1947, in *Quaid-i-Azam Mohammad Ali Jinnah, Speeches and Statements*, p. 47.

9. For a detailed position of the author concerning these aspects, cf. Diethelm Weidemann, 'Gefährliche Identitätssuche. Pakistan zwischen Orientierungslosigkeit und Indien-Fixierung', *Blätter für deutsche und internationale Politik*, Bonn, vol. 47, no. 2, 2002, pp. 846–54; Diethelm Weidemann, 'Divergent Perceptions of History', in *Indian Culture: Continuity and Discontinuity: in Memory of Walter Ruben (1899–1982)*, ed. Joachim Heidrich, Hiltrud Rüstau and Diethelm Weidemann (Berlin: Trafo Verlag 2002), pp. 241–56; Diethelm Weidemann, 'Die Krise des Staates in Pakistan', Chapter 1, pp. 237–53.

10. *Inter alia*, see Ayesha Ayal, *Self and Sovereignty: The Muslim Individual and the Community of Islam in South Asia since 1850*, Oxford: Oxford University Press, 2000.

11. Khursheed Kalam Aziz, *Pakistan's Political Culture: Essays in Historical and Social Origins*, Lahore: Vanguard Books, 2001.

12. Quoted from Mahim Maher, 'Paradoxes of Muslim Identity', *Friday Times*, Lahore, vol. 13, no. 3, 2001, p. 16.

13. Ghulam Kibria, *Pre-Independence Indian Muslim Mindset*, Karachi: City Press Bookshop, 2001.

14. Saeed Malik, 'The Third Generation Since Pakistan Resolution', *Nation*, Lahore, 23 March 2001, p. 3.

15. For an interesting view, see Tariq Rahman, 'Language and Ethnicity in Pakistan', *Asian Survey*, Berkeley, vol. 37, no. 9, 1997, pp. 33–9.

16. Quoted from Werner Adam, 'Pakistans Suche nach Identität. Zur Problematik einer religiösen Staatsgründung', *Europa-Archiv*, Bonn, vol. 33, no. 20, 1978, p. 676.

17. Ibid.

18. See, f.i. S.S. Bindra, *Politics of Islamisation with Special Reference to Pakistan*, New Delhi: Deep & Deep, 1990; John L. Esposito, 'Ideology and Politics in Pakistan', in *The State, Religion, and Ethnic Politics in Pakistan, Iran and Afghanistan*, ed. A. Bauazizi and Myron Weiner, Lahore: Vanguard, 1987, pp. 333–69.

19. Text in G.W. Choudhury, *Documents and Speeches on the Constitution of Pakistan*, Dacca 1967, p. 197.

20. *The Constitution of the Islamic Republic of Pakistan (Passed by the National Assembly of Pakistan on the 10th April, 1973, and Authenticated by the President of the National Assembly on the 12th April 1973)*, Karachi 1974, pp. 1-2.

21. G.W. Choudhury, *Transition from Military to Civilian Rule*, Burkhirst Hill, 1988, pp. 146ff.

22. Stephen P. Cohen, 'State Building in Pakistan', in Banuazizi and Weiner, *The State, Religion, and Ethics Politics*, pp. 299-300.

23. Akmal Hussain, 'The Crisis of the State', in *The Pakistan Experience. State of Religion*, ed. M.A. Khan, London: Zed Books, 1985, p. 225.

24. Diethelm Weidemann, 'The Crisis of the Post-Colonial State as the Key Conflict in the South Asian Conflict Constellation', *National Development and Security,* Rawalpindi, vol. 5, no. 1, August 1996, pp. 1–35.

25. In 1996, after all, one-third of the Pakistanis were not convinced that Pakistan could survive the next fifteen years. T. Aslam and H. Zaidi, 'What Do Pakistanis Really Want?', *Herald,* Karachi, Annual 1997, p. 146.

26. Concerning the state of affairs after 11 September 2001, see Khaled Ahmed, 'Split Down the Middle', *Friday Times,* vol. 13, no. 32, p. 10; Khaled Ahmed, 'Pakistani Mind in 2001', ibid., vol. 13, no. 34, 2002, p. 10.

27. Herbert Feldman, *From Crisis to Crisis*, London: Oxford University Press, 1972.

28. For a detailed overview, see Diethelm Weidemann, 'Die pakistanische Dauerkrise', *Blätter für deutsche und internationale Politik*, vol. 42, no. 3, 1997, pp. 323-30.

29. Syed I.H. Gilani, 'Don't leave us short', *News*, Karachi, 1 December 1996, p. 6.

30. M.S. Karim, 'The People's Mandate. Results of a Nationwide Opinion Poll', *Newsline*, vol. 8, no. 8, *Election '97 Special*, p. 98.

31. Mohammad Malick, 'Change of Face, Not Fate', *Tribune*, Lahore, vol. 1, no. 4, 11-17 October 1998, p. 4.

32. Aziz Siddiqui, 'For a Licence for Execution', *Dawn*, Karachi, 22 November 1998, p. 13; Mohammd Malick, 'Destroy Senate, and You Destroy Pakistan', *Tribune*, vol. 1, no. 18, 17-23 January 1999, p. 32.

33. Inamul Haq, 'Zia-Nawaz Doctrine: Justice of Convenience', *Tribune,* vol. 1, no. 18, 17-23 January 1999, p. 9.

34. Shafqat Mahmood, 'Decoys and Deadly Games', *News,* 21 November 1998, p. 7; Amin Saikal, 'No Taleban-style Rule in Pakistan', *Frontier Post*, Peshawar, 25 November 1998, p. 6; Eqbal Ahmad, 'Turning Islam into a Liability', *Dawn*, 15 November 1998, p. 13; Inamul

Haq, 'Theological Monsters', *Tribune,* vol. 1, no. 11, 11–18 September 1998, p. 25.

35. Mohammad Malick, 'Touching On a Few Things', *Tribune,* vol. 1, no. 15, 27 December 1998–2 January 1999, p. 32.
36. See *inter alia* Asad Rahman, 'Worsening Political and Economic Woes', *Nation,* Lahore, 11 December 1998, p. 9; M. Akram Sheikh, 'Chronic Dependence', *News,* 7 December 1998, p. 6; 'Pakistan Armed Forces Ordinance, 1998', *News,* 21 November 1998, p. 16.
37. For details, see Diethelm Weidemann, 'Kargil—Background and Fallout of a Misperception', in *Considering the Future of Democracy in Pakistan,* South Asia Working Papers, no. 1, Institute of Asian and African Studies, Humboldt University of Berlin, Berlin 2001, pp. 9–16; Diethelm Weidemann, 'Pakistans Weg in den Militärputsch: Hintergründe und Perspektiven', *Asien. Afrika. Lateinamerika,* Berlin, vol. 28, no. 5, 2000, pp. 505–32.
38. 'The Creeping Coup', *Herald,* vol. 30, no. 5, May 1999, pp. 26–30.
39. See Weidemann, Die Krise des postkolonialen Staates.
40. See Banuazizi and Weiner, *The State, Religion and Ethnic Politics,* Introduction, p. 7.
41. For the central function of state-nationalism in the post-colonial process of state formation, see Diethelm Weidemann, 'Vom antikolonialen zum postkolonialen Nationalismus, *Humboldt-Journal zur Friedensforschung,* Frankfurt/M., nos. 10–11, 1993, pp. 39–64.

CHAPTER 5

# Bangladesh's Crisis of Democracy

*Rehman Sobhan*

## INTRODUCTION

It is popularly believed, particularly in the West, that holding 'free and fair' elections will usher in a democratic government. This chapter seeks to establish, drawing on Bangladesh's experience, that holding free and fair elections is merely a prelude to building a democratic order. Sustaining democracy is a more arduous process. If we go behind the façade of an electoral process we may see that democratic systems are exposed to serious malfunctions which compromise the sustainability of the democratic process. Such malfunctioning democracies perpetuate malgovernance, which further undermines the working of the democratic order.

## I. UNDERSTANDING BANGLADESH'S POLITICAL SYSTEM

### 1. BANGLADESH'S POLITICAL ASSETS

This chapter focuses on the ongoing crisis that has compromised the sustainability of Bangladesh's fragile democratic order. Yet such a crisis was far from inevitable. From a structural perspective Bangladesh is indeed one of the most favourably equipped amongst South Asian countries and indeed most developing countries (DC), in building a working democratic and pluralistic political system. Bangladesh is a relatively homogeneous country with regard to language and culture. This overwhelming cultural homogeneity has tended to marginalize the tribal minorities and thus demands sensitive handling which unfortunately has not been the case under Bangladesh's democratic order. Little headway has been made by successive regimes to honour the commitments made to the tribals as part of the original Peace Agreement signed in 1997 to end an ongoing separatist insurgency in the Chittagong Hill Tracts (CHT). This is due in part to the divergent perspectives on the Peace Agreement between the Awami League (AL), which originally signed the agreement when in power, and the Bangladesh Nationalist Party (BNP), which was returned to power in 2001. This has left a strong sense of grievance amongst the tribals of the CHT, which is compromising both stability and development in the area.

Bangladesh also has a sizeable religious minority who may have reason to feel that they have been marginalized in their access to power and economic opportunities. The minorities remain vulnerable to assaults on their personal security and property, which often does not elicit the requisite protection of the law enforcement agencies. These threats to the minorities become particularly manifest during elections when persistent efforts are made in particular areas, where their vote is of some consequence to the electoral outcome, to intimidate them from exercising their franchise.

Notwithstanding the sense of democratic deprivation of Bangladesh's minorities, religion and communalism have emerged as much less of a variable in influencing political behaviour in Bangladesh politics compared to the dominant role that ethnic issues have played in Sri Lanka or caste has influenced Indian politics. This is no doubt owing to the fact that minorities in Bangladesh do not feel empowered enough to assert themselves. Nor do the minorities constitute any challenge to the hegemony or interests of the majority community even at the local level, except perhaps in the CHT. The beneficial by-product of this disempowerment of minorities has meant that debates in Bangladesh can afford to focus on mainstream social, political, and economic concerns rather than make political appeals on religious, tribal, caste, or ethnic grounds. This de-communalization of the political discourse should not imply that fundamentalist forces from the majority religious community in Bangladesh have secularized their politics. Such communal forces have, for tactical reasons associated with the compulsions of alliance politics, temporarily kept their ideological agenda in abeyance. However, even mainstream political parties have not been averse to playing the communal card, when they have felt it expedient to do so, though it is not certain how electorally advantageous this has been. Under more propitious circumstances, fundamentalist political forces could therefore assert themselves in the future.

Social stratification in Bangladesh has grown in recent years but is not institutionalized in the way that feudal elites have been embedded in the social structures of Pakistan or in parts of India and Nepal. Bangladesh's society remains much more fluid with considerable scope for upward mobility. Few, if any, people in Bangladesh can lay claim to power through an inherited social legitimacy. In Bangladesh, upward mobility does not always originate from competitive processes but through inequitable access to resources and opportunities, which tends to compromise the legitimacy of the prevailing social disparities in the country. Such manifestations of illegitimate and sudden affluence lend an element of instability to the social order. Thus, Bangladesh's prevailing social hierarchies remain exposed to challenge from below as well as from competing aspirants because the legitimacy of these differences is not widely accepted.

## 2. A STRONG DEMOCRATIC TRADITION

Bangladesh has a long tradition of political struggle for the assertion of its democratic rights which goes back half a century. These struggles first challenged Pakistani rule and the usurpation of democratic rights by the military regime, which culminated in a war of national liberation in 1971 associated with the emergence of an independent Bangladesh. This struggle continued against the usurpation of power by military regimes which again culminated in the ouster of the autocratic regime of Lieutenant General Ershad at the end of 1990. This tradition of struggle has left a legacy of an assertive civil society, the urge for a free media, and recognition that any usurpation of democratic rights will not go unchallenged for long.

## 3. THE EMERGENCE OF A TWO-PARTY POLITY

The principal feature of Bangladesh's democratic political tradition lies in the emergence of a stable two-party system. Its two principal political parties, the Awami League and the BNP, command together an overwhelming plurality amongst the voters and demonstrate strong grass-roots support. Each party has held office and has demonstrated that it can win elections. Each party remains well represented in Parliament and is sufficiently strong on the ground to be able to challenge any attempt by a ruling party to impose its will on the national polity.

Such a bipolar political system has introduced a measure of stability into Bangladesh's political system. A party once elected to office does not have to depend on the shifting loyalties of its political allies, as is the case in India today. At the same time the ruling party remains conscious of the fact that it does not have any security of tenure in office beyond the five years it is permitted to hold office under the Constitution. The introduction of the 13th Amendment to the Constitution in March 1996, which mandates that the ruling party must vacate office at the expiry of its tenure and surrender the control of the government to a non-party caretaker government which will conduct the elections, gives credibility to the competitive nature of Bangladesh's political process. A government which lives under a serious threat that it will have to vacate office at the end of five years remains under pressure to perform whilst in office. Indeed, within the prevailing social configurations of Bangladesh an incumbent regime cannot easily invoke primordial loyalties to compensate for its poor performance in office.

This bipolar political system has permitted for three highly competitive elections in 1991, 1996, and 2001. All these elections were held under caretaker governments which have, by Third World and even South Asian standards, been relatively free and fair. The elections have permitted the BNP to be elected to office in 1991 against the political forecasts of that period, to be voted out and succeeded in office by the Awami League in 1996, and to again return to power in 2001 by inflicting an electoral defeat on the Awami League. Thus the electoral system has worked to ensure changes in the regime in office and has permitted both parties to have a taste of power. In the process it has ensured both competition as well as unpredictability in the outcome of the next election.

## II. BANGLADESH'S CONFRONTATIONAL DEMOCRATIC ORDER

### 1. The Emergence of a Political Duopoly

A bipolar polity has, however, also contributed to the confrontational style of Bangladesh's national politics, which is undermining the working of the parliamentary system. The emergence of two parties of equal strength has contributed to the emergence of a duopoly over the national political system. This duopoly has served to stifle any challenge by smaller parties.

The duopolistic dominance of the two major parties in Bangladesh's political life has encouraged their insensitivity to the concerns of minor parties, their direct supporters, their voters, and even to the concerns of their party rank and file. This arrogance within the leadership structure of both parties is premised on the belief that within a duopolistic political system the supporters have no option but to support one or the other party. This duopolistic structure has thus eroded the pluralism as well as the challenge within the political system contributing to the emergence of structural weaknesses within the two parties and reduced the choices available to the electorate.

### 2. Exclusionary Democracy

This hegemonistic perspective of the two dominant parties within the Bangladesh polity has eroded some of the benefits of better governance that might have been reaped from a competitive and stable two-party political system. In a better functioning two-party system both parties should have been aware that they do not speak for the whole country and that the views and concerns of the rival party always need to be taken into account in building a viable system of governance. This would require some attempt to build a consensus in setting the rules of the game which would ensure that the ruling party respects the rights of the opposition to have equal voice in parliament, in the national media, and on political platforms across the country. Both parties thus collectively need to work out the rules of parliamentary business, as well as the chairing and working of parliamentary committees. The ruling party should, as a routine procedure, consult with the opposition on major legislation prior to its introduction in parliament and indeed should take account of their views and concerns arising from important executive actions. Within such a consultative process norms of constructive and decent discourse in parliament could be established, built around the unquestioned recognition of the political legitimacy of either party to occupy the political space of Bangladesh.

In practice, however, the bipolar system has yielded results which remain largely contrary to popular expectations. Successive ruling parties have demonstrated a high degree of intolerance for the concerns of the political opposition. In the present parliament the ruling BNP-led coalition commands over two-thirds of the seats even though the opposition Awami League won 43 per cent of the vote in the 2001 election. In the outgoing parliament, when the Awami League held office, the opposition represented over 50 per cent of the electorate. The first past the post system of elections permits for this disparity between actual political support in the country and representation in the parliament. This disparity creates an illusion of overwhelming power within the domain of parliament, which is at variance with the political reality on the ground. It has, however, served to perpetuate the exclusionary exercise of parliamentary power demonstrated by the BNP and the Awami League in their earlier respective ascendancy in parliament after the 1991 and 1996 elections. Thus, over three successive parliaments the majority parties have denied equal time to the opposition both in parliament and over the official electronic media. Nor have successive regimes made any more than token attempts to consult the opposition on issues of policy and governance. Under three regimes, opposition workers have been periodically exposed to harassment and detention through a partisan use of the law enforcement agencies.

In response to the perceived unfair behaviour of the ruling party, successive oppositions across three regimes have moved on to a highly confrontational political path, leading to the boycott of parliament, invocation of *hartals,* and a relocation of opposition political activity away from parliament and into the streets. This confrontational political behaviour has now persisted for over thirteen years and the tenure of three parliaments. It may be argued that this response by the opposition appears disproportionate to the provocation and must seek its origin in the highly confrontational perspective of either party towards the other. Thus today, the two principal parties question the very legitimacy of their rival to participate in politics. One does not consult the other on any major issue and they barely speak to each other so that negotiated solutions to their divisions remain unusually difficult. Successive opposition parties have demanded that the ruling party vacate office even though it commands a majority in the parliament and has a secure tenure in office under the provisions of the Constitution.

## III. A DYSFUNCTIONAL PARLIAMENT

The immediate results of this confrontational approach to national politics has been to erode the effectiveness of parliament in discharging its designated responsibilities. These areas of parliamentary dysfunction are summarized in this section:

### 1. DEBATING ISSUES OF PUBLIC CONCERN

Over the last thirteen years very few major policy issues have been fully and constructively discussed on the floor of the house where parliamentary debate has been characterized by incendiary and personalized rhetoric. Allowing for distinguished exceptions, the quality of debate has been poor and largely uninformed.

The successive oppositions complain that they were not given time to discuss vital issues.

Part of the problem associated with insufficient discussion on important issues is that a needless amount of time is spent on procedural issues over who will speak for what length of time. These procedural wrangles end in stalemate because of the inflexibility of either party to accommodate the concerns of the other side, and invariably end in walkouts from the parliament by the opposition. These walkouts cut short debate and explain the lack of floor time invested on debating important issues.

In turn, it could be argued that the opposition in both the outgoing and current parliaments would have been much better off taking the government of the day to task on the floor of the house where their criticisms would have been listened to on the national radio network which broadcasts the entire floor debate. Indeed newsworthy and sensible criticism on the floor would also have been reported in the largely independent print media, leaving television as the only part of the media monopolized by the government through BTV, the state controlled station. The previous AL government gave permission to a privately owned terrestrial channel, ETV, which served as a significant competitor to BTV. However, ETV was closed down by the incumbent BNP regime. This still leaves several privately owned satellite cable channels on the air where they present a more balanced news coverage and could have given exposure to the opposition voice in successive parliaments. Unfortunately the private channels are denied the scope of giving live coverage to proceedings in parliament which remains the exclusive monopoly of BTV.

Another area where parliament could have been better used was through the Question Hour, which remains a useful vehicle for keeping the government accountable. Unfortunately, the first BNP government had given little attention to Question Hour, which had largely been ignored by the then PM. In the previous parliament, the Awami League regime attempted to invigorate Question Hour in parliament through the presence of the Prime Minister, to directly answer questions on a particular day every week when the house was in session. This represented a promising initiative in making the Chief Executive publicly answerable for the government's actions. Regrettably, the AL gesture proved to be unfruitful because the BNP opposition chose to deliberately boycott such sessions as a challenge to the authority of the PM. In the current parliament, the ruling BNP alliance has again rendered Question Hour unproductive by excluding questions from the opposition addressed to the Prime Minister. The PM's Question Hour is, thus, used to plant tame questions which are of little public interest.

## 2. The Role of the Parliamentary Committee

The parliamentary committees (PC) in the outgoing parliament have functioned somewhat more effectively than the parliament itself. Indeed, notwithstanding the protracted boycott of parliament by the opposition BNP, all PCs in the last parliament continued to function with the regular participation of the opposition members. Some of the committees had, as a result, shown promise in seeking accountability from the executive. Here again the effectiveness of the PC was improved under the previous Awami League regime through the expedient of appointing non-ministers as committee chairmen. Whilst all chairmen were drawn from the ruling party, unlike the practice in India where they are elected from the opposition, this move was an improvement over the arrangements in all previous parliaments in Bangladesh where the PC was chaired by the concerned minister. As a result, in those previous parliaments most meetings of the PCs remained anodyne affairs where the executive chose to deal with the queries of MPs on a *need to know* basis.

The new arrangements in the outgoing parliament had led to some improvement in the functioning of the PCs. The non-official chairmen, even if they were members of the ruling party, were more inclined to challenge the authority of the executive. PC members often came together on a bipartisan basis in seeking accountability from the ministries and agencies under their jurisdiction. Under the current parliament, the PCs have yet to be fully activated. The ruling party complains that the opposition Awami League has refused to nominate its members until it extracts an agreement from the ruling alliance to give them an opportunity to chair some of the PCs. The ruling alliance is quite content to let this stalemate continue so that three years have gone by without any active attempt being made by the ruling party to activate all the PCs.

## 3. Parliament and Accountability

Notwithstanding the potential demonstrated by some PCs in the previous parliament successive parliaments have proved ineffective in discharging their primary function of adequately representing the concerns of their electorate and holding the executive responsible for its actions. In this failure the opposition in successive parliaments bears a particular responsibility. The tendency to use rhetoric as a substitute for reasoned as well as informed argument and the indiscriminate use of the walkout and boycotts have effectively taken the government off the hook in having to respond to an informed, vigilant, and present opposition everyday that the parliament is in session. No matter how partisan the role of the Speaker or inequitable the allocation of speaking time, a strong opposition can, with imagination and perseverance, make itself heard on the floor of the house. Since all the proceedings are broadcast live on the national radio network, which is widely listened to throughout Bangladesh, an effective opposition could have kept the government under perpetual challenge in the house.

The incapacity of the opposition to discharge the very responsibilities for which it is elected to parliament has meant that for the best part of thirteen years three incumbent governments have not really had to expose themselves to the regular scrutiny of parliament for their executive acts or to expose their legislative efforts to serious debate. As a result, the weak accountability of the GOB, which has contributed to misgovernance throughout the long years of autocratic rule, has now been compounded by the failure of the principal institutions within a system of plural democracy, namely, parliament and the opposition, to ensure more accountability and transparency from the government.

## 4. The role of Members of Parliament

Few members of parliament (MP) feel strongly inclined to push any clearly articulated policy agenda during their tenure in parliament. Their principal concern is to use their political presence in parliament to persuade the GOB to channel some government projects into their constituency. Less attention is given by MPs to monitoring the state of governance within their constituency or to see how development projects are being implemented or operated. Parliamentarians, even from the ruling party, do have views on policies, particularly on such issues as the price and availability of fertilizer, which impinge on their constituents. MPs therefore, tend to be resentful at not being regularly consulted on legislation or budget formulation.

Neither party appears to have a clearly conceived programme in place to consult MPs or party members on a regular basis either on policy-making or on governance. A party, when in office, tends to believe that parliamentarians are unqualified to offer policy advice or that they will use the opportunity to press particularistic agendas. In practice, consultations initiated by the Centre for Policy Dialogue (CPD) with MPs have at least pointed to a willingness on the part of MPs to take policy and governance issues seriously. Such MPs remain willing to expose themselves to a learning process to prepare themselves to play a more constructive role in parliament. They remain receptive to the idea of outside professional inputs into the work of the PCs. However, left to themselves MPs are not overactive in seeking such assistance and need to be regularly exposed to the possibility of such support.

This dysfunctional role of MPs to discharge their primary mission as legislators has posed a serious problem in the functioning of the system of local government. These under-employed MPs have, over the years, increasingly intruded into local politics and governance. They spend time lobbying the executive for spending public funds in their constituencies and take undue interest in how such funds are spent. Since the average parliamentary constituency is broadly coterminous with an *upazilla* (a subdistrict), MPs have reincarnated themselves as surrogate *upazilla* chairmen. With the abolition of the *upazilla* system in 1991 the MPs have emerged as the principal source of public resource patronage in their constituencies and as major players in the system of local politics. This intrusion by MPs into local governance has served to undermine their interest in reviving representative institutions at the *upazilla* level ever since the BNP regime abolished the system in 1991. The Awami League government did pass legislation to resurrect the *upazilla* system but it could not be activated due to the boycott of *upazilla* elections by the opposition. After the BNP returned to power in 2001 there have been strong divisions in the ruling party over reviving the *upazilla* precisely because some cabinet members apprehend that an elected *upazilla* chairman could emerge as a challenge to the prevailing authority of the sitting MP in the *upazilla* that overlaps with a particular parliamentary constituency.

## IV. THE STATE OF THE POLITICAL PARTIES

### 1. MALFUNCTIONING POLITICAL PARTIES

The malfunctioning of parliament has its roots in the degeneration of the principal political parties themselves. Over the years, both political parties have been witness to infiltration by a breed of activists who increasingly tend to be motivated by private agendas. Today the ideological divide, as it impinges on immediate issues of development policy, is virtually non-existent between the two parties. Thus, both parties have developed party manifestos which serve as little more than proforma obligations to their electorate and rarely intrude into their legislative practise or executive behaviour. Party agendas tend to be designed by a few professionals in consultation with a few leaders and are rarely exposed to debate within the party or consultation with the rank and file let alone with the public. The manifesto thus means all things to all people, with little binding value as a guide to action by party workers. In turn, the public has also remained disinclined to take these manifesto commitments seriously. People are reminded of the manifesto as and when the opposition takes the government to task, largely for rhetorical purposes, for their failure to discharge their commitments to the electorate.

Both parties have a large number of political workers. A party such as the Awami League, with a fifty-year history has a large and loyal cadre of workers many of whom have long records of service and sacrifice for the party as well as the people in their respective areas. They remain close to the people and can serve as effective conduits for carrying through party programmes. The BNP has also built up a significant base across the country with a large number of workers. Regrettably, neither party has any clearly identified role for its party workers who are thus mostly used as mobilizers and organizers during election campaigns. Opposition party workers are also used to mobilize people for public agitations whilst corresponding ruling party workers are deployed to oppose or frustrate such agitations. Party workers, paradoxically, feel particularly neglected when their party comes to power. There is no perceived role for such ruling party workers either in disseminating the policies of the government before the electorate or in monitoring the state of governance at the local level. Some workers do spontaneously take some initiatives in both these areas but this does not originate from any organized initiative by the ruling party.

Successive ruling parties tend to demonstrate more faith in the bureaucracy which emerges as their instrument of choice in not just implementing government decisions but in also guiding their policy choices. As a result party workers feel devalued at a time when their links with the grassroots should have been put to good use by the ruling party. This sense of purposelessness, particularly when a party is in office, drives workers into using their political access to the party in power to seek official patronage for enhancing their material fortunes either as intermediaries with the executive or for direct benefit. In this role, ruling party workers increasingly develop either collusive relations with the bureaucracy or conflictual relations when their particular expectations cannot be satisfied. Such tensions constrain the process of governance at various levels and contribute to the alienation of the ruling party from its traditional sources of support.

## 2. The Democratic Deficit

The de-professionalization of political parties and the demoralization of its workers originates in the democratic deficit within the two principal parties. Both the Awami League and the BNP are led by all-powerful leaders who are rarely exposed to challenge from within the party. This elevation of the leadership of a democratic party into a position of absolute power reflects the weakness in the party organization as well as the political authority of second rank leaders and their own internal divisions. As these secondary leaders tend to neglect their links with their party workers they become more dependent on the patronage of the party leader in sustaining their authority and even retaining their constituency. Personal and political divisions within the party further encourage this surrender of power to the leadership to a point where most key decisions are made by the party leader. Within the prevailing structures of the two parties their financing also remains both centralized and non-transparent, which further concentrates power in the hands of the leadership. In response to this other party leaders seek to build their own financial treasure chest which remains unaccountable and spreads corruption.

## 3. THE CRIMINALIZATION OF POLITICS

The ineffectiveness of party workers is increasingly driving them towards extra-legal activities. This tendency is aggravated by the increasing presence of *mastaans* or hoodlums in the major political parties. This ascendancy of the *mastaans* is associated with the progressive criminalization of politics and the disconnection of a growing number of party workers from any political goals beyond using politics as a source of livelihood.

The patronage extended by a political party to *mastaans* or hoodlums derives from the dependence of many political figures on these forces to ensure their election and the retention of their political authority in their constituency area. Many politicians now increasingly use *mastaans* as a political resource in the contention for political office and state patronage to access public resources. The resultant nexus between politicians, business, *mastaans* and law enforcement agencies is now embedded in the social structure of Bangladesh.

Partisan law enforcement in favour of the ruling party serves as the key instrument for the criminalization of politics. Opposition complaints of political victimization are legitimate not because their own affected political workers are honest people dedicated to public service but because of the inequitable enforcement of the law against them. The BNP, when in office from 1991–6, heavily depended on *mastaans* to capture the institutions of education and to enforce their political presence in particular constituencies. The law was used ineffectively against these elements and was instead directed to detain *mastaans* in the service of the opposition. From 1996–2001 the Awami

League's treatment of opposition workers was the mirror image of the behaviour of the BNP when it was in office. When the BNP returned to power in 2001, it perpetuated the earlier tradition of victimizing the workers of the Awami League whilst giving a free hand to the ruling party *mastaans* to live off the fat of the land whilst oppressing opposition supporters. As a result both parties have tended to depend on such undemocratic instruments as integral political resources for realizing their electoral ambitions. Thus both parties have abused the system of law enforcement to protect their own workers and to persecute those of their opponents, and, in the process, have exposed ordinary citizens to a system of institutionalized anarchy where they have little relief from the depredations of the *mastaans*.

This criminalization of politics is presumed to be inhibiting private investment in Bangladesh. This linkage between constrained law enforcement and its impact on investment was articulated during the tenures of successive regimes since the liberation of Bangladesh. It was particularly visible during the Ershad regime, was manifest throughout the BNP regime, was seen as an important constraint under the Awami League regime, and is today cited as the principal factor in inhibiting investment under the BNP regime. *Mastaans* reportedly use their immunity from law enforcement to exact tolls from business, demanding their tithes in particular from construction contracts and as part of any investment activity. In many areas the claims of the *mastaans* have become a recurrent cost for doing business. This politically patronized *mastaan* culture has institutionalized itself over successive regimes. It is, however, less clear whether they constitute a fundamental constraint to new investment or operating a business or merely represent a transaction cost along with political and bureaucratic pay-offs for the privilege of doing business in Bangladesh. This proposition deserves closer analysis, which remains outside the scope of this chapter.

The real problem in Bangladesh politics lies in the fact that every party harbours *mastaans* because they play an integral part in the election system and in securing a support base in particular areas. *Mastaans* are not always just common or garden variety thugs, but may be people of considerable local influence with a capacity for getting things done. Thus each party feels the need for their *mastaans* and will be reluctant to abandon them for potential but indeterminate gains in public esteem unless its opponents are willing to do likewise. Thus, expecting political leaders to abandon such proven political resources is an unreal exercise however important this may be on the agenda of governance reform.

## 4. MONEY AND POLITICS

The emergence of the *mastaans* as a political as well as governance variable has been accompanied by the growing presence of money as a factor in Bangladesh's politics. Elections have over the years become a costly process and have thus increasingly become a rich man's game. The growing presence of men of property in the political arena has further driven up the cost of elections. Once upon a time businessmen contributed to party coffers, particularly during elections. This permitted people of modest means to contest elections as long as they had the financial backing of the party. Most party financiers hoped to use their support to promote their business fortunes when the party came to power but there were always some party loyalists who invested their wealth in particular parties out of a sense of political commitment. In this respect Bangladesh politics is no different from any other country. The main difference lies in the growing presence in Bangladesh politics of a class of people who view politics as a business investment and will spend large sums of money in the process, which needs to be recouped. Such a commercialized perspective on politics is encouraged by the lack of transparency in the system of electoral and political financing or the protection of law to enforce such transparency.

Businesspersons, however, appear to have moved beyond party financing to invest in particular political persons who thereby became captives to the business agenda of their patrons. Over successive regimes the politician as a business intermediary, whether in or out of office, is a familiar figure in the corridors of the secretariat of the GOB and the drawing rooms of particular ministers.

The final stage in the commodification of Bangladesh politics was attained when businessmen themselves directly entered electoral politics or politicians chose to graduate from being intermediaries and themselves became businessmen. The increasing presence of politicians as indentors, traders, contractors and term-loan borrowers from the banks to finance investment projects, has already made its contribution to the perpetuation of the default culture.

In such an environment politics is increasingly being divorced from any public purpose and is being used as an instrument to promote private material interests where the dividing line between government and opposition parties is becoming indistinguishable. Elective office is seen as a mechanism to improve access to scarce resources. Being part of the ruling party is advantageous but is not essential to this process.

The societal implications of such a transformation in the political culture of Bangladesh lies in its exclusionary effect on a large segment of the population. People without wealth, or the patronage of wealth, or who do not aspire to wealth have little prospect of surviving in politics. Such a perspective applies for election not only to parliament but also the local elective bodies. It is not surprising that those of modest means who now contest local elections are becoming increasingly dependant on the patronage of some of the wealthier NGOs. However few if any NGOs can afford to finance the election of a poor farmer or schoolteacher to the *Jatyo Sangshad* where considerably larger resources are required. In such a milieu politics is becoming a game played by the rich for the rich and for the accumulation of riches. This perspective on politics is of crucial significance in the disempowerment of the poor through their distancing from public affairs. This development has important implications for agendas of poverty alleviation and governance reform where sustainability depends on giving a political voice to the deprived members of society.

## V. FROM DEMOCRATIC DYSFUNCTION TO CRISIS IN GOVERNANCE

Bangladesh's crisis of democracy has contributed to a crisis in governance, which is reflected in the progressive degeneration in the functioning of the machinery of administration and law enforcement. Most of these problems have aggravated over the years and have acquired structural features that originate in the malfunctioning of the democratic system. The two major manifestations of malgovernance in Bangladesh relate to

- The Politicization of the Administration.
- Partisan law enforcement.

## 1. The Politicization of the Administration

The dysfunctional nature of the political system is increasingly impacting on the functioning of the machinery of government. The same political dynamics that has undermined the working of the machinery of law enforcement is compromising the working of the administration. If politics is to serve as an instrument for accessing resources, then political persons will remain inclined to subordinate the administration to this objective. Bureaucrats thus have to be incorporated into the business-political nexus because they remain the direct instrument through which public resources are accessed. Thus officials in the development financial institutions (DFI) or nationalized commercial banks (NCB), the ministries awarding public tenders for procurement or construction, the agencies for allocation of public lands, the revenue collection agencies, at the level of the ministry and the operating agencies, have to be coopted into the system. In such a dispensation the politicization of the bureaucracy emerges as a logical outcome of such a system.

In the Bangladesh context, politicization of the bureaucracy does not mean using bureaucrats to serve a particular party ideology. Here politicization means the use of bureaucrats to promote the private agendas of politicians. Bureaucrats thus need to be compatible with their ministers rather than a party. At the local level they need to be compatible with an MP or the local political leadership. The idea that bureaucratic power is used to promote particular party agendas is thus a misleading notion. Police may be deployed to arrest an opposition *mastaan* or worker at the behest of a minister or even some local leaders. Officials may be willing to manipulate tenders or make land allotments or reschedule a loan, ostensibly in the service of the ruling party. But in practice such interventions are designed to serve the electoral and material interests of a particular politician. The bureaucrats recognize this particularist element in their links with politicians and are happy to serve these interests for both their own material gain as well as their career advancement. Thus, the politicized bureaucrat is no more than a malfeasant bureaucrat who rationalizes his behaviour in the name of serving some higher political purpose, but in practice is embedded in more mundane acts of collusion for material gain. Such bureaucrats remain happy to reinvent themselves over successive regimes by proclaiming largely mythical political loyalties to the party in power in order to advance themselves.

Whatever may be the underlying logic of the politicization of the bureaucracy, the end result has been the erosion of good governance. Bureaucrats embedded in collusive links with their political patrons use these links to advance themselves beyond their merit, to acquire private wealth, and to accumulate power within the bureaucracy by promoting collective interests. The official who can access a minister to use his influence to realize some benefit for a section of public employees uses this influence to consolidate his leadership of this group. His command over such bureaucratic constituencies is used as a bargaining resource with particular political leaders to then promote the individual ambitions and appetite of the bureaucrat. Such arrangements to extend political patronage to particular bureaucrats undermine bureaucratic discipline, erode accountability, promote inefficiency and encourage corruption.

## 2. PARTISAN LAW ENFORCEMENT

The deterioration in law and order has become endemic to the system of governance. The breakdown of law and order during the tenure of the Awami League was the principal theme of the election campaign by the BNP alliance in its 2001 election campaign. Today the breakdown in law and order under the BNP alliance is again seen as a source of governance failure. The BNP regime was sufficiently concerned by the state of law and order during the first year of its incumbency to bring in the armed forces on 16 October 2002 as part of an emergency measure code named 'Operation Clean Heart', to stem the deterioration in law and order. Under this operation, which extended for two and a half months, around 11,000 people were arrested of whom 2,482 were designated as 'listed criminals'. The provenance of the remaining detainees remains unclear. Such draconian measures contributed to some temporary improvements in the state of law and order but also led to serious abuses of human rights involving a large number of cases of torture of detainees which resulted in around fifty-five custodial deaths. The public outcry against such abuses compelled the government to pass a law ensuring immunity from prosecution to all those involved in Operation Clean Heart.

It has been argued that the armed forces were eventually withdrawn after two and a half months in the field because too many ruling party workers were attracting the wrath of the law enforcers. Such impartial law enforcement threatened to become prejudicial to the capacity of the ruling party to contest the forthcoming elections to the primary institution of local government, the Union Parishad, held in early 2003. The withdrawal of the armed forces rapidly led to a restoration of the *status quo ante*. Once the army was withdrawn the hoodlums came out of their hideouts or were released from custody and were believed to have played a serviceable role in influencing the outcome of the local elections.

The degeneration of law and order after the suspension of Operation Clean Heart has compelled the incumbent BNP administration to once again resort to extra-curricular means of law enforcement. The government has constituted a special force known as the Rapid Action Battalion (RAB), drawn from the armed services, paramilitary forces, and the police. This unit has generous resources at its disposal and special equipment not available to the police. But its special feature appears to be a license to kill criminals or those presumed to be criminals in staged 'encounters' without any application of due process of law. This has led to the death of nearly 300 prisoners while in the custody of the RAB. There has been some reduction in crime in some areas, but its sustainability remains open to question, as was the case with Operation Clean Heart.

Both Clean Heart and RAB have failed to address the structural sources of the problem. Similar ritual invocations by citizens and aid donors to successive governments to improve law and order have not had much effect because of their non-structural approach to the problem. In Bangladesh, whatever may be the time-trends for crime, over several decades criminals have operated with immunity from law enforcement agencies because they already have collusive and mutually rewarding links with them. These links are ubiquitous across regimes, parties, and areas. However, the ruling party enjoys a special privilege in protecting its own *mastaans*. Thus, more than any other area of governance, the crisis in law enforcement has become systemic. We have observed that the problem is embedded in the working of Bangladesh's political system so that regime changes will, at best, have a limited impact on the problem. Unless each party commits itself to marginalize the *mastaan* elements in its party and to apply the law of the land, without reference to the political colour of the wrongdoer, attempts to reform law and order are going to be more rhetorical than real.

In focusing on the political patronage that sustains malfeasant law enforcement, one should not ignore the structural constraints within the machinery of law enforcement. Aided and abetted by their incestuous links with the political parties, the law enforcement agencies have built their own structural links with the criminal classes where, in each area, they collude for mutual benefit. In every area there is very limited prospect that the police will move, *suo motu,* against the major criminals. They will only do so if they receive categorical, unambiguous political orders to clean up an area and are threatened with the prospect of dire action if they do not comply with such orders. However, once such orders are diluted by the instructions of the government of the day or its factotums, that rigorous law enforcement must remain discretionary, the police will simply be encouraged to believe that business may continue as usual.

Business as usual for the police means treating law enforcement as a commercial enterprise where any citizen can secure the degree of law enforcement he is willing to pay for. This means that law enforcement is commoditized, personalized, and parochialized to a point where no citizen can feel entirely secure against criminals or feel immune from the use of the law enforcement system against them for political, private or predatory purposes. In such circumstances, the commitment by any regime in Bangladesh to an agenda of comprehensive non-partisan law enforcement will always involve structural interventions. The entire culture and institutional basis of law enforcement will thus need to be overhauled. Such a process could be resisted by the agencies which would be able to draw upon support from within the political system and from interest groups who have benefited from a system of personalized law enforcement. Thus, as in the case of administrative reform, a political consensus will have to be built up so that one party cannot take political advantage if a ruling party seeks to impose structural changes in the machinery of law enforcement.

## VI. CONCLUSION: SUSTAINING DEMOCRACY

Bangladesh's crisis of democracy, which has originated in its confrontational style of politics, is being aggravated as the next general elections in 2006 approach. Today, democratic politics has become not only more confrontational but increasingly violent. The proliferation of arms, manifested in periodic discoveries of arms shipments coming into the country, is particularly troubling because the arms merchants remain undetected and appear to enjoy immunity from the law. A bomb attack in August 2004 in the centre of Dhaka on a public rally of the opposition Awami League party nearly succeeded in killing the leader of the opposition, Sheikh Hasina, killed or injured other AL leaders and a significant number of party workers. The public assassinations of Awami League MP, Ahsanullah Master, and, more recently, of a former finance minister under the previous AL regime and sitting MP, Shams Kibria, have led to the arrest of some low-level functionaries of the ruling party as instruments of the assassinations. But the higher-level patrons of the assassins remain undetected. Nor has an earlier attempt to assassinate the British High Commissioner to Bangladesh yielded any clue as to its progenitors. Failures in detection point to the ineffectiveness of the law enforcement agencies, including the RAB, in dealing with such political killings. This aggravation in the confrontational style of politics has raised strong demands by the political opposition for further reforms to ensure the neutrality of the caretaker government to oversee the next elections and the credibility of the Election Commission. Such a state of affairs suggests that the build-up to the next elections could be fraught with danger not just to the security of the political participants but to the sustainability of Bangladesh's democratic institutions.

## SELECT BIBLIOGRAPHY

Adnan Shapan, 2004, *Migration, Land Alienation and Ethnic Conflict: Causes of Poverty in the Chittagong Hill Tracts*, Dhaka: Research & Advisory Services.

Ain O Salish Kendro, 2002, *Human Rights in Bangladesh 2002*, Dhaka: Ain O Salish Kendro.

Asia Foundation, 2002, *Election Day 2001 Nation Wide Observation: A Report of the Election Monitoring Working Group*, Dhaka: Asia Foundation Group.

Barkat Abul (ed.), 2004, *An Inquiry into the Causes and Consequences of Deprivation of Hindu Minorities in Bangladesh through the Vested Poverty Act*, Dhaka: PRIP Trust.

Centre for Policy Dialogue, 1998, *Crisis in Governance: Independent Review of Bangladesh's Development*, 1997, Dhaka: University Press Ltd.

Centre for Policy Dialogue, 2001, *Development Debates: Perspectives for Policy Dialogue*, vol. I, Dhaka: Pathak Samabesh.

Rahman Husain Zillur and S. Aminul Islam, 2002, *Local Governance and Community Capacities*, Dhaka: University Press Ltd.

Seabrook Jeremy, 2001, *Fundamentalism and Popular Resistance in Bangladesh*, London: Zed Book.

Sobhan Rehman, 1993, *Bangladesh: Problems of Governance*, Dhaka: University Press Ltd.

———, 1998, *From Two Economies to Two Societies: Honouring Bangladesh's Social Contract*, Nazmul Karim Memorial Lecture, Dhaka.

———, 2001, 'Misreading the October Election', in *Daily Star*, 8 October 2001, Dhaka.

———, 2002, 'The Evolving Political Economy of Bangladesh in an Age of Globalization', BIDS Millennium Lecture, Dhaka.

————, 2002, 'Clean Politics as a Way to a Clean Heart', in *Daily Star*, 20 February 2002, Dhaka.

————, 2004, 'Structural Dimensions of Malgovernance in Bangladesh', *Economic and Political Weekly*, 4 September 2004, Mumbai.

World Bank, 2002, *Taming Leviathans: Reforming Governance in Bangladesh*, Washington D.C.: World Bank.

UNDP, 2005, *Beyond Hartals: Towards Democratic Dialogue in Bangladesh*, Dhaka: UNDP.

CHAPTER 6

# Ethnic Conflict, State Reform, and Nation-Building in Sri Lanka

*Siri Gamage*

## INTRODUCTION AND BACKGROUND

The nature of Sri Lanka's state and its relationship with various components of the nation has been the subject of a long-standing tradition of scholarship and commentary—both academic and popular. Aspects of the nation thus examined include religion, ethnicity, bureaucratic and ruling elites, castes, classes, colonialism and independence, international relations, development, and now peace and conflict. Both the nation and the state have been changing their character during the last few decades. Despite broad and fundamental changes in society and culture, however, certain aspects of the traditional values, habits, practices and customs still continue. There is also a high degree of hybridization in these as well as the key institutions coming under the state.

Recently, those writing about Sri Lanka have commented on the multiple crises facing the nation, in particular its state.

The development of multiple levels of crises suggests that the country has lost its centre of gravity and is being propelled into mutual self-destruction. It seems to me that we have lost analytical categories which can truly comprehend and understand the chaotic and turbulent period to which the country is heading. If our leaders, Sinhalese, Tamil and Muslim, do not act with a sense of responsibility the country will be drawn irrecoverably into a vortex where further fragmentation of the polity could result in a period of escalating domestic violence and increased external intervention. It could also lead to an inadvertent war. A war that nobody wished but which was propelled by circumstances and events which are unfolding before us. (Rupasinghe 2004: 9)

A question raised and discussed by Sri Lanka observers and commentators is whether the so-called ethnic conflict in Sri Lanka is a result of failed attempts at nation building by those who held power in the post-independent period. The need for further nation building has emerged because of the centralizing tendencies of the state, the deterioration of democratic norms of government, the alienation of the youth segments from the political and governance processes, the development of counter-political and paramilitary forces, the so-called ethnic conflict, and the continuing instability in the state and the nation emanating from the 'politics of conflict'.

By their very nature conflict situations, especially political conflicts, their causes and consequences, are complex phenomena. Stability or change in the state and any crisis situations in the nation have to be investigated in their relevant historical, socio-economic and political contexts. This chapter looks at the causes that led to political conflicts, particularly the so-called ethnic conflict, in Sri Lanka and the indications of crises in the state and nation in the last three decades. A noteworthy feature here is that though in the 1980s and 1990s, academics, analysts, and politicians concentrated on the causes of the ethnic conflict, the focus has shifted to finding solutions in the early years of the twenty-first century.

Periodic crises of state and nation in Sri Lanka, especially since the 1970s, can be ascribed to several factors:

1. The introduction of a new economic liberalization policy in the late 1970s, the role of state and the prescriptions of the international monetary agencies such as the world bank in facilitating the same at the expense of a declining welfare state;

2. The centralization of power in the hands of an 'executive president' created in the Constitution of 1978, the politicization of society and the institutions of the state; the curtailment of political and democratic freedoms, tampering with the democratic political process, attacks on political opponents and political violence, especially during and after the elections; and the legacy of the one-party rule from 1977–94;

3. The rise of counter-movements from the north and the south against the backdrop of declining democratic governance, freedoms, and broken promises by the politicians in power; the counter-terrorism measures taken by the state to curb these;

4. The practical inability to change the Constitution to abolish the presidency as it requires a two-thirds majority in the parliament, and the inability to resolve the northern Tamil question.

There is a distinction between nation state and nation *vs.* state. Nation state is defined as 'a particular type of state, characteristic of the modern world, in which a government has sovereign power within a defined territorial area, and the mass of the population are citizens who know themselves to be part of a single nation' (Giddens 1989: 745). 'A state exists where there is a political apparatus (governmental institutions, such as a court, parliament or congress, plus civil-service officials), ruling over a given territory, where authority is backed by a legal system and by the capacity to use force to implement its policies' (ibid.: 301). A nation state includes the characteristics associated with the state.[1] A nation is a community of diverse people bound together by place, culture, history, identity, and often ethnicity. There are nations without states but there cannot be states without nations. Government refers to the administrative process enacting policies and making decisions within a political apparatus (ibid.: 301). In the case of Sri Lanka, the Tamils in the north and east, who have been claiming separate nationhood have developed their own political apparatus, a military and a government led by the Liberation Tigers of Tamil Eelam (LTTE). They do not wish to belong to the Sri Lankan state. Balasingham (2001: 31–5) explains the reasons.[2] A strong and separate ethno-nationalism has also been developed and utilized in the political campaigns launched by the LTTE leaders.

According to Held and colleagues (1999: 29) modern nation states claim 'a proper symmetry and correspondence between sovereignty, territory, legitimacy, and with the passage of the nineteenth and twentieth centuries, democracy. The concept of sovereignty lodges a distinctive claim to the rightful exercise of political power over a circumscribed realm. It seeks to specify the political authority within a community which has the right to determine the framework of rules, regulations, and policies within a given territory and to govern accordingly'. Thus they describe sovereignty as the entitlement to rule over a bounded territory. To them, state autonomy is the actual power the nation state possesses to articulate and achieve policy goals independently; the capacity of state representatives, managers, and agencies to articulate and pursue their policy preferences. (ibid.: 29). 'Moreover, to the extent that modern nation-states are democratic, sovereignty and autonomy are assumed to be embedded within and congruent with the territorially organized framework of liberal democratic government: 'the rulers'—elected representatives—are accountable to the ruled—the citizenry—within a delimited territory. This is, in effect, a 'national community of fate', whereby membership of the political community is defined in terms of the people within the territorial borders of the nation-state; this community becomes the proper locus and home of democratic politics'. For various reasons, in the postcolonial world of nation states, those who feel that they are not ruled by inclusive regimes have contested these concepts and their interpretations. The case of Sri Lanka is no exception.

The Ceylonese[3] nation as it existed at the time of independence from Britain in 1948 does not exist today. The nation has been fragmented. The Sri Lankan government authority is non-existent in substantial parts of the northern and eastern provinces. Even though it has not received international legitimacy yet, the controlling authority is the Liberation Tigers of Tamil Eelam (LTTE). Under the existing ceasefire agreement entered into in February 2002, the government and the LTTE remain each in charge of the areas over which they have operational control. In between there are European monitors. Even though the violent armed clashes have since largely ceased, the reasons that led to the conflict have not disappeared.

Fragmentation of the state happens when a section of the population, in particular a minority population, refuses to accept the legitimacy of the central state and develops its own decision-making and implementation institutions and processes by identifying itself as forming a distinctive self-governing entity.

The idea of the unitary state, including sovereignty over the so-called Tamil homeland, has been challenged by the LTTE politically, militarily, judicially, bureaucratically, economically, and culturally. The Sinhalese conception of the nation, supported by the state, is one that encompasses the northern and eastern provinces in a unitary state. The LTTE by contrast claims for the Tamil population the powers for self-determination, or in the extreme a state separated from the central government based in Colombo. These divergent positions are contributing to a significant conundrum in terms of nation building in contemporary Sri Lanka. This chapter examines this conundrum, its history, the players involved, and the challenges ahead.

If the state or indeed the concept of nation is to be accepted, these constructs have to be representative and widely supported by the population. In other words, the diverse population has to find self-expression in these macro-constructs symbolically as well as in reality. Whether all segments of the society can find expression in the social constructs of the nation and the state and closely identify with them in Sri Lanka is open to question. The state has been characterized by various writers as an exclusionary construct run by the ruling elites who work more hand in glove with international players than to care for the general population and its requirements. The dominant conception of the nation as Sinhalese Buddhist has been characterized as an exclusionary one in regard to ethnic minority interests. The centralized administration of the country operated from Colombo by the ruling elites has also been questioned. These contestations have not only been verbal. In order to achieve political objectives, the competing political camps have employed physical violence. In the history of post-independent Sri Lanka there have been several occasions when the state faced a crisis situation. In political and military terms, the continuing differences between the state and the LTTE, and the past conflicts between the state and the Janatha Vimukti Peramuna (People's Liberation Front) (JVP), led to a crisis situation on more than one occasion.

In this context, the nature of the state and its current forms have been criticized both by insiders and outsiders on various grounds, and the state itself is seen by some writers as facing a crisis (Uyangoda 2003, 2004; Rupasinghe 2004). Discussions on the national question primarily centre around the ethnic issue. At the time of writing, several questions dominate the thinking and aspirations of the national community:

1. How far can the society be held together by means of a centralized, semi-authoritarian state, and whose interests are served by the existing framework of governance?
2. What role does the democratic form of governance play in keeping the nation together, and how can human rights violations be avoided?
3. What are the possibilities of devolving centralized power to resolve the conflict between the government and the ethnic minorities, mainly northern Tamils?
4. How can the growing disparities between the rich and the poor, the powerful and the powerless be reduced?
5. What reforms are necessary in the state structures and electoral processes in order to assure the well-being of the civil society?

## HISTORICAL BACKGROUND AND THE MARCH TOWARDS MULTIPLE CRISES

When Sri Lanka (then Ceylon) gained independence, it inherited a democratic state. This was the result of hard-fought constitutional battles by the nation's leaders from all ethnic communities with a foreign power that had occupied and administered the island since early 1800. The seeds of democracy had been planted in the minds of Sri Lankan elites by way of education. They centred upon democratic principles, and institutions such as the rule of law, equal vote, a parliamentary system of government, an independent judiciary, a constitution, and a party system. The political, legal, and socio-economic developments that took place after independence have brought the country and its population to a crisis situation on a range of issues. These include the high cost of living, the ethnic conflict, post-colonial complexities in thinking and behaviour (e.g. the primacy of English and convoluted Western habits) leading to the alienation of average Sri Lankans from the ruling and managerial elites. Other crisis symptoms relate to the diminished rule of law, politicization of the judiciary and bureaucracy, the erosion of the traditional moral order, the waning quality of education and mismatch of skills and the employment market, infrastructural inadequacies, a widening gap between the electors and the elected, lack of transparency in decision-making, downgrading of the parliament, lower quality and behaviour of politicians, and much more.

Those who acquired the mantle of leadership after 1948 came from not only an Anglicized Christian but also colonial bourgeois and professional backgrounds. However, with the introduction of universal franchise, they were compelled to seek the support of other classes or segments of society like the Sinhalese peasants, workers and intermediary classes, like salaried employees of the government. Consequently the Sinhalese polity and the electorate started to bifurcate along a different logic. Up to then the bifurcation had been along the two bourgeois parties.

Even though the intermediary classes and the Sinhalese peasants supported the two main parties initially, the socio-economic and political changes that took place in the 1970s did not benefit the children of these strata. Significant segments were alienated and made to feel excluded from the social institutions, processes, and opportunities in society. The children of the lower strata of Sinhalese society, e.g. poor farmers or farm workers, tradesmen, and labourers, were specifically affected. With the expanding *Swabhasha* education system they obtained qualifications including university degrees. However, the political, class, cultural and geographical dialectics did not work in their favour. By contrast, the city-based, English-speaking children of the middle and upper-class enjoyed better status in society. Even without a degree they could obtain employment by using old boys' networks, superior knowledge of English, sporting skills, etc. These experiences of discrimination and exclusion led to the formation of the JVP. The JVP not only became the advocate of these disadvantaged people, mainly youths, but also developed a critique and a party organization to counter the ideological and political platforms used by the mainstream political parties including the socialist parties such as the Communist Party (CP) and the Lanka Sama Samaja Party (LSSP). After two failed attempts to capture state power through armed intervention, in

1971 and 1988–9, the JVP has now become a potent political force in the south to the extent that it has become the main coalition partner in the current United People's Freedom Alliance (UPFA).

Following Sirima Bandaranaike's and her coalition governments import substitution policy many middle- to upper-class professionals and even the average Sri Lankan faced considerable and continuing shortages of daily consumables. As a result, the people voted with their feet to elect the government of J.R. Jayewardene in 1977 advocating an open/liberalized economy and society based on moral principles. The 1977 elections were conducted according to the Westminster principles of parliamentary democracy. Until then the party with majority power in the parliament elected the prime minister who in turn appointed the president whose duties were purely, ceremonial. Jayewardene, who got an overwhelming majority of seats in parliament, had been impatiently waiting in the wings to secure such power since the Senanayake years. He used this mandate to change the constitution into one centred upon a strong 'executive presidency'. The powers entrusted with the new position of president can only be described as 'absolute'. He/She is not accountable to the parliament or judiciary for his/her actions, can prorogue parliament, dismiss ministers, and make high judicial appointments. Since the new system was introduced, executive presidents have generally held key portfolios such as defence and finance and appointed close confidants to other important portfolios such as foreign affairs, media and home affairs. A separate and highly powerful bureaucracy under the command of the president was systematically established. Government ministers, police, and defence chiefs, heads of departments all are accountable to the president as he/she is the head of the executive and in some cases the relevant minister.

In essence, since 1978, when the new constitution was adopted political leaders in Sri Lanka have gained their legitimacy through two elections: the presidential and the parliamentary. The system was described as one that combines the French and Westminster systems of governance. What ensued was the slow but steady erosion of the Westminster part of the system in favour of an all-powerful executive president directly elected by the people.

The only significant accountability check is every six years at the elections. Any changes to the constitution require a two-third parliamentary majority. Looking back at the many efforts made by the state to address the issues arising from the ethnic conflict one can see how difficult this has been.

The crisis of state in Sri Lanka has thus been a man-made one primarily due to the centralization of effective power in the hands of an individual for a period of six years and the political and constitutional changes that gave effect to this new venture.[4] Jayewardene justified the introduction of a strong executive by saying that previous governments were paralysed by the inability to make hard decisions, and if the government is to make key decisions in areas concerning economic development along the Singapore style, this was necessary. To some extent, when we look back on the open economic policies and programmes implemented by the governments since 1978 as well as the changes brought about by them, one can see the validity of the point made by him. In major economic development programmes such as the Mahaweli River development, the establishment of free trade zones, and import liberalization, the governments used powers acquired through the presidential system to streamline and accelerate the decision-making process and implementation. Nonetheless, in terms of democratic principles, rights, instruments, and processes many politicians and people in the north and south have started to feel that the system is unfair and alienates the population from the leaders they elect. Furthermore, a separate apparatus, line of command and control structure have been established parallel to the central bureaucracy creating duplication, waste, and at times conflicts among bureaucrats and politicians. Those who are close to the president's office are seen as movers and shakers compared to others who feel they are simple functionaries of a state machinery, marginalized not only by the growing influence of the presidency but also by the private sector. The lack of a formally constituted forum where the electors can debate and challenge the president face-to-face has been a key shortcoming in the new system. The president as the head of state almost operates like the former kings of Sri Lanka whose word was the ultimate in matters of governance.

The president also heads one of the two main political parties, and the extent to which any democracy prevails in decision-making within the parties is anyway open to question. As the Sri Lankan party system is very much based on personalities rather than principles and policies, the incumbent wields great influence within the party, especially after coming to power. More than any other factor, the crisis of state and nation in Sri Lanka can be ascribed to the nature, functioning, and tensions of the polity, which has led a schizophrenic existence. The issue of power-sharing between the executive and the legislature is a key one creating tensions and periodic crises.

According to political observers and academic and popular literature, there are at least two interconnected areas of major concern in terms of the crises:

1. Development and poverty related crises emanating from the implementation of liberal economic policies favouring the private sector multinationals and advocated by the World Bank, IMF, Asian Development Bank, associated technocrats and bureaucrats while simultaneously eroding the welfare state/system, and

2. Political and constitutional crises emanating from the creation of a centralized state, disaffection of youths, increasing violence, erosion of democracy, conflict with the Tamil militants, and the disagreements within the ruling elites about the way to resolve the Tamil question.

## DEVELOPMENT AND POVERTY RELATED CRISES: MYTH OF GROWTH WITH WAR?

The war in the 1980s and 1990s has had devastating economic and social consequences resulting in destruction of property and displacement of people. On the other hand, war and anti-terrorism related enterprises developed in the country. While some criticized the war economy others emphasized the need for economic growth and reconstruction as a solution to the ethnic conflict. The government continued on a path of 'war for peace'.

For both the state and the nation, development and poverty alleviation are significant issues. The social and economic disparities can make or break a nation. Sri Lankan leaders were mindful of the disadvantages faced by *Swabhasha*-educated segments, those in outlying areas, and other underprivileged backgrounds (e.g. caste groups) in the early decades of independent governance. With the introduction of neo-liberal economic policies which give priority to market forces with states playing a minimalist role, and the adoption of the doctrine of 'growth with war' the predicament of the underprivileged and disadvantaged groups has been less emphasized. A society based on competition among individuals and groups for private gain has been constructed. Those who succeed are the winners. Those who do not are the losers. Welfare measures that were available to the poor and disadvantaged have been reduced to the minimum over the years. According to Jayasuriya, 'In restructuring welfare policies, the post-1977 neo-liberal regimes departed from a redistributive strategy, abandoned universalistic social policies, encouraged the delivery of welfare by the private sector, and adopted residualist welfare measures (e.g. food stamps) to relieve poverty' (Jayasuriya 2000: 182).[5] The effects of these new policies were felt in the north and the south.

Focusing on the post-1977 period, Bastian (2004: 10) states that 'The liberal capitalism of the post-1977 period has had much negative impact on southern society. Growth of inequality, dismantling of rural livelihoods, political decay, development of an extensive patronage system and political violence are some of the features that characterize this period'.[6] Commenting in particular about the UNF's development policy package enunciated in *Regaining Sri Lanka*, he claims that the 'unstated assumption in the document is that the absence of economic growth is a major reason for conflicts; generating economic growth can lead to taking care of factors that underlie conflict' (ibid.: 10). He claims that this assumption was not correct, and in fact, the UNF policies alienated significant sections of the population, e.g., intermediary classes.

What impact did the neo-liberal economic policies have on the north and east? In the late 1970s and 1980s, it was believed that some segments of the Tamil society benefited from these policies while others were badly affected. Colombo-based Tamil entrepreneurs started some industries with the backing of the state in the north. However, the influx of imported goods such as onions and potatoes almost destroyed the northern farmers. During the 1970-7 period they had enjoyed better times.

According to Rajasingham-Senanayake (2003: 15), it is important for the peace negotiators to address the issues of economic and social inequality. If they fail 'to adequately acknowledge and address issues of economic and social inequality that structured the conflict it may result in an unstable peace that becomes a blueprint for renewed violence'. Her view is that in the current post-conflict settlement discussions, the issue of power redistribution via a devolved and federated system has received high priority at the expense of remedies for social and economic inequality. The public debate influenced by global recipes for post-conflict reconstruction focused on (neo-liberal) institution-building, constitutional design, and good governance. She highlights the economic hardships and social disaffections caused by spiralling costs of living, unemployment exacerbated by lay-offs, a sealing on public sector hiring, and privatization of essential services including public utilities (ibid.: 15-16). Questioning the role of the World Bank as custodian of the post-conflict reconstruction fund, she asks: will the peace dividend become available to those marginal communities and social groups that were most brutalized and instrumentalized by the war economy? According to Rajasingham-Senanayake a neo-liberal post-conflict peace will exacerbate socio-economic disparities potentially leading to further violence. To her growth with war, the fiction in policy circles in the 1990s, is an unsustainable myth as was evident in the failure of Japanese efforts to revive the negotiation process between the government and the LTTE in 2004.

Some writers observe that the war between the government and the LTTE was not simply an ethnic affair.

The war was sustained and fuelled by a range of global and local factors including rural poverty, unemployment, and caste marginalization (particularly in northern Tamil society and in the deep south). The majority of those who fought, died, and were disabled on both sides were drawn from the urban and rural poor. Additionally, in the last decade a war economy that developed a self-sustaining momentum emerged, as a number of transnational actors and networks, from the diaspora to the military and humanitarian industry stabilized and sustained the conflict dynamic as the economy structured into a war economy. (Rajasingham-Senanayake 2003: 15)

## RESISTANCE POLITICS AND ATTEMPTS AT COUNTER-HEGEMONY

The centralizing tendencies described earlier and the feelings of exclusion experienced by significant segments of the population—particularly the youthful segments—gave rise to paramilitary radical movements from the south and the north. The nature of these counter-movements, their goals and strategies, successes and failures are now well known.

Sri Lanka, which used to be proud of its democratic institutions, traditions and processes, quickly assumed the role of its own destroyer. Mechanisms set in place to elect leaders and govern the country along democratic principles and procedures started to crumble or were fatally tampered with by the elected leaders after the mid-1970s. Party politics started to erode the social fabric based on traditional values and modern aspirations as much as it seriously divided the population. Means of representation and governance started to be questioned in the north and south of the country. The ruling elites, in combination with minor parties and lower social classes, divided themselves into two main parties, i.e. the Sri Lanka Freedom Party (SLFP) and the United National Party (UNP). They started competing with each other for legitimacy of a state and nation so much that at times they could barely hold together while singing the mantra of 'unitary state' and state sovereignty. The country has seen many episodes of significant human rights abuses, violence, destruction of property and people's livelihoods, and displacements. One observer recently wrote (Bastian 2004: 10):

The inauguration of the period of liberalized capitalism coincided with the Sri Lankan Tamils contesting an election on a separatist platform. Immediately after the 1977 election, several rounds of ethnic riots and violence affected the country. Riots in August 1977, 1981 and 'Black July' of 1983 are the key events of violence that affected the south. In the meantime, military confrontation between the Tamil militant groups and Sri Lanka Army escalated. The southern politics also turned violent.

The attack on strikers and students in the eighties, the notorious referendum in 1982, the period of violence accompanying the Indo-Lanka Accord and the JVP violence from 1987 to almost the end of 1990 characterized this period.[7]

People in the north and the south felt that they were alienated from the rulers and that their elected representatives were operating from another planet. Their frustrations and sentiments surfaced in the public arena in various forms. These included the introduction of political violence, tele-dramas and literary expressions of the situation and tensions, and the emergence and expansion of political forces such as the JVP in the south and the LTTE in the north. The crisis of the state that existed in the late 1980s due to the struggle between the JVP and the government reached a peak with the capture and annihilation of the JVP leaders by the government. This episode was characterized by extra-judicial killings and violence of an unprecedented nature leading to charges of human rights violations of considerable scale on both sides.

The power struggle among the ruling elites in the south continues primarily between the two main political parties and their allies, i.e. minor parties including the JVP. As neither of the two major parties is able to enjoy a majority in the parliament, the role of minor parties has become crucial in forming and maintaining a government. In the last decade, there were occasions when some members of the two main parties as well as the minor parties changed their party allegiances. This movement of members of parliament from one alliance to another has been a destabilizing factor in Sri Lanka's political landscape. However, the most visible factor contributing to the relative destabilization of the state has been the so-called ethnic conflict or the conflict between the government and the LTTE from the early 1980s. At the core is the issue of power-sharing between the Tamil Tigers who claim to represent the Tamils in the north and the east of country and the elected government of Sri Lanka.

The state includes the Legislature, the executive or the government, and the judiciary. In the past separation of powers between these three arms of the state has been a key pillar of democracy. However, with the introduction of a presidential system of government in 1978, the concept and practice of separating powers assumed a new meaning. The powers and the role of the prime minister in the government became less important compared to those held by the president in whose hands powers became centralized. Politicization of the judiciary and the public administration was another trend. Tensions and conflicts between the three arms of the state continue to exist and are manifested publicly from time to time, such as in cases when parliamentarians make attempts to impeach the president. The tension between the Legislature and the president can be described as a main source of the crises of state in Sri Lanka in recent years. This was especially apparent when the president representing one main political party, i.e. the SLFP, and the prime minister and cabinet representing another main party, i.e. the UNP, ruled the country between 2002–4. This period of tension ended when the president abrogated the parliament and called for fresh elections in 2004.

Until it joined forces with the current government after the last elections in 2004, the political and armed struggles of the JVP had been a factor contributing to the periodic destabilization of the state. The JVP holds views that are appealing to the masses in the Sinhalese south. In political terms, its rising fortunes in the 1990s and up to now are seen as a destabilizing factor within governing circles of the two main parties. The JVP, which has an active political programme at the grass-roots level and presents itself as the advocate for the down-trodden Sinhalese masses, has a platform and employs rhetoric which counter the ideology and platform of the SLFP as well as the UNP. The media abounds with stories of tension between the two main parties forming the current alliance government, i.e. the SLFP *vs.* the JVP. This was evident after the recent tsunami disaster and relief efforts. However, some sections of the SLFP, are known to be working closely with the JVP.

The crisis of the state is best understood when it is examined in the broader national and socio-economic context. The inability of the UNP or the SLFP, to obtain a clear majority in the national parliament, the foreign debt and the continuing need for international aid, and indeed the heavy dependence created by this syndrome are important contextual factors.[8] As mentioned elsewhere, some minor parties that assist in the formation of a government after an election tend to change sides at unpredictable times. This creates a situation of crisis in the state and nation leading to the formation of another coalition or the need for general elections. Thus the leader of the major party in power tends to provide a share of power as well as other material benefits to members of minor parties in order to keep their trust and loyalty. This political play and patronage in the top echelons of power has become very intriguing and disturbing. For example, an astonishing number of MPs from the governing coalition have been appointed as ministers and deputy ministers. Yet from a public point of view, key problems in the country remain unresolved.

The tensions created by the ethnic factor, especially the demands for autonomy in the north and east of the country by the Tamils, have led to serious drawbacks in the governance of Sri Lanka. While the ceasefire agreement currently in place has given breathing space to politicians and civilians, lack of substantial movement in peace negotiations is generating anxieties among the public. It is almost as if a dark cloud is always hanging over the space. If there is one factor that can lead not only to further the crisis of the state and nation but also to continued violence and even the break-up of the nation, it should be this ethnic factor. While the LTTE with its demands for regional autonomy has been waging a campaign against the state seeking fundamental changes to the constitution and the way Sri Lanka is run, neither the main parties nor the JVP nor the other minor parties representing different communities have been forthcoming with constructive proposals for meaningful and effective devolution of power.

On numerous visits to the country, the present author has observed that there is very little indigenous planning for resource generation and utilization. Any planning at the government level occurs in relation to the vast international aid and loans secured by the government. It has come to such a situation that the people in a given area, who lack access to electricity, water, roads, schools, etc., totally rely on the government to do the planning, resource generation, and resolution of their problems. Very few government-community partnerships can be seen in these activities. Planning happens at the elite level involving the top politicians, technocrats, and bureaucrats. The government in turn expects the donor agencies to provide funding for the problems of the population, as they have been laid out in various proposals prepared by the instrumentalities of the government. However, a significant percentage of such funding remains dormant as the agencies responsible are unable to spend it in a given fiscal year. When the trust between the electors and the elected is eroded, when the local communities are not mobilized to resolve local problems, and when the politicians and bureaucrats are looking for foreign funding to resolve almost all problems in the country (and until this happens keep their hands tight), then it is no wonder a crisis of the nation develops in terms of the trust people have or do not have in the leaders, in the community ownership of the decisions, and in the system in operation.

The JVP and the LTTE have developed their own methods for mobilizing people for various activities under the banners of their respective parties. This became more visible during the recent tsunami and its aftermath. The civic organizations and the media mobilized people in numerous ways even before the government swung into action. While government as a whole waited for international aid to address the many issues emerging from the tsunami disaster, the JVP and LTTE opted for local participation and solutions. Even though the JVP was a partner in the governing coalition, tensions existed about the international aid and personnel coming to the country by way of NGOs. The point being made here is that the international aid syndrome has created a 'dependency mentality' among the political leaders, policy-makers and the general population as well that extends as much to day-to-day matters of existence as to long-term projects requiring extensive planning and resources. This dependency has created a crucial divergence or cleavage between the state and the community, or the population. This cleavage is counterproductive when it comes to finding solutions for Sri

Lanka's main problems whether they be poverty alleviation, sustainable development, free education, health care, local government, road and traffic matters or anything else. In a sense, then, this cleavage replicates the other gulf described earlier, between the electors and the elected where the electors experience alienation and deprivation of power, resources, and human and civic rights, especially after each election.

## CITIZENSHIP, IDENTITY, PATRONAGE AND A UNITED NATION

Even before the Tamil militancy started in the north, the country had introduced measures like starting to educate emerging generations in Sinhala and Tamil which divided the population along ethnic lines. In countries like Singapore and even Bhutan, the medium of instruction is English. Though it had been a colony of the British empire, Sri Lanka did away with English as the medium of instruction and introduced education through the mother tongue. Tamil children began to be taught in schools in Tamil and Sinhalese children in Sinhala. In the south, Sinhalese became the language of administration. In the north, Tamil assumed the same significance. In essence a segregated population started to be formed by way of education. The media also assumed a similar character. Thus generations of young people who go through the schooling system, often including university, do not know their own countrymen and women—except in terms of the ethnic stereotypes that circulate among their own people. These stereotypes propagate hatred, discrimination, condemnation, and exclusion. Rare are the examples of ethnic interchange in pockets of society, encouraged by government policy and the role played by NGOs. In the commercial as well as the religious sphere, there has been some interchange. But not in terms of intermarriage. These interchanges are not sufficient to counter the hatred and mutual suspicion created by the other forces that exist in the society. Without radical changes in the education system, and partly in the media, it is impossible to imagine the formation of a harmonious multi-ethnic community in Sri Lanka. Leaders may have to think hard about the necessity of a common language like English, which can cut across ethnic hatred and facilitate inter-ethnic communication in the schooling system. However, only little hope can be placed on this possibility because the present system of education and mutual suspicion seem to provide benefits to the politicians who can address and nurture their respective Sinhala or Tamil constituencies using the conflict to gain personal advantage. Issues of common identity and language are not even at the forefront of political discourse.

Not all people who cast their vote in elections are members of political parties. Once a party or parties come to power, not all their members benefit from government decisions either. Many adhere to a party only symbolically. They keep their membership simply following in the footsteps of their parents and grand-parents. Others become members for material gain and the promises that politicians make during the elections. A few become members on the basis of the policies and programmes of the parties. Politics has become a vocation in Sri Lanka, not only for those who contest a seat in the national Legislature, but also in the provincial councils. A majority of the politicians in the national assembly are from the upper middle or upper classes. If they are from a lower class before the elections, they move to upper class status while holding power. The system allows for this. It is no wonder then that the majority of the population, which belongs to the lower classes and remote regions, feels alienated after the elections as the politicians move to Colombo to take up their respective roles and the high life. The gulf between elected representatives and the electors is very significant in Sri Lanka. Many of the former do not even bother to visit the electoral offices of the parliamentarians. Among those who do only a few return satisfied. The general distrust in the system of governance has been increasing in all areas of the country since the introduction of the presidential system, and it has been more so in the north and the east as reflected by the ethnic conflict. When the JVP, which fought for the rights of the downtrodden in the south, became a key partner in the recent coalition government, many of those who had high expectations of the JVP began to question its credibility and credentials.

The rule of law is non-existent. One only has to observe the primordial rule of the jungle that prevails on Sri Lanka's roads and in the government institutions. In the latter, without personal contacts one cannot expect just solutions to (one's) problems in a reasonable period of time. If one goes to a police station in Sri Lanka for any small matter, one will spend hours there, which then become days, to get a matter addressed. Sri Lanka's court system is another sad story where decisions can take decades. In the so-called modern and open economy renting out premises is a risky proposition because reclaiming the property after the rent agreement or lease expires is nearly impossible. Law professors who became powerful ministers in previous governments have not done much to address a simple matter like this. Thus the people have to face immense hardships by way of court cases which go on for years if not decades. Those who lead are not in fact leading the country by reforming what is not right or introducing new measures to assist the population to live a decent life. The example of Singapore is not followed. In practice, law is applied depending on who the persons involved in a case are—not necessarily what the persons have done. When the people are uneducated and compelled to follow rules, they start breaking them. In this context, breaking rules has become the norm.

A society based on personal favours at the expense of a commonly understood system of rules and norms of governance which includes rewards and sanctions depending on the merit or the offence, as the case may be, is bound to face crises of one sort or another. In fact, Sri Lankans are now facing crises all the time. Even to get a small matter attended to they have to wage a struggle. The question has to be asked, who benefits from a chaotic situation when the people are unable to resolve the day-to-day matters of existence through the civil society and the institutions of the government (part of the executive)? From the sociological and social contextual points of view, such a situation assists the politicians and department officials because the affected people have to run after those in authority even for minor matters. There is a general malaise sweeping the governing institutional regime in the country irrespective of the changes that have been introduced in the private sector in the name of open or liberalized economic policies. Generally speaking the political leaders who are familiar with Western democracies and operations of the governments there, as well as the relations between the electors and the elected, have not used their knowledge or positions of power to resolve the country's civic issues to the satisfaction of the population. This includes the infrastructural developments needed in the capital and suburbs and in the provinces. The international aid syndrome and the colonial habits are partly to blame for this.

## THE NORTHERN QUESTION AND
## THE PEACE PROCESS

At the heart of the ethnic conflict in Sri Lanka is the issue of power-sharing, generally labelled as the 'devolution debate'. Efforts made so far by successive governments have been characterized as state-centric approaches and researchers involved in the development processes in the conflict zone have highlighted the need for approaches where devolution is taken to present not only challenges but also opportunities (Mayer et al. 2003).

Tamils, especially the young Tamils experienced alienation and disenfranchisement after each election. Faced with the widening gulf between the electors and the elected post-1978, including the failed promises given to them by their elected Tamil representatives in the national assembly, they searched for other options to secure power within or without the existing political and judicial system. Thus we saw the emergence of the LTTE and other Tamil political organizations—some having armed wings affiliated to them. Among these organizations, after a period of to-ing and fro-ing, and internal fights and murders, the LTTE has become the dominant force in the Tamil areas of the north and to some extent in the east. Their demand is for more power to the northern and eastern province taken as a whole even though the latter consists of three different ethnic communities: Sinhala, Tamil, Muslim. The LTTE argues that these areas comprise the traditional homeland of the Tamils as they have lived there for over a thousand years. They seek self-determination in order to govern the province in its own right with the least involvement of the central government headed by the executive president. However, the LTTE's ultimate aim is to establish a separate state called Eelam in the north and east of the country. Both these aims have drawn sharp criticism and response not only from the government but also from the Sinhala population at large. Much criticism against the LTTE has been framed in terms of preserving the unitary nation-state, as we have known it after independence. Yet the ground reality is quite different as the LTTE controls substantial parts of the north and east.

The fact that the conflict was interpreted as an ethnic conflict and several wars were waged for nearly two decades, is crucial in understanding the crisis of state and nation in Sri Lanka as this had a very significant impact on the instruments of state, rule of law, democracy, civic life, and so on. In fact, one has to wonder whether Jayewardene, being a veteran politician with experience in the Legislature from pre-independence times, conceived the new presidential system partly to address the problems he foresaw would come from the Tamils. For a decade or more, Sri Lankans lived in a war like situation and many soldiers lost their lives. The Tamil insurgency was described as terrorism and laws were passed to enable the defence forces and the police to arrest suspected people and keep them in custody for long periods without producing them in court. A large security establishment developed in the private sector to cater to the needs of army camps, and to provide security to government and private sector establishments. Mutual suspicion developed between the two populations. Images of terrorists out to destroy democracy and create a separate state dominated by the Tamils (and ethnically cleansed) on the one hand, and a hegemonic race of Sinhalese that does not want to give the Tamils their due rights and peaceful existence on the other were propagated. The use of suicide bombers by the LTTE in Sinhala areas, in particular the capital Colombo, was a key factor in destabilizing civic life, tourism, and trade. The attack on Sri Lanka's main airport by the LTTE in July 2001 epitomized such warfare which created tremendous economic loss. The counter-insurgency measures taken by the government were equally destructive.

To a considerable degree Sri Lanka has now passed the stage of mutual suspicion, hatred and violence after the signing of the ceasefire agreement in 2002. People want lasting peace between the government and the LTTE. Many in the population, including Sinhala people, understand that it is necessary for the Tamils in the north and east to have reasonable rights, and are in fact critical of the national political leaders who do not move the peace process forward. However, there is no desire or willingness on the part of many to agree to a separate state of Eelam for the Tamils. A self-autonomous region based on ethnicity has instead become the focus of activity. Thus, the crisis facing the Sri Lankan state, and to an extent the LTTE and the nation is how to share power in a political system where all communities can play a part. Various models have been looked at such as those found in India, Switzerland, Canada, Australia, and Malaysia. Peace secretariats have been established in Colombo and the north, and many conferences have been organized. Rounds of negotiations were held. Governments changed. But the peace process is stagnating. There is a real possibility of a return to war at any moment as extra-judicial killings by the LTTE are continuing in the north and east and to a limited degree in Colombo also against members of the Karuna faction.[9]

Notwithstanding the various national and international efforts made to reconcile the two sides and arrive at a negotiated settlement of the conflict, a permanent solution has not yet been found. A volatile ceasefire agreement continues and people on both sides of the country have found this a temporary blessing. They want their leaders to find a permanent solution so that they can live in peace. However, Sri Lankan polity, which has evolved from the pre-colonial, colonial and post-colonial modes of thinking and behaviour, is too complex for it to easily fulfil the desire of the population for a truly democratic society or the achievement of a satisfactory resolution of the conflict.

The United People's Freedom Alliance (UPFA), came to power in 2004 largely because the LTTE issued its response to the previous UNF (United National Front) government's proposals in an idealistic manner. Electors could not differentiate between the LTTE's desire for provincial administration powers and a separate state. Chandrika Kumaratunga, the president (also the president of the SLFP) used this situation to characterize the UNP, the main partner in the UNF, as a party willing to give Tamils more powers than necessary and appealed to the national sentiment. She took over several key ministries from the UNF after the LTTE issued its response, and prorogued the parliament while the prime minister was in Washington and called for new elections. After the 2004 elections, Kumarantunga formed a government with the JVP and other minor parties but the peace process has stalled. Within the coalition government itself there are differing emphases and approaches to the peace process and the granting of autonomy to the northern and eastern provinces. As already stated, since independence the main crisis of the state and nation has been this power-sharing issue with the Tamils, and it continues to be the case. No political leader or party has ever been able to prepare the ground for a satisfactory dialogue and resolution of the matter. There has not been a shortage of all-party conferences or peace negotiations, lately with the assistance of foreign countries such as Norway and Japan. Yet the problem persists, the mistrust remains. The Singapore ideal for the country, which Jayewardene talked about, still hangs in the balance. The general frustrations of the people with the malfunctioning bureaucratic institutions and the unfulfilled promises regarding the improvement of infrastructural facilities, reduction in the cost of living, and creating a society based on the rule of law rather than personal favours and employment of physical power and violence—in short, a peaceful society—have reached a crisis point. This is evident from the emergence of third parties in Sri Lankan politics such as the JVP and, more recently, the entrance of a minor party of Buddhist monks, Jathika Hela Urumaya (JHU), to the national parliament.

## THE WAY FORWARD?

While it is not difficult to find explanations for the reasons for the crisis of state and nation in Sri Lanka, it is not quite as simple to find solutions. Some of the solutions that have been proposed have already been discussed. Establishing and promoting democratic institutions and processes of governance is a key issue which involves both the north and the south constituencies. This is an approach favoured by India and other countries involved in the peace process. Within such a framework of governance, where the rights of all citizens are guaranteed, the substantial devolution of power to the northern and eastern regions has become the other key focus.

The role of international agencies and players is another issue. The overarching framework of international aid, and the associated liberal-economic paradigms, have been criticized on various grounds. In this context, the need for regaining the peace process has been emphasized by some writers:

The role, value and exit strategies of international actors in the post-conflict reconstruction process needs to be constantly evaluated, monitored and assessed. Indeed the GoSL and the LTTE must co-operate on this issue, if Sri Lanka is to regain the peace process and chart its own post-conflict development policy. This is necessary if the post-conflict process is to benefit the people who have been affected by the war rather than the global post-conflict industry, and if aid is not to become a cause for a new cycle of war. (Rajasingham-Senanayake 2003: 14)

The two main political parties and their associates also need to concentrate on the long-term future of the country and its people rather than on temporary political expediencies of devising strategies to remain in power by using the crises in the state and nation. They have to make a concerted effort, with or without mediation, to seek and find common grounds between the government and the LTTE. When addressing the core issues in the north and the east, it is inevitable that the leaders have to think of reforming the politico-legal systems in operation in the rest of the country as well.

Mainstream Sinhalese political parties have not yet moved decisively away from the politics of narrow Sinhalese nationalism, although in power they may demonstrate some limited capacity for pluralism and multi-ethnic accommodation. Indeed, these mainstream Sinhalese political parties continue to produce leaders and policy spokespersons who are quite comfortable with both extremes of the political discourse—Sinhalese nationalism and accommodationist pluralism. The trouble with this type of duplex politics is that it has never enabled the Sinhalese ruling class to make a decisive move towards managing or resolving the most destabilizing crisis with which the polity has been beset for decades. It goes against the grain of ruling class capacity to govern a modern and complex society in deep crisis. (Uyangoda 2002: 8).

As Uyangoda does, in terms of political analysis, the crisis of the state and nation can be explained away as a failure on the part of the ruling class. But what about the way forward in resolving this failure as well as the crisis?

A precondition for averting further crises in the Sri Lankan state and nation is the abolition of the executive presidency and a return to the Westminster style of government with a prime minister and cabinet. Given the negative impact that the executive presidency has had on Sri Lanka's body politic and the contribution it has made to the generation of resistance from the north and the south, it is hard to imagine how Sri Lanka can be a champion of democracy again without such a reversal. The concentration of power in one individual irrespective of parliamentary elections amounts to rule by one individual—the head of a mainstream party who is eventually bound neither by parliamentary elections, not by decisions made in the Legislature. Recent history shows that the president can hold on to power even when opposition parties form the government. While this ability provides a degree of continuity in terms of centralized power, the question being asked is how far does the presidency represent the diverse population of the country? How far are the decisions made by the president in the best interest of the diverse population?

The powers of the president are defined in the constitution. Having two centres of power, the president and parliament, has also led to a duality of interests and associated politicking. Clashes—open and not so open—between the two centres have created inefficiencies. It is obvious that the minority Tamils from the north and east do not see the presidency as representing their rights and interests. They have elected some parliamentarians from their areas to the national parliament. These members function as a proxy team for the LTTE. The leadership of the northern Tamils is clear-cut, i.e. the LTTE, which runs an administrative, political, judicial, educational, and security machinery in the areas under its control. It is possible that in a truly democratic system of government whereby members are elected from each electorate and the prime minister and the cabinet are selected from these parliamentarians, the LTTE will display better involvement in national politics, policy development, and implementation as opposed to its current absence. Once the duality is removed the LTTE will realize that to take part in national politics is really to share power. In the current context, this can't happen because the real power is concentrated in the hands of the presidency.

In the new scenario, like the JVP the LTTE also can be the kingmakers by aligning with one of the mainstream parties in Sri Lanka, the SLFP or the UNP.[10] Such a situation, as that in Singapore, will be for the benefit of the country as minority involvement on the highest levels of the power hierarchy will allow the LTTE to reduce their anxieties about discrimination and exclusion. The leaders in Colombo will also benefit from such involvement as all will be operating in a national system of government without the talk of a separate state or a violent struggle for power. In such a scenario, the Colombo-centric ruling elites of the Sinhalese will not be able to manipulate power in the same way as they have done until now. Give and take will be necessary, but the key will be the re-establishment of trust between them and the LTTE, not with words but with actions. Lack of trust on the part of the ethnic minorities, particularly the Tamils from the north, has been a critical factor in the current crisis.

Devolution of power under a federal system to the north and east is another key issue. The reluctance on the part of the mainstream political leadership to give up the power bestowed upon it by the existing centralized political system has been a factor leading to the current stalemate. Some suggest that the talk of a unitary state is now meaningless as the ground reality is almost two states. If the federation is one of two states, then, they say, the federation or unity of the nation can have some meaning. Otherwise it is only political rhetoric on the part of Sinhalese leaders. The temporary peace as a result of the ceasefire agreement provides an excellent opportunity to consider the options available for power sharing. The approach this author suggests is direct consultation and negotiation with a degree of good faith between the government and the LTTE—even though the latter may seek international guarantees for any lasting agreement.

## CONCLUSION

Many writers on Sri Lankan society, especially the so-called ethnic conflict and the state, have been critical of the supposedly continuing hegemony of the Sinhalese as opposed to the ethnic minorities such as the Tamils, Muslims, Burghers, and religious minorities like the Christians. Others go a step further and point to the Sinhalese ruling elites comprising well-to-do families whose ancestors accumulated wealth, power, and status as well as cultural capital during the previous periods of royal rule, and colonial occupation.[11] As this elite group cannot rule the country on its own due to the electoral system and its requirements, it has forged various links with other strata of society in the capital Colombo and outlying provinces through the party system. The politically active members of parties have multiple links with each other through family, kinship, caste, region, schools, class, professions, and businesses, and as landowners. Once in power, the politicians promote and foster these close links further, materially and symbolically. Tamil and Muslim leaders too have been doing the same.

However, large segments of Sinhalese and Tamil society in the island fall outside this mutually reinforcing 'patronage system'. Even the majority of those from the lower strata of society who supported the two main Sinhala political parties, or their counterparts in the Tamil areas such as the Tamil United Liberation Front (TULF), continually experienced broken promises by the elected politicians. This created a reservoir of frustration and anger which led to the formation of a counter-political culture and leadership culminating in the formation of the JVP, the LTTE and other parties. These counter-parties also armed themselves in order to confront the so-called state terrorism (or the use of extra-judicial powers to attack political opponents). This made it easy to brand them as terrorists trying to destroy the 'democratic framework of governance' (no mention was made of the widely practised patronage system that led to the frustrations of the young people).

By now we have seen the various stages of this conflict between the political and social forces of the establishment and the counter-forces of what is termed liberation or resistance. The

JVP has become a mainstream party ending up in parliament and entering into coalition governments. In fact, it is described as the 'third force' in southern politics. Until recently, the LTTE had been maintaining a dual face by way of its armed struggle with the state and its presence in the parliament through its proxies, i.e. the Tamil National Alliance (TNA). The current ceasefire—signed after the 11 September attack on the World Trade Center in New York—has given breathing space to both the state and the LTTE to reflect on their respective strategies without the bloodshed experienced before.

The issue before the LTTE is whether to get involved in patronage politics and a system of governance based on the same and supported by the international monetary agencies and other states in the international system, which it fought against in the early years of its struggle, or continue the current arrangement where it has control over certain areas of the country and some status nationally and internationally as a legitimate political force, or go back to armed struggle to seek more power and control in the north and the east. It is, however, impossible to think of a scenario in which the LTTE will want to either join hands with or become a party to the system of 'patronage politics' found in the south and give up the ideals for which it has fought for several decades.

In this respect, we ought to note the differences between the respective administrative systems found in the south and the north. Not much has been written about this aspect but it is known that the system in the north is far more efficient and functional even though it is operated under a hegemonic political power like the LTTE. By contrast, the system found in the south is highly inefficient, corrupt, and reinforces rather than diminishes the patronage political system, ignoring the needs and aspirations of the whole society. In fact, large numbers of Sri Lankans have emigrated and settled elsewhere because of their unhappiness with this system. Those at the top strata of society, especially those who can muster political or administrative muscle via their multiple links, benefit more from the system compared to others.

Thus the political conflicts in post-independent Sri Lanka are very much rooted in the socio-economic inequalities, power imbalances, lack of equal opportunity and fair play, and the

reproduction of elitism and self-perpetuating practices of
patronage, as well as the cultural and identity connotations
associated with these. The disadvantages and disempowerment
felt by the youthful sections of society in the north and the south
because of the hegemonic and exclusionary political party system,
the administration, and a system of governance which presents
a façade of 'democracy, development and poverty alleviation',
while reinforcing certain elite families and their coterie of friends
and close confidants in Colombo and the provinces, have been
contributing factors in the rise of conflicts and, ultimately, of
periodic crises of state and nation.[12]

The question for the LTTE is how to address this issue of
family rule in the south or at least circumvent the hegemony of
elite rule predicated upon close networks of family, etc. It doesn't
seem to have a strategy for this. All it is asking for is more
power to the north and east without pushing for fundamental
change in the southern polity by joining hands with those who
are seeking the same in the south. State reform is the need and
aspiration of the masses in the south—currently labelled as 'good
governance' by academics, parliamentarians, and technocrats.
The LTTE has not given much attention to this aspect. This
neglect has given considerable space for the politicians in the
south to continue with the corrupt patronage system without
much hindrance. They are more interested in devising strategies
for retaining the political, administrative and patronage system
in the south than in what happens in the north—except when it
comes to a crisis point. Even Muslim politics is currently governed
by patronage politics linked to the mainstream Sinhalese party
system, as is the politics of Indian Tamil plantation workers.

The rise of the Jathika Hela Urumaya—the party of Buddhist
monks—in the last elections provides a different scenario. It has
become yet another segment of the Sinhalese population frustrated by the practices of the mainstream Sinhalese political
parties and their leaders. The monks are demanding more rights
for the Sinhalese because they feel that the politicians who are
willing to heed the Tamil demands have downgraded their rights
and status. They foresee the threat of a divided country. Their
appeal is to the same electorate that the two main parties and

the JVP are competing against each other for votes. Unlike the JVP, the JHU at this stage is an urban-based phenomenon.

Thus the crisis of state and nation in Sri Lanka is a complex one to which the tsunami added a new dimension. We are yet to see if the unfolding post-tsunami activities and agendas become another leaf in the book of Sri Lanka's failed state. To some extent, tsunami aid prevented the crisis of the state from breaking out as the world yet again came to focus on Sri Lanka's humanitarian needs. Sri Lanka politicians, instead of being involved in power struggles, suddenly became busybodies receiving world sympathy, assistance, and aid. The redistribution of such aid and the mechanisms in place have become another issue of contention among parties.

Every society has various contradictions. When they turn into open conflicts, they become difficult to manage without the express agreement of the parties involved. The dominant power may attempt to subjugate the subordinate one. However, the conflict itself defines who the dominant and subordinate powers are in given situations. New situations of equilibrium emerge from time to time. This is what has happened in Sri Lanka. The Sri Lankan state cannot now claim to be the dominant power in certain parts of the country—north and east. Power in the Colombo-based state has been and is being contested politically, militarily, culturally, and within and beyond the framework of a modern nation. Leaving aside the political rhetoric on both sides, instead of sharing power, the contending parties are after total power. This has been the reason for the failure of peace negotiations, the state, and the nation thus far.

As Uyangoda (2002: 4) states:

Indeed, one infinitely complex task involved in a comprehensive peace project is the restoration of the formal Sri Lankan state in the two provinces while re-introducing liberal political institutions as well as practices. Such a journey from the collapsed state to a 'liberal state' is profoundly a difficult one.... At one level, there already exist rudimentary structures of two competing states that are not 'liberal' by any means—the military—administrative structures of the collapsed Sri Lankan state in the region and the military-administrative structures of the LTTE-led *quasi state*.

A constructive approach would be to conceptualize the post-civil war peace and state formation in transformation terms. The idea of transformative peace could offer a creative way out from the divisive debate on 'liberal peace' vs. 'totalitarian peace'. A transformatory peace agenda can focus on a broad political program for reconstituting the state not merely in the sense of restoring the state in the north and east, but also reforming the Sri Lankan state in general. This view could be easily anchored on the premise that a further democratized state in Sri Lanka would provide a greater impetus for post-conflict democratic state formation in the north and the east.

The points made by Rajasingham-Senanayake (2003: 18) can be applied to other societies faced with crises of state and nation in the region and elsewhere:

It is arguable that trans-historical ethnic readings of the violence in Sri Lanka and neo-liberal myths that growth with war is possible in the dependent economies of the *global south* have obscured issues of economic and social inequality that structured the two decades-long armed conflict in the north and east of Sri Lanka. They also obscured how the war had transformed the island's society and political economy. But issues of political representation and economic justice are in-extricably linked: self-determination will remain an unfulfilled promise without economic and social rights.

In this context, we have to ask whether the participants in the peace negotiations in Sri Lanka have been following a broader approach which involves self-determination as well as the economic and social inequalities faced by the aggrieved parties or whether they have indeed been one-track approaches where at some point in time one aspect was emphasized over the other? Since uneven development, can lead to conflicts and conflicts for power can retard development, it may be useful to adopt a holistic approach involving both aspects. Rajasingham-Sena-nayake highlights this: 'Post-conflict reconstruction must have a holistic approach and move beyond a formalist legal appro-ach to devolution and power sharing among the armed actors and the state, and address issues such as poverty, inequality and their relationship to macro-policies of economic adjustment and conflict' (2003: 19). Moreover, 'building a sustainable peace would entail political and economic reform aimed at achieving substantive rather than ritual or procedural democracy and the need for re-distributive justice' (ibid.).

## NOTES

1. According to Giddens, all modern states are nation-states, and they are associated with the rise of nationalism. 'Nationalism can be defined as a set of symbols and beliefs providing the sense of being part of a single political community' (1989: 303).

2. He describes the four cardinal principles that Tamil representatives presented the Thimphu talks in (1985) and their rejection by government officials saying that the principles contravened the rights of sovereignty and territorial integrity of Sri Lankans. We have to be aware of the legal vs. socio-political definitions and differences here.

3. Sri Lanka was called Ceylon during the British colonial period. The name change occurred when it became a republic and a new constitution was adopted in 1972.

4. Bastian explains this development and the challenges posed to the centralized state from the Tamil militants (Bastian 2004: 9–12).

5. Jayasuriya advocates the need for charting a new political agenda for social democracy which is different from economic liberalism, the operation of market forces and political liberalism encompassing the rights of citizenship. The ideological rejection of state welfare meant a departure from the principles of social democracy.

6. Bastian differentiates between the economic policies of the UNF government led by the United National Party (December 2001-4) and the UPFA government led by the Sri Lanka Freedom Party (SLFP) that came to dominance after the 2004 parliamentary elections. While the UNF achieved much in terms of the peace process such as the signing of the Ceasefire Agreement with the Tamil Tigers and the mobilization of international support for the peace process, it lost the 2004 parliamentary elections because it could not communicate its message to the electorate effectively. 'The UNF economic policies were dominated by the interests of the big capitalists and informed by the traditional trickle down growth theories. These policies alienated many who could have formed the social base for the peace process among the southern voters' (Bastian 2004: 9).

7. The referendum was conducted to obtain a mandate to extend the parliamentary term of the governing party by another six years. As this was held not long after the presidential elections accompanied by a lot of disturbances and improper practices, the legitimacy of the referendum was open to doubt.

8. Some commentators have argued that the stalemate in negotiations between the Government of Sri Lanka and the LTTE in 2004, amidst many efforts made by Japan, etc., to revive it, was caused because of the emphasis placed by the government and its international supporters on check-book diplomacy. It is also believed that the closeness of the USA and Japan to the government and the exclusion of the LTTE from the Washington talks of donor countries were other factors which created doubt in the LTTE ranks.
9. Karuna, who was the LTTE commander in the eastern province, defected in 2004 along with his followers. The two sides are engaged in a killing spree to regain dominance.
10. During the UNF government led by Ranil Wickramasinghe between 2002–4, there was a semblance of such alignment, especially when the two parties signed the ceasefire agreement and continued the peace dialogue.
11. The ancestors of current leaders who are included in the elite group or the ruling class as the case may be held positions in the British colonial administration and the state Legislature after being educated in English in England or Ceylon. Some even participated in the independence movement. Among these ancestors were a number of Tamil and Muslim personalities.
12. If one were to make an analysis of the backgrounds of current members of parliament from the two main parties in terms of family, kinship, and other close contacts, one would be in for many surprises. The building and nurturing of political dynasties has not been limited to the Bandaranayakes. At the regional levels the same model has been applied. With rare exceptions, when a minister, deputy minister, or a member of parliament passes away, it has been the practice of the party leadership to appoint his or her son or daughter or another close relative to take over the party organizer's role at the electorate level. In the 1970s, Janice Jiggins published a study on family and kinship among parliamentarians. To this author's knowledge, no such research study has been conducted since.

## SELECT BIBLIOGRAPHY

Balasingham, A., 2001, *The Will to Freedom: An Inside View of Tamil Resistance*, Mitcham: Farimax Publishing Ltd.

Bastian, S., 2004, 'How Development can Undermine Peace', *Polity*, vol. 2, no. 2, Colombo.

Gamage, S. and I.B. Watson (eds.), 1999, *Conflict and Community in Sri Lanka*, New Delhi: Sage.

Giddens, A., 1989, *Sociology*, Cambridge: Polity Press.

Held, D., A. McGrew, D. Goldblat and J. Perraton, 1999, *Global Transformations: Politics, Economics and Culture*, Cambridge: Polity Press.

Jayasuriya, L., 2000, *Welfarism and Politics in Sri Lanka: Experience of a Third World Welfare State.* Perth: The University of Western Australia.

Mayer, M., D. Rajasingham-Senanayake and Y. Thangarajah (eds.), 2003, *Building Local Capacities for Peace: Rethinking Conflict and Development in Sri Lanka*, New Delhi: Macmillan.

Rajasingham-Senanayake, D., 2003, 'The Economics of Peace: The World Bank, Information Asymmetries, and the Post-Conflict Industry' *Polity*, vol. 1, no. 1, Colombo.

———, 2003, 'The International Post-Conflict Industry: Myths, Rituals, Market Imperfections and the Need for a New Paradigm', *Polity*, vol. 1, no. 3, Colombo.

Rupasinghe, K., 2004, 'Multiple Crises in Sri Lanka', *Polity*, vol. 1, no. 6, Colombo.

Uyangoda, J., 2002, 'Peace Watch', *Pravada*, vol. 8, nos. 1&2; vol. 8, no. 3, Colombo.

———, 2003, 'Peace Watch—Road Map to Interim Administration', *Polity*, vol. 1, no. 4, Colombo.

———, 2004, 'Peace Watch—Crisis of Democratic Institutions', *Polity*, vol. 2, no. 1, Colombo.

Wijemanna, A., 2002, 'The Rhetoric of Impotence', *Pravada*, vol. 8, no. 3, Colombo.

# CHAPTER 7

# Sri Lanka—State and Nation in Crisis

*John P. Neelsen*

Like many other post-colonial countries, independent Sri Lanka being a multi-ethnic and multi-cultural society was conceptualized as a secular democratic state. Back in 1948 the task of nation-building appeared comparatively easy since the island faced no border problems, disposed of a rich plantation economy, and was administered by a highly qualified professional and political elite which had imbibed the British tradition of government. Moreover, democracy was well entrenched. After all, universal suffrage for men and women was introduced in 1931, i.e. earlier than in many European countries, and a plurality of parties, including communists and trotskists, presented the voters with real political alternatives.[1] Colonial rule ended without war, government being handed over to the United National Party which represented a broad spectrum of political currents. At first this optimism appeared justified. Until the early 1970s, Ceylon was even held up as a model for other Third World countries because its high standards in education, health, infant mortality, longevity, etc., were on par with those in the West. It proved that a high standard in human development was possible despite a low per capita income.

Today, more than half a century after independence, all that has changed. It is in name only, that the country represents a 'secular socialist democracy'. In reality, it has turned into a 'security state' with a democratic façade. State power has been instrumentalized to advance the interests of the majority community at the expense of the minorities. Class conflict and political ideologies have been superseded by ethnic nationalism. The latter has so deeply infected the body politic that even the massive aid being made available in the aftermath of the tsunami of December 2004 that left 40,000 people dead and huge destruction behind, was not distributed according to need. As a result, a long-running civil war threatens not just the social cohesion of society but puts into doubt the territorial integrity of the country as a whole.

This chapter analyses first the evolution of the process of nation-building based on a secular democratic state to a narrow exclusive authoritarian nationalism. In a second part, the crisis of the state focusing on the privatization of violence and the question of self-determination, are analysed. The article concludes on outlining the major requirements and problems that will have to be addressed to eventually usher in a lasting and just peace.

## I. CRISIS OF THE NATION: FROM NATION-BUILDING TO ETHNIC NATIONALISM

### 1. SRI LANKA AS A MULTI-ETHNIC MULTI-CULTURAL SOCIETY

Ceylon as the island was called during the 450 years of colonial rule and until 1972, is a multi-cultural, multi-ethnic society. Separated from the Indian subcontinent by the narrow Park Strait, the 2500 year history of the island has been strongly influenced by its huge neighbour. It is from India that the majority of its peoples have migrated, it is from there that a strong influence on its culture has been exerted throughout. Natural factors have proved to be further determinants. Endowed with good harbours, rich in gems and spices, it came to occupy an important position in the network of international maritime trade going back to Roman times. Starting in the early sixteenth century, European colonialists arrived having learnt the sea-route between East-Africa and the coasts of the South Asian subcontinent from Arab navigators. Portuguese, Dutch and British in succession occupied the island coveting its spices, especially cinnamon, and valueing it as a strategic port between Europe and the Far East as much as a springboard for the control of India. This long-standing double exposure to the outside world, i.e. to India in general, to foreign trade in particular, became increasingly reflected in the composition of its people. Rich in its cultural and ethnic diversity, the country has been turned into a social laboratory.

The official census classifies Sri Lanka's population according to religion and race in addition to the usual demographic criteria of sex and age. A break-down of the current 20 million people shows that about 3/4th are Sinhalese. Largely concentrated in the centre, the south and the western part of the country, their mother tongue is Sinhala, an Indo-European language, indicating their origin in northern India. Most Sinhalese (69 per cent) are Buddhists making Buddhism the foremost religion in the country. The second largest group, the Sri Lankan Tamils (12 per cent) originally from south India crossed the Park Strait more than 2000 years ago. They are overwhelmingly Hindu and speak Tamil, one of only five Dravidian languages. They are mostly settled in the north and east of the island. The third group, the Indian Tamils (6 per cent) are for the most part concentrated in the 'up-country', a mountainous region that stretches in an arch from the centre of the island to the south. They came to the island only from the middle of the nineteenth century onward to work in the recently established plantations. Next come the Moors (7 per cent) who while speaking Tamil distinguish themselves by their religion, Islam. Living mostly along the eastern and the north-western coast, they are the descendents of thirteenth century Arab and Persian merchants who controlled the external trade of Ceylon before the Europeans came to replace them. There is, furthermore, a small but (once) influential Christian community (7 per cent) recruited from members of both, the Sinhalese and the Sri Lankan Tamil communities. Composed of Catholics and Protestants of different denominations, they reflect the dominant religious convictions of the successive occupiers of the island. Finally, there are very small groups of Burghers (of European stock), of Malays and of the Veddas—the remainders of the original inhabitants or marginalized low caste people—which complete the ethno-cultural mosaic of Sri Lanka.

## 2. MINORITY, NATION, UNDERCLASS— SOCIOLOGICAL CATEGORIZATION

At first sight mere statistical categories, the plurality of ethnic groups assumed in the course of independent Sri Lanka ever more socio-political significance. In this context, it has to be recalled that the island had been ruled by indigenous kings as a single entity only until the end of the twelfth century, if at all.[2] In the following centuries, the unitary reign dissolved into several kingdoms,[3] and the capital was transferred from Polonnaruwa in the centre to the south-west. In fact, when the Portuguese Lorenzo de Almeyda landed in 1505, he found the island divided into three major states, a Tamil kingdom in the north (Jaffna), the kingdom of Kotte in the south-west, and a third one in the interior with Kandy as capital. Only the latter remained independent for the next three hundred years, while the Portuguese and Dutch ruled over the coastal areas.[4]

It was only at the beginning of the nineteenth century that the whole of the island came once again under a single administration. The British East India Company replaced its Dutch rival in 1796, and became the undisputed master of the country with the military defeat of the last king of Kandy in 1815. Soon after the country was declared a British crown colony and was eventually subjected to one and the same centralized colonial administration in the aftermath of the Colebrooke-Cameron reforms of 1832. In addition to the politico-administrative unification, large-scale changes in the legal and social system were implemented. They built on and extended the measures taken by the Portuguese and Dutch providing for individual private property and personal (monetary) taxes by instituting the legal framework for a private market economy in place of the traditional system of land ownership (Asiatic/tributary mode of production) and related service obligations. They also appropriated huge tracts of crown and temple land to be freely sold and bought on the market. They paved the way for the introduction of an export economy of primary products in Ceylon. Against the backdrop of the abolition of slavery in the British colonies, thousands of immigrant, factually bonded labour, was brought in from southern India to cultivate coffee, then tea and rubber on large plantations in what has been called 'military agriculture'. Running parallel to the beginnings of industrial capitalism in Europe, the ground was laid for a *complementary* international division of labour and exchange. Internally, however, a different socio-economic configuration emerged. With the estates socially and economically largely isolated in the interior, a 'dual economy' was established with the export driven enclaves exerting relatively little impact on the indigenous economic system of subsistence production. Until well into independence, the country's economy remained concentrated around the plantation sector so much so that the industrial sector not only remained small, but was essentially confined to tea processing in the estates.

As a result, while British colonial rule unified the administration, it did not break-up the stability of the rural character of the socio-economic order with their largely closed localized communities structured by ethnic and caste-cum-occupational criteria. The unequal structure inherent in a 'dual' economy restricted the modernization of society in terms of horizontal and vertical mobility, of transport infrastructure or of urbanization. Consequently, the distribution of the population was largely retained as were the traditional criteria of social stratification and collective identity. Outside the city of Colombo with its international harbour and modern commercial and financial centre, there was little intermixture of peoples from different caste, religious, ethnic or cultural backgrounds. In other words, the formation of a modern class society remained incomplete and fragmentary.

As a first result, from a sociologist's point of view the formally multi-ethnic Sri Lankan society can be conceptualized as follows:

- Sri Lankan society is composed of two distinct nations, the Sinhalese and the Sri Lankan Tamils. According to the Kirby definition they qualify as 'nations' given that the members of each group distinguish themselves by a specific language and culture, share a common history and destiny and are united by a collective identity as expressed in a common political will. Each finally disposes of a circumscribed territory as that community's particular historical settlement area or homeland.
- As to the Moors, they represent a religious minority, their group identity being predominantly based on Islam. They are spread over different locations with seizable concen-

trations apart from Colombo in the western and, not least, in the eastern part of the country.

- The Indian Tamils, finally, represent legally an ethnic minority. While sharing language and religion with the Sri Lankan Tamils, they differ with regard to the typical settlement area, historical experiences, caste and class background. In the framework of Sri Lankan society as a whole, the Indian Tamils form an ethnically defined underclass being in their majority estate workers characterized by a collectively low socio-economic status combined with a limited degree of internal social differentiation, and a generally underprivileged political position.

The challenge for the Sri Lankan polity at the time of independence consisted, therefore, in welding together two nations and the various minorities into a new common Sri Lankan identity superseding without necessarily eliminating the traditional more restrictive group identities. Economic development in conjunction with equal economic opportunities and social justice would be the cornerstone of such an endeavour. A participatory political system safeguarding minority rights and allowing for collective (ethnic) group interests to be constitutionally represented would, finally, allow for a successful experiment in nation-building. Yet, on the economic as much as on the politico-institutional front, soon different developments took place. It was particulary left to the political system to energize society, to create not just competing, but conflicting interest groups and parties. In the given fragmented context, traditional and ethnic forms of group formation prevailed not least in order to advance particularistic interests in the new socio-political order.

## 3. FROM CLASS TO ETHNIC POLITICS

With the end of European colonial rule, the common identity as subjects of British India, that comprised not only the populations of then Ceylon but also of today's India and Pakistan, lapsed and a new national identity had to be created. There had not been an armed struggle for independence which under the banner of national liberation could have forged a new Ceylonese identity out of the different population groups. Instead, this task was left to the Ceylonese social and political elite. Ethnically mixed, this power elite was bound together by the English culture and language which its members had typically acquired in a small number of missionary run boarding schools. However, whereas socio-economic class and Western cultural background united the heirs to the colonial rulers, it separated them at the same time from the 'indigenous' populations with their different traditional local cultures, languages and belief systems. Apart from legal questions of citizenship, the socio-economic policies to be pursued were also to materially bolster the new political status as an independent nation. This implied at least a partial reorientation away from the plantation economy towards the build-up of an industrial sector, and the development of an internal market as against the total dependence on foreign trade. This would necessarily entail a reconfiguration of the social structure. Industrialization in conjunction with urbanization would draw peoples from different ethnic, regional and cultural origins together eventually creating common new class identities.

However, whatever the original intentions of policy-makers and independently of ideology and party affiliation, the politics of successive post-colonial governments have invariably had an ethnic bias in favour of the majority community at the expense of the minorities. As a result, society has increasingly tended to split along ethnic lines, with social conflict manifesting itself as communal confrontations which furthermore, turned, ever more violent.

DISENFRANCHISEMENT OF THE INDIAN TAMILS

The question of the citizenship of the Indian estate labourers proved a landmark in the history of independent Ceylon. It was their treatment right after sovereignty was transferred that set the tone for the future developments of majority-minority relations. What at first appeared like a normal undertaking of any new state, i.e. to decide on which basis and to whom to confer citizenship, became in fact a question of racial discrimination and class warfare. It was a political and class alliance of the elite Ceylonese Tamils and Sinhalese that in two acts of parliament in 1948 and 1949 deprived the vast majority of the estate Tamils of the citizenship rights which they had hitherto enjoyed like everyone else as subjects of British India.[5] More than a million were disenfranchized. In consequence, a regression set-in, their political organization dissolved reverting to a simple trade union. Made stateless, even though they had lived in Sri Lanka for several generations, a majority of Indian Tamils was forced to leave the island for India as a result of bilateral agreements between India and Colombo beginning in 1964. Today, the share of Indian Tamils in the total population has been reduced by half from about twelve per cent in 1946. In reverse, it is important to note, that it was the up-country Sinhalese who profited in parliamentary representation from the former's disenfranchisement.[6]

More than a civic question of nationality, the discrimination meted out to the Indian Tamils involved also dimensions of class struggle.

The leftist parties which rose to prominence in the early part of the twentieth century had identified in the plantation workers the core of the Sri Lankan proletariat and the primary subject of societal change. The super-exploitation of the workers combined with the miserable living conditions on the estates lend credence to this analysis advanced in particular by Western educated Marxist intellectuals. Moreover, it was the exports of plantation crops which until recently constituted the mainstay of the Ceylonese economy, the sweat of the Indian estate labour on which the other social groups thrived. While the impact of the semi-feudal production relations on the plantations on class consciousness were probably underestimated, still, powerful trade unions were formed and a political party emerged in the plantation districts long before independence. But early on, another, ethnic factor came to play an increasingly important role. However depressed the socio-economic conditions of the Indian labourers, they were considered aliens working on estates which encroached on limited land resources hemming in the

Sinhalese villagers in the valleys and threatening their livelihood. The various factors combined to turn the Indian Tamils into a group of pariahs, physically and socially excluded from the rest of the population. Ethnicity came to dominate class position and ideology preventing any major role in social transformation. Inversely, by disenfranchising the estate labour force, the Ceylonese political class successfully weakened the working class, split it moreover along ethnic lines while securing a docile hardcore of super-exploitable labour. From discrimination to disenfranchisement proved only a first step. In the late 1960s and early 1970s, the Indian Tamils were denounced as a fifth column of Indian imperialism by the Janatha Vimukti Peramuna or JVP (People's Liberation Front), as part of their ideologically motivated attack of the existing state. In the 1980s, finally, they were drawn into the increasingly violent confrontation between the Sinhalese and the Sri Lankan Tamils. Victims to pillage, arson and murder by Sinhalese mobs, thousands fled the up-country searching for security in the Tamil dominated north-east.

CULTURAL DECOLONIZATION—THE LANGUAGE ISSUE

The United National Party (UNP), established in 1946, led the country into independence. Much like the Congress party in India it united within its fold the major centrist political currents. In the early 1950s, one of its leaders, Salomon Bandaranaike, broke away to found the Sri Lanka Freedom Party (SLFP) which was to become the second most important party alternating in power with the UNP ever since.[7] The SLFP appealed more explicitly to the Sinhala electorate, especially the non-English speaking middle classes. Programmatically inclined to social democracy, the party has favoured a policy of state intervention giving priority to the development of the internal market and indigenous industrialization. Socio-culturally, it proclaimed a policy of cultural decolonization and indigenization. Not surprisingly, it became the quasi natural alliance partner for the parties on the left, including communists and trotskists. Until this day, they have formed many coalition governments. It is hypothesized that it was precisely this laudable and typically left orientation which has tragically been turned from an emancipatory to a repressive policy.

To tap the vote of the traditional middle class, Bandaranaike during the 1956 election campaign successfully addressed the Sinhala educated Ayurvedic doctors, monks, and teachers. In a world dominated by modern science, education and research, their knowledge had been devalued depriving them of their earlier elevated social status. They had, in turn, come to resent the Western trained, English speaking elite and the liberal professionals. Bandaranaike's pre-election promise to do away with English in favour of Sinhala as sole official language had an anti-colonial ring, but carried also a internal discriminatory bias. The Jaffna or Sri Lankan Tamils had more than any other ethnic group taken advantage of the missionary schools that offered a modern English education and the prospects of occupational advancement in the professions and state administration. A programme aiming at the abolition of English and the simultaneous downgrading of Tamil to the level of a minority language carried, therefore, serious implications for the internal labour market in general, the competitiveness of its various ethnic components in particular. Violent communal conflicts ensued. A compromise formula providing for Tamil to be employed as language of administration in the north-east and to allow this largely Tamil inhabited region a certain degree of administrative autonomy had to be withdrawn in the face of forceful resistance not least by the Buddhist clergy. It was a monk also who in the aftermath of the language controversy assassinated the prime minister in 1959. In the 1978 constitution, Tamil was finally accorded the status of 'national' language alongside Sinhala which was additionally designed as sole 'official' language.[8] While not on a par, Tamil can since officially be used in parliament and for administrative purposes in the north and east. In reality however, not much has changed. According to international reports parliamentary proceedings, textbooks for higher, including university education, etc., are—contrary to the stipulations of the law—translated and published in Tamil after long delays only, if at all. Furthermore, since public servants are almost exclusively recruited from among the Sinhalese for whom there is no obligation to learn Tamil, government institutions remain for many Tamils not just inaccessible. An apartheid system based on language has come into operation with Sinhala being the code of the masters. With the linguistic competence of judges and in particular the police restricted to Sinhala, government loses its representative character being perceived as a foreign, if not repressive institution.

AFFIRMATIVE ACTION AS ETHNIC DISCRIMINATION

In the aftermath of the 1971 revolt by Sinhalese educated youth which was bloodily suppressed leaving behind 15-20,000 dead, the government instituted a policy measure that materially affected the race relations even more. In the name of positive discrimination, the ethnic imbalance in the recruitment to higher education was addressed with the aim to increase the number of Sinhalese students. A score system was introduced upgrading the marks of applicants from low performing districts. Rhetorically a progressive social measure to equalize opportunities, it turned out to be a discriminatory device at the expense of Tamil students. Even though better performing, the latter's share not least in subjects with promising occupational avenues, e.g. in science and medicine, was drastically reduced. In the long-run not only in higher education but in all branches of public service the ethnic composition was changed.[9] Faced with ever fewer professional opportunities in the state sector as by far the most important employer coupled with the barrenness of the Jaffna peninsula, frustration and communal resentment among the Tamil youth set in. Eventually, an ethnically based political movement, the New Tamil Tigers, a militant student group was formed, that was to evolve into the Liberation Tigers of Tamil Eelam (LTTE).

In sum, it was once again a left government, that in the name of greater social justice resorted to (and instrumentalized) a political device—designed to uplift underprivileged minorities— to further the interests of the majority community. More specifically, confronted with a politically dangerous unemployment problem affecting the new middle class, the government used state power to 'politicize' and 'ethnicize' an economic problem.

## LAND SETTLEMENT POLICIES OR COLONIZATION AS INTERNAL COLONIALISM

The final and in the long-run most important government measure that planted the seed of communal violence concerned the resettlement of Sinhalese peasants from the overpopulated south-western zone in the more fertile east. Initiatives of the 1930s were taken up again soon after independence and reinforced in the late 1970s when the construction of huge dams and systems for irrigation were launched. They were fiercely opposed by the peasants already settled in the area, namely Muslims, and in particular Tamils. To counter the resistance, the security forces of the state were employed and local armed militias formed; armed ethnic conflict ensued. To be clear: there is no doubt as to the poverty of the Sinhalese peasant coupled with the high population density in the south. There is similarly no question as to the right of every citizen to circulate and settle freely within one's country's frontiers nor of a government to encourage people to move to other regions in the pursuit of its overall social and economic programmes. What happened in Sri Lanka, however, was that a one-sided dramatic change in the demographic and political composition of the east was officially effected accompanied as it were by a militarization in the implementation of this policy. In quite a number of cases a strategy of dispossession of the original settlers and a replacement of former Tamil by Sinhala names of villages have been reported. Where fifty years ago, the proportion of Sinhalese was minimal, they represent now about a third of the population. Totally new electoral districts dominated by Sinhalese have been carved out of the former Eastern Province which the Tamils claim as part of their historical homeland.

In this situation, it is significant that the plans for a new constitution not only put the merger of the northern and eastern province into question, but provide for separate regional referenda coupled with an eventual territorial secession of the now Sinhalese dominated districts.[10] In sum: once again, government policy aimed less at promoting the common weal than to curry favour with the majority Sinhala electorate. By contrast, loss of confidence in its impartiality and overall legitimacy seemed less to matter; while ethnic consciousness and communal confrontation became ever more pronounced.

## 4. THE SACRILIZATION OF THE ISLAND— BUDDHISM AND 'JUST WAR'[11]

Given the plurality of ethnic groups and the presence of four principal religions in Sri Lanka, a secular state appears to impose itself as one of the fundamental constitutional principles. And indeed, this conception governed also the first constitution. However, in 1972 the secular and republican character of the country was modified, prominence accorded to Buddhism and to the symbols of the Sinhala majority in the national flag. Originally introduced by a left government of social democrats (SLFP) and marxists (CP, LSSP), the changes have been incorporated in all subsequent constitutional projects.[12] In practice, this means, the state continues to financially support the various religions in proportion to their share in the population and their respective representatives are consulted from time to time by the government. As to Buddhism, by contrast, a special council has been instituted to advise the government on a permanent basis. Thus, Buddhism alone occupies not just a *special* place, the government is constitutionally called upon to protect and foster the Buddhist faith. Not surprisingly it has been remarked, that in official allocutions the country's president singles out the leaders of the principal orders of Buddhist monks for special mention. The impact on society at large proved divisive. The conviction entertained by members of the majority became reinforced that they were the only really authentic representatives of Sri Lanka. The minority communities, by contrast, increasingly felt reduced to the status of second class citizens.

With the spread of secularism the role of religious doctrine together with the status of its principal bearers, whether church, *imam* or *sangha*, lose in importance in the daily life of the community. But this is not necessarily a process of long-term inevitable decline. The secular socio-political order namely opens up in its institutions and technologies a new space for ideological work and for religious mobilization. But to successfully use them, organized religion, the church, the *bhikkhus*, the sangha have to adapt and become politicized. In this process, confronted with a world of competing powers and ideologies, including religions, the individual doctrine is transformed into an armour, its believers into religious soldiers.

The history of Sri Lanka, or at least the one of the majority community is closely linked to Buddhism. According to the *Mahavamsa*, the sixth century mytho-historical chronicle, the Sinhalese, i.e. 'the offsprings of the lion', under the leadership of king Vijaya landed in Sri Lanka the same day that Gautama Buddha died. Moreover, in the Temple of the Tooth in Kandy one of the most important reliquary of Buddhism is venerated; in addition, saplings of the very same bodhi tree under which the Buddha found enlightenment have been preserved and replanted here. Finally, it is in Sri Lanka that Buddhism in its pristine form (*Theravada*) has survived. Given this framework, a double transformation in the religious-ideological sphere took place in the modern period: on the one hand, the island in its entirety became the sacred home to Buddhism. On the other hand, the Sinhalese, a small community of people on the Indian subcontinent, surrounded as it were by hundreds of millions of Hindus in general and tens of millions of Tamils specially, have been entrusted with the mission to preserve and foster the *dhamma* (the teachings of the Buddha, the four noble truths). Thus, the *bhumiputra* (sons of the soil) became identified with the *buddhaputra* (sons of the Buddha). As a result, according to the *Mahavamsa* ideology an unbreakable bond exists between the island, Buddhism and the Sinhala people.[13]

As to the latter, the monks among them have a special role to play. In the course of time their role and self-perception changed. They were no longer simple disciples and followers of the Enlightened One leading an ascetic life and seeking individual liberation (*nirvana*). An alternative path to liberation gained ever more prominence first in the form of a special obligation for the spiritual welfare of the lay Buddhists in general. In a further step, these were identified as the Sinhalese people. Thus, the Buddhists monks in general, the *sangha* in particular, became the guardians of Buddhism and the avant-garde of the Sinhalese people in their struggle for survival: the *buddhaputra*, on their part, turned into *bhumiputra*.

Helped on by developments in the political sphere, the transformation in the religious domain took on an increasingly communal and militant connotation. From the 1930s onward, Westernized English educated politicians eager to establish links with the Sinhala electorate directly sought the Buddhist vote. Furthermore, they tried to rope in the monks appealing to them to engage in politics. This mobilization of the Sinhalese couched as it were in Buddhist terms soon acquired a communal edge. The terrain had been prepared from the late nineteenth century onward by people like Anagarika Dharmapala who had not only advocated a political role for monks seeking to exploit their prestige as opinion leaders but introduced negative stereotypes of Tamils at the same time. Adding 'Aryan' as further epithet to Sinhala and Buddhist to characterize the ethnic majority, they introduced 'race' as differentiating trait with the objective to posit the former's racial superiority over the Dravidian Tamils. Moreover, harking back to ancient times, the history of the island was reconstructed as a perennial struggle against the Tamils. And until today, Dutugemunu, the warrior king of the second century BC, is conjured up as an everlasting symbol of the victorious battles of the Sinhalese people over the Tamils.

The implications for race relations in Sri Lanka are as follows:

- For the politicized Buddhists, all other religions are inferior to Buddhism and are in fact alien to the island, having their final locus of reference elswhere, in Rome, in Mecca or various locations in India. By contrast, Buddhism, the island of Sri Lanka, the Sangha/the Sinhala Buddhists have merged into a single entity that must be protected at all cost.
- Buddhism has been transformed from a religion based on 'peace' and 'loving kindness' (*metta*) as core values

practised by monks leading an essentially ascetic life into a belief system closely allied with politics with the monks being turned into the guardians of the faith. It is the Sinhalese spearheaded by the monks' orders who are entrusted with the preservation of the true teachings of the Buddha (Theravada Buddhism).

- It is the island of Sri Lanka that in its physical entirety has been sanctified as the true abode of Buddhism. To preserve the territorial integrity of the country is therefore a supreme religious obligation. To guarantee it, a centralized unitary state is required. Any concession for power sharing and internal autonomy has to be resisted as a first step to the country's dismemberment and thereby a sacrilege.

Thus a combative religiosity has evolved that can be called *Buddhist fundamentalism*. In combination with its socially exclusive character in the sense that the bearers of the faith are Sinhala Buddhists who in turn constitute the only true representatives of the country and the nation in contrast to all others who are termed later-day foreign migrants,[14] they closely resemble the 'cultural nationalists' of the *Hindutva* movement in India. Finally, this exclusive, if not xenophobic ideology is being transformed into a political programme. Its most recent *avatar* is the Jathika Hela Urumaya (JHU) or 'National Heritage Party', which is essentially recruited from among Buddhist monks. Created only in 2000, the party has gained importance far above its few MPs. Competing for support among a clientele similar to the one of the hard-line nationalist JVP and given the razor thin majorities of all recent coalition governments, their total opposition to any devolution of power, their religiously reasoned condemnation of the Tamils demand, can only tilt the political balance among the Sinhalese to ever more chauvinist positions. The ultimate step in the ideological evolution of the Buddhist doctrine of peace has been taken with the teaching of 'just-war' which is now advocated by various Buddhist representatives. The disastrous results of the 'war for peace' strategy pursued during Mrs Kamaratunga's reign notwithstanding, a negotiated settlement is considered a betrayal. Only an unconditional war of annihilation of the Tamils that puts forever an end to any aspirations for autonomy or even independence, would be good enough.

In sum: it is precisely the evolution of race relations, the growing sense of futility of parliamentary methods in conjunction with the ever growing socio-economic discrimination and finally, bloody persecution that tightened the bonds among the Sri Lankan Tamils, sharpened the awareness of a collective identity and common destiny, eventually leading to the ethnic split of the country. Inevitably, the other smaller communities followed suit. While in the first decades of independence ideology separated political parties and programmes, these have been superseded by ethnically based organizations. Today, party allegiance is first of all based on ethnic identity, with the result that the socialist and communist Left has almost disappeared. As to the two principal Sinhalese parties, the SLFP and the UNP, with regard to the 'ethnic problem' they are as much prisoners of their own past chauvinist policies and rhetoric as they are caught in a perennial power struggle which leaves very little room for manouevre.

## II. CRISIS OF THE STATE

### 1. CHARACTER AND FUNCTION OF THE MODERN STATE[15]

Before speaking of a crisis of the state in Sri Lanka, its general characteristics and typical functions are enumerated:

CHARACTERISTICS OF THE IDEAL-TYPICAL MODERN STATE

- Division and classification of the population according to territory and no longer by familial, ethnic (racial, caste) or any other real or imagined blood lines.
- Establishment of a (separate) public power. It manifests itself in the form of publicly armed and maintained security forces, including their material adjuncts, such as prisons.
- State monopoly in the use of force. Physical violence as applied by the state's security apparatus for the maintenance of public order is both legal and legitimate.
- Formal separation of economic and political power. In

contrast to preceding societal types (modes of production), the economically dominant class is no longer identical with the politically ruling one. Political power is based on universal suffrage and exercised in the name of the people whose ultimate sovereignty is thought to be best guaranteed by a division of the powers of the state and democratic institutions.

## FUNCTIONS OF THE MODERN STATE OR OF 'RATIONAL' RULE

In line with the characteristics enumerated above, specific functions are attributed to the modern state.[16] Their implementation determines the legitimacy of government. According to Max Weber, five principal tasks can be identified:

- Legislation. This has to be performed in conformity with international standards and commitments, e.g. human rights conventions.[17]
- The administration of justice. In its pursuit, the acquired rights and the impartial and equitable implementation of law have to be guaranteed.
- The promotion of common interests in the fields of social policy, education, public health, culture, etc.
- The safeguard of personal security and public order (police).
- The organized armed protection of society against external threats (military).[18]

## 2. FROM THE RULE OF LAW TO A SECURITY STATE

The US State Department's yearly survey on the situation of human rights around the world, routinely states in its report on Sri Lanka, that the country is a democracy. For sure, regular elections based on universal adult franchise are held, a multiparty political system has been established after independence, there is a formal separation of powers and no explicit legal discrimination. However, this is only the formal façade. The reality is quite different. The developments in post-independence Sri Lanka, especially in the last 25 years, reveal a deepening crisis not only in that the state has failed in the fulfilment of major functions but in so far as successive governments have turned it into an arbitrary instrument of majority rule and transformed it into an authoritarian repressive apparatus.

Sri Lanka has a long history of violent confrontation that can be traced to two originally distinct types. The first one originated in social discontent and aimed at the overthrow of the then economic and political order. It crystallized in an 1971 armed uprising of educated youth led by the JVP, a self-proclaimed marxist anti-imperialist and anti-capitalist party, that was bloodily suppressed. Another attempt to capture state power was undertaken at the end of the 1980s. This time also, the JVP was defeated, its leaders killed in a general climate of civil war, terror, and murder. In the 1990s the JVP reemerged once again. Having renounced armed struggle in favour of parliamentary politics, it entered parliament and even joined a coalition government in 2004. Having its chief electoral basis among the younger generation of rural Sinhalese, it is still a party opposed to neo-colonialism and favouring state intervention. At the same time, an increasingly ruthless Sinhala nationalism has been added. At this point, the original socialist ideological orientation merged with the second type of violent confrontation that has marked the history of Sri Lanka: the communal issue. This combination of exclusive or organic (ethnic/race based) nationalism with socialism has much in common with similar movements not least in Europe during the 1930s: fascism. It contributed to the sharpening of the ethnic conflict between the Sri Lankan Tamils and the majority Sinhalese. Erupting into open war in 1983 it has for ever reconfigured the country's political landscape. In combating both types of confrontation successive governments irrespective of party composition and ideological orientation have violated all legal constraints, and eventually undermined the rule of law. Even more ominous, this collapse of the rule of law has come about legally, i.e. within the framework of the law and the constitution. Major events were the following:

- In 1978, a presidential system of government was introduced. It concentrates the powers of head of state, head of government, and head of the military in the hands of the president at the expense of parliament. The president appoints and dismisses the prime minister and all other members of the cabinet; he has also a decisive voice in the appointment of judges. At his discretion, he can dissolve the parliament any time twelve months after the last elections.[19] Since the president typically retains also the position of head of his party, the exercise of his duties tends not only to follow partisan political considerations but to be highly personalized encouraging favouritism.

The extraordinary powers invested in the president extend to civil society and have led to the erosion of basic civil rights. While the law provides for freedom of association, including the formation of trade unions, an 'Essential Services Act' empowers the president to include in this category any branch of economic activity rendering worker's action automatically a criminal offence. Faced with a general strike in July 1980, then President Jayewardene in fact resorted to this law and had an estimated 80,000–100,000 striking workers simply dismissed.

- Since colonial times the country's constitutions have always contained provisions for the imposition of a state of emergency to cope with natural calamities, internal disturbances or external threats to the country's security. The normal laws of the land are temporarily and for specific circumstances suspended in favour of extraordinary powers given to the executive and the forces of law and order. The most important safeguard against abuse lies in the period of its imposition which in Sri Lanka is contained in an obligatory monthly review by parliament. Despite this constitutional provision a state of emergency has, however, been in force for the better half of independence. Indeed, with very few interruptions, it has been in force during the last 25 years. Considering that parliament has renewed the state of emergency invariably month after month throws light not just on the separation of powers in the country. It indicates that 'the rule of law' carries little meaning in Sri Lanka, existing as it were only in the formal sense of the word. Moreover, democracy itself is put on hold. The role of governers and governed has been reversed with the former no longer accountable to the sovereign. On the contrary, the people have been turned into an object of arbitrary rule.

- In 1979, the Prevention of Terrorism Act complemented the executive's arsenal of oppressive laws. Together they have only served to augment the role of the security forces, allow the invasion of the private sphere of the citizens, to interrogate and detain at will, to resort to extrajudicial killings. Thus, the state's security services were responsible for the disappearance of over 16,800 persons as reported by the official inquiry commission set-up to investigate the second half of the 1980s when the JVP staged its second uprising.[20] Similarly, torture, including rape in custody, unlawful and incommunicado detention, etc., have been committed on a massive scale and repeatedly been castigated by national enquiry commissions, by Amnesty International as well as other human rights organizations and also by the special rapporteurs of the UN's Human Rights' Commission.[21]

- The enabling national legislation has provoked the criticism of international bodies as not conforming to the minimum requirements of United Nations' conventions to which Sri Lanka is a signatory. Thus, torture in custody even though prohibited under any circumstances in international human rights' law, has never been invoked as a criminal offence in Sri Lanka. Indeed, considered an indispensable means of interrogation, it is routinely resorted to by the police and the military. Moreover, confessions made under torture are allowed as evidence in court, with the burden of proof at the trial stage being placed on the victim.[22] As successive official commissions of enquiry have concluded, 'torture is deeply entrenched in the country's criminal justice system'.[23]

- More than just a break-down of the police system and a crisis of democratic government, it signals an outright collapse of the rule of law. A general militarization of the security forces and of society can be observed. Beyond maintaining law and order, and the investigation of crimes, the police has been regularly employed in armed confrontations. Inversely, the military's mandate has been extended from the defence of the country to fight an all-out civil war. An enormous increase in power has accrued to the police and the military, right down to the individual officer. They have become a law unto themselves knowing that there is no effective instance of accountability for them. Unauthorized places of detention may no longer exist, mass graves no longer be dug,[24] the impunity of state agents for violations of human rights persists, rooted as it were both in legal provisions as well as in institutional and procedural limitations. Apart from the emergency and anti-terrorist legislation, there is the Evidence Act, the Public Security Act(s), the Indemnity (Amendment) Act which effectively exclude the prosecution of crimes committed by the state. Not a single officer in charge of a police station has been charged with 'death in custody' nor a single conviction because of torture been pronounced even though Sri Lanka signed the respective UN Convention in 1994. Thus, the culture of absolute impunity, horrendous torture, non-dependability of the system *in toto*, continues.[25]

## 2. ON THE PRIVATIZATION OF VIOLENCE AND ITS ROLE IN POLITICS

As stated above, for Max Weber a modern state is the particular polity which successfully claims and is considered the sole source of the 'right' to violence within a clearly defined territory.[26] Coupled with the institutionalization of a public authority and exercised within the framework of the law, the use of violence by the state's security apparatus is both legal and legitimate. It is precisely in this domain of the monopoly and legitimate use of violence by the state, that Sri Lanka has witnessed one of its most important symptoms of crisis, if not outright failure as a modern state. Three major areas stand out:

- The state has resorted to arming private militias thus delegating the use of violence to private groups and individuals. A political space has been created where every citizen in the name of 'self-defence' can arrogate to himself the right to decide when, where, and against whom to use arms. Thereby, the essential achievement of the modern state to have substituted the use of violence to regulate conflict by legal process—which is moreover entrusted to specially empowered and publicly accountable institutions—has been surrendered. It represents a socio-political regression, a break-down of public order and the state's retreat from one of its primary functions.

- This conclusion is reinforced when the use of the militias is examined. There are on the one hand, Muslim and Sinhalese settlers in the east. There are on the other Tamils opposed to the LTTE. Trained, armed and officially controlled by the army, they can operate outside all laws governing warfare. The latest example is the 'Karuna faction', a rebellious group that split off from the LTTE in 2004 and has been engaged in attacks against them ever since. Even though supported by the government, the latter denies any involvement. Colombo furthermore rejects the demand for their disarmament as stipulated in the Ceasefire Agreement of February 2002 arguing that the group has been formed only after that date.

- In the early 1980s, the government allowed politicians, including parliamentarians, the recruitment of four to eight, armed body guards for their protection. Since then, these protective guards have developed into privately financed groups of hired thugs who do whatever it takes to promote the interests of their employer, including break-ins, threats and outright murders. Business people followed suit. In consequence, business fortunes have increasingly flourished less by traditional market mechanisms of productivity and price, but more by the twin mechanisms of access to government and intimidation of competitors. Finally, even individual citizens have been reported to hire private thugs to take revenge or regulate disputes over inheritance. The civil war accompanied as it were by massive human rights violations has greatly contributed to the decay of civil

virtues and the brutalization of society. The material
underpinnings for this societal crisis has drastically been
augmented by the tens of thousands of soldiers who have
deserted the army taking their weapons with them.

- Not just individuals and groups have taken the law into
their own hands, it is the political parties and the government that have resorted to violence. Intimidation of opponents, political murder, including assassinations of
opposition party leaders, or violence at election rallies,
have frequently occurred suggesting their use as normal
means in the struggle for power and for the promotion of
particularistic interests. Thus the Jatika Sevaka Sangamaya
(JSS), a powerful trade union close to the UNP, has been
less of an organization fighting for workers' rights and
interests but—at least in the 1980s and early 1990s—an
instrument of the ruling party to advance government
policies, if necessary by violence and terror.

Furthermore, violence, including rampage, murder and pillage
committed against the minorities has been consciously employed
as means of mass mobilization for political ends. Thus, the
pogrom of 1983, when the properties and businesses of Tamils
were ransacked, the Sinhala mob was directed by people close
to the government. Similarly, in the struggle against the JVP in
1987-89 people were arbitrarily apprehended in broad daylight,
and corpses were left for days at the roadside (or floating in a
tank in the centre of Colombo) as a warning and as a deterrent
for the general public. In the most recent past, critics of the
government whether journalists or other public figures have been
threatened, some assassinated even in areas closely guarded by
the police. Similarly, governments agents, including prison
wardens have cooperated with inmates or outside mobs to have
defenceless Tamil prisoners hacked to death.[27] Subsequent
investigations have invariably been stalled, accused acquitted,
key witnesses disappeared, occasionally murdered.

In sum: a culture of violence and impunity has come to reign
in Sri Lanka. Physical violence has become a favourite means to
settle private accounts, in politics as in business affairs to gain
an advantage over competitors. State terrorism has been used to

subjugate minorities and to secure the government in power by initimidating the population at large. When Max Weber sees in the state's monopoly of violence not only an advance in the development of the modern state, but also a sign of its legitimacy, this does not apply to Sri Lanka. Here, the state has frequently resorted to repression in an arbitrary manner, as an instrument of rule and control. Violence has been privatized both by the operation of private militias and as an instrument in political and economic affairs to further partisan or personal interests often in league with or even initiated by politicians themselves. It is not an inadvertedly occurring crisis emerging out of a civil war situation. In fact, it precedes it and is not confined to the armed conflict. It represents a process of vulgarization of violence for which the state bears responsibility. As a consequence of this erosion of the monopoly of violence the state has not just become weak but delegitimized being unable to provide its citizens with that most basic needs of all—physical security. Yet, still more than a crisis of the state is at stake. Not only the belief in due process and recourse to law have been undermined, the widespread insecurity rooted in an increase in crime and accompanied by high levels of suicide signal a state of anomy and a societal collapse.[28]

## III. FROM CRISIS OF THE POLITY TO FAILING STATE

### 1. FROM COMMUNAL REPRESENTATION TO THE DEMAND FOR TAMIL EELAM

In Sri Lanka, the problem of class versus ethnicity, of class versus communal interest articulation goes back to the nineteenth century. In fact, there were anti-Christian riots in 1883 and in the early twentieth century inspired by Sinhala Buddhists in an attempt to gain a greater share of power and privileges in colonial society. More important still were the anti-Muslim riots of 1915 rooted in earlier economic rivalries by Sinhala merchants against 'the alien (here dominant Muslim) traders' or the anti-Malayali agitation against immigrant workers from the present state of Kerala in the 1930s.[29] With regard to the Sri Lankan Tamils

there was no conflict at the beginning of indigenous representation in the colonial political dispensation. Increasingly
coopted into the colonial administration via membership in the
State Council, for the emerging local elite ethnic background
was secondary compared to the commonality of class and
Western education. This changed when the question of universal
suffrage arose in the 1930s. It became vital with the advent of
independence. The representatives of the Sri Lankan Tamils feared
to become systematically and for ever relegated to the background
in view of their position as an ethnic minority. To reinvent their
power, explicitly ethnically based political parties, the Tamil
Congress (1944) followed by the Tamil Federal Party (1949)
were founded. Programmatically, the slogan of a parliamentary
representation equal to the Sinhalese was raised based on the
concept of the 'Tamil-speaking people', that included the Muslims
as well as the Indian Tamils. While this advocacy never succeeded
in uniting for any length of time all Tamil-speaking peoples in a
common front, it lend itself to raise fears in the majority community to become a minority in their own country.[30]

Attempts by two prime ministers (Bandaranaike of the SLFP
in 1957–8 and Senanayake of the UNP in the middle of the
1960s) to after all bridge the ethnically dichotomized society
and find a compromise in the increasingly violent conflict with
the Tamils came to nothing. Accords concluded had to be
abandoned in the face of their unconditional rejection by the
political opposition and rival for power catering to the very
same Sinhalese clientele. Such repeated failures inevitably
undermined the moderate Tamil leadership. The peaceful methods
of struggle advocated by them ranging from parliamentary
intervention to civil disobedience, appeared more and more
doubtful in their efficacy. Their goal envisaging an arrangement
within the existing institutions and political system came under
fire. Eventually, they were sidelined and an overall radicalization
under a different leadership took place.

Indeed, the minorities cannot draw comfort from the constitution or the political institutions. They are anything but
reassuring. The present constitution established in 1978 after
the overwhelming election victory of the UNP while introducing

an all powerful executive presidency did not reinstate the few provisions of the Soulbury Constitution to safeguard the rights of the minorities. These had been removed in 1972 despite strong opposition of the Tamils and the UNP. Inspite of the sharpening communal tensions in the intervening period, even the most recent proposals for a new constitution which have been under discussion for almost a decade contain no protective devices for the minorities. While formally proclaiming a 'devolution of power' they cement the unitary state and the concentration of absolute power at the centre. They maintain the myth of a single united Sri Lankan nation and while the proposals contain a lengthy catalogue of civil and political rights, including the right to practise one's religion, language, etc., together with others, these pertain to the individual, but do not constitute collective rights. Moreover, following the British (and French) tradition, the constitutions of 1972 and 1978 rooted as it were in the principle of the supremacy of parliament as ultimate representative of the people, provide at best for a formal review of legislation, but none in terms of their constitutionality as to substance. However, without legal (veto rights) or institutional safeguards (a second chamber) the unfettered rule of the majority carries the day. Finally, constitutional changes are rendered next to impossible because they require a two-third majority in parliament to be followed by an absolute majority in a popular referendum. As a result, the democratic principle of one man-one vote has in the Sri Lankan context been used to instrumentalize the powers and resources of the state primarily to advance the interests of the majority community without much regard for the minorities. In combination with the concentration of power in the presidency democracy has effectively been transformed into the tyranny of the majority.

The experiences of systematic collective discrimination compounded by repeated post-election communal violence eventually led to a radicalization in the demands and methods of struggle of the Tamils. In 1976, a congress of all Tamil parties, including representatives of the Indian (estate) Tamils was held to review the situation of the community at large and propose solutions. The Tamil United Front (TUF), later renamed into

Tamil United Liberation Front (TULF) was born. The feeling of shared oppression by the Sinhalese majority and its state led to the formulation of a common platform for the elections in 1977, the so called Vaddukoddai Resolution. It has served ever since as programmatic reference and was reinforced in the 'Thimpu principles' of 1985 during the India-sponsored talks between Colombo and the six principal Tamil (guerrilla) organizations.[31] It centres on four principal demands symbolizing the aspirations for the future:

1. Recognition of the Sri Lankan Tamils as a nation;
2. Recognition of their right to self-determination;
3. Recognition of the north and east as their traditional homeland; and
4. Citizenship and political rights for the Indian Tamils.[32]

Reflecting the overall despair and not wanting to confine one-self to rhetorics, the congress called on the Tamil people, not least its youth, to struggle to realize these aims, if possible by peaceful, if necessary by violent means, if possible within the framework of the Sri Lankan state, if necessary by setting up an independent state 'Tamil Eelam' precisely in the north-east. In the following year, the Tamils voted overwhelmingly along ethnic lines and for the TUF making the front the largest opposition party in parliament. The election victory of 1977 came to be considered as democratic legitimation of the Vaddukoddai resolution as charter of the Tamil nation and popular mandate for the struggle for independence. It retained this unique role until the parliamentary elections of 2004, when the newly formed Tamil National Alliance (TNA) which had declared the Liberation Tigers (LTTE) as sole authentic representative of the Tamil people obtained a resounding victory vindicating the latters' leadership, and armed struggle.

In the aftermath of the Vaddukoddai Resolution the logic of ethnic confrontation became aggravated. An amendment to the constitution of 1978 declared even a verbal demand for self-determination and independence a criminal offence against the integrity of the state. The Tamil parliamentarians were thus faced with the alternative to either renounce their electoral promises or give up their parliamentary seats followed by criminal prosecution or exile. The Tamil leadership opted for the latter, the MPs resigned and emigrated to south India.

## 2. FROM POLITICAL STRUGGLE TO WAR FOR INDEPENDENCE

It was, however, the post-election pogrom of 1983 which really sparked off the civil war. An estimated 3000 people fell victim to the massacre of innocent civilians; an unaccounted number of homes and businesses of Tamils were looted and burned. It led to a huge population exodus from the south, especially from multi-ethnic Colombo to the northern peninsula, driving home to the Tamils that security for them existed only in an own state. It was not the first pogrom against them; others had similarly occurred in connection with elections, as in 1956 or in 1977. What characterized the one of 1983 was not only its scale. It was not even the fact that the president kept silent for four days, and when at last he addressed the public he laid part of the blame on the Tamil victims. Most important was the fact, that what appeared to have been an uncontrollable outburst of mob violence, was in fact condoned, if not instigated by the party in power. Apart from inflammatory chauvinist speeches by cabinet ministers, government vehicles were used, and electoral lists employed by the mob in order to identify Tamil houses and businesses.

The logic of war has since then taken hold of the country. The large scale cleansing of Tamil and Christian personnel in the army that begun after the attempted *coup d'état* of 1962 has continued with the result that today's security forces are almost exclusively recruited from among Sinhalese Buddhists. Since hardly anyone speaks Tamil they are already for that very reason considered a foreign occupation army in the north-east. The same holds for the bureaucracy and the law enforcement authorities: largely Sinhalized and without any legal obligation for government servants to acquire Tamil language skills, they increase the communication gap between the communities, transform 'public service' into institutions of oppression.[33] At police stations violent measures of interrogation have been reported, with the Tamil detainees made to sign papers and approve statements in Sinhala, even if they do not understand. An overall *racist* attitude—following the UN definition—manifests itself when routinely people are rounded up in so-called cordon and search operations, identity checks performed at numerous checkpoints and people eventually put into prison simply because of their ethnic origin. Being a Tamil is enough to be a suspect. The climax in ethnic confrontation was reached as part of the 'war for peace' strategy after 1995. The then introduced sanctions on medicine, food, kerosene, cement, fertilizers and agricultural implements imposed on LTTE controlled areas in the name of 'dual use' lead to widespread misery, sickness, and undernourishment not least among the most vulnerable sections of the civilian population; the policy has been qualified as 'genocide' by specialists in international law. As a result, society has been dichotomized, and the government delegitimized in spirit and form, it no longer represents the people as a whole.

## 3. BETWEEN INTERNAL AND EXTERNAL SELF-DETERMINATION

An internationally recognized state is characterized by a territory within well-defined boundaries, a people with all the citizenship rights, an internally uninhibited economic space, including a special currency, a common legal system, an administration and a government. A whole set of symbols, such as a national anthem, a flag, etc., signify the distinct character of a state. The linchpin of a state as an actor is its territorial integrity. When this is threatened, the survival of the state itself is at risk.

And this possibility has loomed large ever since 1983 when militant groups among the Sri Lankan Tamils took up arms in a war of secession for an independent state of Tamil Eelam. After 19 years of civil war with at least 65,000 dead, 800,000 internally displaced persons (IDP), over half a million emigrants, with the north and east devastated by war, and the economy of the country in ruins, the two sides entered into a ceasefire agreement in February 2002. At immense costs the Sri Lankan Tamils under the LTTE have gained control over large parts of the north and east where they have successfully set-up a parallel administration with their own security forces, including border police, established their own legal system, including tribunals and law colleges, and levy taxes. In other words, in fact, even though not legally already two separate contiguous politico-administrative entities exist side by side. Still, there are alternative future developments short of fragmentation. Apart from government controlled territory around Jaffna and large tracts of disputed areas in the east, also claimed by the Tamils to be incorporated in an eventual Tamil Eelam, important institutional links have been retained between the territories under different control. Thus, Colombo continues to transfer pensions, pays teachers, and maintains local government institutions all over the island, even though they may follow LTTE directives in their daily operations. Moreover, while there is a border, and foreign visitors' passports are stamped with a special seal once they cross into LTTE territory, there are no independent economic or monetary systems. In other words, some sort of hybrid, even dual system of government and administration has been established.[34]

The then UNP government realizing that the war could not be won on the battlefield, decided to lift the proscription of the LTTE as a terrorist organization, recognize them as representative of the Tamil people and negotiating partner in the search for a settlement. With Norway as facilitator and subsequent talks at different international venues, from Berlin to Thailand, an internationalization of the conflict has taken place, raising at least formally the profile of the LTTE from a guerilla force to an internationally recognized actor. In substance, however, in an international system made up of mutually recognized states, a non-state actor, here the LTTE, remains systemically in a subordinate position. This disequilibrium of forces becomes paradoxically particularly pronounced at the time of a ceasefire and negotiations. Superior strategy, firepower, popular support, all the factors that determine the balance of forces between a guerilla and government troops on the battlefield, are in peace-time unilaterally replaced by the internationally recognized government representatives of the state. Thus, it is the government that controls and protects the external borders, allows or denies visits to foreign dignitaries and decides over their itinerary; it continues to conclude treaties, enters into exchange and training programmes with foreign militaries, contracts credits, receives foreign aid and imports weapons, etc. All these measures are, by contrast, structurally denied to the non-state actor independently of the extent of any formal international recognition. It was this realization more than the formal exclusion from participation in the talks of the Sri Lanka Aid Group in Washington—for being listed as a terrorist organization in the USA—that contributed to the suspension of the peace-talks by the LTTE in March 2003. The meeting symbolized in a nutshell that these foreign governments together with Colombo appeared solely empowered to decide on the future developments of the country and its peoples. Peace alone reversed the gains obtained on the battlefield!

In the Oslo declaration of December 2002, the government had agreed to seek a peaceful solution within the framework of a federal structure for Sri Lanka. Already prior to the beginning of negotiations, the LTTE had offered to give a settlement within the boundaries of the existing state a chance. In other words, they were prepared to give up their long-standing demand for an independent state in favour of a power-sharing arrangement within an autonomous north-east, their traditional homeland.[35] It was a major concession in view of the huge sacrifices, including the 18,000 fighters who had died so that their community could at last find peace, security, and prosperity in a country of their own. Even assuming that for the LTTE only the methods may change, but not their final aspiration for a Tamil Eelam, to publicly favour internal over external self-determination provides a major challenge to the ruling political establishment in Colombo and the Sinhala Buddhist public at large.

Yet, a strong opposition that included the then president and her party, the SLFP, the JVP and the JHU, the Buddhist clergy, and parts of the military has from the beginning resisted the ceasefire and even more so any change in the political system to accommodate the minorities. Indeed, within days of the LTTE's proposal for an Interim Self-Governing Administration (ISGA) in November 2003, President Kumaratunga citing the threat to the integrity of the country first dismissed three important ministers and subsequently dissolved parliament.[36]

It was not the first time, that in the pursuit of power, the competing factions within the Sinhalese ruling class, the recent destruction in men and material suffered by the population at large notwithstanding, sacrificed the common weal on the altar of their particularistic interests. Since then, a dramatic deterioration in the overall situation has set in. Murders of political cadres and assassinations of journalists have multiplied, as has the harrassement of civilians. Attacks on army personnel have increased. The ceasefire has become ever more fragile. The parliamentary elections of April 2004 did nothing to improve the situation. A coalition led by the SLFP and dependent on the Sinhala extremist parties came to power. Even the promise of billions of aid by foreign governments, provided progress was made on the peace front did not have the desired impact. The same hardline Sinhala Buddhist alliance of SLFP, JVP and JHU succeeded at the presidential elections at the end of 2005. The new president had already during his campaign declared his total opposition to any dilution of the unitary state. He even contested outright the nationhood of the Tamils and the notion of homeland thus negating the very basis for negotiations. And as to his competitor, the former PM and signatory of the ceasefire, a close confident revealed only a few days before the elections the former's *machiavellian* political manoeuvres: While he had negotiated with the LTTE, he had simultaneously helped to engineer an armed rebellion in the LTTE's fighting ranks (Karuna group in the east).

As a result, not only the Sinhala ruling class, the nation itself is divided along ethnic lines, with Sinhala Buddhists and Sri Lankan Tamils having both developed an increasingly exclusive nationalism. With talks having been suspended for many months, officially an uneasy calm prevails while a shadow war is fought with paramilitaries cooperating with Colombo in the forefront. Negotiations with the sole objective to strengthen the ceasefire are to be held in early 2006. But whatever their outcome, they will just buy time; not peace but the renewal of hostilities appear the most likely future.

## 4. THE CHANCE OF A BREAK-UP OF SRI LANKA

In theory, the obstacles to conflict resolution within the framework of a (con-)federal structure appear low. Still, the forces opposed to any kind of negotiated agreement dominate. If the above analysis is correct, even a ceasefire is nothing but a continuation of war by other means, decidedly tipping the balance of forces in favour of the powers that be. Moreover, in contrast to the south the war affected people in the north-east still wait for a peace-dividend. Moreover, while the guns have remained silent for the greater part of the last four years, the High Security Zones installed by the army in civilian areas have remained, the occupation of educational and religious institutions continues, and the paramilitaries pursue their deadly work. Quite the reverse holds for the civil population: insecurity and harrassement have not ended, the internally displaced persons continue to languish in shelters unable to return to their homes, and the fishermen are prevented from following their livelihood. The aftermath of the tsunami has revealed in a nutshell the eventually unbridgeable division of the polity. While neighbourhoods and NGOs immediately went into action in the face of the common human desaster, soon communal politics took over and gained the upperhand. Even the lure of billions of foreign aid could not convince the Sinhala extremists from denouncing an official accord between the government and the LTTE for the establishment of an agency charged with the management and distribution of funds, the so called P-TOMS. And the principal parties? They kept out of the limelight, thus leaving the political arena and the major issues facing the country to the extremists.

When reflecting on the basic measures that would have to be implemented in order to start regaining mutual trust between the communities, fill the divide that separates them and provide new legitimacy and representativity, the difficulties become apparent. To name but a few:

- In order to remove the war related destruction and equalize the living standards between regions and communities, a huge transfer of resources would have to be channelled to the north and east. For many years, it would have to be disproportionately much higher than for the rest of the country. Given that the country is small, of the typical import-export economic type with a negative trade balance, nationally and internationally indebted, such unequal transfers would require a sustained sense of collective identity and national solidarity which is greatly missing today.

- The Sinhalization of the army, the bureaucracy and social institutions would have to be reversed. However welcome such a 'de-ethnicization' would be in principle, a strong recruitment drive among the minorities, not least the Sri Lankan Tamils, would neither be easy nor without any political risks in practice. After all, many decisions over the last decades that eventually sharpenend the ethnic conflict were inspired by the experience of two bloody uprisings by educated (Sinhalese) youths dispairing over the lack of employment opportunities and disillusioned with the political system. This aspiration-expectation gap remains essentially intact and could only become worse in case of a more balanced ethnic recruitment to public service since this could only be implemented at the expense of the majority community.

- The polity would have to be overhauled far beyond a simple return to a 'secular' state. Not only the executive presidency, the concentration of power at the centre together with the unitary state would have to be dismantled in favour of not just a general 'symmetric' or regional devolution, but substantial self-government coupled with veto powers for the different nationalities, the minorities respectively. The same holds for the system of justice. Its independence would have to institutionalized; the 'culture of impunity' would not only have to end but those responsible for past crimes be at last brought to justice.

- The civil war started because the state did not even guarantee the physical security of all its citizens. On the contrary, parties and state institutions, the police and army share responsibility in the persecution of minorities. It is inconceivable that the same security forces which have waged war against part of its own population, have committed massive human rights violations against the Sri Lankan Tamils will tomorrow assume responsibility for the protection of today's enemies and victims.

It is hard to see how these problems can even be addressed given the present political alignment among the majority community and the state of ethnic relations. After all, the present situation has developed over decades strengthening the ideological, cultural and social divides within and between the different communities in the process. Moreover, hard-boiled class interests were involved when the members of other ethnic groups were persecuted and eliminated as business or professional competitors. Finally, a political and business class has emerged over the last two decades of conflict profiting directly or indirectly from the war economy.

While all these arguments run in favour of an independent Tamil Eelam, the major stumbling block appears to come from outside. International law knows nothing of internal colonialism. It reserves the right to external self-determination essentially only to the former European colonies overseas, otherwise upholding the principles of national sovereignty and territorial integrity. Exceptions are possible only in cases of separation by mutual consent, exemplified by the peaceful dissolution of Ethiopia or Czechoslovakia or when the fragmentation of a state lies in the interest of the hegemonic powers. Then, even armed intervention otherwise banned under international law is resorted to as demonstrated in the case of Yugoslavia or the Kososo.[37] But neither India as regional super-power nor the US advocate at present such a course of action. On the contrary, apart from having both proscribed the LTTE, they do not have an interest in the emergence of an independent Tamil Eelam with a capital in Trincomalee. Without any external recognition, however, one cannot really foresee a formally independent state flourishing in an increasingly interdependent global system.

In brief, an end of the time of turmoil and suffering for the peoples of Sri Lanka is not in sight; what appears still a political or system crisis shows already signs of evolving into a general crisis of society and polity going beyond a simple question of ethnic confrontation. From an increasingly corrupt and repressive regime, accompanied by a militarization of society to a failed state is not a great step.

## NOTES

1. The Lanka Sama Samaj Party (LSSP) founded in 1935 was in fact the first ever trotskist party.

2. One of the last and greatest was Parakrama Bahu I the Great whose reign lasted from 1153 to 1186. As to the historical evidence, Prof. Peter Schalk from Uppsala University comments: 'A unitary government never existed other than as an ideological concept; the term *ekachatta* or "one umbrella" was used by kings only as a metaphor for a unitary state. In the 11th century the Cōḷas ruled for more than 70 years and there is no indication that Sinhala Kings ruled continuously in the north. The settlement in the north is in the dark before the Jaffna Kingdom.'

3. Apart from an interlude in the fifteenth century under the long reign of Parakrama Bahu VI (1411-66).

4. Primarily motivated by commercial interests, they gave up the attempt to seize the Kandyan kingdom as the supply of spices from the interior was assured anyway.

5. The Ceylon Citizenship Act of 1948 created two categories of citizens, one by descent, the other by registration. The 1949 Indian and Pakistani (Residents) Citizenship Act provided citizenship under rather stringent conditions to those who had become stateless under the law of 1948, e.g. proven uninterrupted residence for 10 years. According to the pacts of 1964, resp. 1974, India agreed to accept 600,00 whereas Sri Lanka was to grant citizenship to 375,000 Indian Tamils. However, many more wanted to stay. As a result of this imbalance in addition to administrative delays in awarding nationality around 30 per cent were still stateless in the early 1990s, i.e. without identity cards, with no right to own property, to be legally employed or to move about freely. The state of repatriation was similar: 135,000 were still awaiting passage to India in early 1990. Only at the beginning of the twenty-first century has Sri Lanka at last agreed to 'naturalize' the remaining stateless persons.

6. In the election of 1947, the Indian Tamils had sent eight members to parliament. As a result of the subsequent disenfranchisement and the redrawing of electoral districts in favour of the Kandyan Sinhalese [cf. Ceylon (Parliamentary Elections) Amendment Act] no Indian Tamil MP got elected between 1952 and 1977; and even the four MPs thereafter were nominated, not elected.

7. S. Bandaranaike is reported to have left the UNP for reasons of personal ambition. He is said to have felt slighted because the party's founder and first prime minister, D.S. Senanayake, favoured John Kotelawala, his nephew, as his successor.

8. Cf. chapter IV of the 1978 Constitution, esp. Articles 18, 19, 22.

9. Apart from the changes in education, a broad-based nationalization programme, especially of plantations, was initiated that profited the small Sinhalese cultivator and broadly opened up the estate labour market for Sinhalese. Lamballe 1985, esp. Appendix.

10. The Indo-Sri Lankan accord of 1987 to end the civil war, had stipulated an amalgamation of the northern and eastern province. While coming immediately into force and enshrined in the constitution, it still remains to be confirmed in a popular referendum.

11. Silva, Bartholomeusz, 2001; Bartholomeusz, T.J., 2002.

12. This applies to the current constitution enacted in 1978 as much as to the reform proposals.

13. Before the tenth century the term 'Sinhala' signified all people living on the island. Only afterwards was this *territorial* category transformed into an *ethnic* one and became reserved for the Singhalese-Buddhists thus excluding the Tamils/Hindus.

14. Even President Bandaranaike-Kumaratunga expressed such sentiments during an official visit to South Africa.

15. F. Engels, Der Ursprung der Familie, des Privateigentums und des Staates, pp. 151-301, in K. Marx, F. Engels, *Ausgewählte Schriften*, Band II, Dietz Verlag Berlin 1981. V.I. Lenin , *The State and Revolution*, pp. 264-351, in V.I. Lenin, *Selected Works*, Progress Publishers, Moscow 1968. M. Weber, 1972, pp. 516, 519.

16. Kristian Stokke 2006, following Clark and Dear's study of the capitalist state apparatus in his analysis of the emerging Tamil Eelam, identifies three state functions with their corresponding institutional mechanisms: consensus (political, legal, repressive); production (public production, public provision, treasury control); and integration (health, education, welfare, information, communication and media). For the present purpose, the Weberian approach appears better suited.

17. Among them the principles of non-discrimination, prohibition of torture, rule of law and due process; no retroactive applicability; proportionality of crime and punishment, etc.

18. Apart from the (implicit) right to go to war, two other functions, the right to levy taxes and to print money, have to be mentioned. A final essential function of the state concerns the guarantee of the existing socio-economic order. This touches on a basic theoretical question: is the modern state in principle a representative of 'the' people, 'the' common weal or does it reflect and is essentially charged with the

maintenance of an antagonistic class structure rooted in exploitation.

19. While all parties have regularly called for the abolition of the constitution as undemocratic and authoritarian, once in power they
have enjoyed its prerogatives. Only recently the chief justice appointed
at the behest of the president has come under fire because he heard
and adjudicated a case that was brought against him personally. It
only strenghtened the widespread conviction that the judicial system
in Sri Lanka is corrupt.

20. Cf. Final Report of the Commission of Inquiry into the Involuntary
Removal or Disappearance of Persons in the Western, Southern and
Sabaragamuwa Provinces, Dept. of Government Printing, Colombo
1997. Another 10,000 cases were to be investigated by a fourth
commission.

21. Asian Legal Resource Centre (ALRC), 2004. Asian Centre for Human
Rights, 2003. Asian Human Rights Commission, 1999.

22. The same applies in cases of complaints of rape in custody where the
Evidence Act provides that the woman proves that there was no prior
consent on her part.

23. Cf. the commissions appointed to inquire into the police, i.e. Justice
Soertsez's Commission of 1947, Justice Basnayake's Commission of
1970, Subasinghe's Salaries Commission of 1978, and Jayasinghe's
Commission of 1995. All pointed to institutional problems showing
that 'torture is entrenched in policing in Sri Lanka'. ALRC 2004,
p. 13; see also UN Committee Against Torture, Geneva A/53/44,
para 243–57 (p. 13).

24. The mass grave of Tamils at Chemmani on the Jaffna peninsula has
acquired notoriety because of the circumstances of its discovery
(testimony of a soldier implicated in the rape and murder of a young
Tamil woman) and the government's procrastination. There are at
least 13 others, this time located in the south-west and containing the
bodies of Sinhalese murdered by the state in the 1980s.

25. Asian Legal Resource Centre 2004, p. 20. Cf. also UN Committee
Against Torture: A/53/44, para 243–57.
To illustrate major defects in the system of law enforcement: there is
for example no independent investigative authority, i.e. the police/
security forces are charged with the investigation into complaints
against their own members; there is neither a time limit on investigations nor a proper record kept at police stations. Complainants
are frequently intimidated, and must fear reprisals, including false
accusations, etc.

26. And Weber continues: 'The state represents a power relation of human
beings over other human beings based on legitimate (or as legitimately
perceived) violence as means. In order to last, it is therefore necessary

that the dominated people submit to the authority claimed by the respective rulers. . . . There are in principle three inner justifications or bases of legitimacy for the exercise of power: customs, charisma, and, finally, domination/authority based on 'legality' founded on the belief in the validity of legal statuation as much as on the material competence rooted in rationally created rules.' Weber, 1972, p. 822. Weber also argues that the pacification and enlargement of the market society go hand in hand with the monopolization of legitimate violence by the state and the rationalization of the rules for its application which become eventually crystallized in the concept of a legitimate order of law. Ibid., p. 519.

27. The murder of 53 Tamil political prisoners in the high security prison Welikada in July 1983 and the more recent slaughter of Tamil youth in the rehabilitation camp in Bundunuwewa are referred to here.

28. Other more mundane illustrations are cited by the Asian Legal Resource Centre: E.g. strikes by health workers result simply in suspension of work by doctors, nurses and hospital staff '. . . Donations received for poverty alleviation are arbitrarily used, creating divisions among the poor and the system has developed clusters of control, manipulation and violence.' ALRC 2004, p. 5.

29. Jayewardene 1985, Chapter II-V.

30. Particularly when presented not as a demand for all Tamil-speaking peoples, that includes the Muslims, but only one of and for the Sri Lankan Tamils. The Sinhalese, moreover, tend to consider the Tamils of Sri Lanka as mere spearhead of the larger community of over 50 million Tamils in India.

31. These were the LTTE, ERPLF, TELO, and EROS which had earlier joined forces in the ENLF (Eelam National Liberation Front); to which have to be added PLOTE and the TULF.

32. This fourth demand was later dropped; the united front with the Indian Tamils did not survive for long.

33. In violation of the constitution, legislation and educational textbooks are not at all or very late translated into the other national language, Tamil.

34. See Stokke 2006.

35. See Heroes' Day speech 2002 of LTTE leader Pirapaharan; Bala-singham, 2004, pp 400f.

36. It is important to note, that then UNP Prime Minister Wickremasinghe had accepted the ISGA as basis for discussion.

37. It would, by all accounts, not be the only new state emerging from the fragmentation of existing ones; it was after all Bhutros Bhutros Ghali, then General Secretary of the UN, who prognosticated a doubling in UN membership in the first half of the twenty-first century.

## SELECT BIBLIOGRAPHY

Abeysekera, C. and N. Gunasingha (eds), 1987, *Facets of Ethnicity in Sri Lanka*, Colombo: Social Scientists Association.

Asian Centre for Human Rights, 2003, *The State of Civil and Political Rights in Sri Lanka*, New Delhi.

Asian Human Rights Commission, 1999, *Sri Lanka: Disappearances and The Collapse of the Police System*, Hongkong.

Asian Legal Resource Centre (ALRC), 2004, *Report 'to conduct a study on the exceptional collapse of rule of law in Sri Lanka'*, Commission on Human Rights, UN, Economic and Social Council, Geneva June 2004, E/CN.4/Sub.2/2004/3 (Annex 3, pp. 3–51).

Athukorala, P.C. and S. Rajapatirana, 2000, *Liberalization and Industrial Transformation: Sri Lanka in International Perspective*, New Delhi: Oxford University Press.

Balasingham, A., 2004, *War and Peace*, Mitcham: Fairmax Publishing.

Bartholomeusz, T.J., 2002, *In Defense of Dharma: Just-War Ideology in Buddhist Sri Lanka*, London/New York: Routledge.

Brass, P., 1991, *Ethnicity and Nationalism: Theory and Comparison*, New Delhi: Sage Publications.

Bush, K., 2003, *The Intra-Group Dimensions of Ethnic Conflict in Sri Lanka*, London/New York: Palgrave Macmillan.

Fricke, D., 2002, *Der Tamilen-Singhalesen-Konflikt auf Sri Lanka*, Berlin: Verlag Dr. Köster.

Guntalilleke, G., 2001, *The Ethnic Dimensions of Socio-Economic Development*, no. 10, Marga Monograph Series on Ethnic Reconciliation, Colombo: Marga Institute.

Jayawardena, K., 1985, *Ethnic and Class Conflicts in Sri Lanka*, Colombo: Centre for Social Analysis.

Jayaweera, S., 2001, *The Ethnic Conflict and Sinhala Consciousness*, no. 5, Marga Monograph Series on Ethnic Reconciliation, Colombo: Marga Institute.

Jean, F. and J.C. Rufin (eds), 1996, *Economie des guerres civiles*, Paris: Hachette.

Kaldor, M., 2000, *Neue und alte Kriege*, Frankfurt: Suhrkamp Verlag.

Korf, B., 2003, *Ethnicised Entitlements? Property Rights and Civil War in Sri Lanka*, no. 75 Discussion Papers, ZEF, Bonn: Centre for Development Research, November.

Lakshman, W.D., C.A. Tisdell (eds), 2000, *Sri Lanka's Development since Independence: Socio-Economic Perspectives and Analyses*, New York: Nova Science Publishers.

Lamballe, A., 1985, *Le problème tamoul au Sri Lanka*, Paris: Harmattan.

Manor, J. (ed), 1984, *Sri Lanka in Change and Crisis*, London/Sydney: Croom Helm.

220        *John P. Neelsen*

Meyer, E., 1994, *Ceylan—Sri Lanka*, Que-Sais-Je? (3rd edn.), Paris: Presses universitaires de France.

Nayak, S.C., 2001, *Ethnicity and Nation-Building in Sri Lanka*, New Delhi: Kalinga Publications.

Nesiah, D., 2001, *Tamil Nationalism*, no. 6, Marga Monograph Series on Ethnic Reconciliation, Colombo: Marga Institute.

Paul, L., 1997, *La question tamoule au Sri Lanka 1977–94*, Paris: Harmattan.

Rösel, J., 1991, Geheimnis, Terror und der Zerfall staatlicher Macht auf Sri Lanka, pp. 204–19, in Th. Scheffler (ed), *Ethnizität und Gewalt*, Hamburg: Deutsches Orient Institut.

Silva, C.R.de and T. Bartholomeusz, 2001, *The Role of the Sangha in the Reconciliation Process*, no. 16, Marga Monograph Series on Ethnic Reconciliation, Colombo: Marga Institute.

Silva, K.M. de, 1986, *Managing Ethnic Tensions in Multi-Ethnic Societies: Sri Lanka 1885–1985*, Lanham/London: University Press of America.

Sri Lanka: Racism and the Authoritarian State, *Race and Class* XXVI, 1, 1984.

Stokke, K., *Building the Eelam State: Emerging State Institutions and Forms of Governance in LTTE-controlled Areas in Sri Lanka*, Workshop on 'War and Peace in Sri Lanka', Uppsala University, 26–27 January 2006.

Südasien Büro, 1986, *Der autoritäre Staat—Die Institutionalisierung von Gewalt in Sri Lanka*, Wuppertal.

Thomas, C.Y., 1984, *The Rise of the Authoritarian State in Peripheral Societies*, New York: Monthly Review Press.

Weber, M., 1972, *Wirtschaft und Gesellschaft*, Tübingen (5th rev. edn.).

Wilson, A.J., 2000, *Sri Lankan Tamil Nationalism*, London: Hurst.

Winslow, D. and M.D. Woost (eds), 2004, *Economy, Culture, and Civil War in Sri Lanka*, Bloomington: Indiana University Press.

# CHAPTER 8

# The End of Shangri-La: Self-Perpetuating Tendencies and Invisible Displacement in the Nepalese 'People's War'

*Gil Daryn*

## INTRODUCTION

The Maoist insurgency in Nepal, or the 'People's War' as it is locally called, reached its 10th anniversary in February 2006, appears to have come to an end with the signing of a peace agreement in June 2006. This calls for reflection and retrospective examination of the war and its corollaries, which the present chapter attempts to do via a discussion of two of the most disturbing aspects of the conflict. First is its tendency to perpetuate itself, that is, to recreate the initial conditions which led to it and exacerbate the grievances that fuelled its incipient stages. The second is the relative invisibility of both the war itself and particularly of many of its victims. Prior to embarking upon this, and in order to place the ensuing discussion in the appropriate historical context, I shall briefly outline some of the main 'milestones' and features of the conflict.

The insurgency was officially launched by the CPNM (Communist Party of Nepal, Maoist, referred to as Maoists herein) on 13 February 1996, just four days before an ultimatum they delivered to the government, requesting that the latter respond to a list of forty demands, was due to expire.[1] Among these were the demands to end discrimination on any basis, be it gender,

*This paper, which is based on research which began in 1994, was written while the writer was a British Academy Postdoctoral Fellow. Recent fieldwork (October 2004 to October 2005) was funded by a British Academy Larger Research Grant.

ethnic, caste and the like, the need to guarantee the freedom of
press and publication, the call for substantial land reforms giving
land ownership rights to those who cultivate it, the implementation of a minimum wage for workers, free education and
health services, and the provision of drinking water, road and
electricity to the rural population.[2]

The initial Maoist strongholds were in western Nepal, in
Rukum and Rolpa districts, which were the first to be declared
'liberated' (with the establishment of the 'people's governments')
and where the Maoists still enjoy considerable public support.[3]
These include some of the remotest and most neglected districts
in Nepal where the presence of the state was rarely felt. At the
time, the democratic government headed by the then Congress
leader, Sher Bahadur Deuba, failed to perceive the full potential
of the Maoist threat, which, within a few years became the
major national concern in Nepal. Hence, initially, Deuba's and
subsequent governments were reluctant to engage the army in
fighting. This task was left solely to the under-equipped and ill-
trained police force. Only in November 2001, a few months
after the palace massacre of 1 June 2001, in which King Birendra
and his entire family lost their lives and the king's younger
brother, Gyanendra, inherited the throne, did the government
(once again under Prime Minister Deuba) decide to deploy the
army against the rebels and declare a state of emergency. This
period saw a marked escalation in the scale of the conflict, and
by mid 2002 the Maoists had gained influence at the village
level across much of rural Nepal. Since then there has been a
gradual yet steady intensification of the conflict and at present
it is believed that the Maoists have strong influence, at times
even de facto control, over all of Nepal's 75 districts, while
government rule is limited to district headquarters and the
kingdom's few urban centres, including the capital Kathmandu
and its immediate surroundings.

This is, however, not to say that the Maoists have no influence
or presence within urban Nepal. Many Maoists, including high-
ranking individuals, are said to enter the Kathmandu valley on
a regular basis, often staying there for long periods of time.
Nevertheless, the majority of Nepalese urban centres rarely
experienced any serious Maoist activity, and on the whole, Maoist

presence was virtually invisible and hardly felt by ordinary citizens. There were of course exceptions such as the rather rare and relatively harmless waves of sporadic bombings, and the occasional well-targeted individual assassination in urban regions. The Maoists have so far refrained from launching a full scale attack on the capital itself and have limited their actions to attacks on small police posts on its outskirts. However, throughout the insurgency, frequent general strikes have disturbed ordinary life in Kathmandu, and intermittent Maoist blockades have created short-term inconveniences for the capital's dwellers. Yet on the whole, the capital has not been exposed to the horrors experienced elsewhere. Thus life in Kathmandu has continued almost uninterrupted with one major inconvenience—extortion.

The Maoists have been very successful in bringing Kathmandu (and other urban centres) within their network of enforced 'donations'. Throughout rural parts of the country most people, belonging to almost all parts of society, have been forced to contribute either in cash (by giving a percentage of their salary or expected profits) or in kind (mainly providing food and lodging for Maoist fighters or, far more seriously, through the enforced conscription of one member of the family to the Maoist revolutionary army). In contrast, in urban areas it is only major businesses, tourist and other industries, private schools and the like who 'buy' their safety via regular 'contributions', while government employees and ordinary citizens are usually spared. As in similar circumstances elsewhere, the Maoists' secretive extortion networks know few boundaries.[4] Thus, for example, although international development agencies continually deny being under any Maoist threat and extortion, many of them have had to enter negotiations with the local Maoist commanders and pay their own share indirectly, to ensure their activities could continue. This indirect donation is made via the contractors engaged in development projects, who pay 15 per cent of their budget (the current 'norm') to the Maoists. Furthermore, there is also evidence that the Maoists are able to obtain 'donations' from at least some of the Nepalese who have fled the war and migrated to India.

In recent years it has become clear that neither the Maoists nor the government are either prepared or able to engage in a full scale war; the Maoists have neither attempted to retain the few government strongholds over which they temporarily took control nor made any serious attempts to attack the capital, Kathmandu, while the government rarely initiated wide scale operations, and did little to undermine the insurgency. Most incidents of fighting were not initiated by government forces but occurred in response to Maoist attacks. In addition, with little exception, leaders and top ranking officials on both sides have enjoyed immunity; although they are clearly able to do so, Maoists have mainly targeted low ranking army and police personnel, government employees, and in particular teachers and local politicians.[5] Similarly, they have never made any attempts to harm a member of the royal family. Likewise, the government seems to avoid direct attacks on the Maoist leadership. From the early days of the insurgency, with few exceptions, the rebels and particularly their leaders appear to have found a safe haven in India, despite the fact that India was the first to label them as terrorists, even before the Nepalese government did so.

The general failure of the democratic governments to end the conflict appears to be behind King Gyanendra's decision to unofficially take executive powers into his own hands in October 2002. Following civil unrest in Kathmandu and the continuous failure of the three successive prime ministers to resolve the conflict, the king dismissed the government and officially assumed executive powers on 1 February 2005. This time a state of emergency was imposed, senior politicians were placed in jail or under house arrest, the media were put under strict censorship, all lines of internal and external communication were cut, Kathmandu's international airport was closed and the king placed himself at the head of an appointed council of ministers. The move was personally explained by the king during a long televised speech that morning as a move towards the restoration of peace, security, democracy and progress in the country. He further declared his intention to rule for an interim period of three years, after which the multi-party democracy would be reinstated.

A few months later, when the state of emergency was lifted and most political leaders were freed, the latter gradually launched a public campaign of agitation against the king. This initiative has so far enjoyed very limited public support. This is not surprising in view of the political parties' record during Nepal's democratic era between 1990–2002, which was characterized by corruption, opportunism and mis-management. In what appears to be a major attempt to regain their lost popularity and relevance in Nepalese politics and society, the top leaders of the seven party alliance (SPA) have put aside almost ten years of deadly Maoist persecution against their activists and began direct negotiations with the Maoists in New Delhi in the autumn of 2005. Unlike previous rounds with the government, this time the talks ended with a 12-point mutual understanding document, which agreed, among others, on the need to establish 'absolute democracy' and end the autocratic monarchy. Not surprisingly, the royal government bluntly rejected the agreement and refused to join the unilateral Maoist ceasefire (declared in September 2005) which ended in early January 2006.

Following this initial agreement and after earlier efforts to stir up a mass movement in order to topple the king failed the SPA decided to coordinate their agitation against the royal regime with the Maoist rebels. This turned out to be a highly constructive move: within less than a month of joint demonstration-cum-general strike during April 2006. The united movement spread to almost all corners of the country, forcing King Gyanendra to submit to the parties' key demands. These included returning sovereignty to the people and an immediate restoration of the parliament, which was dissolved back in 2002. This historic return to democracy cost the lives of 21 young men and women and left some 5,000 people injured.

The new SPA government, together with the reinstated parliament, moved swiftly to curtail the king's power and transformed Nepal into a secular state. The government declared a ceasefire, removed the terrorist tag off the Maoists, set free many of the Maoist prisoners, and invited them to the negotiation table. This time, the negotiations were held far from the media and the public eye, and finally came to a successful, if somewhat premature conclusion on 16 June 2006, with the signing of a peace treaty by the top Maoist leaders and the government. Its main components were the consensus regarding the need to hold elections for a constituent assembly, seeking UN assistance for managing the weapons of both the Maoists and the (formerly

Royal) Nepalese army, drafting of an interim constitution, the establishment of an interim government (including the Maoists)and dissolution of the recently re-established house of representatives.

Although spirits are currently very high in Nepal and optimism reigns, not only did it immediately become clear that the timetable set in the peace agreement is not realistic but there are also serious signs that the road to a permanent peace is paved with obstacles. Hence, for example, the peace agreement failed to address the issue of the conflict's victims, including the millions who were forced to leave their homes, and remained vague regarding the decommissioning of the Maoist army. Moreover, not only do the Maoists seem inclined to continue their intimidation and extortion campaigns, but they appear to have intensified the latter significantly. Furthermore, the Maoists' reiteration of their demands for an immediate dissolution of the newly established parliament and their subsequent inclusion in an interim government prior to full disarmament, and their threat of an 'October revolution' if their demands are not met, cast serious doubts regarding their long term intentions and the future of the peace process as a whole.

According to INSEC (Informal Sector Service Center, a leading human rights NGO), a total of 13,253 people have been killed during the conflict (8,336 by the state forces and 4,917 by the Maoists) as of 16 June 2006.[6] Many more were wounded and traumatized, and were subject to continuous violations of human rights, including torture, by both sides. Keeping in mind the fact that almost all of the fighting took place in remote mountainous areas of Nepal and the state of public record-keeping, it seems clear that the above figures should be taken as rather conservative approximations. Moreover, though the total number of people who have been displaced due to the conflict cannot be verified, in July 2005 this number was estimated to be as high as two million people.[7] This situation and the fact that in recent years Nepal continues to head the list of countries with the largest number of annual 'disappearances',[8] has led to great international concern, concluding in the formation of a special team of human rights inspectors who work under the auspices of the UN throughout Nepal in April 2005.

# I. A VICIOUS CYCLE IN THE MAKING?
# THE SELF-PERPETUATING TENDENCIES
# OF THE CONFLICT

## 1. THE UNINTENTIONAL CONSEQUENCES OF DEVELOPMENT

Against the background of the main characteristics of the conflict and its development the changes that occurred in a number of cardinal elements, which were highly instrumental (or at least were declared as such) in the development of the insurgency can be explored. First one of the key factors behind the rise of the Maoist insurgency and part of its indispensable background, namely Nepal's state of poverty, under- and uneven development is examined. The general failure of more than half a century of the massive, multi-million dollar, local and international development enterprise which aimed at promoting Nepal from its position as one of the poorest countries in South Asia, and at providing the rural Nepalese with a real hope for a better future, is no doubt one of the main reasons behind the insurgency. Yet even though substantial improvements were made, for example in the field of health, this was not equally achieved throughout the country. While Kathmandu and Nepal's central and eastern districts had witnessed a substantial improvement, the health situation in some of Nepal's most remote regions, especially in the far western and north-western parts of the country, hardly changed over the years. There, the levels of starvation and inadequate food supply, which are the reasons for the generally appalling health condition and very low life expectancy, are on a par with those in sub-Saharan African countries.[9] Although not stated specifically, it seems obvious that the insurgency, whose heart was and still is in the far western regions of Nepal, has brought little if any relief to these areas as far as health and food security are concerned.

More generally, a DFID, GTZ and SDC report notes the absence of effective government health management in rural Nepal and concludes that the health system has been significantly disrupted by the conflict.[10] Moreover, health workers are beaten, arrested and abducted by both the security forces and Maoists alike. Some health workers, who were abducted by Maoists to provide treatment to the injured rebels, were never seen again.

This situation, the writers argue, has resulted in health professionals becoming too afraid to provide, and local people being too afraid to seek medical treatment. Although Maoists did not necessarily seek to destroy the health infrastructures and services, they were and still are affecting their availability.[11]

## 2. AN ETHOS OF MODERNITY

As may be expected, Nepal's poverty and uneven development is not only evinced in the area of healthcare but engulfs almost every sphere of life. A true understanding of the meaning of Nepalese poverty and unequal development entails going beyond the dry numbers and statistics of absolute poverty, and looking at the ways in which these came to be perceived and imagined in Nepal and their place in modern Nepalese discourse. Thus, Nepal may appear to be on the way to eradicating absolute, 'statistical' poverty, as one recent national report suggests, but these statistics do not reflect the daily lives of most rural Nepalese.[12] What matters at the grass root level, and at least partially lies at the root of the insurgency, is the manner in which poverty is locally perceived. Generally speaking, this can be viewed in terms of unequal development or the gap between village and city, with the capital Kathmandu epitomising the latter. Prior to the conflict and during its early stages, the aforementioned gap dominated the social discourse of youths in rural Nepal to a large extent and was seen to create a common ethos of modernity.

In order to understand how unequal development came to be perceived in Nepal, let us briefly examine the local meaning of development or *bikas* (Nepali). The latter has been one of the most significant buzz words in public discourse in the decades that preceded the conflict. Asked to define development, most young Nepalese usually answer that it is mainly connected to facilities, material needs and amenities, for example, access to a road, phone, electricity, hospital and school. I often heard that having a motorcycle (not to mention a car), TV and the like, as well as having a job are some of the fundamental characteristics of a 'developed' person.[13] Development is mainly seen to be concentrated in urban centres, particularly in Kathmandu, while most villages are deprived of much or all of it because of what they view as the government's failure to deliver it to rural areas.

Hence, it is obvious that from a local point of view, Nepal was and is still largely undeveloped, since while Kathmandu could compete with any small-scale Western town in terms of the availability (though not necessarily the quality) of public services and facilities, modern consumer products and appliances, most of rural Nepal is yet to be connected to the national electricity grid and telephone system. Water is only available in one or two central points in the village and there is no access to safe drinking water. Rural hospitals are few and far between and local health posts, if available, provide very limited and basic care. Many villages have no road access, and most roads are merely gravelled paths, thus transportation is limited to the dry season. Village cooking is still based on firewood, and most kitchens lack a chimney. Permanent toilets are rarely found and almost all modern appliances are not available.

The above perceptions of development are part of a more general modernity ethos, which seems to be able to mould and frame people's identity and consciousness, aspirations and motivations for action. The remote high-caste rural Nepalese village I studied almost ten years ago provides a good example of this. At the time, most village men and all village women above the age of forty were uneducated, most of the women had never visited Kathmandu and many never went as far as the nearest market town. With little exception, people belonging to that age group viewed agriculture as an honourable profession and were quite content with their village life circumstances, provided that their fields produced enough rice and vegetables to feed their families.

In contrast, the perceptions and entire world-view of the younger generation, even if they had little education, were governed by the contradiction between the derogatory state of 'villageness', into which whey were born, and the desired urban existence in Kathmandu. In short, while the first carried strong connotations of ignorance, backwardness, under-development, poverty and the parochial Hindu way of life with its numerous social and other divisions, the latter is characterized by education, modernity, development, wealth, secularism and social equality. Anything vaguely resembling the village was therefore seen as disparaging and hence rejected; young villagers migrating to Kathmandu attempted to shed their past and realize their ideal identity as modern, liberal, educated and wealthy individuals. This modernity ethos was fostered and reinforced as a result of the greater mobility of the younger generation and their exposure to the wonders of the city, particularly the capital Kathmandu.

Very similar perceptions seem to be prominent in rural Nepal as a whole as was demonstrated by Pigg (1992). As Pigg rightly notes, this unintentional consequence of the successful diffusion of an international development perception is indeed ironic, given that so many cautiously designed development projects actually fall short of bringing any significant change to village life. Concomitantly, the dichotomy between 'village' and 'city' was also inculcated and propagated via the curriculum of the national education system taught in village schools.

## 3. THE ROLE OF THE EDUCATION SYSTEM

The modernity ethos and its perception of the rural/urban division in binary terms would have remained a benign social anecdote, were it not for the disturbing, rather explosive and unresolved cognitive dissonance it entails. This becomes apparent when we consider two issues. First is the tendency of 'development' to remain concentrated in urban centres, far from thousands of remote villages. Secondly, while the education system was successful in promulgating the dichotomy between rural and urban, it failed to pave the way for the rural young to turn their modernity ethos into a reality.

The reasons for this are manifold. The education system did not set forth the direction or provide the means for the rural youths to attain 'modernity' within the rural setting; it largely failed to foster values of co-operation, common civil action and public awareness that could bring about the gradual transformation of rural settings. Thus the attitude towards development remained largely passive; either development 'came' to you in the form of government or foreign sponsored projects, or you moved to the city to achieve it. Furthermore, the impressive outreach of the education system throughout rural Nepal was not matched by a concomitant and significant rural transformation, making it difficult for any local development initiative to succeed and confirming that modernity and a rural existence are mutually exclusive. While 'modernity' could not be realized in the village, the education system left the majority of rural youths ill-equipped for making the transition to the city. Education to this day remains neither compulsory nor actually free.[14] And the system still suffers from heavy dropout rates as well as poor pass rates in the matriculation exam or SLC (School Leaving Certificate), which is an indispensable qualification for higher education and employment.[15] Moreover, the SLC pass rates among students from government schools are much lower than those of their counterparts in private schools, most of which are located in urban areas.[16] To further aggravate the situation, the slowly developing Nepalese urban economy did not translate into sufficient employment opportunities to match the supply of young educated migrants, drastically limiting the latter's opportunities to remain in the city. This situation led to an exacerbation of the already growing sense of frustration, helplessness and aggravation among the younger generations in rural Nepal. It is not difficult to see how joining the revolution was therefore deemed a viable opportunity for success, gaining self esteem and earning a living for large numbers of un- or poorly educated youths from difficult economic backgrounds.

## 4. The Ethnic Factor

From its early days, the Maoist insurgency built upon, manipulated and fought in the name of Nepal's excluded and oppressed social groups, among them low castes, various Tibeto-Burman speaking ethnic groups (*janajatis*), landless farmers and women, who constituted their widest support and participation base. In fact, the Maoists were highly skilful in making use of the age old feelings of deprivation, disenfranchisement and discrimination, which converge with the rural/urban gap and unfulfilled modernity ethos discussed above. Thus, the Maoists seem to have transformed and channelled the strong ethnic tensions, particularly the anti Brahman/Chhetri sentiments of the Nepalese ethnic minorities, into a well-orchestrated class conflict that appears to satiate the 'ethnic *jinni*'.[17]

Reflecting this, the Maoists' initial 40 demands from the government back in 1996 included putting an end to patriarchal exploitation and discrimination against women, giving them the right to inherit their parental property, ending caste discrimination, racial exploitation and suppression, eliminating 'untouchability', giving all languages an equal status, establishing autonomous ethnic governments where ethnic communities constitute a majority, and implementation of an agrarian reform through which tenants would be able to own their land. The role played by these grievances and feelings of discontent in the rise of the insurgency cannot be underestimated.

## 5. TEN YEARS ON—THE EDUCATION SYSTEM, RURAL/URBAN GAP AND DEVELOPMENT

From the above discussion it is clear that the education system, the rural/urban gap and local perceptions of development, embody vital reference points in any examination of the initial conditions which led to the insurgency. We shall now turn to examine how the education system has fared during the decade long conflict. Unfortunately, it seems that this already fragile and ineffective system was badly hit during the conflict, particularly in rural areas. From the early days of the insurgency, the Maoists have targeted schools and teachers in particular as they were viewed as extensions of the feudal government and agents of state propaganda. Many teachers were killed, injured or forcibly displaced, while the rest are required to pay between 5-25 per cent of their salary as 'contribution' to the revolution. Schools are the first to be disrupted in times of general strikes (*bandh*), and many are used as barracks by the Maoist and the security forces alike. It also became apparent that while the Maoists have banned large parts of the ordinary national curriculum, they were extremely slow in developing any significant alternatives. With teachers and students often witnessing their schools being transformed into battlefields and being terrorized by the outcome, it is little wonder that they later find it almost impossible to teach and study.

In Maoist controlled areas, students and teachers are frequently forced to participate in re-education programmes that often take them away from school for a number of days or weeks at a time. As one high-school teacher told me: 'The Maoists ask all students and teachers to participate in a cultural programme once every few weeks. We have little choice but to comply. We usually march to an unknown destination for up to five days. There, we watch a cultural programme, are forced to shout Maoist slogans and finally given a meal with a lot of meat. In this way they believe they can buy our hearts and minds.' In 2003 for example, schools were only open for 120 days and many schools have been shut down following their destruction, lack of teachers or due to Maoist threats.[18] Even in those that do remain open, many students do not attend since they are forced to work in the fields while their older brothers and fathers are away. In particular, the Maoists have targeted private schools and forced them to either shut down or pay large donations. The SLC examinations are disrupted almost annually and the data from the last two years is revealing: the national pass rate has declined from 46.18 per cent in 2004 to 38.72 per cent in 2005.[19] Displaced children are often deprived of education altogether; with their parents struggling to make ends meet the children are often sent out to work. The lucky ones attend schools in urban areas, which are overcrowded due to displacement.[20] The emerging picture is thus a very pessimistic one; the major disruption to the education system as a result of the insurgency is giving rise to a new generation of poorly educated young people, for whom joining the insurgency may appear to be an attractive option.[21]

Now we turn to briefly examine the effects of the conflict on the Nepalese rural/urban gap in economic terms. According to ODI's excellent study (2002), it appears that with the exception of improvement to the livelihoods of a small proportion of households in Maoist affected areas, the insurgency has seriously affected rural livelihoods and has resulted in a major economic slowdown.[22] This is a direct result of the widespread reduction in physical mobility and travel, the destruction of infrastructure and bridges, growing insecurity, adverse effects on tourism, the withdrawal of banks from rural areas, and the targeting of businesses for contribution/extortion. Concomitantly and as was mentioned above, there has been a significant rise in the exodus from rural Nepal and many areas now have very few working-age men, hence it is unlikely that the general rural economic situation will improve in the foreseeable future. In addition, with the continuation of the Maoist donation campaign, in cash and kind, and the risk associated with any obvious accumulation of wealth, there seems to be little incentive for people to engage in economic activity.

In sharp contrast with the deteriorating rural economy, it seems that at least some of Nepal's urban centres have fared much better as a result of the conflict. Thus one report mentions that: 'Paradoxically, the unfolding human tragedy of the mid-western districts has resulted in an urban boom in Nepalganj [on Nepal's southern border with India]. Roadside lodges and restaurants are doing a roaring business, and transport operators in Nepal and India have a lot of customers. Wealthier people from the northern districts have moved permanently here, buying property and building houses on the outskirts of Nepalganj.'[23] This trend is even more significant in Kathmandu, where the last five years in particular have seen an unparalleled boom in the construction industry of private and business buildings alike, as well as related businesses. Much of what until recent years was the city's 'green belt' is now covered with the cement of numerous new houses. With the exception of tourist related businesses, which continue to suffer due to the declining tourist numbers, and the large businesses that are forced to pay donations to the revolution, economic life in Kathmandu shows few signs of suffering as a result of the insurgency. Many of the more up-market restaurants in Thamel, Kathmandu's popular tourist hub, which were occasionally empty when tourists failed to arrive, are crowded once again but nowadays the customers are mainly locals.

Similarly, the occasional and expensive entertainment events in five-star hotels have no shortage of enthusiastic participants. Kathmandu's expensive supermarkets which attracted few locals years back are now packed with customers and the streets are bursting due to the influx of numerous imported cars. The city's infrastructure (electricity and water for example) may be on the verge of collapse due to the influx of displaced people, yet the general impression is that Kathmandu, in recent years, is experiencing an economic boom of sorts.[24] Hence, while the Maoists have tried to limit or altogether obviate the existing discrepancy between poor and rich in a Robin Hood-like style and were highly successful in eliciting donations from and driving wealthy people and their families away to the cities, the war has largely eroded the livelihoods of the rural masses, while causing many urban centres to flourish.

One of the Maoists' initial 40 demands back in 1996 was stopping: 'the invasion of colonial and imperial elements in the name of NGOs and INGOs'. Thus, it is not surprising that their attitude towards various local and international development agencies was generally speaking, far from supportive. With the exception of limited development projects introduced by the Maoists, many development and aid activities have been seriously affected, delayed or stopped due to Maoist attacks.[25] Major development agencies gradually restricted their activities, postponing or altogether pulling out from large areas of the country. Some relatively recent examples include the decision of at least ten foreign donor organizations from the UK, Germany, Japan, the Netherlands, the United Nations and World Food Programme to suspend their projects in May 2004, following threats by Maoists rebels. Towards the end of that year the US government decided to pull out its Peace Corps volunteers from Nepal. A year later, in May 2005, following an incident in which four local aid workers from INGOs were beaten by Maoists, the World Food Programme, as well as UK, German and Dutch aid agencies suspended their work in the western Kalikot district. More recently, Canada decided to remove Nepal from the list of countries in which it plans to focus its future development efforts.[26]

## 6. Ten Years On—How Have Nepal's Disadvantaged Groups Fared?

The insurgency has considerably changed Nepalese politics and social agenda and brought previously marginal and neglected social issues, particularly of gender, caste and ethnicity, to the forefront of social life. However it is rather questionable whether the insurgency has been successful in making a tangible, significant long lasting change in the lives of underrepresented, excluded and oppressed groups including women, low castes, various Tibeto-Burman speaking ethnic groups and landless farmers.

The early days of the insurgency saw a concerted effort to attend to the needs of the rural disadvantaged and gain their support via campaigns against sexual abuse, gambling, drinking, and caste discrimination. The insurgency was certainly successful in undermining many, particularly Hindu, ancient social structures, symbols and practices and managed to bring the neglected issue of women's status and rights to the forefront of Nepalese social discourse. One highly visible achievement is the opening of the lower ranks of the Nepalese army and police to women, matching the opportunities offered by the Maoist forces. No less significant was the parliament's decision (at the end of 2001) to provide women with partial inheritance rights (though a daughter has to return her share of inheritance upon marriage). In December 2005, the Supreme Court went even further, ruling that women were no longer required to obtain consent from their father, husband, sons and unmarried daughters if they wish to sell their property. Furthermore, a marked change can also be seen in the marriage patterns in rural Nepal with the Maoists fostering secular marriage by mutual consent and advocating against polygamy. Concomitantly, cases of domestic violence and neglect of women have decreased.[27] Of course, it still remains to be seen whether these changes have long lasting effects.

One major change affecting numerous women is that due to the mass exodus of working-age men from rural areas, they now find themselves empowered as the *de facto* heads of the household. This in itself is not a remarkably new role for many women whose husbands spend long sojourns working out of the village, yet the conflict has literally placed these women on the front line, torn between and having to meet the demands of both the Maoists and the government forces. Thus rural Nepalese women whose normal burden includes looking after their children and house, cooking and doing much of the agricultural work, may have gained more independence, yet the conflict has placed on their shoulders an additional, often excessive burden. Moreover, as observed by many, women seem to be indirectly victimized by the Maoist actions after the male members of the household are forced to flee due to threats made by either of the fighting sides.[28] Thus, a recent report presents a rather mixed picture regarding rural women's view of the changes brought by the conflict, and gives the impression that apart from the increased incidence of violence, which clearly gives rise to general negative feelings, women are both happy about their freedom, new personal and social position, yet they resent their extra burden, increased vulnerability, economic and physical insecurity and the restrictions placed upon the public performance of religious activities.[29]

One could argue that a revolution concerning women's position and social status was already underway prior to the insurgency as may be exemplified by the data from one predominantly orthodox Brahman village.[30] Despite the infamous patriarchal attitudes common among high-castes, it was apparent that the education of girls was fast becoming a priority, not due to a change in people's deep-seated attitudes towards women's roles, but due to a practical concern, since potential suitors were looking for educated brides and it became difficult to marry off poorly educated girls. The increasing levels of education among young women considerably raised their awareness of the often deplorable circumstances of women in Hindu families, resulting in a general determination among daughters not to replicate their mothers' experiences as far as gender relationships are concerned. Although, at the time, many of these young women's aspirations could not be fulfilled, there were clear signs that a real revolution in women's status and gender relations was underway among high-caste Hindus. Ten years on it appears that a general transformation has indeed taken place throughout much of Nepal, but at a rather exorbitant price.

A much less fortunate consequence of the conflict has been the exacerbation of sexual abuse of low caste women. According to the Centre for Human Rights and Global Justice 2005 report, while occasional sexual abuse by the police forces was known long before the conflict, now both the army and the police are reported to have far fewer restraints in entering low caste homes and sexually abusing women.[31] The same report further mentions Maoist rapes of women in the households that host them (let alone in those that refuse to or cannot do so) and sexual abuse of low caste women.[32] Furthermore, there are reports of young female recruits being employed as sex slaves by the Maoists.[33] The conflict has also brought a substantial increase in the number of women of all castes, who work in Kathmandu's dance bars or in Nepal border areas, where they are highly prone to sexual abuse.[34]

As mentioned above, although the Maoists did open their ranks to women, low castes (Dalits) and ethnic groups, which no doubt gave these minorities an unprecedented feeling of authority, control and empowerment, there is still a stark difference between their representation in the lower echelons of the Maoist movement compared with the higher ranks. It is estimated that women (70 per cent of whom come from ethnic communities)[35] make up a third of the rebel army and militia,[36] while ethnic minorities as a whole account for about two thirds.[37] The Maoists recruited heavily among low castes but there is no confirmation of their actual numbers.[38] Whatever these may be, this representation has yet to be translated into equity. In fact, the general makeup of the Maoists' governing bodies appears to replicate the one dominating general Nepalese politics and administration; the two supreme Maoist military and political leaders are both high-caste Brahman males, and Brahmans also constitute an overwhelming majority of the top level standing committee where currently there is not even one low caste or female member.[39] Furthermore, it has often been claimed that many of the female recruits are still mainly engaged in traditional female chores like cooking, washing clothes and the like;[40] and that the monthly allowance of the lower rank guerrillas (predominantly consisting of the above disadvantaged groups), currently stands at Rs. 150 – about \$2.[41] Hence, it may not be surprising that there have been repeated accusations that minority and disadvantaged groups are cynically manipulated by the leadership.[42]

On the positive side, with few exceptions, 'untouchability' is not practised within the Maoist armed forces. Nevertheless, it seems that they have so far been unable to end discrimination against low castes within the general population.[43] Furthermore, many fragile, low caste communities who were often on the verge of starvation prior to the conflict, are said to be further pushed towards grinding poverty, often due to Maoist demands on their limited resources.[44] Not surprisingly, many non-cadre low castes often see the Maoists as exploiters and assert that the conflict has made them weaker and poorer.[45] An additional and unfortunate consequence has been the exacerbation of abuses against low castes by the state security forces, who assume that they are all Maoist supporters.[46]

The picture regarding the Tibeto-Burman speaking ethnic minorities is less clear-cut. The insurgency significantly increased awareness among ethnic minorities of their previous social exclusion. They also developed a growing sense of pride in their culture and traditions and experienced a significant improvement in their relationships with higher castes. At the same time, the Maoists banned religious festivals and cultural gatherings and tried to replace these with less traditional, secular festivals of their own and, in doing so, have contributed to the erosion of local culture and traditions in some areas. Crucially, there has not been any visible improvement in the livelihoods of these groups and they are reported to be among the most badly affected groups due to the conflict.[47] The Maoists did not appear to address their promises regarding ethnic autonomy until the end of 2003 and, as observed by Whelpton (2005: 232–3), this process is inevitably ridden with fundamental difficulties as no single caste or ethnic group accounts for more than half of the population in any given district. Indeed, various ethnic organizations have been parting with the Maoists due to ideological differences and unfulfilled demands. This is well exemplified by the relationship of the Maoists and the ethnic Khambuwan and Limbuwan (Kirat) fronts in east Nepal.[48] It is further estimated that in the future the Maoists will find it more and more difficult to maintain control over the various militant ethnic organizations currently acting under their wings.[49]

Regarding the highly aggravating issues of land reform, it has been claimed that apart from sporadic expropriation and redistribution of land, land reform was low on the Maoist agenda.[50] Furthermore, it appears that wealthy landowners could, in almost all areas, keep their land as long as they paid the large 'donations' demanded by the Maoists, and according to Whelpton (2005: 206), even when landowners were forced to flee, the Maoists took up their place and the workers who continued to cultivate the land were now forced to give them the landowner's share (about 50 per cent of the crops).

To conclude this part, it appears that rural Nepal has borne the brunt of the insurgency, witnessing the significant disturbance to the education system, the breakdown of the local economy in most rural regions and the gradual decline in internationally-funded development activities. At the same time, urban Nepal was relatively unaffected, and many urban centres have benefited economically. It thus appears that in their struggle for an egalitarian society the insurgents have largely contributed to widening the rural/urban gap. In particular, rather ironically and with few exceptions, the insurgency has significantly worsened the circumstances of the people in whose name and for whose causes it was originally launched. The on-going conflict continues to cause suffering and agony on an unprecedented scale, which no words can capture. One need only contrast the alarming increase in the number of those orphaned and disabled during the insurgency and the scores of elderly people left alone in villages across the country with the last of the Maoists' original 40 demands which states that 'Orphans, the disabled, the elderly and children should be duly honoured and protected.'

This situation has significant consequences for the Maoists' rural support base, and could well be behind their decision to enter into partnership with the seven party alliance and sign a peace treaty. It will as doubt determine the outcome of any future elections for a constituent assembly. Since the insurgency exacerbated or at best merely transformed rather than altogether eliminated many of the grievances and frustrations that formed the fertile grounds in which its original seeds were sown—

it appears to have left them ready for transplantation. Thus, if the Nepalese government fails to seriously address the afore-mentioned burning issues, the prospects for a long term sustain-able peace appear slim.

## II. THE CONFLICT'S INVISIBLE VICTIMS

Another unfortunate and most disturbing aspect of the decade-long Maoist insurgency is that with very little exception it has remained highly invisible, not only to the eyes of the international media and public around the world but also within Nepal itself, where private and state media has faced external or self-censorship throughout the conflict. The Kathmandu valley itself, the stronghold of the central government, often seems cut off from the horrors taking place daily only a few miles beyond the hills surrounding it. Were it not for the contact with friends and relatives living in villages, who occasionally visit the capital often with pleas for shelter and assistance, the residents of Kathmandu would be almost totally disconnected from Nepal's rural drama. Yet, not only has the conflict itself remained largely invisible and rarely manifested itself outside rural Nepal, which became largely out of bounds for most foreigners and urban Nepalese alike, but also the insurgency's victims remain almost totally invisible and overlooked, and their hardships remain unattended to. The important and dedicated activities of a small number of Nepalese and international NGOs, which implement projects targeted at physical and mental rehabilitation of the victims of violence, presently seem like drops of medicine in a sea of pain and are yet to reach the vast majority of those who have been devastated and traumatized by the conflict. For example, CVICT (The Centre for the Victims of Torture, Nepal) maintains a shelter for sexually abused women (mainly pregnancies resulting from rape) but it has the capacity to host and treat only twenty women at a time. As the centre is located in Kathmandu, it is obvious that many women in need do not know about it or are unable to access its services. CVICT estimates that at least 2000 other women are in urgent need of admission to the centre.[51]

Families left behind following the death or serious injury of the householder or other family member only rarely receive the meagre government compensation, which currently stands at Rs. 1.5 lakh (about $2,000). No compensation is offered to the families of Maoists killed or to families of suspected Maoist collaborators who 'disappeared'. Most affected families have largely been left to their own devices, doomed to a life of pain and destitution. Yet, not only are the victims who remain in rural areas largely invisible, but this is also true of the masses who decided or were forced to move out of their rural homes to other parts of Nepal or to India. For many of these the huge difficulties and struggle associated with displacement come as additional blows following their previous traumatic mental and physical experiences. The remainder of the present paper will focus on the rather invisible and neglected phenomenon of displacement.

## 1. SETTING THE STAGE FOR A RURAL EXODUS

What began as a minor trickle during the incipient phases of the insurgency during 1996, gradually came to embody what is today recognized to be a major rural exodus.[52] Recent reports (July 2005) estimate there are between 200,000 to 400,000 displaced people in Nepal's urban areas, while the figure for those who have fled to India is much higher and is estimated to be around two million people.[53]

Prior to the onset of the People's War, much if not most of rural Nepal suffered from an age-old vacuum of authority where the central government was felt to be too weak and remote, while the police forces, which were only situated in relatively large rural market towns (*bazaars*), were regarded neither as agents of law and order nor as a source of assistance or refuge. The rule in rural Nepal was that of the might, be it the head of the nearest police station, a strong local landowner and the like, while government officials and elected members of local municipal bodies only rarely held any actual authority. Apart from rare criminal acts, which usually took place outside villages 'in no man's land', violence was almost non-existent. Small crimes like petty theft were regularly settled via ad-hoc councils of village *thulo manche*—literally 'big people'—highly respected and influential (often high-caste) people.

This relatively peaceful existence gradually came to an end with the onset of the insurgency when the Maoists, and to a much lesser extent the army and police forces, began to fill the above authority vacuum, introducing intense terror and a realistic fear for one's property and life. The majority of Nepalese villagers now found themselves the enemies of both the government armed forces and the Maoists alike. The former saw them as (forced or wilful) collaborators with the insurgents, while the latter suspected them of being government informers or, at best, viewed them as a legitimate source of assistance in kind, cash, labour or fighting force. Both sides attempted to influence and exercise their power by systematically terrorizing the rural population. Thus, the rural masses found themselves trapped between the two armed sides, often literally in the centre of a battlefield, totally unprotected against the human rights violations committed by the two fighting sides as well as by various criminals and armed gangs. Not surprisingly, life became almost impossible for many and the intensification of the conflict over the last five years has coincided with a significant increase in migration out of village Nepal.

## 2. INTERNAL DISPLACEMENT[54]

The background, stages, duration and circumstances of displacement vary considerably between individuals and families, yet its primary causes always seem to involve intense feelings of insecurity and an acute fear for one's property and life. It must be stressed that the aforementioned fear and resultant migration are due to threats made by both the government forces and the Maoists alike. Yet, if Maoist-induced displacement is almost 'invisible', the people who flee due to the actions of state security forces literally seem to vanish into thin air.[55] Their increased 'invisibility' is most likely due to their reluctance to expose themselves and disclose the circumstances of their displacement for fear of being labelled as Maoist collaborators, as well as the high likelihood that they have actually fled from Nepal.[56] Their plight, however, is no doubt on a par with that of families and individuals displaced due to Maoist actions, who form the focus of the present section.

The first people to be targeted by the Maoists belonged to rural Nepal's upper social strata. This relatively privileged group mainly consisted of well-off landlords, local leaders and party activists, as well as Village Development Committee (VDC) chairmen and vice-chairmen. Until 2002, these constituted the majority among the people displaced to district headquarters, Nepalese cities such as Nepalganj and the capital Kathmandu.[57] Often seen as belonging to this group are also those 'fortunate' recipients of (usually meagre) government salaries, such as teachers and security personnel, who were especially persecuted throughout the conflict. Although these people often came from very poor backgrounds themselves, they were still seen as the representatives of the feudal and capitalistic enemy state.

The actual decision to leave the village is always difficult. It is usually taken only after a close family member is killed, when death threats are issued or when another major human rights violation (such as rape or torture) occurs. Upendra Bohara, a 55 year-old wealthy villager and an admired pro-democracy Congress politician (who served three years in jail during the Panchayat authoritarian era), used much of his influence and wealth to initiate various development projects in the rural area where he used to live. He tells the following story about the circumstances that brought him to leave the village and migrate to Kathmandu together with his family:

In our area Maoist presence increased only in 2000–1. At first they enjoyed a lot of public support with their coming down on (alcohol) drinking and (card) gambling but very soon they started destroying community buildings and the nearby bridge and made a lot of trouble for ordinary people. Therefore people began to resent them. For example, they [25 people] came to my house around midnight and asked for food. Without electricity or gas, the whole family had to wake up, cook and serve them all night. In the morning they left. They came back three or four days later and asked for food again. Then they started to ask for money and told me:

'You are a respectable person around here, you worked and did a lot for your village, you are not corrupt and hence you should support us with your money.'

I didn't give them. Then they started to threaten to punish me if I would not give them one lakh (100,000 rupees, about $1300) but I refused to give. One day the local Maoist commander [24 years old] came and said that he talked with many of the people in my village about me and they told him about the development projects I introduced and how they liked me. Hence, said the commander, you need not go to Kathmandu and you can stay here. But now I could not trust them. I told him, next month another commander who does not know me will come [instead of you] and what will happen to me and my family then? I packed and moved to Kathmandu.

At least part of the significant rise in property value and the housing construction boom witnessed in the Kathmandu valley (as well as at a number of other urban centres, mainly in the Terai) in recent years is due to such wealthy displaced people who settled in the valley. Yet the majority are not so fortunate; many come from a low economic background or were forced to leave their homes empty-handed. Many did find shelter in a relative's house, however, years after such temporary accommodation is offered open-heartedly, the arrangement often becomes uneasy. Then rent or support towards meeting of the household expenses is requested and if it cannot be provided many displaced families are asked to leave. In addition, urban landowners seem increasingly reluctant to rent out accommodation to strangers, fearing retribution from the Maoist and state forces alike if the tenant turns out to be on the run from either side. Although mainly poorer families usually opt for crossing the border into India, some of them at least try to settle within Nepal's urban centres, along with many better-off village families, who have lost all their property in the conflict but due to age and other concerns do not wish to or can't migrate to India. Without the appropriate (if any) economic means to support themselves, the latter endure dire living conditions and embody a new stratum among the urban poor. In some places this has resulted in the mushrooming of small shanty neighbourhoods and slums in various parts of urban Nepal.

Many people say they managed to buy temporary peace-of-mind by 'donating' a percentage of their government salary to the Maoists. As one high-school teacher recalled: 'At first I was asked to give one day's salary each month, then two days a month, now they are asking us to donate five days' worth every month. I already can't feed my family with what I have left, what shall I do if they will ask for more?' In a similar vein, many large landowners testify that although the property and fields of others were confiscated, they secretly paid up to Rs. 1 lakh ($1,300) per calendar year in order to keep both their village house and fields intact, and were able to enjoy half of the crops their tenants grew on it as they used to do before the conflict. However, many left their village since they were simply unable to meet the Maoists' demands. Such is the case of Mukunda Giri (50), a health assistant and father of six. Mukunda appears to maintain the façade of a light-hearted, happy man, yet when unfolding the circumstances that brought him to leave his village, he often seemed on the verge of tears:

Our problems started only three years ago, when the Maoists arrived in the village. They declared that they first have to destroy everything in order to build the country anew. Among others, they promised to confiscate the land from the rich and redistribute it. They searched all village houses and took all of the women's jewellery and expensive items from their dowries. Four teachers had to flee the village together with their families and their houses were confiscated. Others were forced to donate money to the revolution or permit one member of the family to join the revolutionary army. At first I refused to donate because I did not have enough money. One day, at four in the afternoon when I came home, five armed Maoists were waiting for me. When they saw me they took me away immediately. We walked for hours. In the morning we arrived at a small hut which they called 'People's court'. There I was interrogated about my political opinions for the whole day. They mainly wished to know why I refused to help them. Finally, they told me that they found out that I am an informer. Next they blindfolded me, took me out of the hut and started torturing me. I was first stripped naked apart from my underpants and then they placed nettle plants on different parts of my body. Next they told me to lie on the ground and stretch my limbs, and then they started jumping on my hands and legs. I lost consciousness. When I woke up they tied my hands behind my back, blindfolded me and told me that they will now kill me and asked if I have anything to say. Then they placed two guns at the two sides of my head and shot but the guns were not loaded. Then they pushed me down the hill. I think I fell some six or eight metres. My body was all blue and I could not move due to the pain. Laughing, they took me up once more and pushed me down again and again. At the end of that day I could not walk. They carried me to the hut and asked me how much money I am willing to give. They demanded 50,000 rupees. I told them I don't have it. So they told me they are writing down 25,000 and if I will not give them the money they will kill me. As I was unable to walk, the Maoists called a few people from my village, eight hours walk away, to come and carry me home. The next morning after arriving home I was carried away for medical treatment in the district headquarters. My family joined me after a week. We never went back to the village. Most people stayed in the village, they have nowhere to go. They stay and pay or are punished. If people wish to go to work abroad and want their family to stay in the village they first have to pay one lakh rupees (100,000) to the Maoists as tax.

It seems that almost any public disapproval or expression of dissatisfaction with the situation under the Maoist rule results in an incident that leads to the displacement of an individual or a family. Thus Maheswor Paudel (40), a father of seven, was threatened due to his enforced political activity in elections organized by the Maoists:

The Maoists punish everyone who makes mistakes. For example, if one drinks they may stitch part of his mouth, if someone gambles and plays cards, they will cut his hands. I also made a mistake. The Maoists decided to make our VDC a model VDC and so one day they announced elections and said these would be free. They had their own candidates and they made it compulsory for all former remaining supporters of various political parties to participate. The main political leaders were already out of the village. They also made room for two people to stand as opposition candidates. Indeed the elections were free, without guns. Participation was compulsory: women who had just given birth had to come and old people who could not walk were carried to give their vote. In this way 84 per cent of the people participated in the polls. The outcome was that the parties and the Maoists lost, while a large majority gave their votes to the opposition candidates. After the elections the winning candidates were beaten and had to leave their village with their families, one of them is now in India. Two other people were blamed for helping the winning candidates and had to leave as well. I was one of them.

### 3. LEAVING HOME AND COUNTRY

Hitherto, we have examined conflict-induced *internal* displacement. We now turn to look more closely at *external* displacement, which today mainly involves youths and young people who cross the border into India. Temporary (lasting several months or years) and seasonal migration from rural Nepal to India in pursuit of work was already known to exist in the nineteenth century and possibly even earlier. Particularly during the early stages of the conflict, whole families crossed the border to India. Relatively few had the means to build a house and settle there, yet even this was sufficient for creating a significant rise in the prices of land as reported in certain north Indian localities.[58] Otherwise, many poor families crossed the border with little idea of where they were going to or how they would survive.[59] These first-time migrants probably still constitute the most vulnerable group of Nepalese migrants in India.[60]

About three and a half years ago, the Maoists launched a conscription campaign in the regions under their control, forcing one person from each family to join their militia, thus creating a gradual but mammoth wave of rural exodus and migration, particularly into India. One survey found that the conflict has led to a three to four-fold increase in the numbers of youths and men crossing the border into India.[61] At times, these numbers may have been much higher, for example when a particular locality was threatened by Maoist retribution following the activity of the (government sanctioned) village defence committees.[62] In many areas of rural Nepal, villages are left with only women, young children and the elderly to maintain the houses, cultivate the fields and face the wrath of the war. Although it is mainly young men, often from a low economic and educational background, who flee into India to avoid forced conscription, there are quite a few young women who run away for similar reasons or are forced to leave due to the breakdown of the rural economy. However, most of them appear to remain in Nepal, working in the eateries of its flourishing border towns, or are lured by the (dubious) opportunities offered by the singing and dancing clubs in the cities.[63]

Migrants to India currently make up the largest group of displaced Nepalese. Concentrated mainly in north India, they are usually found working in manual and usually low paid jobs, including agriculture, factories, restaurants and the like. Young, lone migrants to India may be economically better off than many of their counterparts living in Nepal due to the flourishing Indian economy, though many testify that they are hardly able to earn a living. They often feel safer, being further away from either the Maoists or the armed state forces. Yet, unlike internally displaced people (IDP) the prominent Nepalese physical attributes easily expose the origin of many of the migrants to India. Moreover, many of them tend to work and live together thus creating small but prominent enclaves of Nepalese. This clearly makes them vulnerable to further extortion by Nepalese Maoists active in India as well as harassment by Indian criminals and the Indian police.

## 4. INVISIBLE AND NEGLECTED

One of the hardest aspects particularly of internal displacement, which considerably contributes to its invisibility, is the relentless fear the displaced seem unable to leave behind them even within the apparently safer urban setting. IDPs maintain a very low profile and attempt, as far as possible, to blend in unnoticed into existing urban communities. Relatively wealthy displaced people change their address and phone number frequently. Some rent their house in the city to others and move from one rented place to the other like many of their counterparts from less fortunate economic backgrounds. This fear and the resultant feelings of deep mutual mistrust cripple the development of social networks among the displaced and block almost all co-operation, joint economic ventures and mutual help. Their fears are not unfounded; in many cases the Maoists appear to go to great lengths to track down suspected informers and those who have failed to pay up. Maoist persecution of several individuals, such as the February 2002 murder of Ganesh Chilwala, the head of the Maoist victims association (Maobadi Pidit Sangh), which took place in Kathmandu in broad daylight, just two days after he led an anti-Maoist demonstration, was more than sufficient to cause panic and send waves of terror among the displaced hiding in urban centres.

The various difficulties, mental and physical adversities people face following their displacement are usually intense and long-lasting. Many face an uphill economic struggle as they try to find a secure source of income to meet their most basic human needs including accommodation, food, health and education.

This is doubly challenging due to age limitations and an obvious lack of transferable skills needed for city life. To add to this, it seems the memories that people carry with them from the village, particularly of the circumstances that led to their displacement, are equally tormenting. The mental scars of those who were physically tortured, became trapped in the cross-fire, were wounded or lost a close relative are hard to measure or even imagine. The humiliation that displaced life more often than not entails, the economic difficulties of urban survival and the constant fear the displaced must endure exacerbate the mental state of many, who suffer from depression and alcoholism.

Unfortunately, the Nepalese government's reaction to this humanitarian crisis has so far been wholly unsatisfactory. Although various aid programmes were announced from time to time, they failed to reach those most in need and were rather patchy. A recent report by the Norwegian Global IDP Project concludes that: 'since the beginning of the conflict, the government has to a large extent ignored its obligation to protect and assist IDPs. Its response can be described as inadequate, discriminatory and largely insufficient'.[64] In April 2005, the government still claimed the official number of IDPs nationwide was around 8,000 and only relatively recently have there been signs that it is finally beginning to recognise the gravity of the problem.[65]

The response of the international aid and development agencies to this unfolding humanitarian crisis has, with very few exceptions, been almost on a par with that of the government thus far. Most of them have only recently acknowledged the problem and now seem willing to address it, yet there has been little in the way of a coordinated, agreed strategy to deal with the plight of the displaced and it appears that the general international response leaves much to be desired. This comes despite the fact that the magnitude of the problem is clearly evident in many parts of rural Nepal (for example, the visible absence of men in many areas), and in spite of the assessments made by various international agencies, such as the Norwegian Refugee Council's April 2003 report entitled *Nepal: displaced and ignored*.[66] The report called for an urgent assessment-cum-response to the needs of vulnerable groups among the displaced.[67]

This situation may perhaps be partially explained by the fact that, notwithstanding many other reports suggesting the contrary, according to a rather late UN assessment (June 2004), the IDP situation did not merit special targeted programmes.[68] Moreover, the general approach recommended by the aforementioned report was to enhance the protection of civilians and place a greater focus on reducing the threats and abuses that give rise to displacement. Yet how can the protection of civilians be enhanced and threats and abuses be reduced in the reality of a Maoist-controlled rural Nepal? As was mentioned earlier, targeted individual assassinations by Maoists could not be averted in urban areas including the capital Kathmandu, which are the government's strongholds. Thus it seems totally unreasonable to assume that protection and security may be achieved elsewhere. The case studies presented earlier clearly demonstrate the futility of such an approach.

Discussions with INGO representatives revealed that at least a few donor agencies seem to believe that part of the problem may be solved via their current heavy investment in human rights seminars and related activities targeted at army and police personnel. However, even if the latter were persuaded by the enlightened, foreign moral advice, could put aside age-old practices and decide that not all means are appropriate to deal with what they perceive to be an acute national security concern, how could they translate this foreign wisdom into practice when their opponents do not seem to follow similar principles? In light of the previous analysis, it seems doubtful whether this educational approach may bear any fruits.

Two other, highly pertinent issues, which often arise in the context the general international agencies' response to the plight of the displaced people in Nepal, merit further discussion. The first is the aforementioned 'invisibility' of the displaced, while the second, related point concerns the differentiation between the IDPs and the 'ordinary' urban poor who would, no doubt, stand in the same queue for assistance. Unfortunately, the 'invisibility' of the displaced, a recurring theme in most reports ordered by international aid and donor agencies, seems to be a major inhibitive factor for the latter's actions. Yet, while the vast majority of the displaced are dispersed within the ordinary

urban population and cannot be distinguished from the outside,
they are well recognized within the locality that hosts them and
can be identified, located and reached, as indeed was done by a
small number of local and international NGOs.[69] Moreover,
although displaced Nepalese living in urban areas feel deeply
threatened, there is little doubt that those in need will be more
than willing to come forward if only they will see a tangible
opportunity to better their lot and will be assured of their personal
security.

Regarding the second issue, it seems highly questionable
whether the differentiation between the IDPs and the urban poor
is justified in view of the present situation. There is little doubt
that the influx of displaced people into what are often already
unstable socio-economic loci made both disadvantaged groups
compete for exhausted urban resources. Hence the urban poor
should be regarded as being seriously, if indirectly, affected by
the conflict and thus in genuine need of help. Discriminating
against these groups is neither justified nor moral. Of course,
for various other reasons, such as the provision of post-traumatic
psychological assistance, the displaced need to be specifically
identified and in a majority of cases this seems possible via various
governmental channels.

Another major issue that was high on the list of international
donors' concerns, particularly during the earlier stages of the
conflict, was how to avoid creating pull-factors that would
otherwise foster displacement and result in the establishment of
IDP camps. The likelihood of the latter, as previous analysis
clearly demonstrates, is not high as most displaced individuals
and families would do almost anything to avoid living in
designated areas which would form easy targets for Maoist
retribution. Those displaced due to the actions of state security
forces are even less likely to expose themselves and hence it
should be concluded that the nature of internal displacement in
Nepal makes the possibility that aid would promote the creation
of camps unlikely. But could the provision of assistance to
displaced people encourage others to move out of rural areas
and become 'displaced' as well? Can a massive international aid
campaign for displaced people create an even bigger wave of

rural exodus? This is an apparently plausible scenario. However, I wish to recall the degree of suffering and risk which many Nepalese would often be willing to endure before making what is the very difficult, often delayed decision to leave their village homes. Displacement in itself is usually traumatic enough and the prospects of life as a displaced individual or family are so bleak that most people attempt to avoid and delay it as much as possible. Nonetheless, those who already have nothing left may indeed choose to be rehabilitated elsewhere in Nepal rather than join the multitudes of migrant Nepalese in India. Whether a reduction in the exodus to India is indeed a preferred scenario is obviously open for debate, yet I believe that it is certainly better, not only for the future of the individuals concerned but for Nepalese society as a whole.

Statements like: 'So far, the international community at large has preferred to adopt a development-oriented [rather than humanitarian provision focus] approach to avoid undermining the population's coping mechanisms', which attempt to sum-marite the international assistance agenda to Nepalese IDPs, are alarming for two reasons.[70] First, this implies a perceived necessity to choose between either a development or a humanitarian-oriented approach, and the assumed inability to develop a tailored agenda for tackling the unique circumstances of Nepal's IDPs. Secondly, it alludes to what seems like a largely myopic per-ception, namely, the view that 'the population's coping mechanisms' in Nepal, one of the poorest countries in South Asia, were at some point deemed appropriate and capable of dealing with mass internal migration.[71] Addressing the state of 'coping mechanisms' in Nepalese society, Professor Kälin, the UN Secretary-General's special representative on the Human Rights of the IDPs observed that these appear to be near exhaustion.[72] There is no doubt that the unique situation of IDPs in Nepal poses a major challenge for international donor and aid agencies. Yet the recent attention paid to the displacement crisis provides a measure of hope that at least some assistance will be provided to IDPs in Nepal sooner rather than later.

However, this is not the case for the majority of externally displaced Nepalese who have crossed the border into India. The majority of these, whose number are believed to be in the millions, represent the lower economic strata of the displaced, and many of them are very young, which makes them easy targets for exploitation and abuse. One reason for the scant international attention these migrant Nepalese have attracted is the fact that, like their counterparts in Nepal, they also tend not to establish 'camps'. Another major issue revolves around the question of whether these are conflict-affected or simply seasonal-economic migrants, as was the case in previous generations, and how if at all is it possible to differentiate between the two. The report of the Norwegian Refugee Council (September 2004) mentions that it would be difficult to attribute more than a proportion of the accelerating rural exodus over the last five years directly to the conflict. There is little doubt that such queries and the difficulties they raise have been inhibiting factors to the international response to the displacement crisis. Yet, as Rai recently argues: 'In a time when Nepal has been through nine years of conflict and is continuing to do so, who is not conflict affected?'[73] Moreover, for aid provision purposes, it seems irrelevant whether a family leaves its village home as a result of acute food shortage resulting from the government's cut in food supply to Maoist controlled areas, due to the breakdown of the local economy, for fear of Maoist retribution, or following the torture of a family member by either side in the conflict. Urgent assistance for all displaced people from village Nepal is needed, irrespective of the exact circumstances of their migration.

The fact that Nepalese migrants to India do not conveniently fit into existing categories and international definitions further explain the lack of attention they receive from international agencies. First, being Nepalese who have crossed the border to India, it is perhaps unclear whether it is INGOs working in Nepal or India who may be in a position to assist them. Secondly, many of these migrants cannot be classified as either IDPs or refugees, further complicating their position.

According to the UN definition: 'IDPs are persons or groups of persons who have been forced or obliged to flee or to leave their homes or places of habitual residence, in particular as a result of or in order to avoid the effects of armed conflict, situations of generalized violence, violations of human rights or natural or human-made disasters, and who have not crossed an internationally recognized state border.'[74] This definition obviously leaves out the majority of displaced Nepalese who fled the insurgency to India, since they are not *internally* displaced. Neither can the majority of them be regarded as refugees as is evident from the 1951 Convention relating to the Status of Refugees, which defines a refugee as a person who: 'Owing to a well-founded fear of being persecuted for reasons of race, religion, nationality, membership of a particular social group, or political opinion, is outside the country of his nationality, and is unable to or, owing to such fear, is unwilling to avail himself of the protection of that country . . . ' since those who migrated as a result of Maoist actions are theoretically able to return to (urban) Nepal to seek the 'protection of the Nepalese government'.[75] Those who have fled due to the actions of the state would of course qualify for refugee status.

The question of definition would remain an academic one were it not for the fact that the allocation of international resources is considerably influenced by Western public opinion and institutional policies, within which the 'IDP' and 'refugee' buzzwords carry special merit. The above discussion makes the case for moving away from formal definitions and focusing international effort on assessing, addressing and alleviating the suffering of all of these 'invisible' migrants.

The recently signed peace agreement may theoretically signal a foreseeable end to the IDP problem, yet not only have the Maoists' sporadic invitations for people to return to their villages proved rather hollow so far,[76] but even if allowed to go back safely, most people have little to come back to in terms of housing and sources of subsistence. Most unfortunately, despite a number of declarations to the contrary, both sides in the conflict have paid only scant attention to the IDP crisis, as is well reflected in the recent agreements between the govenment and the Maoists. Since any fundamental future rural transformation and development will largely depend on bringing rural Nepal back to life and resettling the millions who were forced to flee their homes, an urgent international and national response is essential, if peace is to prevail in this former Shangri-La.

## NOTES

1. Yet clashes with members of political parties and the police in far western Nepal as well as attacks on individuals began a few months earlier.
2. For the full list of demands see for example Thapa (2003: 391–5).
3. Mercy Corps International. 2003. Sowing the Wind . . . History and Dynamics of the Maoist Revolt in Nepal's Rapti Hills, p. 79 (by Robert Gersony).
4. See Gambetta (1993).
5. The Maoists assassinated the head of Nepalese police, his wife and bodyguard in Kathmandu in January 2003.
6. INSEC (Informal Sector Service Center) Kathmandu, personal communication.
7. Norwegian Refugee Council. July 2005. Nepal: Displacement Crisis Worsens in Wake of Royal Coup. Global IDP Project, p. 1.
8. According to *World Report 2006*, Human Rights Watch, Washington, reported in the *Kathmandu Post*, 19 January 2006.
9. S. Bezruchka, 2006. A Healthy Nepal, Health Care is Not What Makes People Healthy, *Nepali Times*, 280, 6–12 January 2006.
10. DFID, GTZ and SDC (2003), *Conflict and Health in Nepal: Action for Peace-Building* (by O. Delfabbro, J. Pettigrew and M. Sharma).
11. On the adverse consequences of the conflict on Nepalese health services see also IRIN December 2005, *Between Two Stones—Nepal's Decade of Conflict*, Web Special, OCHA, UN, pp. 9–10.
12. National Planning Commission June 2005. *An Assessment of the Implementation of the Tenth Plan (PRSP). Second Progress Report, On the Road to Freedom from Poverty.* Kathmandu: Singha Durbar.
13. As Yuba-Raj Kumar (23, born in a village in Dang, western Nepal, and currently studying in Kathmandu) put it during a discussion: 'If I have a mobile phone, I feel I am fully developed'.
14. The education system is supposedly free yet involves various expenses that the poorest cannot afford.
15. Only about 75 per cent of primary school aged children are enrolled in school while only 44 per cent of those who begin grade one reach grade five (Norwegian Refugee Council, September 2004, *Profile of Internal Displacement: Nepal*, Global IDP Database, p. 91).
16. Whelpton (2005: 227).
17. These had escalated in Nepal in the late 1980s and were further raised following the success of the democracy movement in 1990.
18. Norwegian Refugee Council, September 2004, *Profile of Internal Displacement: Nepal*, Global IDP Database, p. 91.
19. KOL (Kantipur On Line) report, 14 June 2005. <http://www.kantipuronline.com/kolnews.php?&nid=42820>.

20. In one school for example, 14 teachers were in charge of 1400 students (Norwegian Refugee Council, September 2004, *Profile of Internal Displacement: Nepal*, Global IDP Database, p. 90).

21. On the consequences of the conflict on the education system see also IRIN, December 2005, *Between Two Stones—Nepal's Decade of Conflict*, Web Special, OCHA, UN, pp. 10–11.

22. ODI, December 2002, *The Consequences of Conflict: Livelihoods and Development in Nepal*. Working Paper 185 (by D. Seddon and K. Hussein).

23. Norwegian Refugee Council, September 2004, *Profile of Internal Displacement: Nepal*, Global IDP Database, p. 60.

24. The sustainability of this boom is however open for debate, particularly since it involves very little industrialization.

25. ODI, December 2002, *The Consequences of Conflict: Livelihoods and Development in Nepal*. Working Paper 185, pp. 31-2.

26. An interview with Marc Mangin, First Secretary (development) in the Canadian embassy in Kathmandu, published in the *Nepali Times*, 20-6 January 2006, p. 5. See also the comprehensive report on the suspension of aid in rural Nepal in Norwegian Refugee Council, September 2004, *Profile of Internal Displacement: Nepal*, Global IDP Database, pp. 108–12.

27. The World Bank, January 2004, Social Development Notes, Conflict Prevention and Reconstruction, no. 15, pp. 1-2. The above is a summary of DFID'S 2003 REPORT: *Social Change in Conflict Affected Areas: Assessment Report*.

28. See for example, Thapa and Sijapati (2003: 160–1).

29. Samanata (Institute for Social & Gender Equality), 2005, *A National Study on Changing Roles of Nepali Women due to Ongoing Conflict and its Impact*, Samanata Studies no. 6 (by A.R. Deuba), pp. 27–9.

30. Fieldwork conducted by the author during 1995-7.

31. Centre for Human Rights and Global Justice, 2005, *The Missing Piece of the Puzzle, Caste Discrimination and the Conflict in Nepal*, pp. 34–5.

32. Ibid., pp. 38–9.

33. Cited in Thapa and Sijapati (2003: 162).

34. Save the Children USA, 2005, *The Movement of Women—Migration, Trafficking, and Prostitution in the Context of Nepal's Armed Conflict* (by S.L. Hausner).

35. The World Bank, January 2004, *Social Development Notes*, no. 15, p. 1.

36. Ibid., p. 16.

37. Ibid., p. 3.

38. Center for Human Rights and Global Justice, 2005, *The Missing Piece of the Puzzle, Caste Discrimination and the Conflict in Nepal*, p. 37.

39. Ibid., pp. 34–5.

40. Shyam Bhattam Samay 19 January 2005, the *Nepali Times*, 20–26 January 2006.
41. Magar (2004: 95).
42. ICG, October 2005, *Nepal Maoists: Their Aims, Structure and Strategy*, Asia Report no. 104, p. 15.
43. DFID, August 2003, *Social Change in Conflict Affected Areas: Assessment Report*, pp. 23–4.
44. Center for Human Rights and Global Justice, 2005, *The Missing Piece of the Puzzle, Caste Discrimination and the Conflict in Nepal*, p. 38.
45. Biswokarma (2004).
46. Center for Human Rights and Global Justice, 2005, *The Missing Piece of the Puzzle, Caste Discrimination and the Conflict in Nepal*, p. 32.
47. DFID, August 2003, *Social Change in Conflict Affected Areas: Assessment Report*, pp. 24–8.
48. Shrestha (2004).
49. Puran P. Bista, Conflict and Ethnicity, *The Kathmandu Post*, 11 January 2005.
50. ODI, December 2002, *The Consequences of Conflict: Livelihoods and Development in Nepal*, Working Paper 185, pp. 21, 31.
51. Interview with Shailendra Guragain, CVICT Director of Operations, Kathmandu, 13 December 2005.
52. See for example, Norwegian Refugee Council, September 2004, *Profile of Internal Displacement: Nepal*, Global IDP Project, Global IDP Database.
53. Norwegian Refugee Council, July 2005, *Nepal: Displacement Crisis Worsens in Wake of Royal Coup*. Global IDP Project, pp. 5–6.
54. All identifying details in the case studies mentioned in this paper have been altered.
55. That the case studies presented herein do not include accounts of state-induced displacement should not be taken as indicative of their relative incidence within the total number of displaced Nepalese. There is currently no estimate of the numbers of state-induced displacement.
56. Martinez (2002: 8), Norwegian Refugee Council, July 2005, p. 5.
57. Martinez (2002: 12).
58. *The Kathmandu Post*, 11 April 2005.
59. *The Nepali Times*, Issue 123, January 2002.
60. Norwegian Refugee Council, September 2004, p. 45.
61. Ibid.
62. Such was the case during March 2005, when following violence between Maoist and vigilante groups in Kapilvastu, some 30,000 people crossed the border into India. T.P. Pokharel, 'Displaced Families, Children languish in India. KOL, 19.3.05. <http://www.kantipuronline.com/kolnews.php?&nid=34815>
63. A recent report found that women rarely cross the border to India

unaccompanied, and most plan to join their husbands or other male relatives already there. Save the Children USA, 2005, *The Movement of Women—Migration, Trafficking, and Prostitution in the Context of Nepal's Armed Conflict* (by Sondra L. Hausner), p. 61.

64. Norwegian Refugee Council, July 2005, *Nepal: Displacement Crisis Worsens in Wake of Royal Coup*, Global IDP Project, p. 8.

65. According to Professor Kälin, the Representative of the UN Secretary-General on the Human Rights of IDPs, *The IDPs are Overlooked and Neglected*, Press Conference given on 22 April 2005.

66. By Fredrick Kok.

67. See also: INSEC, March 2003, *Idea Paper on Internally Displaced Persons*; GTZ, INF, SNV, UNDP/RUPP, March 2003, *Nepal IDP Research Initiative Findings*; Norwegian Refugee Council, September 2004; IDD, April 2005, *Report on the Inter-Agency Internal Displacement Division (IDD) Mission to Nepal*; Terre des Hommes, September 2005, *Nutritional Status of Children Victims of the Armed Conflict in Nepal, a Survey Report of IDP Children in Banke District.*

68. OCHA, June 2004, Report to IDP mission to Nepal.

69. SAFHR, March 2005, *A Pilot Survey on Internally Displaced Persons in Kathmandu and Birendranagar* (by D.R. Rai), p. 42.

70. Profile of Internal Displacement: Nepal, Global IDP Database, September 2004, p. 126.

71. Ibid.

72. Press conference, 22 April 2005.

73. SAFHR, March 2005, *A Pilot Survey on Internally Displaced Persons in Kathmandu and Birendranagar*, p. 35.

74. http://www.reliefweb.int/ocha_ol/pub/idp_gp/idp.html

75. http://www.unhcr.ch/cgi-bin/texis/vtx/basics
opendoc.htm?tbl=BASICS&id=3b0280294

76. See, for example, *The Kathmandu Post*, 16 and 27 June 2006.

## SELECT BIBLIOGRAPHY

Biswokarma, B., 2004, 'Dalits and the Conflict', in *People in the 'People's War'*, Center for Investigative Journalism, Himal Association, Lalitpur: Himal Books.

Center for Human Rights and Global Justice, 2005, *The Missing Piece of the Puzzle, Caste Discrimination and the Conflict in Nepal*, New York University, School of Law (by R. Goyal, P. Dhawan and S. Narula).

DFID (UK Department for International Development, Nepal), August 2003, *Social Change in Conflict Affected Areas: Assessment Report* (by M.S. Lama-Tamang, S.M. Gurung, D. Swarnakar and S.R. Magar).

DFID, GTZ and SDC (2003), *Conflict and Health in Nepal: Action for Peace-Building* (by O. Delfabbro, J. Pettigrew and M. Sharma).

Gambetta, D., 1993, *The Sicilian Mafia: The Business of Private Protection*, Cambridge: Harvard University Press.

GTZ, INF, SNV, UNDP/RUPP, March 2003, Nepal IDP Research Initiative Findings, An Initiative of Concerned Agencies in Nepal, GTZ, INF, SNV, UNDP/RUPP in Co-operation with NHRC and the Global IDP Project.

ICG (International Crisis Group), October 2005, *Nepal Maoists: Their Aims, Structure and Strategy*, Asia Report no. 104. Kathmandu/ Brussels: ICG.

IDD, April 2005, *Report on the Inter-Agency Internal Displacement Division (IDD) Mission to Nepal (11-22 April 2005)*.

INSEC, March 2003, *Idea Paper on Internally Displaced Persons* (by S.R. Pyakurel), Kathmandu: INSEC.

IRIN, December 2005, *Between Two Stones – Nepal's Decade of Conflict*, Web Special, OCHA, UN. <http://www.irinnews.org/webspecials/nepal/ nepal-webspecial.pdf>

KOL (Kantipur On Line) report, 14 June 2005, http://www. kantipuronline.com/kolnews.php?&nid=42820.

Magar, U., 2004, Financing the 'People's War', in *People in the 'People's War'*. Center for Investigative Journalism, Himal Association, Lalitpur: Himal Books.

Martinez, E., July 2002, *Conflict-Related Displacement, Nepal*.

Mercy Corps International, 2003, Sowing the Wind . . . History and Dynamics of the Maoist Revolt in Nepal's Rapti Hills (by Robert Gersony).

National Planning Commission, June 2005, *An Assessment of the Implementation of the Tenth Plan (PRSP). Second Progress Report, on the Road to Freedom From Poverty*, Kathmandu: National Planning Commission.

Norwegian Refugee Council, April 2003, *Nepal: Displaced and Ignored* (By Fredrik Kok), Geneva: Norwegian Refugee Council.

_____, September 2004, *Profile of Internal Displacement: Nepal*, Global IDP Project, Global IDP Database.

_____, July 2005, *Nepal: Displacement Crisis Worsens in Wake of Royal Coup*, Global IDP Project.

OCHA, June 2004, Report to OCHA/IDP mission to Nepal, Kathmandu: OCHA.

ODI (Overseas Development Institute), December 2002, *The Consequences of Conflict: Livelihoods and Development in Nepal*, Working Paper 185 (by D. Seddon and K. Hussein), London: ODI.

Pigg, S.L., 1992, 'Inventing social categories through place: social representations and development in Nepal', in *Comparative Studies in Society and History*, vol. 34 (3), pp. 491–513.

Samanata (Institute for Social & Gender Equality), 2005, *A National Study on Changing Roles of Nepali Women due to Ongoing Conflict and its Impact*, Samanata Studies no. 6 (by A.R. Deoba), Kathmandu: Samanata.

Save the Children USA, 2005, *The Movement of Women—Migration, Trafficking, and Prostitution in the Context of Nepal's Armed Conflict* (by Sondra L. Hausner), Kathmandu: Save the Children USA.

Shrestha, D.K., 2004, in *People in the 'People's War'*. Center for Investigative Journalism, Himal Association, Lalitpur: Himal Books.

SAFHR (South Asia Forum for Human Rights), March 2005, *A Pilot Survey on Internally Displaced Persons in Kathmandu and Birendranagar* (by D.R. Rai), Kathmandu: SAFHR.

Terre des Hommes Nepal, September 2005, *Nutritional Status of Children Victims of the Armed Conflict in Nepal, a Survey Report of IDP Children in Banke District*, Lalitpur: Terre des Hommes.

Thapa, D. (ed.), 2003, *Understanding the Maoist Movement in Nepal*, Chautari Book Series 10, Kathmandu: Martin Chautari.

Thapa, D. and B. Sijapati, 2003, *A Kingdom Under Siege, Nepal's Maoist Insurgency, 1996 to 2003*, Kathmandu: The Printhouse.

The World Bank, January 2004, *Social Development Notes, Conflict Prevention and Reconstruction*, no. 15.

Whelpton, J., 2005, *A History of Nepal*, Cambridge: Cambridge University Press.

# CHAPTER 9

# Nation-Building Process in Bhutan

## Rajesh Kharat

The post-Cold War period, dominated by an era of globalization, had a direct impact on the countries of the Third World, especially South Asia where the socio-economic and political situation is deteriorating day by day. For example, Bhutan and Nepal, the only surviving monarchies in the region, are suffering from the problems of dissidents, secessionist movements, ethnic crisis, cross-border terrorism, insurgencies, and a series of human rights violations. In response to this, militarily weak countries like Bhutan are incapable of defending themselves on their own as these states are backward and exposed to enormous threats from many directions such as socio-political instability, under-development, corruption, and vulnerable geostrategic locations. As a result, these states are still in the process of a resurgence of nation-building activities.

However, one cannot also overlook the efforts made by the Himalayan kingdom of Bhutan at the institutional level in nation-building. To mention a few here, the country took the decision of devolving political power to avoid any fragmentation or threat to nation-building. Bhutan introduced a constitutional monarchy recently, in 1998.

In view of this background, this chapter seeks to examine the existing mechanism to protect the nationhood of Bhutan and also to discover what the challenges there are to its nation-building process. For instance, in Bhutan the problem of ethnicity between Drukpa Bhutanese and Bhutanese of Nepali origin is still not resolved, and as a result, for the last two decades these societies have remained divided making Bhutan one country with two nations, at least ideologically. Thus, it appears that despite the efforts made by the government, the process of establishing a national cohesion and identity is, (a) far from being completed, (b) the unity of the nation will remain fragile, and (c) the process is not only not linear but apparently even reversible.

## I. GOVERNING INSTITUTIONS IN BHUTAN

### 1. THE MONARCHY

In Bhutan, up to 1952, the institution of absolute hereditary monarchy not only centralized power and integrated all the other areas of administration but also represented the highest court of appeal and controls in both religious and spiritual matters. Since 1952, under the guidance of King Jigme Dorji Wangchuk, 'Bhutan moved towards a new direction of a more liberal and modern administrative system, seeking recognition as a sovereign independent country, with its own distinct identity and culture'.[1] He introduced liberal trends and many reforms in the economic and social fields for the development of the country. At the same time, the king treated with respect the feelings of the traditionalists in Bhutan, as total neglect of the traditions and customs would have resulted in the people being attracted to and being influenced by alien ideas and cultures. Thus the institution of monarchy introduced major changes in the political as well as economic field similar to those of its friendly neighbour, India. For instance, whereas the head of state is the king of Bhutan, the head of state in India is the president. India has a prime minister, so Bhutan created an analogous position to correspond with its Indian counterpart in bilateral dealings.[2] However, the title of prime minister was not officially conferred on either Jigme Dorji or Lhendup Dorji. According to B.S. Das (who served as Indian ambassador to Bhutan), a deliberate decision was taken to combine the offices of the head of government and state, preventing parallel seats of power from emerging.[3]

Despite these efforts, there were two major incidents which have challenged the process of nation-building in Bhutan when the Royal Government of Bhutan (RGB) was in its infancy period of political and economic development. First, the assassination of a Tibetan origin prime minister, Jigme Paldan Dorji, in April

1964, resulted in a crisis within the government and posed a possible threat of civil war.[4] Secondly, an attempt was made on the life of Jigme Dorji Wangchuk himself in July 1965. According to Nari Rustomji, then Indian adviser to the Royal Government of Bhutan, the reasons for the assassination of J.P. Dorji could be Dorji's constant support for Indo-Bhutan friendship and Bhutan's alignment with India.[5] He, in addition, ignored the institution of traditional groups, especially that of the Buddhist lamas, while introducing development in Bhutan. To quote Rustomji again: 'Apart from the threat to religion, the lamas apprehended that their own influence and hold over the people would be undermined by changes they saw looming ahead.'[6]

This apprehension among the Bhutanese was based on a strong feeling that the Indians might be behind the murder, particularly Nari Rustomji himself.[7] Hence, after the completion of his term, the post of Indian adviser was abolished. To fill the vacuum caused by the abolition of this post the monarch decided to establish a Royal Advisory Council in 1965 in which he gave representation to the Buddhist lamas in the decision-making process of Bhutan's internal as well as external affairs. Two members are nominated from the clergy to the council. Thus the monarch himself decided to involve the monks in development programmes and to make them aware of the importance of the latter for the country's development and new image.[8] Moreover, on 13 November 1968, in the National Assembly the king of Bhutan expressed his desire, 'to form a government combining the monarchical and democratic systems in order to ensure the stability and solidarity of the country'.[9] Since then the *Druk Gyalpo* has taken advice from the National Assembly and the Royal Advisory Council in running the affairs of state. So the institution of monarchy though it appears to be absolute is limited by the institutional arrangements whereby the king is to function according to the advice given by these councils. By this resolution, the members of the National Assembly can impeach the king in the national interest. However, most of the members did not support this idea and it remained merely an announcement. This change in the political system of Bhutan from absolute to constitutional monarchy was aimed at giving the people a decisive voice in the country's affairs.[10] This devolution of power can be

seen in the efforts made by the king to counter the various un-
happy developments that have threatened the nation-building
process in the kingdom.

## 2. *TSHOGDU* (THE NATIONAL ASSEMBLY OF BHUTAN)

The idea of *Tshogdu* or a national assembly was conceived by
King Jigme Dorji Wangchuk in 1952 on his accession to the
throne,[11] because he realized that for the rapid progress of
the country all sections of the people must participate in the
deliberations on national issues and must advise on the formulation of any policies that would have an impact on the country
and the people of Bhutan.

The National Assembly comprises three categories of members;
the People's Representatives who are directly elected by the people
of their respective constituencies through consensus or by secret
ballot.[12] They occupy 70 per cent of the seats in the Assembly;
the Monastic Representatives who are nominated to the Assembly
by the *Dratshang* (Central Monastic Bodies) located in the main
*dzongs*, i.e. the headquarters of the main districts of the country;[13]
and the Official Representatives who are mainly government
officials nominated by the king. They include ministers, members
of the Royal Advisory Council, senior civil servants, judges of
each *dzong* area and subdivisional revenue officers.[14]

The Speaker and the Deputy Speaker are elected by the
National Assembly from amongst its members. The National
Assembly plays a very important role and works at three levels:
it enacts laws, approves senior appointments to the government,
and advises on all matters of national importance. Practically
speaking, the *Tshogdu* performs legislative functions and also
acts as an advisory body. Decisions are passed by a simple
majority. A secret ballot is taken on all matters of national
importance. Any Bhutanese citizen above the age of 25 can be
a candidate for membership of the National Assembly.[15]

According to official documents and records as well as the
resolutions passed at the various sessions, political power is
decentralized and the king of Bhutan appears reduced to being a
mere constitutional monarch for good governance. But in reality,
the National Assembly can be considered a quasi-final authority

in the decision-making process as its members are mostly nominated and not directly elected by the people as in other countries on the subcontinent. They are dependent on the monarchy rather than the people for their survival due to the absence of other organs of democracy like political parties and pressure groups. Thus the *Tshogdu* simultaneously embodies the principles of democracy and monarchy.

Till 1968, to become law, the approval of the king was mandatory for all legislative bills passed by the National Assembly as the king had veto power over an issue or bill. This he surrendered voluntarily at the autumn session of 1968. At the same time, he expressed his desire for a stable government to maintain the future peace and tranquillity of the country, and to safeguard it from any threats, internal as well as external. The king introduced this clause because Bhutan has a hereditary monarchy and in turbulent times there could emerge a passionate feeling for a radical change.

In his speech in the National Assembly at the spring session of 1969, the king observed,

Rebellion will only bring disaster and disgrace to the country accompanied by loss of lives and chaos which will be exploited by outsiders to the detriment of the country. In case of misunderstanding between the king and the people, or if the king resorts to repression, the people, instead of rebelling, should convene the National Assembly.

He added,

I did not say that the system of hereditary monarchy should be abolished. My intention was to empower the National Assembly to change by peaceful means any king, including myself who is found unfit to rule the country.[16]

Finally, in order to ensure the stability and solidarity of the country and to form a government combining the monarchical and democratic principles, the National Assembly unanimously decided that the system of hereditary monarchy should depend on popular approval. Under this act, the reigning monarch is obliged to abdicate if two-thirds of the Assembly's membership supports a vote of no-confidence in his conduct of affairs.[17]

However, the 1973 spring session of the Assembly took the decision to abolish the system of expressing confidence in the king,[18] because the National Assembly felt that since Bhutan was a small and landlocked country, undesirable elements, both within and outside the country, could use this system to destabilize the country to further their own evil designs.

After studying all of Bhutan's reforms one can say that as a part of the nation-building process, the hereditary monarchy was transformed into a constitutional monarchy, which has had the effect of liberalizing the political system of Bhutan in modern times.

It should be noted that the National Assembly has been playing an important role in the nation-building process. For instance, in July 1979, on the issue of Tibetan refugees, it recommended to the king that 'all Tibetans refusing to accept Bhutanese nationality should be sent back to Tibet'.[19] More recently it resolved that boundary talks with China should be continued in order to maintain the current cordial relations with China.[20] The National Assembly has also banned the employment of Nepalese nationals in government and private organizations.[21] This action was taken in view of the recent ethnic problems and to avoid adverse developments in future. At the same time, the National Assembly has urged the Bhutanese government to negotiate with Nepal regarding the settlement of the question of the *ngolops* in Bhutan.[22] These instances illustrate the active role in the nation-building process played by the National Assembly.

## 3. THE ROYAL ADVISORY COUNCIL

The Royal Advisory Council, or *Lodoi Tsokde*, was established by the king in 1965. The Royal Council is the main advisory organ of the state. It is just like a cabinet. Its main function is to render advice to the king whenever it is sought and also to his Council of Ministers on all matters of national importance, especially foreign affairs. It also offers advice on domestic issues to promote the welfare of the people and to safeguard the interests of the kingdom, to develop friendly and harmonious relations between the government and the people. In addition to this, it makes its advice available to ensure that the laws and resolutions passed by the National Assembly are faithfully implemented by the government and generally followed by the people.[23] In 1975, the membership of the Council was increased from nine to ten. Two members represent the monks, five members represent the people of the various regions, the Nepali-origin Bhutanese community and the women are represented by one member each, and the tenth member is appointed by the government as the chairman.[24]

With regard to the Royal Advisory Council, a major event took place in 1984, when King Jigme Singye Wangchuk further strengthened its role. Although the Council had the authority to advise the king and to watch over the performance of the government, His Majesty felt that it lacked the necessary clout to carry out its responsibilities. Therefore a revised set of rules and regulations for the functions and the responsibilities of the Royal Council was formulated by the king. The important new clause states that:

[I]f any person, including His Majesty the King, does anything harmful to the interest of the Kingdom and the people, the Royal Advisory Council, without suppressing such matters and free of fear from any quarter shall bring it to the attention of His Majesty the King and, if necessary, even report it to the cabinet and the National Assembly.[25]

Although the king of Bhutan incorporated this clause in the revised rules of the Royal Council, the National Assembly took objection to it. The Assembly felt that it was a gross violation of traditional values and that it undermined the sacred principles of unflinching loyalty to the throne. However, the king explained that the real purpose was to inculcate a sense of responsibility in the future rulers of the nation and to commit them to certain accepted norms of behaviour. In a way, the clause was to act as a check on any unscrupulous behaviour of the monarchs. It removed the dangers of too much power being concentrated in the hands of the ruler. A harmonious linkage was thus established between legal opinion and public opinion.

## 4. COUNCIL OF MINISTERS

The National Assembly of Bhutan took a major step when the Council of Ministers was formed on 16 May 1968, with only four portfolios, namely, home affairs, finance and trade, industry, and development. However, three additional departments, namely, the ministries of communication, tourism, and foreign affairs, were added in 1973.[26] In the absence of the institution of prime minister, the king himself discharged the functions of the head of the government as well as head of state until June 1998. It was during the 76th session of the National Assembly that the king introduced profound changes. And through an unprecedented royal edict he called for greater people's participation in the decision-making process and devolved full executive authority to an elected council of ministers.[27] The old cabinet was dissolved and the National Assembly elected six new cabinet ministers through secret ballot. With the same spirit of a royal edict, the National Assembly also adopted a mechanism to register a vote of confidence in HM, the King of Bhutan. The 77th session of the National Assembly in July 1999 also debated and endorsed the mechanism for a vote of confidence in the king. It is appropriate to mention here that the 81st session of the Assembly, during August 2003, elected an expanded council of ministers of 10 members thereby strengthening the government.[28]

The principle of collective responsibility has not yet been effectively introduced in the council of ministers as they are all responsible to the king in their individual capacity and serve at his pleasure. Although the position of the ministers is vulnerable and their appointment is at the discretion of the king and the National Assembly, they do exercise a moderate amount of influence. They are responsible for the implementation of policy and as such play some role in the decision-making process. The *Druk Gyalpo* is thus dependent upon the ministers for effective administration and advice on policies and programmes, and also for the implementation of policy decisions.

## 5. TOWARDS CONSTITUTIONAL DEMOCRATIC GOVERNMENT

HM the King of Bhutan announced in December 2005, that he had offered to step down in 2008 and hold the country's first election for a parliamentary democracy after the completion of 100 years of absolute hereditary monarchy (1907–2007). This decision was not taken in haste, but as a result of a gradual process of introducing political reforms started by HM Jigme Dorji Wangchuk, father of the present King of Bhutan.

In 2000, the king emphasized the need for good governance to provide useful services to the people through decentralization and people's participation in the decision making process, with a compact, efficient, transparent and accountable civil service.[29] To do so, he formed a 25-member Special Task Force to review, rationalize and recommend ways to further strengthen the government's structures and functions based on the three pillars of good governance: efficiency, accountability and transparency.[30] In continuation of the devolution of political power, thus the RGB decided to formulate the ninth Five Year Plan which is geog-based. New ordinances and legislation are being drafted to strengthen the judicial system. For instance, in order to strengthen the rule of law, it has submitted the Bill for Civil and Criminal Procedure for approval by the National Assembly during its 79th Session in June 2001.[31] Besides, a Committee of Secretaries has been formed to enhance inter-ministerial coordination and co-operation in order to facilitate the development of the system of governance.

Another milestone in the process of political reforms and change was an announcement on 30 November 2001 by the king constituting a 39-members Constitution Drafting Committee. On this occasion, the Head of the Government expected that the

Constitution, being a supreme law should assimilate the salient features and the present and future functional principles of Bhutan. Moreover, provisions of organizations and governance as well as fundamental rights of the society should be incorporated in the Constitution.[32]

In addition in order to enhance the mechanism of checks and balances more effectively among the three branches of government, the king had commanded in July 2002 the delinking of the legislature from the executive.

In view of these political developments, one could say that Bhutan has decided to draft the written constitution as the only remedial measure available to counter the allegations of anti monarchical forces that the monarchy is discriminatory and must be abolished. Secondly, it is always better to take initiatives and decisions towards any political reform on your own, rather than have it imposed by outside forces. At the same time, the respect and dignity of the throne are maintained. Moreover, the world has been witnessing the struggle for more liberal civil and political rights and the demand for more autonomy of the economic and political institutions. Even in the Indian subcontinent there are various organizations which raise their voices against the military dictatorship in Pakistan, against the rise of fundamentalism in Bangladesh, the suppression of human rights of minorities in Sri Lanka and recently, the suppression of democracy and democratic rights by the monarchical system in Nepal as well as the autocratic behaviour by President Abdul Gayoom of Maldives. At this juncture the king of Bhutan has taken the wise decision to draft a written constitution for the future politically stability and economic development of the country. Accordingly, the first draft of the Bhutanese constitution was prepared in March 2005 and the second draft was released in August 2005.

One important characteristic of the Constitution is its preamble which begins with the words,

We, the people of Bhutan . . . Blessed by His Majesty, His Majesty King of Bhutan . . . Solemnly pledging ourselves to strengthen the sovereignty of Bhutan, to secure the blessings of liberty, to ensure justice and tranquility and to enhance the unity, happiness and well-being of the people for all time;[33]

It is the first time, the people of Bhutan probably have realized that it is their country and they belong to it. Very interestingly, Article I says that the form of government shall be that of a Democratic Constitutional Monarchy, and Sovereign power belongs to the people of Bhutan.[34]

Any other form of government shall be unconstitutional and is prohibited. The Constitution is the supreme Law of the State.
and
The Druk Gyalpo shall abdicate the Throne for willful violations of this Constitution or for being subject to permanent mental disability, on a motion passed by a joint sitting of parliament. . . .[35]

The proposed constitution has also made provisions for civil and political rights.

A Bhutanese citizen shall have the right

- to life, liberty and security of person and shall not be deprived of such rights except in accordance with due process of law,
- to freedom of speech, opinion and expression,
- to information,
- to vote and exercise of adult franchise, and
- to freedom of peaceful assembly and freedom of association.[36]

But apart form human rights it contains also fundamental duties principles of state policy and all the other provisions which are expected in any democratic constitution.

According to the Draft Constitution, Bhutan will introduce a two-party system. The future parties are however, cautioned concerning their operation in the following words:

Political parties shall ensure that national interests prevail over all other interests and ... shall promote national unity and progressive economic development and strive to ensure the well being of the nation.[37]

The Opposition Party shall play a constructive role to ensure that the government and the ruling party function in accordance with the provisions of this Constitution ... shall promote national integrity, unity and harmony and co-operation among all the sections of society.[38]

The Constitution not only describes the role of ruling and opposition parties it defines also their structure, functions and provides that their sources of finance will be regulated by the parliament.[39] It is the first time that the RGB formally allows representation in the National Assembly by two political parties registered with the election commission.[40] Thus to strengthen its democratic set-up through the election commission, in May 2006, Bhutan has signed an agreement with the Government of India for a Joint Election Commission.

Therefore, the recent announcement of the king of Bhutan to hold elections within a two-party system in parliamentary democratic fashion is not a sudden decision but an outcome of concerted efforts taken by the RGB.

## II. MECHANISMS OF SOCIAL INTEGRATION

### 1. RELIGION AND TRADITIONS

The nation-building process of any country is always influenced by its religion, traditional values; and customs. This is particularly so in a small state which does not have any material assets to assert its position and integrity. The culture and tradition become an inherent part of the nation-building institutions.

In the case of Bhutan, monarchy and religion are 'inseparable, as a monarch is not only the head of the state but also the protector of the Buddhist faith and culture'.[41] As mentioned earlier, the neglect of this culture was one of the causes that led to the resentment against and the eventual assassination of Prime Minister Jigme Palden Dorji. It must be pointed out that Bhutan is still largely a traditional society. Each and every act in the life of the Bhutanese is directed by rituals and religion. Performing religious duties and traditions is not only a private matter but also a part of the public life of Bhutan. For example, when a child is born, only a lama can decide the day and date of the naming ceremony. Similarly, after the death of any person, it is the lama who decides the place of cremation and other rituals.[42] In this context, one cannot ignore the importance of religion and tradition in Bhutanese society. In Bhutan, practically all activities, including socio-eco-political ones, are influenced by traditional values.

The recent experience of introducing the policy of *Driglaham Namzha* (a revival of traditional Bhutanese culture) proves the influence of religious and traditional institutions in the nation-building process. This cultural underpinning of society helps emotional integration and smoother evolution of a socio-political consensus which is vital for nation-building.

### 2. NON-GOVERNMENTAL INSTITUTIONS

Non-governmental institutions which influence the decision-making process comprise public opinion, political parties, pressure groups, mass media, etc. However, such institutions are not yet developed in Bhutan due to lack of education, absence of a functioning democracy, and the lack of a modernized social sector.

Bhutan's monarchical system is relatively more sensitive to socio-political developments, therefore, the role of non-governmental institutions in the nation-building process is almost negligible. For instance, there is very limited scope for the influence of public opinion on nation-building due to the absence of the usual channels of communication, except for the official media, which is used as a mere channel for information. However, there are certain other factors in Bhutan which influence nation-building, particularly the emergence of the elite or middle class, which is engaged in the economic and social activities of the state. Basically this class is rich, in many instances it is related to the royal family, and has links to business and the professions. It is comprises the educated, the young and less traditionalist elements of Bhutanese society who are interested in replacing the traditional monastic institutions with a modern state structure.[43] Since they have already tasted the fruits of modernity either in India or abroad, they want to change the psychology of the people and establish their dominance in the state.

Besides these institutions, Bhutan also maintains its secret Internal Intelligence Services at an informal level.[44] It keeps a vigilance on the developments that are taking place in the country. It keeps the king informed of developments so that he may take preventive and corrective measures.

Thus, it can be stated in conclusion that whatever the records or books might say about the nation-building institutions in Bhutan, in practice, the decisions on any policy with regard to nation-building are taken by one authority alone, i.e. the king of Bhutan, in association with his trusted ministers and professionals. Apart from the existence of the monarchical system, this nation also suffers from the lack of a well-informed and advanced bureaucratic set-up, which is necessary to channellize decisions of the state.

### III. CHALLENGES TO NATION-BUILDING PROCESS IN BHUTAN

#### 1. THE INDO-BHUTAN TREATY OF 1949

In the summer of 1949 Chinese communists captured almost all parts of the Chinese mainland and went on to establish their own government. This development was seen as a threat not only to Bhutan's security but also to India's. Thus security considerations compelled both countries to sign the Indo–Bhutan Treaty of Friendship and Co-operation on 8 August 1949 at Darjeeling, India. Although the treaty recognized the independent and sovereign status of Bhutan, this has always remained a bone of contention between the two countries. Article 2 of the treaty says, 'the Government of India undertakes to exercise no interference in the internal administration of Bhutan. On its part, the Government of Bhutan agrees to be guided by the advice of the Government of India in its external relations.'[45] As far as the first part is concerned, 'non interference in the internal administration of Bhutan', it did not create any misinterpretation concerning the sovereign and independent status of Bhutan. But Bhutan was not happy with the second part of Article 2. It implied that the treaty restricted Bhutan from extending her relations beyond India. From the Indian point of view, Article 2 has its own significance. According Prime Minister Nehru, India should take care not to get involved in the internal squabbles of Bhutan. In a private meeting with B.M. Kaul, Nehru said

[H]ow important it was from India's point of view to strengthen Bhutan's friendship in view of her key position on our border and how we must do everything possible to help her. He also said we must treat smaller countries like Bhutan as our equals and never give them an impression that they were being 'civilized' by us.[46]

From the point of view of defence, Bhutan provides a natural barrier to protect the Himalayan frontier of India. However, the Sino-India war of 1962 had shaken Bhutan's confidence in India's capability to defend it against a Chinese attack. It therefore demanded a revision of the treaty.[47] Relations between the two countries remained tense at least till 1965 because of the assassination of Prime Minister J.P. Dorji and the attempt on the life of King Jigme Dorji Wangchhuk. Gradually these strained relations changed into cordial ones, and in the mid-1970s, the present king of Bhutan, Jigme Singye, Wangchuk said, 'The treaty is working well and India had been helping us a lot to accelerate the pace of economic development set forth by my late father. We are receiving very good technical and financial assistance from India or through India'.[48]

However, in July 1978, Bhutan expressed its concern over the interpretation of Article 2 of the treaty of 1949. In a circulated statement Bhutan reminded the Government of India that, 'in regard to its external relations, it would be entirely up to the Royal Government of Bhutan to decide whether to accept such advice or not. It is not correct to say that Bhutan's future still depends on Indian goodwill and friendship'.[49] These statements reflected Bhutan's eagerness to opt for more and more independence from the Indo–Bhutan Treaty of 1949.

Two incidents which compelled Bhutan to assert its independence of action can be cited. One was Indian Foreign Minister S.N. Misra's unsavoury remarks about Bhutan's support of the Kampuchean regime at the Havana Non-Aligned Summit. He said Bhutan had given vent to the feelings of some of the small countries by taking that particular stand (in support of Pol Pot) at Havana.[50] The other incident was the circulation of newspaper reports to the effect that the Chinese were intruding into Bhutan, creating a crisis situation there. There was the further allegation that Bhutan was moving closer to China.[51] The king reacted strongly and asserted that, 'it was utter nonsense to say that Bhutan was turning towards China.'[52] On the basis of the above evidence, one can observe that Bhutan's foreign policy had become both more sensitive and more assertive. But a major regional initiative and diversification occurred in 1984 when boundary talks with China were held in Beijing. In 1985, at the SAARC meeting at Thimpu, when a Nepalese correspondent asked whether Bhutan had taken India's permission before holding direct talks with China on the border issue, the foreign minister replied that as a sovereign country Bhutan did not seek anybody's consent but always had consultations with India.[53]

From the events of 1984–5 it is clear that both India and Bhutan do not adhere to the literal meaning of the treaty; indeed they have adopted a more liberal interpretation of the words 'aid and advice' as used by the Government of India in Article 2 of the treaty.[54]

This soft-peddling of Bhutan's stand *vis-à-vis* the Indo–Bhutan

Treaty of 1949 can be understood in the light of the following factors: (1) frequent Chinese incursions into Bhutan and the need for India's countervailing power; (2) the need not to antagonize India in view of its substantial economic and technical assistance; and (3) the general realization by landlocked countries of their geographical dependence on a neighbouring power or powers, despite their desire for greater autonomy of action.

## 2. THE PRESENCE OF TIBETAN REFUGEES IN BHUTAN (1959–79)

The suppression of the Tibetan uprising sent alarm signals in Bhutan as many Tibetans came into Bhutan and stayed on as refugees creating a number of problems for the country. Hence Bhutan officially closed its border with Tibet in 1959 and imposed a ban on trade with it as well as China.[55] This dealt a blow to the Bhutanese economy. And due to the setback to Bhutan's trade with Tibet, there was widespread resentment. In addition, the Chinese invasion of Tibet triggered in Bhutan a deep concern about the very survival of the nation, and it was now eager to abandon its policy of isolation and therefore sought an alliance with India. This in turn led to the growth of anti-Indian feelings and the emergence of a pro-Chinese lobby among the local Bhutanese, which works as a pressure group even today.

Many Tibetan refugees who entered Bhutanese territory in 1959 stayed there because of the sympathy shown to them by the local population.[56] However, this influx of refugees created many problems in the country's domestic affairs and affects its internal socio-political structure even today. By 1961, more than 2,000 Tibetan refugees had entered Bhutan,[57] and later on settled there, taking up whatever occupation was available to them. The Government of Bhutan offered them Bhutanese citizenship to integrate them into the national mainstream but the Tibetans refused this and maintained their separate identity, a move of which Bhutan disapproved. This attitude of the Tibetans clashed with the national consciousness and pride of the Bhutanese. The other reason for the growing differences between the two communities was that 'the Tibetans living in Bhutan kept their loyalty to the Bhutan king at a lower level than that to the Dalai Lama'.[58]

Finally, between 1974 and 1979, the Royal Government of Bhutan decided to deport Tibetan refugees from the country. It contacted the Dalai Lama at Dharmshala in Himachal Pradesh, India and after a long process of discussion in 1979, Bhutan decided to repatriate there Tibetan refugees who declined to accept Bhutanese citizenship.[59] By doing so, Bhutan hoped not only to keep its nation intact but also to maintain correct relations with China.

### 3. THE SINO–BHUTAN BOUNDARY DISPUTE

On the occasion of the 74th session of the National Assembly in 1996, His Majesty, the King of Bhutan declared that,

[T]he boundary talks between Bhutan and China began in 1984, when there were more than 1,000 square kilometers of territory under dispute. After the past rounds of talks, there are essentially only three areas in the western sector which are still under negotiation. These are 89 square kilometers in Doklam, 42 square kilometers in Sinchulumpa, and 138 square kilometers in Shakhatoe, a total of 269 square kilometers.[60]

He also said that the Bhutan–China boundary is an important issue because it affects Bhutan's national interest and the well-being of the Bhutanese people.

During the tenth round of talks in Beijing in November 1996, the Bhutanese delegation put forward Bhutan's claim to Doklam, Sinchulung, Dramana and Shakhatoe in the western sector of the northern border and stressed that these were vital as pasture land for the people of the Haa Valley in Bhutan.[61] The delegation also informed its Chinese counterpart that Tibetan herdsmen had been intruding into Majathang and Jakarlung in the central sector of the boundary and had even constructed sheds.[62]

In response, the foreign minister of Bhutan said, 'Chinese officials did not make any comment on the Bhutanese territorial claims but on the question of intrusion by Tibetan herdsmen, they pointed out that since there was no agreement on the proposal (offered by the Chinese during the seventh round of talks) they could not control the activities of Tibetan herders along the borders'.[63]

The twelfth round of bilateral border talks between Bhutan

and China in Beijing on 8–12 December 1998 concentrated on three important points:

1. The establishment of diplomatic relations with Bhutan,
2. The establishment of trade relations with China,
3. The question of the exchange of land.[64]

On this occasion Bhutan and China signed an agreement to maintain peace and tranquillity on the Bhutan–China border.[65] This has remained the only Sino–Bhutanese agreement or treaty till today. There was no final decision on the exchange of territories as the proposed area to be exchanged has borders with Sikkim, a state in India. The agreement shows Bhutan's concern about protecting its boundaries with its immediate neighbours, India and China, while maintaining its formal relations with China.

During the fourteenth round of boundary talks in Beijing in November 2000, the Bhutanese Foreign Minister, Jigmi Thinley, met Chinese Premier Zhu Rongji and the Chinese Foreign Minister, Tang Jiaxuan. During this round of talks, Bhutan extended its claim of the border-line beyond that offered by the Chinese government. Bhutan had also proposed technical discussions using maps between experts from each side.

In this way, till April 2004, seventeen rounds of talks had been completed but there was no sign of a permanent resolution to this issue. Therefore, we can surmise that the Chinese are reluctant to reduce their claims on the western sector, which is strategically important for them, or to interfere in the question of Tibetan yak herders' intrusion into Bhutanese territory unless and until the Bhutanese accept the proposal of exchange of an area of 495 sq. km. with the pastureland, an area of 269 sq. km.

On the other hand, Bhutan cannot accept this kind of proposal from the Chinese: large numbers of Bhutanese people depend on livestock for their livelihood, as thus and these pasturelands are vital for their survival. Besides, the Bhutanese claim that both areas have always belonged to them.[66]

On the issue of a further delay in final decisions on boundary talks, Bhutan gave typical diplomatic answers. To quote the foreign minister of Bhutan: 'Big objectives take time to fulfil'.[67] He added, 'it would be better to conduct the talks without haste and with great care and patience as it involves the national interest of the country'.[68] Thus Bhutan wants to ensure that its traditional grazing land is not affected and that the boundary is demarcated according to traditional lines.[69]

As China is one of the largest and most powerful nations in the world today, the foreign minister said that a small country like Bhutan must be tactful in its approach to boundary negotiations with its large neighbour because it cannot afford to lose even a single sq. km. of land.

Thus, the resolution of the demarcation of the boundary line with China and the question of Tibetan intrusion into Bhutanese territory remain as major objectives in the nation-building process of Bhutan.

### 4. THE PROBLEM OF PEOPLE OF NEPALI ORIGIN IN BHUTAN

An important domestic component which has a long-term impact on the nation-building process in Bhutan is the presence of the population of Nepali origin in Bhutan and its clandestine activities against the Royal Government of Bhutan. The question of the role and treatment of the Nepalis has not only affected the country's socio-economic structure but also compelled the government to calibrate its political system in line with modern times. Moreover, apart from Nepal the ethnic crisis has also affected Bhutan's relations with India because of the possible spillover into the border states of Assam, Sikkim, and the north-eastern region.

The ethnic crisis has its roots in history, when more than 60,000 Nepalese labourers known as *Lhotshampas* were brought to Bhutan by the Dorji family at the end of the nineteenth century to clear the land. Since then, due to the existence of open borders with Nepal, there has been a constant influx of Nepalese, most of whom settled down in southern Bhutan.

Till the 1950s, the government did not involve the Nepalese in any part of national affairs. 'A despotic regime had reduced them almost to the level of dumb animals.'[70] Hence, the ethnic Nepalese decided to launch a protest movement against the discriminatory policy of the government and established a political platform known as the Bhutan State Congress, through which they submitted a memorandum to the Maharaja in 1953. The maharaja realized the necessity of integrating the Nepalese into Bhutan's national mainstream. The Nationality Act of Bhutan was enacted in 1958, which granted equal and full citizenship rights to all Nepalese who had settled in the kingdom prior to 1958.[71] In other words, the process of accommodating people of Nepali origin only started in 1959–60.

In the beginning of the 1960s, the king announced many development programmes and plans which included free health care and education for labourers and a hike in wages.[72] This was attractive to the Nepalese who continued to immigrate in rising members. The uninterrupted flow of labourers across the borders alarmed the Bhutanese. They were sure that the foreign ethnic groups would outnumber them and they could soon become a minority.[73] This fear was strengthened by the merger of Sikkim with India where the massive influx of Hindu Nepalese into Sikkim had turned the original inhabitants, i.e. Mahayana Buddhists, into a minority. With the help of the majority Nepalese moreover, the ruler of Sikkim, the Chogyal, had been removed from power,[74] and another Himalayan state lost its independent identity and became part of India.

Against this background Bhutan apprehended that the silent influx of Nepalese migrants might create another Sikkim-type situation, if preventive measures were not taken immediately. Therefore, in order to restrict the entry of Nepalese, the king of Bhutan introduced a new law in 1977 by which fresh labourers and recruits of Nepalese nationality had to possess a valid Nepalese passport and travel documents. They were also asked to seek government clearance before their appointment.[75] Also in the same year, the government introduced the new Marriage Act in Bhutan. 'It imposes the denial of a number of benefits to those who marry non-citizens. It was strictly followed against the Bhutanese of Nepali origin and not against the Drukpa Bhutanese.'[76] According to the 1981 census, 53 per cent of Bhutan's population is of Nepali origin. But they are treated as second-class citizens.[77] They are denied high positions in the civil bureaucracy, the Royal Bhutanese Army, the Royal Bhutanese Police, the Royal Advisory Council, and the National

Assembly.[78] They are also underrepresented in the fields of agriculture, education and industry. As a result they continue to nurse a grudge against the ruling Bhutanese elite for denying them their due share in national life in proportion to their population. The negative attitude of the Nepalese population towards the government is resented by the Drukpas who treat the former as a major threat to their very existence.

Therefore in 1985, a New Citizenship Act was introduced which nullified the previous Act of 1958.[79] According to this new Act, the Royal Government granted citizenship retroactively only to those inhabitants who could prove that they were inhabitants of the country since 1958.[80] Meant to control the illegal migration of Nepalese into southern Bhutan. The new law created problems of identity for those who were either born after that date or held no record from that period.[81]

In 1988, the government launched a census exercise to determine the population status of its inhabitants. According to this census, claimed the Bhutan authorities, a great number of 'illegal immigrants' were living in Bhutan's southern districts'.[82] The disproportionate presence of an ethnic people in a tiny kingdom of 600,000[83] created a feeling of apprehension among the ruling Drukpas, of their being outnumbered, as had happened in Sikkim. To quote the foreign minister of Bhutan, 'if this trend continued the Bhutanese in another two decades will become a tiny minority and Bhutan would be turned into another Sikkim and Darjeeling'.[84] This realization compelled Bhutan to enforce the immigration laws vigorously and forced those who were unable to produce sufficient proof of their domicile prior to the cut-off year 1958 to leave the country. This action resulted in widespread resentment among the *Lhotshampas*, or southern Bhutanese, who felt that they were being ill-treated and alienated in their own land due to their ethnic identity.

Thus anti-Drukpa activities by Bhutanese of Nepali origin compelled the government to bring them into the mainstream and forcefully integrate them into Bhutanese culture which sparked an ethnic crisis between these two communities. To counter their feelings of alienation the king participated in many Nepalese festivals and encouraged intermarriage between different ethnic groups. The king himself said in one interview, 'we are trying to intellectually integrate them into our society by means of a common education; we see to it that their language and religious beliefs are maintained. Nepali and Hindi are officially recognized languages here. The Government has declared Hindu festivals as official holidays'.[85]

The king of Bhutan introduced the ideology of 'One Nation, One People', which led to the imposition of a code of conduct, which is the Drukpa language, religion, and dress on all Bhutanese citizens, through a policy of *Drighlam Namza* (a revival of traditional Bhutanese culture). Enforcement of the code of conduct raised an outcry by the southern Bhutanese. They protested against this cultural domination. Defending the policies of integration and the ideology of 'One Nation, One People', Lynopo Dawa Tsering, Bhutan's foreign minister said: 'There is a bottom line for citizenship. If a group of people come here they must integrate into the mainstream. They must wear the national dress and learn the national language. It is important to preserve our sovereignty and independence by ensuring that we have a distinct national identity. We are worried that we may disappear.'[86]

In this context, it is important to quote from the pamphlet of the banned Bhutan Peoples' Party which mainly represents the Nepalese: 'We may see the day when the majority Drukpas of northern Bhutan are nepalized by the Gurkhas of southern Bhutan. We must create a Gurkha state in Bhutan to extend the borders of Nepal.'[87]

The origin of this thought stems from 'the success of the democratic struggle in Nepal that had a direct impact on the Nepalese of Bhutan'.[88] Moreover, 'during 1987–8, the activists of the Gorkha Liberation Movement in the hill districts of West Bengal had live contacts with the Nepalese in Bhutan for shelter and financial support'.[89]

The fear expressed by the foreign minister is justified, as the Bhutanese know that the Nepalese in Bhutan are able to outnumber them as was seen in the Indian state of Sikkim, and towns like Darjeeling and Kalimpong. That is why the government of Bhutan is firm on implementing the *Drighlam Namza* programme, and putting a check on the flow of illegal Nepali immigrants into Bhutan.

To seek an amicable solution to this problem, several bilateral talks have been held between Nepal and Bhutan. After 1990, due to the rigorous implementation of the policy of cultural integration pursued by the government, most of the Nepalese of southern Bhutan had taken refuge in the border areas of Nepal. These refugees, as mentioned earlier, created problems for Nepal and caused a heavy financial burden on the national economy.[90] Therefore, both the countries had several rounds of bilateral talks and agreed to classify the refugees into four categories:

1. Bhutanese who have been forcibly evicted,
2. Bhutanese who have voluntarily emigrated,
3. Non-Bhutanese, and
4. Bhutanese who have committed criminal acts.[91]

According to Bhutanese officials, out of the four categories only the first group qualifies for true refugee status and has a chance of repatriation. Most of the refugees in the UNHCR camps in eastern Nepal are Nepalese and Indian citizens looking for free food, shelter, and health care.[92] But in one of these meetings, strangely enough, the Nepali delegation deviated from its earlier stand and argued that the problem was between the Royal Government of Bhutan and the refugees in the camps, and that the Bhutan Government should take back all these people.[93] As a result, Bhutan felt that the Nepalese government was not interested in solving the problem through bilateral talks. We can also infer that the Nepalese government felt that bilateral talks with Bhutan had not gone very far in finding a workable solution to the ethnic problem. In addition, progress in the bilateral talks had stalled because of the political instability in Nepal with each new government changing that country's stand on the refugee issue. The Bhutanese held discussions with seven governments in as many years on the refugee problem.[94] All these factors led to a deadlock which lasted for three years, 1996–9.

At the eighth round of bilateral talks which were held in September 1999, it came to be known that due to international pressure, particularly from the funding agencies and human rights organizations, the RGB agreed to take back the legitimized refugees under category two. But these people were forced to sign the so-called Voluntary Migration Forms (VMF), which were written in *Dzonkha*.[95] So, during the ninth round of bilateral talks in May 2000, both Nepal and Bhutan agreed on the terms of reference for a Joint Verification Team (JVT), which would go into the camps in eastern Nepal to identify the people: 'they agreed on the proforma for verification; on the modalities of verification and the practical time frame to start the verification process'.[96] During the tenth round of talks, which were held in Kathmandu in December 2000, both countries decided to finalize the mechanism of verification into a four-step process: the terms of references for the verification team, the composition of the verification team, the modalities of verification; and the proforma that would be used to record the personal details of the refugees.[97] Both countries agreed on the unit of verification, that is, the team would first validate the family units and then proceed to verify heads of families and individual units.[98]

Looking back at these several rounds of bilateral talks, one can see that Bhutan has always maintained an upper hand in the meetings. This was due to clever diplomacy and farsightedness, and the desire to protect its interests. Moreover, a well planned and positive campaign dwelling on the potential threat to this tiny nation state, its unique ethnic cultural identity, had created a favourable world public opinion towards Bhutan. The possible nexus between the United Liberation Front of Assam (ULFA), Bodo outfits and Bhutanese refugees, might also have compelled Bhutan to mellow its rigid stand on the issue. The recent killings of innocent Bhutanese on the Indo–Bhutan border close to Assam were a grave shock to Bhutan. Also, the political and economic survival of Bhutan must have indirectly influenced Bhutan's domestic as well as international postures forcing it to adjust to the existing situation and consider available options in regard to Bhutanese refugees living in Nepal.

But in reality, the local inhabitants, especially Drukpa Bhutanese, are not ready to accept these refugees as citizens. For instance, the 77th Session of the National Assembly, held from 22 June to 4 July 1999, saw most of the *Chimis* (heads of villages) arguing that the 'Government must never agree to take back these people who had left the country on their own free will and a ban must be imposed on their return'. The reason according to

Bhutan's home minister is that, 'a large number of these people in the camps are not Bhutanese. The main objective of the *ngolops* has been to come to Bhutan and take over political power, so that all of them can be made Bhutanese citizens and given employment'. [99]

The 78th Session of National Assembly, held in July 2000, discussed again the issue of a ban on the repatriation of refugees. This time the members were very hostile in their reaction to the refugees. They were asking questions like, 'How can the people in the camps in Nepal possibly return when they are still making false allegations against the country?'[100] Moreover, the home minister of Bhutan, Lynpo Thinley Gyamtsho, repeatedly stated that, 'people who have left Bhutan should not be allowed to return. Because, they were making repeated demands for a change in the Bhutanese political system into a multiparty system, [and for] changes in the citizenship laws.'[101]

## UPDATES ON CRISIS OF BHUTANESE OF NEPALI ORIGIN

By October 2003, fifteen rounds of bilateral talks had been held between the two counties. During this time,

It was decided that the Category 3 Non-Bhutanese Nationals appeals would be re-examined by the Joint Verification Team when they next convened. It was reconfirmed that persons under C1, C2 and C4 who voluntarily apply to return would be repatriated as per the harmonized position on these categories and the Government of Nepal would give the people in C2 who did not wish to come to Bhutan the option to apply for the Nepalese citizenship as per the harmonized position in the category.[102]

However, in December 2003, refugees from Khudunabari camp hurled stones at the Bhutanese officials, saying the verification was discriminatory.[103] Since then no further bilateral talks between the Nepali and Bhutanese governments have been held and the whole process of repatriation of refugees was halted. At present the RGB have shown keen interest in resolving the refugee problem, in view of recent developments in Nepal, especially, when the Monarchy was thrown out by the democratic forces in May 2006. The other reason could be that the alleged Maoists' influence and association within the Bhutanese refugee camps might have compelled Bhutan to mellow its rigid stand on the issue. According to Bhutanese officials, a Bhutan Gorakha Liberation Front (BGLF) and a Bhutan Communist Party (BCP) have been formed with the latter having links with the Maoists in Nepal. It is also said, that the Maoists were recruiting people in the camp and that some of them had been participating in Maoist attacks in Nepal.[104] Apart from this, the political and economic survival of Bhutan must have indirectly influenced Bhutan's domestic as well as international postures leading it to adjust to the existing situation, and to consider available options with regard to Bhutanese refugees living in Nepal. As a result, during the recent 15th ministerial Meeting of the Coordinating Bureau of the NAM at Malaysia, the Bhutanese Foreign Minister expressed his desire to resume the bilateral talks that have been in limbo for a long time, and was positive about finding a solution to the festering Bhutanese refugee problem.[105]

Unfortunately, despite the curtailment of the wings of the monarchy in May 2006 and the emergence of new democratic forces in Nepal, the issue of Bhutanese of Nepali origin is still unresolved. On its part, the UNHCR too has been unable to find a solution which would be acceptable to both parties.

Thus, with all this evidence, one can visualize the fate of the poor, ignorant and innocent Bhutanese refugees, who, even if they are being repatriated to Bhutan, will surely not get a warm welcome by the Drukpa Bhutanese. They will find it difficult to survive in an atmosphere of animosity. Any attempt to earn a livelihood would also become difficult for them after their return to Bhutan. Furthermore while in the camps these Bhutanese refugees have tasted the fruits of democracy, and a free atmosphere, they may find it difficult to adjust to a monarchical type of government. Under these circumstances they may have second thoughts about returning to their homeland. Thus the issue of Bhutanese refugees is likely to not only remain but also become more problematic in due course of time.

The implications of an ethnic crisis could be both positive and negative. If Bhutan solves this problem effectively, it would be setting a good example for other countries suffering from a similar conflict. This requires a lot of soul-searching, a long-term approach, and statesmanship on the part of the Bhutanese rulers. Bhutan might have to introduce both the Nepali and the Dzonkha languages as state languages, it should also allow the Nepalese to share in the economic development process and its benefits. Thus the Royal Government of Bhutan should adopt the policy of an honourable and equitable aggregation of the interests of the two principal communities.

## 5. CAMPS OF ASSAMESE MILITANTS IN BHUTAN

At the beginning of the 1990s-many militants from Assam, especially the United Liberation Front of Assam (ULFA) and the National Democratic Front of Bodoland (NFDB), had taken shelter in Bhutan. Today these militants have multiplied into a few thousand cadres working for various similar organizations like the Bodo Liberation Tigers Force (BLTF) and the Kamtapuri Liberation Organization (KLO), as the geostrategic location and mountainous terrain of Bhutan provide a safe sanctuary. The Royal Government of Bhutan took objection to the influx of these militants and protested.

On 24 July 1998, in an interview the Bhutanese foreign minister, Jigme Thinley, described the issue of ULFA and Bodo insurgents as the domestic problem of India but said it had spilled over into Bhutan. The issue formed the core agenda for discussion in the country's National Assembly[106] and 'every member saw this problem as a threat to the security and sovereignty of Bhutan since the armed people entered our land and have forcibly occupied our areas'.[107] When asked why the RGB did not drive the insurgents out of Bhutan, he said, 'Bhutan did not have the military capability,' and that 'in terms of weaponry the insurgents were superior to Bhutanese forces'.[108]

Since the basic demand of these organizations is independence from India they are fighting against the Indian Army, the government of Assam, and the police force. The Government of India (GOI) on its part decided to meet the secessionist challenge and to go after their hideouts along the Indo-Bhutan border, particularly in Assam. When the GOI proposed to initiate a Joint Indo-Bhutan Army (JIBA) operation to drive out these militants from Bhutan, the RGB did not respond and decided to take action on its own. In June 2000, Bhutan's National Assembly, *Tshongdu,* passed a resolution of a Four-Point Action to flush out insurgents from Bhutanese territories.

1. Cut-off ration supplies to the militants,
2. Punish all groups and individuals found helping the militants by invoking the National Security Act,
3. Pursue the process of dialogue with the militants to make them leave peacefully, and
4. If all efforts fail, take military action as a last resort.[109]

However, in reality, according to various intelligence and security agencies, many Bhutanese government officials were involved in supporting the ULFA militants through economic and military aid. To quote Jaideep Saikia: 'A certain Bhutanese army Brigadier V. Namgel, Security-in-Charge and Military Adviser to [the] Bhutanese King, has been actively helping the ULFA in obtaining arms and ammunition from foreign countries.'[110]

Apart from this evidence there were many other incidents which proved Bhutanese personnel's involvement in supporting ULFA militants. For instance, Wangchuk Dorji and Lhaba Tshering, on the staff of the protocol division in the Foreign Ministry, were involved in transferring US $ 38,000 and Rs. 300,000 in diplomatic pouches. They were caught by their own police.[111] Responding to this, the RGB denied all these reports and stated that these two officials 'had acted on an individual level and their actions had nothing to do with the RGB'.[112]

In this respect, one can see the persisting fear in the minds of Bhutanese statesmen that military operations by the JIBA to flush out these militants will increase apprehension among the ultra-nationalists and traditionalists in terms of a breach of the country's sovereignty and independence by the GOI. For a variety of reasons, the RGB is not prepared to officially concede any involvement in support of the ULFA militants. Concerning foreign relations: it will raise Chinese apprehensions and hamper smooth Sino-Bhutanese relations. For, any military assistance from the GOI to Bhutan might provoke the Chinese to send their observers not only to monitor and protect their border with Bhutan but also to assist the Royal Bhutanese Guards to prevent illegal entry of Tibetan herdsman into Bhutanese territory. In this case it would be very difficult for Bhutan to say 'no' to the Chinese if it allowed the Indian military into Bhutan to deal with the ULFA militants seeking refuge there. In view of this security scenario, and being a small and militarily weak state sandwiched between two powerful neighbours, India and China, Bhutan may face a serious setback to its attempts to protect its territorial integrity, sovereignty, and independent status in the region.

On the other hand, the ULFA militants are compelling the RGB to provide them with safe shelter, failing which they pressurize the RGB, resorting to violent tactics and sometimes even kill innocent Bhutanese civilians and businessman on the Assam-Bhutan border. Bhutan has experienced this on many occasions. Besides, ULFA leaders are demanding that Bhutan protect their human rights, which they allege are being violated by the state government of Assam and the GOI. To quote ULFA Chairman, Arabinda Rajkhowa:

We reiterate that ULFA is not going to occupy Bhutan permanently, nor is there any plan to include Bhutan in a sovereign Assam. Our camps in Bhutan are not for such purposes. As a result of the Indo-Assam conflict, our freedom fighters had to establish camps in Bhutan. It is a basic human right to be able to go to a place even when one's life is in danger. . . . We appeal to the Government of Bhutan and the Bhutanese people again that the cadres of ULFA must be given the universal right and to maintain the centuries old Assam-Bhutan cordial relationship intact.[113]

Caught in a pincer-like situation, the RGB has been in a dilemma of how to cope with threats to its internal as well as external security posed by the ULFA militants on its southern border which lines the north-east regions of India, an area notorious for its militancy and its role in the arms and narcotics trade in South Asia. The camps of armed insurgent groups in north-east India and their 'close proximity to the Bhutan border (just 20 km. away) has made procurement of small arms ridiculously easy. It has spawned a new "gun culture" in the region'.[114]

Thus, to avoid any further complications by the insurgents from Assam, the RGB has recently adopted a few conciliatory policies which may help to resolve this crisis. At the military level, the RGB took the decision to provide small-arms training to its Forest Guards to protect its forest resources and to provide border security support to the RBP (Royal Bhutan Police). In 2003, the RGB made a budgetary provision of Rs. 13 million to raise a voluntary force of young men able to fight against the insurgents. As a result, at present more than 5,000 soldiers of the RBA and 174 officers have been deployed between Diafam in the east and Sibsoo in the west and are being readied for action in the event of an attack by the insurgents.[115] The RGB has recently purchased AK 101 and AK 104 assault rifles worth Rs. one million from a third country. Moreover, it also receives advance military training and weapons like infantry rifles machine guns and 81 mm mortars from the GOI.[116]

During his visit to India in September 2003, H.M. Jigme Singye Wangchuk conveyed his serious security concerns over the presence of ULFA camps in Bhutan and said that the National Assembly had already taken a decision to make a last attempt to invite the leaders of the ULFA, NDFB, and KLO militants for talks to resolve the crisis through a process of dialogue.[117] Obviously, the RGB did not want to use armed force to tackle this problem, to avoid any antagonism from India or any other side. However, when confronted with an evidently direct threat to its sovereignty and security by the militants from Assam and West Bengal Bhutan had no other choice but to opt for the military action, known as Operation Flush Out, as envisioned in its Four-Point Action Programme of 2000.[118]

However, one cannot overlook the fact that Bhutan, being militarily weak, cannot resist the consequences of a backlash. Moreover, the use of armed force may cause the suppressed anti-monarchical forces within and outside Bhutan to extend a helping hand to the militants. Therefore, it is in the interest of Bhutan's security to continue a peace dialogue with the ULFA militants while taking the GOI into confidence.

## IV. PROSPECTS: SOCIO-ECONOMIC DEVELOPMENT AND POLITICAL INDEPENDENCE

As to the 1980s and early 1990s, the nation-building process in Bhutan can be characterized as being carefully assertive and constructive. This trend was shattered in the late 1990s due to internal crises resulting from the ethnic clashes between Bhutanese of Nepali origin and native Drukpas. There were widespread allegations of the violation of the rights of the former by the latter. Voices were raised on behalf of the former in international forums and their cause was championed by various NGOs. The ethnic crisis has its own implications for Bhutan's nation-building process. To solve this problem, Bhutan and Nepal have held many rounds of bilateral talks. Unfortunately, till today, no concrete results have been achieved.

On the domestic front, socio-economic problems have led Bhutan to launch a series of development plans in a vigorous effort at nation-building. For instance, during the initial Five-Year Plans, top priority was given to end its isolation from the rest of the world and to open channels for communicating with Third World countries. Thus the three main national highways in Bhutan were completed. In addition, Bhutan concentrated on agriculture and social services like health and education, the power sector, and irrigation development schemes. By 1971, Bhutan had become a member of the UN and its name appeared on the list of Least Developed Countries (LDC) as prepared by the UN General Assembly.[119] Thus, by joining the United Nations, Bhutan tried to mobilize some financial resources from UN agencies for the nation's development.

In its fifth Five Year Plan (1982–7), the Bhutan government tried to achieve economic self-reliance to ensure the continued progress of the country. To this end, Bhutan changed the priorities and concentrated on mobilizing internal resources to meet the challenges. Hence the king travelled and toured each district of Bhutan and drew up development plans. These plans aimed at promoting export-oriented industries based on forest and mining products. This was done in order to fetch a good market price in India. The king of Bhutan encouraged his countrymen to participate in these projects voluntarily to save the cost of labour.

In the sixth Plan (1987–92), priority was given to the development of power and industries. Convinced that economic growth could be achieved more efficiently with the help of private enterprises, Bhutan privatized the Gedu Wood Manufacturing Corporation in 1990. During the eighth Five-Year Plan (1997-

2002), Bhutan's priorities were mainly the service sectors, particularly training for personnel in administration, building of industrial and agricultural projects, preservation of natural resources, infrastructural development and management, mass communication, and data processing and statistics.[120]

In the ninth Five Year Plan (2002-7), the Royal Government of Bhutan announced new basic parameters together with its objectives and general strategies: (1) rural infrastructure, (2) upgrading the quality of health and education facilities, (3) private sector development, and (4) decentralization of planning and implementation.[121]

Apart from these five-year plans, Bhutan made concerted efforts to boost its infrastructure and indirectly help to diversify its economic relations.

Communication was one of the basic problems confronting the country and restricting its economic development. With Indian assistance telephones were first introduced in 1963 and the department of telephones was established in April 1971.[122] Moreover, for a faster communication the Indo-Bhutan microwave link was instituted in 1984, which facilitated telephonic contacts with India and other countries.[123] Another landmark in the history of Bhutanese telecommunication was 'the commissioning of the Thimpu Satellite Earth Station in March 1990'.[124]

Bhutan also invested in other means of communication like a wireless system and a medium-wave radio service. This has helped the country to disseminate and propagate information about its developmental and cultural activities.[125] The well-developed communication system plays a very important role in maintaining the separate cultural identity of Bhutan, strengthening and mobilizing support for the nation's development efforts.

As Bhutan is an underdeveloped country, its planners realized the pressing need for electric power to boost economic growth. In order to achieve this objective, in September 1961, Bhutan and India signed an agreement for a joint hydro-electric project on the Jaldhaka River which runs along the south-western Indo-Bhutanese border for about twelve miles.[126] Bhutan received its first electricity in the spring of 1968. But most of the benefit from the project went to West Bengal. However, Bhutan received Rs. 2.5 million as royalty from West Bengal for the use of Bhutan's river water. Over and above this, Bhutan was able to get 250 kilowatts of electricity without cost.[127]

After the successful implementation of this project two more hydroelectric projects were completed with Indian assistance. The fourth project, the Chukha Hydropower Project, began in 1974. It was set-up according to an agreement between the governments of India and Bhutan and is located at Chukha, about 55 miles from the country's capital, Thimpu, along the Raidek river. It is the largest power project in Bhutan with a capacity to generate 336 megawatts (MW). These projects are stepping-stones for the development of the economic infrastructure, besides being a major source of revenue through the sale of electricity to India given the latter's growing need of power. Moreover, while these power projects help to upgrade the standard of living of the people, they are also treated as symbols of the nation's spirit in Bhutan.

With regard to foreign aid, India has been the principal source for development programmes, apart from smalled grants received from the UNDP, the World Bank, the Asian Development Bank, the Kuwait Development Fund and other international funding agencies. Bhutan also obtained financial inputs from Australia, Great Britain, New Zealand, Canada, Singapore, and Japan through the Colombo plan and some bilateral aid from Switzerland.[128] They were, however, much too insignificant to have a major impact on its developmental programmes.

There was therefore a big question before the Bhutanese elites, how to solve the problem of being dependent on a single source of economic and technical assistance. Apart from this, Bhutan had some complaints about the quantity of aid received from India and the non-availability of ready aid for its development programmes. In the circumstances, it might have been inclined to approach other major powers for economic aid. But since such aid might come with political strings attached, it refrained from doing so. To quote the foreign minister:

We are looking for economic assistance from countries other than traditional donor nations, but we are determined to ensure that such aid has no political strings attached. We shall not seek aid from either the US or the USSR, as we do not wish to get involved in the superpower racket.[129]

Thus Bhutan took a very discreet stance while receiving foreign aid, given the influence that the donors could exercise over its domestic and foreign policies.

In conclusion, we may say that Bhutan is a society which, after centuries of isolation and stagnation, has taken decisive steps to safeguard its independence and integrity and at the same time modernize its polity and economy. Due safeguards are provided for its traditional culture, religion, and language while promoting the harmonious co-existence of various ethnic groups. In an age of globalization, a parochial mind-set and institutional set-up will be singularly out of place for Bhutan no less than for other small landlocked states, hence Bhutan's efforts to reach out to other states through trade, aid and investments.

An acute dilemma persists about foreign aid. Should a nation receive foreign aid and go for speedy economic development or skip aid and take the long and strenuous path of self-reliance? Very few nations have successfully tackled this dilemma.

Bhutan strongly desires to project the image of a sovereign and independent state in the world. Hence Bhutan started taking an active part in SAARC, the South Asian Association for Regional Co-operation, and extended its foreign relations with Nepal and Bangladesh. It also became active in resolving the problem of border disputes with China, attending many rounds of talks independently. Moreover, Bhutan is playing a very active role at the United Nations and its various agencies as well as in the non-aligned movement.

An important factor in Bhutan's nation-building is its ability to keep its giant neighbours, China and India, in good humour while protecting its national interests by creating enough political space for itself. In stark contrast to other crisis-ridden states in South Asia like Nepal, Bangladesh, and Sri Lanka, Bhutan has shown signs of a stabilizing and modernizing state that bids fair to create a comfortable little niche for itself in the comity of nations.

## NOTES

1. B.S. Das, 'Bhutan', in U.S. Bajpai (ed.), *India and Its Neighbourhood* (New Delhi, 1986), p. 300.
2. In Bhutan there is no institution of prime minister as such. But it should be noted that 'Jigme P. Dorji was designated as Prime Minister as a matter of courtesy only. The title originated at the time of the visit of India's Prime Minister Nehru, 1958, out of sheer consideration for protocol'. See, Nagendra Singh, *Bhutan: A Kingdom in the Himalayas* (New Delhi, 1972), p. 100.
3. Das, 'Bhutan', p. 301.
4. It was reported that after the assassination, civil war in Bhutan broke out between Dorji's and Wangchuk's families. Dorji's anti-king groups wanted to modify the royal order and Bhutan's relations with India. For a detailed report, see Madusudan Bhattacharya, 'Bhutan in Turmoil', *Mainstream*, 19 December 1964, p. 8.
5. Nari Rustomji, *Bhutan: The Dragon Kingdom in Crisis* (Delhi, 1978), p. 12.
6. Ibid.
7. Ibid.
8. B.S. Das, 'Economic Development and Social Changes in Bhutan', in Phadnis, Muni and Bahadur (eds.), *Domestic Conflicts in South Asia*, vol. 2 (New Delhi, 1986), p. 86.
9. *The Kuensel*, Thimpu, 30 November 1968.
10. For details see, Ram Rahul, *The Himalayan Borderland* (New Delhi, 1976), p. 112.
11. Singh, *Bhutan: A Kingdom is the Himalayas*, pp. 96-112.
12. Earlier they were elected indirectly by the selection of representatives of villages by consensus, and their subsequent nomination to the *Tshogdu*. See the document, *Tshongdu: The National Assembly of Bhutan* (Gangtok, Sikkim, 1969).
13. Ibid.
14. Singh *Bhutan: A Kingdom in the Himalayas,* p. 101.
15. *Bhutan in Focus* 17 December 2003 (New Delhi, 2003), p. 13.
16. Speech reprinted in *The Hindu*, Madras, 11 November 1992.
17. Rahul, *The Himalayan Borderland*, p. 112.
18. Leo E. Rose, *The Politics of Bhutan* (Ithaca and London, 1977), p. 155.
19. R.C. Misra, 'Tibetans in Bhutan, Problem of Repatriation' *China Report*, vol. 16, nos. 9–10, September–October 1982, pp. 25–32.
20. National Assembly Debates, 75th Session, *The Kuensel*, 9 August 1997, p. 2.
21. National Assembly Debates, 74th Session, *The Kuensel*, 10 August 1997, p. 17.

22. Ibid.
23. Ibid., p. 99.
24. *The Hindu*, Madras, 11 November 1992.
25. Ibid.
26. Rose, *The Politics of Bhutan*, p. 171.
27. For a detailed discussion see, Bhabani Sen Gupta, *Bhutan: Towards a Grass-root Participatory Polity* (New Delhi, 1999), pp. 66–7.
28. *Bhutan in Focus*, 17 December 2003, p. 12.
29. National Assembly Debates, 78th Session, 25 June 2000.
30. Ibid.
31. National Assembly Debates, 79 Session, 28 June 2001.
32. Ibid., 80ᵗʰ Session, 25 June 2002.
33. Second Draft of the Constitution, 18 August 2005, p. iii.
34. Ibid., p. 1.
35. Draft Tsa Thrim Chenmo as on 26 March 2005. The Constitution of the Kingdom of Bhutan, 2005 Article 2.
36. Ibid., Article 7.
37. Ibid., Article 15.
38. Ibid.
39. Article 15 of Second Draft of the Constitution, pp. 22–3.
40. Ibid., p. 24.
41. Manorama Kohli, 'Bhutan: the Making of a Nation State' in Ramakant and B.C. Upreti (eds.), *Nation-Building in South Asia* (New Delhi, 1991), vol. 2, p. 422.
42. The author was told this by a local Bhutanese lama during the former's visit to Bhutan in December 1994 as well as in November 1997.
43. Das, '*Economic Development*', p. 85.
44. Interview with by a senior officer who served in IMTRAT in Bhutan.
45. For the text see Appendix in Singh, Bhutan: A kingdom.
46. Lt.Gen. B.M. Kaul, *The Untold Story* (Bombay, 1967), p. 248.
47. Kapileshwar Labh, *India and Bhutan* (New Delhi, 1974).
48. Ibid.
49. *National Herald*, New Delhi, 24 November 1978.
50. *The Patriot*, New Delhi, 14 September 1979.
51. *New Wave*, New Delhi, 28 March 1982, *The Indian Express* (New Delhi), 11 November 1982.
52. Ibid.
53. Parmanand, *The Politics of Bhutan* (New Delhi, 1994), p. 173.
54. Manorama Kohli, 'Bhutan's Strategic Environment: Changing Perception', *India Quarterly*, New Delhi, vol. 42, no. 2, April–June 1986, pp. 151–2.
55. Peter Hess, 'Bhutan: The Problems of a Buffer State', *Swiss Review of World Affairs*, Stockholm, November 1968, p. 17.
56. Dalai Lama, *My Land and My People* (London, 1962), p. 202.

57. Srikant Dutt, 'A Brief Study of the Bhutan-Tibet Relations', *View Points on the Third World*, p. 82 (N.A.).

58. Misra, 'Tibetans in Bhutan', China Report, p. 25.

59. Ibid., pp. 27-32.

60. National Assembly Debates, *The Kuensel*, 10 August 1996, p. 17.

61. Ibid., 9 August 1997, p. 2.

62. Ibid.

63. Ibid.

64. 'Bhutan–China Border talks', *The People's Review,* 24–31 December 1998, online edition, see website, < www.yomari.com/p-review/1998/12/241298/bhut.html>

65. See *Appendix* III.

66. National Assembly Debates, *The Kuensal*, 9 August 1997, p. 2.

67. *The Kuensel*, 16 September 1995.

68. *The Kuensel*, 9 August 1997.

69. Ibid.

70. D.B. Gurung, 'Political Problem of Bhutan', *United Asia* (Bombay), no. 12, 1960, p. 369.

71. Ram Rahul, *Modern Bhutan* (Delhi, 1971), p. 36. According to Werner Levi, the Bhutan government introduced this Act as advised by Jawaharlal Nehru during his visit in September 1958, see, Werner Levi, 'Bhutan and Sikkim: Two Buffer States', *The World Today*, vol. 15, no. 12, December 1959, p. 494.

72. 'Bhutan: An Introductory Note', *United Asia*, no. 12, 1960, p. 368.

73. Ainslie, T. Embree (ed.), *Encyclopedia of Asian History*, vol. 1 (New York, 1988), pp. 159–60.

74. For details, see article by Ranjan Gupta, 'Sikkim, The Merger with India', *Asian Survey*, vol. 15, September 1975, pp. 786–98. Also see, B.S. Das, *The Sikkim Saga* (New Delhi, 1976).

75. *Times of India*, New Delhi, 12 November 1977.

76. Ibid.

77. Hari Adhikary, 'The Draconian Designs of the Drukpa Regime', *Rising Nepal*, Kathmandu, 3 April 1993.

78. Ibid.

79. Kalyan Choudhari, 'Bhutan in Ferment', *Frontline*, New Delhi, 27 August 1993, p. 58.

80. Ibid., pp. 58-9.

81. 'The Bhutan Tragedy, when will it end?' *First Report of the SAARC Mission on Bhutan*, May 1992.

82. *The Pioneer*, New Delhi, 3 May 1994.

83. *The Statesman*, 26 January 1992.

84. Ibid.

85. Gisela Bonn, *Indo-Asia*, Sp. Edition, 1988, p. 44.

86. *The Statesman*, 4 April 1994.

87. *Indian Express*, Bombay, 16 April 1994.
88. S.D. Muni, 'Bhutan in the Throes of Ethnic Conflict', *India International Centre Quarterly*, New Delhi, September 1995, p. 149.
89. Ibid.
90. Kanak Mani Dixit, 'Bhutan's Depopulation Policy', *The Pioneer*, 27 August 1993.
91. S.K. Pradhan, 'Human Rights Situation in Bhutan, Appeal by PFHRB', *IMADR Review for Research and Action*, no. 4, September 1994, p. 3.
92. Ibid.
93. Ibid., p. 9.
94. *The Kuensel*, 18–24 September 1999.
95. *The Kuensel*, 27 May–2 June 2000.
96. *The Kuensel*, 30 December 2000.
97. Ibid.
98. 'Bhutan' Country Report on Human Rights Practices – 2000, released by the Bureaucracy of Democracy, Human Rights and Labour, US Department of State, February 2001, p. 10, see website <www.terrorismcentral.com/Library/Government/US/StateDepartment/DemocracyHumanRights/2001/SouthAsia/Bhutan.html >
99. Ibid.
100. *The Kuensel*, August 2000.
101. Ibid.
102. National Assembly Debates, 82nd Session, 28 June 2004.
103. Nepal-Bhutan talks on refugee issue, see website, www.nepalnews.com/archive/2006/may/may30/news 14.php
104. National Assembly Debates 82nd Session, 28 June 2004.
105. www.gorakhpatra.org.np/print.php?nid=1572
106. *The Hindustan Times*, 25 July 1998.
107. Ibid.
108. Ibid.
109. *The Kuensel*, June 2000.
110. Jaideep Saikia, 'Terrorism Sans Frontiers: ULFA Digs Deeper into Bhutan', in O.P. Misra and Sucheta Ghosh (eds.), *Low Intensity Conflict and Terrorism in South Asian Region* (New Delhi, 2003), p. 447.
111. Ibid.
112. Ibid.
113. Quoted in ibid., p. 452.
114. Nitin Gokhale, 'In ULFA Country, Life is Cheap', *Outlook*, New Delhi, 19 October 1998. For details, see, <*http:/www.research.ryerson.ca/SAFER-Net/regions/Asia/Bhu_AT03.html*>
115. M.K. Dhar: 'Eviction of Terrorists: Ball in Bhutan's Court,' *International*, September 2003; see website <*http://www.dayafterindia.com/september1/bhutan.html*>

116. Bhutan's Military Profile: see <*http://www.stratmag.com/issuMAr-1/page06.html*>

117. Ibid.

118. *The Hindu*, 16 December 2003.

119. P.C. Adhikary, 'Economic Transition in Bhutan: A Study on the Impact of Indo-Bhutan Trade and Economic Co-operation', *Asian Profile*, Hongkong, vol. 21, no. 6, December 1993, p. 477.

120. Bhabani Sen Gupta, *Bhutan: Towards a Grass-root Participatory Polity* (New Delhi, 1999), pp. 80–1.

121. *Bhutan: Country's Assistance Plans: Bhutan–I* For details see, <www.adb.org/Documents/CAPs/BHU/0101.asp>

122. P.P. Karan, *Bhutan: Environment, Culture And Development Strategy* (New Delhi, 1990), p. 108.

123. *The Kuensel*, 19 June 1993.

124. Ibid.

125. Bhutan has its own radio service known, the Bhutan Broadcasting Service.

126. Valentine J. Belfiglio, 'India's Economic and Political Relations with Bhutan', *Asian Survey*, vol. 12, no. 8, August 1972, p. 678.

127. S. Seymour, 'Strategic Development in Bhutan', *Strategic Digest*, New Delhi, vol. 3, no. 3, March 1978, p. 56.

128. *Indian Express*, 11 November 1982.

129. *Times of India*, 29 September 1985.

# CHAPTER 10

# The State *vis-à-vis* the Periphery: Issues of Identity, Violence, and Peace in North-East India<sup>a</sup>

*Nani Gopal Mahanta*

The challenges that the state is facing in India and other parts of South Asia can be primarily attributed to the nature and formation of the nation state itself. A mechanical application of the nation state idea from the European experience with its monolithic credo and unitary state structure on the deeply divided multicultural society is problematic. The whole process negated diversity and human interaction which were fundamental to the culture of South Asian society. In this complex mosaic of different nationalities, the Indian state is facing some of its gravest challenges, with the entire process of nation-building being questioned. In response to this, various ethno-sub-nationalist movements in India, Bangladesh, Sri Lanka, and Nepal are increasingly questioning the legitimacy of the state to rule over these communities. The violent nature of these movements also precipitates a violent response by the state. The alternative movements fighting against the state, in some form or other, have been reproducing the logic of the state. These movements, like the state are equally afraid of diversity and their attempt to hegemonize a particular community's way of life is problematic in a heterogeneous society.

In this chapter we will look at the Naga movement in northeast (NE) India. The Nagas (a cluster of about seventeen hill tribes, mainly inhabitants of Nagaland) were perhaps the first subnational group in India and in South Asia to launch a violent secessionist movement just after independence. Even after fifty-five years the problem still remains intractable, the recent peace initiative notwithstanding! Subsequently, the other NE states like Assam, Manipur, Tripura, and Mizoram too have witnessed violent secessionist movements, some of them right from the 1960s.

We shall try to see how the sub-nationalist movements are suffering from lack of democracy, and how are they increasingly becoming intolerant of the other ethnic groups in those regions. The crux of the argument is that these movements have failed to produce any viable alternative framework and simply reproduce the same logic of the state. The insurgent groups work under extreme authoritarian principles where dissidence and difference are not tolerated. We shall also try to put forward our logic against the ideology of secession as the panacea of all ills. To conclude, we shall look at some of the possibilities for accommodating these diverse interests of a multicultural society like NE India.

## I. THEORY AND HISTORY:
## THE CONCEPTUAL FRAMEWORK

### 1. State and Nation-building in South Asia

The modernist school of thinking has primarily shaped our notion about the state and identity. Its main thesis is that nation states are created by certain causal factors, that bind together the diverse communities living within a territorial boundary.[1] The rise of nationalism in India is explained through a dominant, centralizing idea which organizes different sections of people and social groups into one single nation state. The nation state and the modernization framework as adopted in developing countries like India and other South Asian countries is supposed to have created a framework which would gradually accommodate all the divergent regional, ethnic, caste identities into one pan-Indian identity.[2] From the very beginning the Indian nation state tried to impose one pan-Indian identity. As Ashis Nandy points out the nation state fears diversity.[3]

The premises of subaltern studies in Indian history reject such attempts to unify the plural social reality with a centralizing ideology—'the domain of politics was structurally split and not unified and homogeneous as elite interpretation has made out to be'.[4] Recognizing and giving social, cultural, and political space to people, social groups, and nationalities lies at the heart of the post-modernist approach. If the modernists' world-view is shaped by a top-down approach which views the assertion of the subnational groups as a threat to the nation state, the post-modernists study 'the peoples and the movements' in their own right.[5] However, as has been shown by some writers, one cannot possibly agree with all the premises of the post-modernists' approach, particularly their idea of doing away with the state which conjures up the spectre of potentially uncontrollable fragmentation, perhaps anarchy.[6] This presents a challenge to redesign the state structure to give a voice to the plural realities of a multicultural society like India's. Navnita Chadha Behera already talks about such an approach, which is deeply federal and decentralizing in nature; evolved in the spirit of a bottom-up approach. The remedy lies in creating for indigenous civil society a voice in the political structure of the country.[7]

The crux of the argument is that the modern nation-state allows recognition of a single nation only. This principle, applied to a plural democracy when governed through electoral democracy, is inherently problematic. A mechanical application of the nation state idea with its monolithic credo and one unified identity negates diversity and freedom which are fundamental to their culture. Trying to manage and enforce ideological and political conformity on the subnationalities in the interest of the nation state is to 'impose a monolithness and homogenization that are alien and alienating'.[8]

In India, the Congress leadership, although sensitive to the plural identities of India, finally decided on a strong centre with some subsidiary powers attributed to the states in the light of the disturbances that India faced during the time of independence.[9] The result was that the Constitution of India provided enormous social, economic, and political power to the centre to organize and manage social relations among diverse communities and subnationalities to ensure their allegiance to the Indian nation.[10]

We shall argue that this disjuncture between the plural social realities and unitary political structure is the root cause of separatist challenges to the Indian polity. Also, the logic of electoral politics has led the Indian nation state to reproduce state power.[11] The identification of the political parties with the interests of the majorities by appealing to categories such as 'ethnic', 'religious', 'linguistic', or a combination of some or all of them, is problematic. Such a situation not only puts pressure on the less powerful communities to organize their separate identities, but also 'deepens the hatred between the well defined communities or nationalities, particularly when the nation-building is organized and measured in terms of the will of the majority', which exercises state power.[12]

This brings us to the question, what are the viable options to be taken up? Our argument will be that a military or 'law and order' approach, exclusively focusing on the internal security dimension to address the separatist and secessionist demands will not solve the problem unless we address some of the structural issues. There is a need to create a political system which allows healthy nurturing of the subnational and sub-regional identities and develops stakes for them so that the polity holds together because its myriad identities desire a voluntary union with the state and not because the dominant identity believes it is in its interest to do so. This calls for a serious rethinking of the notion of 'national identity' and for restructuring the Indian state.

## 2. NAGA IDENTITY: ROOTS AND ASSERTION

In the post-independence period the first major challenge to the Indian state as one unified nation came from north-east India, a region which is a conglomerate of seven predominantly tribal states. The NE, comprising the states of Assam, Meghalaya, Manipur, Nagaland, Tripura, Arunachal Pradesh, and Megha-laya, is perhaps the most heterogeneous region of India with 250 social groups and more than 75 languages. Only 2 per cent of the landmass is connected with India and the rest of the territory shares more than 4,500 km of international border, with South and South-East Asian countries like Bangladesh, Nepal, Bhutan, China, and Myanmar.[13] Proximity to these countries provides a new dimension to the whole identity issues of the subnational groups in the region.

The Nagas, an Indo-Mongoloid people, are among the proudest and most distinctive communities in the north-east.[14] What initially appeared to be a demand for autonomy for safeguarding the 'Naga way of life' soon evolved into a people's revolt led by the Naga National Council (NNC). Today the Naga armed struggle is the oldest secessionist movement in India's post-independent history. The Indian state, however, has shown considerable resilience in resisting the movement and created a separate state by accommodating the Naga interest in the Constitution of India.[15] The democratic process initiated by the Indian state notwithstanding, some of the issues still remain unresolved. Regarding the role of the Indian state, a scholar from the region remarks: 'Ignorance and prejudice have long marked New Delhi's approach towards this proud race of people who had been leading an independent existence, except for some seventy-odd years of half-hearted British control, at the periphery [of] what today constitutes [the] Indian nation state.'[16]

As the Indian leaders set about building the nation state, deeply infused with the ideas of nationalism and emboldened by the overthrow of the British, they were highly taken aback when certain communities within India challenged their notion of nationalism. They were not at all prepared to appreciate the demands of the Nagas since they were outside the ambit of Indian nationalism. Various attempts were made to discredit the Naga movement. It was dubbed a secessionist movement that was inspired and abetted by foreign Christian missionaries who had been exploiting the fierce feeling of independence of the hill tribes to break up the Indian nation.[17] The long struggle against the state brought various factions of the Naga tribes onto one common political platform although there is no common language among the tribes.[18] A distinct tribal economic pattern, local traditions of self-governing institutions, a deep sense of attachment to the native soil, a desperate urge to protect the traditional laws, customs, and tribal authority are a few factors which gave a tremendous sense of unity to the Naga tribes, to what they claim to be the 'Naga way of life'.[19] Today the Nagas have achieved a 'sense of peoplehood',[20] which very few subnational groups have attained.

It would be wrong to say that the Indian state did not take any democratic steps to accommodate the rights of the Nagas. After the initial blunder of dubbing the Naga movement anti-national and resorting to force of arms, the central government took some corrective measures. Some of these steps included the creation of the state of Nagaland in 1963, providing protective provisions under the constitution, etc.[21] The central government in the subsequent period granted heavy funds to the state of Nagaland to cajole the disgruntled elites.[22]

However, civil society groups and the Naga traditional authorities still support the self-determination demand of the Naga insurgent groups.[23] In other words, the constitutional and democratic process of the Indian state is yet to incorporate a vast section of the Naga people who still don't consider themselves to be Indian. This strong sense of Naga peoplehood is defined by a long Naga history of independence and fierce opposition to subjugation by various forces of history. It is also marked by the Nagas' intense attachment to their native soil and to common local tradition which, they argue, is distinct from the Indian Hindu ethos and culture. Nagas never allowed themselves to be ruled by any foreign rulers.[24]

## II. FROM TRIBES TO PEOPLEHOOD

### 1. THE CONQUEST OF THE BRITISH: SELF-RULE FOR THE NAGAS

The Ahoms who ruled Assam from the middle of the thirteenth century adopted a policy of reconciliation backed by force. But the Ahom rulers had never any plans for the conquest and annexation of the Naga territories. 'The Ahom rulers considered it enough to receive the submission of the Nagas and to allow them to enjoy their tribal autonomy—so long as the Nagas lived near the plains ... (and) did not raid Ahom territories.'[25] Regarding the Ahom-Naga relationship, it can be said that while the Nagas submitted to the strength of the Ahom rulers, the latter respected the Nagas' love for independence and desisted from interfering in their internal affairs.[26] The British after annexing Assam with the Treaty of Yandaboo followed a policy of cautious non-interference in Naga affairs. This was followed by the speedy consolidation of British rule in the Naga Hills. The Nagas, particularly the Angamis, put up a resistance to the British for eleven days in 1879–80 mainly led by thirteen Angami village states. For the first time the Nagas had to accept a totally alien power as a ruler in the midst of their territory. The British decided not to tinker with the village democracy of the hill tribes—in other words, tribes like the Nagas were left to themselves to manage their own state of affairs. Various legislative Acts like the Excluded Areas Act and to Partially Excluded Areas Act put an end to any interaction between the hill tribal and the non-tribal populations. This isolation that was primarily done for political manageability proved useful in later times as the Nagas were almost left out from the anti-British struggle. 'This is not surprising that the Nagas were not in any way drawn into the anti-British struggle led by the Congress and they were practically untouched by the force of Indian nationalism.'[27]

Meanwhile the introduction of a monetized economy and the spread of education by Christian missionaries created a middle class that became conscious of its interests and identity. As early as 1929, the Naga Club[28] submitted a memorandum to the British Simon Commission that the Nagas be excluded from the proposed constitutional changes and be kept under the direct control of the British. In the memorandum, the Naga Club said 'You (the British) are the only people who have conquered us and when you go we should be as we were'. Apprehending that they could be merged with the Indian rulers or left at their mercy the petition said 'If the British Government, however, wants to throw us away, we pray that we should not be thrust at the mercy of the people who could never have conquered us themselves, and to whom we were never subjected; but to leave us alone to determine for ourselves as in ancient times'.[29]

It is clear from the memorandum that the Naga people preferred to be ruled by the British rather than the Indians and there is a sense of gratitude towards the British in Naga Hills. It was primarily the socio-cultural role of the Christian missionaries and the ability of the Britishers to give a sense of identity and unity to the heterogeneous Naga population. To quote from the memorandum: 'Our country within the administered area consists of eight tribes, quite different from one another with quite different languages which cannot be understood by each other and there are more tribes outside the administered areas which are not known at present. We have no unity among us and it is only the British Government that is holding us together.'[30]

## 2. NAGA NATIONAL COUNCIL (NNC) AND FORMATION AS AN ETHNIC GROUP

The formation of the NNC marks an important phase in the formation of Naga peoplehood. Representatives of individual tribal councils held a meeting in February 1946 and reorganized and renamed the erstwhile Naga Hills District Tribal Council the Naga National Council. Here the word 'national' was used for the first time, and it was the first ever attempt to bring various Naga tribes under one socio-political platform. The movement of solidarity launched by the NNC contributed to the lessening of inter-tribal feuds and the consequent emergence of a 'Naga identity' the so-called 'Naga way of life'.[31] Thus it was a remarkable success for the NNC that it could bring diverse groups of Naga people under one banner. Urmila Phadnis, the noted scholar on ethnic movements in South Asia, describes five components of such ethnic groups: (a) a subjective belief in real or assumed historical antecedents; (b) a symbolic or real geographical centre; (c) shared cultural emblems such as race, language, religion, dress, and diet, or a combination of some of them which though variegated and flexible, provide the overt basis of ethnic identity; (d) self-ascribed awareness of distinctiveness and belonging to the group; and (e) recognition by others of this group differentiation. It is thus a self-defined and 'other recognized' status.[32] The self-awareness process has already begun; now there is a long struggle looming ahead for the Nagas to be recognized by others as a separate nationhood. Prior to the advent of the NNC, most of the tribes lived in isolation and the role of the village council was restricted to the 'village republic'. The NNC utilized all the arsenals of ethnic mobilization such as customs, tradition, village-level self-governing institutions, religion, a definite sense of territoriality, and so on. These factors were sufficient to highlight the issue of cultural incompatibility with the Indians. In the later period (in the 1980s) the Naga ethnic leaders developed a historically defined Nagaland with an irredentist claim over the territories of other subnational groups.

The NNC soon called upon the Nagas to prepare for self-determination. Initially the Naga leaders were not so sure about the demand for an independent Nagaland.[33] According to Udayan Mishra, initially the NNC was talking more along the lines of full regional autonomy.[34] However, the Naga leaders soon realized that if they did not ask for independence their case would be marginalized. In its pursuance of the demand for an independent state, a delegation led by Zapu Phizo[35] met Lord Mountbatten, the last British Viceroy in colonial India, with the suggestion that India, after partition, should act as the guardian power for a period of ten years after which the Nagas would be free to determine their political future. There was very little recognition of the Naga cause, but Mahatma Gandhi provided the much-needed support and said: 'We want you to feel India is yours. . . . I feel Naga Hills is mine just as much as it is yours.' He also ruled out the possibility of using any force against the Nagas. 'I will come to Kohima and ask them (Indian soldiers) to shoot me before they shoot one Naga'.[36]

Meanwhile, the governor of Assam, Akbar Hydari, had arrived at a nine-point agreement with the NNC in Kohima on 29 June 1947. The agreement acknowledged the NNC's right of control over all spheres of Naga life ranging from tribal laws to the ownership of land and taxation. But problems emerged with regard to Article 9 of the Agreement,[37] which the Nagas argued had given them the right to complete independence once the interim government's term was over. This was not at all acceptable to the Government of India which argued that the said article gave the NNC the right to suggest administrative changes but not that of secession. The NNC under Phizo declared independence on 14 August 1947, thus transforming the NNC into a full-fledged militant political organization. A series of incidents took place in the period from 1947–52. The NNC rejected the Sixth Schedule of the Constitution,[38] conducted a plebiscite (May to August 1951) in which 99.9 per cent of the Nagas favoured a sovereign state, organized a total boycott of the 1952 general elections, and so on. Nehru, the first prime minister and the icon of Indian nationalism whose popularity was at its height, was completely boycotted when he visited Nagaland in 1953. The Indian army and the police intervened when Phizo announced the formation of the Republican Government of free Nagaland on 18 September 1954, and thousands of Naga youths went underground to wage battle against the Indian state.

Here it would be pertinent to understand the views of the Indian national leaders on the Naga assertion of independence. Nehru, who understood very well the heterogeneous character of Indian society, was opposed to forceful assimilation. On several occasions he opposed the military approach of various regional and national leaders and said: 'I refuse to accept the proposition that the battle for Indian independence should be fought in Naga Hills. I appeal for a more positive and fuller approach to the problem'.[39] It is a real irony that in the days to come Nehru did not look into the widely reported issues of human rights violations and army and police atrocities. Such tactics further alienated the people from the unification attempt of the Indian state. Except for Jawaharlal Nehru and some regional leaders of Assam like Gopinath Bordoloi and Bimala Prasad Chaliha,[40] the ruling elites at the centre lacked the sensitivity to understand the psyche of the Naga people and could not appreciate their way of life and customs. Many wanted to brush aside the Naga movement as a secessionist one instigated by anti-Indian forces. Leaders like Ram Manohar Lohia described the Naga assertion as a ploy of the Christian missionaries and the British to break up the territory of India. He urged the Government of India to take stern action as it was not so much Assam's provincial autonomy as the unity and integrity of the country that was at stake.[41] This is a typical reflection of what we have formulated at the theoretical level: the developing countries of South Asia like India, in their quest to achieve a homogeneous and unified state and nation negated some of the basic ingredients of their societies. Here the observation of Rajat Ganguly regarding the situation in South Asia is noteworthy: 'The over-centralization of state power mainly came from the obsession of the post-colonial elites in South and South-East Asia, who, irrespective of the political system and type of government, wanted to produce a pulverized and uniform sense of national identity at any cost. . . . However, the attempt to forge a uniform political national identity in the space occupied by numerous and distinct ethnic identities generated an 'ethnic backlash'.'[42]

## III. A STATE FOR THE NAGAS AND INTERNAL CONFLICTS

### 1. CREATION OF THE STATE OF NAGALAND AND PEACE MISSION

Meanwhile, New Delhi encouraged a group of Naga moderates to work for a negotiated settlement—which ultimately led to the formation of a full-fledged state for the Naga people within the Indian Union in December 1963. There was fierce opposition from Phizo and his group and he slipped away to Pakistan into self-imposed exile. The 13th amendment to the Constitution that led to the formation of the state provided considerable clauses for the protection of the 'Naga way of life'.[43]

To disrupt the ongoing political process, the NNC launched a series of violent activities. Concerned by this, the Nagaland Baptist Convention in 1964 unanimously resolved to request the government to invite Jayaprakash Narayan, B.P. Chaliha, and Rev. Michael Scott to help restore normalcy in Nagaland.[44] The mission succeeded in concluding an agreement for a ceasefire with the Federal Government of Nagaland.[45] The peace mission while appreciating the Nagas' claim for self-determination stated that the 'Naga Federal Government could on their own volition, decide to be a participant in the Union of India and mutually settle terms and conditions for that purpose.' The Government of India too could recast and reshape its relationship with Nagaland 'so as to satisfy the political aspirations of all sections of Naga opinion'.[46] The peace mission proposal failed as the rebels insisted on the issue of sovereignty which the Government of India promptly rejected.

The overwhelming participation of Naga people in the 1964

state assembly elections essentially marked two things. It marked a new era for the state of Nagaland as an integral part of India; and it led to the gradual marginalization of the NNC as the sole representative of the Naga people. There was recurring inter-tribal fighting for leadership and supremacy, especially after Phizo's self-imposed exile in London. The centre's policy of liberally granting money to the state brought several changes in the internal functioning of the Naga society as it increased their dependence on Indian market forces and the government. The idea of private property was gaining ground; the Nagas were increasingly being absorbed in various government departments, and the life of the community was changing as modernization spread. These developments also helped to curtail the powerful role of the tribal council—which had been utilized by Phizo for spreading the message of Naga self-determination. The new class of politicians, ministers, and members of parliament (MPs) emerged as the new power centre of society who got elected on clan and tribal lines. However, this is not to suggest that the idea of sovereignty had lost its relevance, as is evident from the incidents described in the following section.

## 2. SHILLONG ACCORD: EMERGENCE OF NSCN AND FIGHT FOR SUPREMACY

The Indian state, in its effort to gain ground in Nagaland brought a sizeable number of underground rebels to the table to sign what has become known as the Shillong Accord of 1975. The Shillong Accord was rejected by Phizo, and it created divisions within the NNC organization. Two leaders of the NNC, Thuengaling Muivah and Isak Swu felt that the NNC 'isolated itself from the people'. Thus, to save the people from the 'process of domination, exploitation and assimilation', the National Socialist Council of Nagaland (NSCN) was formed. During this period Khaplang, a Hemi Konyak Naga of Burma, was the president of the rebel Federal Government. Both Muivah and Swu were able to win over Khaplang. A new government of the Peoples' Republic of Nagaland with Isak Swu as the president, Khaplang as the vice-chairman, and Muivah as the general secretary was declared elected. It declare its objectives as: (i) the unquestionable sovereign right of the Naga people over every inch of Nagaland; (ii) the dictatorship of the people through the NSCN and the practice of democracy . . . as long as it is deemed necessary; (iii) faith in God and the salvation of mankind in Jesus Christ, that is, Nagaland for Christ; and (iv) the ruling out of saving Nagaland through peaceful means.[47]

Unlike the NNC which drew considerable support from all sections of the people, the NSCN made it absolutely clear that Nagaland was meant for the Christians and urged its people to fight against the Hindu forces, the Hindu government of India. The NSCN virtually ruled out any possibility of challenging the organization by other political parties: 'there must be a single organization of the people'. Other political parties would not be tolerated as they 'could never accomplish anything except leading to ruination'.[48] Thus the formation of the NSCN marked the beginning of a new authoritarian and military organization which would never tolerate any opposition to its policies. However, it did not take much time for the NSCN military leaders to start fighting with each other. Meanwhile, around 1988, feelers were sent out both by the government and by the rebel groups for a negotiated settlement. There were rumours that Swu and Muivah had sold out and planned to oust Khaplang, seize arms from the Konyak (to which Khaplang also belonged) national workers and surrender to India. In a pre-emptive strike, the Muivah group was attacked by Khaplang's men and Burmese troops at dawn on 30 April 1988. About 140 men, women and children were killed (most of them were Thangkhuls Nagas, the tribe to which Muivah belonged). Some elements are said to have accused Kahplang and his group of having spread the canards about Muivah's and Swu's 'treachery' at the behest of Indian agents.[49] The massacre of the Muivah group was a serious setback to the Naga struggle. It led to a vertical split of the group into the NSCN (Khaplang, Hemi-Konyak Naga) and the faction around Muivah-Swu, Thangkul-Sema Naga which became more popular as the NSCN (I-M).

The Naga intra-tribal feud is well known, but this incident was by any account one of the bloodiest internal conflicts. The recent Naga-Kuki clashes,[50] which claimed hundreds of lives, have clearly shown that there are serious problems with the demands of the NSCN. The NSCN (I-M) and the NSCN (Khaplang) are leading a number of insurgent groups in the region. It was at the initiative of the latter that the Indo-Burma Revolutionary Front (IBRF) was formed in May 1992, which included the principal groups opposed to the NSCN (I-M), such as the United Liberation Front of Manipur (UNLF), the United Liberation Front of Assam (ULFA), the Kuki National Organization, and the Kuki National Army. Not very happy with such a formation, the NSCN (I-M) declared the formation of the 'Self Defence United Front of the South–East Himalayan Region (SDUF) in November 1994. It included among others the Hynnieewtrep Achik Liberation Council of Meghalaya, and the National Democratic Front of Bodoland (NDFB).[51]

## IV. FROM NAGALAND TO NAGALIM: DISPUTED CLAIMS

### 1. Peace Talks, Irredentist Claim and the Fight for Nagalim

We have argued earlier that a hurried and homogenized application of the nation state created an 'ethnic backlash' in a multi-ethnic society like India. The subnational groups in the north–east, particularly the Nagas who had never developed an Indian identity immediately fought back in defence of their own Naga identity. Thus the very process of national integration in South Asia, by over-centralizing power and encouraging policies of assimilation, provided the stimulus for insurgent secessionist movements.

However, the irony of the situation is that these subnational militant groups want to replace the existing nation state by creating another nation state.[52] The problem with these violent articulations in South Asia is that they have never tried to take into confidence the opinions of the diverse communities whom they claim to represent. The homogenizing and standardizing principles that guide the nation state also regulate the internal and external functioning of these alternative militant movements. This is the problem with the Tamil nationalists in Sri Lanka, the Kashmiri militants, the Naga NSCN leaders, the Bodos, and also with the ULFA who want an independent state for the people of Assam. The subnational groups thus also follow the same alienating logic of the nation state. They have failed to go beyond the narratives of colonialism that solidly erected the pillars of the nation state. The social movements in South Asia (whether violent or non-violent), when they are fighting against the over-centralizing and the homogenizing tendencies of the nation state to protect their distinctiveness, reproduce the same logic. These social groups fighting against the injustice of the state are themselves extremely diverse and plural. But once the ethnic groups have captured state power at the provincial level or are aspiring to attain it, they operate not differently from the state. They are as authoritarian and centralized and bent on repro-ducing their hegemony. This is particularly true with regard to the Naga movement whether under the NSCN (I-M) or the NSCN (Khaplang). In other words, the pathology of the nation state as being afraid of diversity has infected these movements also. However, this phenomenon has been facilitated by a variety of factors. For a more coherent analytical purpose, we should mention the following interrelated issues:

1. The tendency of establishing one community's dominance in an otherwise extremely diverse region is a development in South Asia which has far-reaching consequences. The Nagas' claim of incorporating the neighbouring areas like Assam, Manipur, and Arunachal Pradesh as the traditional homeland of the Nagas has created violent protests and feelings of mistrust and hostility between the Nagas and other communities of the region.

2. Of course this is not a straightforward development, the state in India too has developed entrenched interests in the continuation of these inter-ethnic clashes. The state on many occasions has developed counter-insurgency forces by instigating rival ethnic groups to fight against the dominant group. We have argued elsewhere that this helps the state in two ways: (a) it prevents a particular ethnic insurgent movement from becoming too powerful, and (b) it legitimizes the authority of the state in front of the civil society as neutral umpire among contending forces.[53]

3. The approach of the Indian state to the resolution of the ethnic insurgency in the north-east particularly can best be described as 'tribal-to-tribal', cosmetic, and devoid of addressing the core structural issues. The centre has signed a number of accords with the ethnic groups, which have created more discord and dissatisfaction.

4. This requires some soul-searching on the part of the Indian state as the north-east is too sensitive to be tinkered with by the dirty tactics of Indian intelligence. Until and unless there is some effective civil society intervention to respect the diversity and the rights of other ethnic groups, the states like Nagaland and Assam are going to witness more turbulence and violence.

The insurgency in Nagaland has become more complicated with the emergence of the NSCN as the sole custodian of Naga grievances. While the NNC was in control, it was the Federal Government—the political wing of the NNC—and not the Naga Federal Army that called the shots. Decisions taken by the political wing of the NNC had to be ratified by the *Tatar Hoho*.[54] The NSCNs of both the factions are more authoritarian, militaristic, and indiscriminate in their approach. The NSCN (I-M) has killed hundreds of innocent Kuki men, women, and children in its ethnic cleansing drive.[55] The Nagas and the Kukis have lived in harmony for generations and the present struggle has been precipitated by territorial claims. However, the Nagas claim that their animosity towards the Kukis is justified on historical grounds[56] negates the true reasons. In reality the Kukis are the main obstacle to the realization of Greater Nagaland, what the Nagas call 'Nagalim'.

There are also allegations of Kuki militant groups being helped by the state apparatus to counter the supremacy of the NSCN (I-M). There are a number of writings which corroborate the state's involvement in the continuing fight between the Nagas and the Kukis. Commenting on this, a very senior historian from the region, the ex-president of the Indian Historical Association, H.K. Borpujari, comments: 'Kuki militants who were said to have received moral support from official agencies both of Manipur and Union Government had been demanding financial assistance, in arms and materials to "fight and finish" the NSCN (I-M)'.[57]

After a series of informal discussions the Government of India and the NSCN (I-M) came to a ceasefire agreement with effect from 1 August 1997, which has been extended periodically. Both parties have agreed to talk to each other on certain conditions: (a) talks will be held in a third, neutral country, (b) talks will be conducted at the highest political (prime minister) level; and (c) talks will be held unconditionally. Ground rules and modalities to implement them finalized on 12 December 1997 and further revised on 13 January 2001, were set-up to facilitate the negotiations on the politically substantive issues that underlie the five-decade-old' war.

## 2. Contest over Sovereignty and Territoriality

The ceasefire of January 2001, led to massive violent protests in Assam, Manipur, and Arunachal Pradesh as the agreement envisaged to extend the ceasefire without territorial limits. At this point it would be pertinent to look into the issue of Greater Nagaland, or 'Nagalim'. This is the only aspect on which there is complete unanimity among all the overground and underground groups of Nagaland in that they seek to incorporate the territories of the neighbouring states and also some areas in Burma.[58] The controversy took a new turn with the Nagaland Assembly unanimously adopting a resolution in December 1994 seeking the integration of Naga inhabited areas in Manipur and Arunachal Pradesh. Greater Nagaland would include vital districts of Manipur, namely, Ukhrul, Senapati, Sadar Hills, Tamenlong, and Chandel, including Moreh where Kukis and Nagas are evenly divided.

Of all these states Manipur launched a vehement protest both to the resolution of the Nagaland Assembly and to the extension of the ceasefire. Why should the people of Manipur, particularly the populace of Imphal Valley, express such violent discontent at the extension of the Naga ceasefire to their land? Literally, a ceasefire is an arrangement in which people or countries stop fighting in order to discuss their disagreement. How does the territorial aspect apply?

The extension of the ceasefire beyond the present state of Nagaland has always been considered a springboard for the realization of the concept of Greater Nagaland. Even before the Naga ceasefire was announced in July 1997, the issue of the integration of Naga-inhabited areas leading to the dismemberment of Manipur had come to the fore. Various Naga tribes inhabit four of the five hill districts of Manipur comprising 70 per cent of Manipur's total area of 22,372 sq. km. The only other hill district, Churachandpur, not inhabited by the Nagas but by the Zomis (Paites) and Chin-Kuki groups, constitutes nearly 20 per cent of the state. This means the valley districts—Imphal East, Imphal West, Bishnupur, and Thoubal—which house nearly 65 per cent of the total population of Manipur, occupy a mere 2,000 sq. km. or 10 per cent of the state's total area. The Manipur Valley people mostly comprise Meiteis,[59] the most dominant group of Manipuri society, and also some Pangals (Manipuri Muslims) who constitute 6.5 per cent of the total population.

Thus, statistics clearly indicate that, were it not for the meiteis supported by the Chin-Kuki-Zomi groups of Churachandpur fighting to preserve the integrity of Manipur, the consolidation of Naga-inhabited areas into one unit would imply Manipur surrendering at least 70 per cent of its territory. The Valley people, proud as they are of their 2,000-year-old history, are not prepared to give any leeway to the mechanisms of Naga integration. Like the Nagaland Assembly, the Manipur Assembly too passed several resolutions to protect the territorial integrity of the region at any cost.[60] The pent-up anger against the political elites culminated, on 18 June 2001, four days after the decision by the Government of India to extend the ceasefire beyond the territorial limits of Nagaland, in unprecedented violence in Manipur. Thousands of protestors marched towards Raj Bhawan, the only seat of power in the absence of a popular government. On being prevented from proceeding further, the angry mob began targeting the political establishment irrespective of party affiliation, and burnt down the historic Manipur Legislative Assembly building. They also set fire to many other buildings including the official residence of the Speaker of the Legislative Assembly, Sapam

Dhananjoy, as well as the offices of the Congress party. Similarly ransacked were the offices of the BJP, the Communist Party of India (CPI), and the Samata Party. The only common thread in the violent action in which fourteen persons lost their lives was that the target was the political establishment alone. During the course of one and a half months of agitation, popular resentment against local politicians was reflected repeatedly. Similar incidents if not of the same magnitude also occurred in Assam under the leadership of the All Assam Students Union (AASU), where the Congress government also opposed any such move of territorial compromise.[61]

It is very clear from the above analysis that the main demand of the Nagas, i.e. unification of all the Naga tribes into one Nagalim, is structurally problematic and a recipe for ethnic clashes in the north-east region. This process has already created wide-spread animosity and mistrust. It would be wrong to think that the government is worried about such developments. In certain ways it is beneficial for the state if such conflicts remain within a certain level.[62] Very soon after there agitations fratricidal clashes erupted between the NSCN (I-M) and the NSCN (K), and the latter expressed deep anguish over the fact that it had been left out from the ongoing peace process.

The issues of Greater Nagaland and ceasefire beyond territorial limits have already caused sufficient bloodshed and put the Naga-Kukis, Naga-Meiteis, and the Naga-Assamese in a hostile situation. There is no sign however that the NSCN and the Naga civil society groups like Naga Hoho, the Naga Students Federation, are going to compromise on the issue of Nagalim. This recalcitrance is due to the fact that the Nagas as recent developments suggest have already come a long way from their demand of an independent Nagaland.[63] It could be a face-saving device which the NSCNs want to fulfil. There is also no sufficient logic on the part of the Nagas for this irredentist claim. How can the Nagas speak of one historical Nagaland when 'prior to the coming of the British, the idea of a well-defined territory for the Nagas or the other tribes was virtually non-existent? It has therefore, been a long journey from the "Naga village republic" to the concept of a unified Nagalim covering some 120,000 km.

of land which would include all those who consider themselves to be Nagas, irrespective of whether they reside in Assam, Manipur or Arunachal.'[64]

Donald L. Horowitz, one of the great names in the study of ethnic groups in conflict worldwide, made some remarkable observations on secession and territorial claims. He said in a recent publication, 'One reason for the greater danger that often follows secession is the activation of irredentist claims. . . . And when irredentism gets going, it usually involves ethnic cleansing, so as to eliminate troublesome minorities in the region to be retrieved.'[65]

The scattering of one tribe over different territories is not a unique Naga problem. For example, the Ghana-Togo border divides the Ewe, the Nigerian-Benin border divides the Yoruba, the Bakongo are divided between Zaire, Zambia, and Angola. There are Somalis in Somalia, Ethiopia, Kenya, and Djibouti. Coming to South-East Asia, there are Malays in Malaysia, Thailand, Brunei, Indonesia, and Singapore. Likewise, there are Tamils in Sri Lanka and India; Baluch and Kalash in Afghanistan, Pakistan, and Iran, not to speak of the Basques in France and Spain; the Saami (Lapp) people in Norway, Sweden, and Finland—the list is endless. These are ethnic people who are divided across sovereign borders. The Nagas are living contiguously within the same north-eastern region. On top of this, they did not have this cohesive identity till the beginning of the twentieth century. Even now it would be wrong to treat the Nagas living in Nagaland itself as a homogeneous tribe—this is reflected in the fierce battle between NSCN (I-M) and NSCN (Khaplang).

This trend of identifying one territory as belonging to a specific group does not augur well for the future in a highly mixed ethnic society like that of north-east India; this trend is becoming contagious as it is spreading to the neighbouring areas of Manipur, Assam, Tripura, and Meghalaya. There are separatist and secessionist groups in all these states who are trying to create an independent (or within India) or homogeneous land for their respective communities.[66] Such domination of one group is simply neither possible nor desirable in any of the states as they are a mix of diverse groups and languages.[67]

The ethnic groups who are fighting for an independent space want unqualified ownership of their history. They claim to be the real custodians and interpreters of history—the outsiders are simply ignorant who will distort their authenticity and originality. At least this is what the Naga Students Federation (NSF)— perhaps the most powerful student body and a non-violent organization in Nagaland—wants us to believe. The support of the NSF for the Naga sovereignty movement and Greater Nagaland is well known. It issued a directive and a warning requiring non-Naga scholars to secure its permission and clearance before undertaking any academic research pertaining to the Naga people and their history.[68] The president of the NSF said that 'people from outside the community' would not be allowed to undertake any research on Naga history without the organization's permission. It is really surprising that such a directive comes from a so-called non-violent student group and not from an insurgent group.

This feeling of insecurity regarding Naga history originates from the 'genome project' that has been going on in Nagaland University for the last two years. Among other things, the project requires the collection of blood samples from every Naga tribe. It is felt that the project attempts to establish that all the Naga groups are actually totally unrelated, and not one nation.[69] The leaders feel that if the genome project does make any such claim at this hour, it will considerably weaken the Naga's stand of being one nation, which they have built up so laboriously for so many years.

## V. ON SOVEREIGNTY, SELF-DETERMINATION AND POSSIBLE COMPROMISE

The Naga's struggle for the last fifty-five years is essentially centred around two demands: (a) the establishment of a Greater Nagaland, and (b) an independent Nagaland or the issue of self-determination.[70] We have seen how the issue of Greater Nagaland has opened up a Pandora's box in north-east India.

Initially the leaders of the NNC were themselves not clear about what they meant by self-determination. But after the 1951 plebiscite, conducted by the NNC, the latter solemnly declared that 99.9 per cent[71] of the people wanted independence. The right to self-determination has been misread as the unqualified right to secede.[72] The basic point here is that although there is some confusion, international law in contemporary times does not allow the right to secede unless there is a major sanction by the UN and other powers of the world.

In spite of its best efforts to internationalize the issue, the NSCN did not achieve much success except to get admission into the Unrepresented Nations and Peoples Organization (UNPO)—an NGO based at The Hague. Udayan Mishra, who has been writing on the issue of Naga identity for quite a long time, has said: 'Whatever the legalities involved in the NNC's position on self-determination/sovereignty, the situation today is such that a separate, independent Nagaland outside the Indian Union does not appear feasible.'[73] The Naga leaders must realize that independence cannot be won by emotion and by putting forward the argument that Nagaland is not a part of India. Even the members of the peace mission of 1964, who were very sympathetic to the Naga cause, urged the leaders to settle within the Indian Union.

Rev. Michael Scott, who was expelled from India for his close alliance with the underground Naga leaders, said, 'Independence conceded to Nagaland might stimulate secessionist tendencies, which would threaten the integrity of India as a whole.' Commenting on the NNC's demand to secede from India, Scott remarked,

What does India require of Nagaland other than the security of the border? Far from exacting tributes from the Nagas, the flow is rather from India to Nagaland in the form of a large proportion of its annual revenue. . . . As compared with African or colonial territories, Nagaland under the present set-up has the ownership of land and settlement under its control. Nagas cannot be forcibly or constitutionally deprived of their land as the indigenous people of South Africa for example have been deprived.[74]

The developments in international politics after 9/11 have once again brought the security issues to the forefront. Using the pretext of state security *vis-à-vis* terrorism, the states have developed coercive mechanisms as there is a growing realization that the greatest threat to them are from non-state terrorist groups.[75] In the context of such developments the claims of smaller nationalities for an independent homeland are unacceptable. Thus the Nagas, claim for independence is not feasible in a multi-ethnic region like the north-eastern region of India. Again to quote Horowitz: 'Secession, I shall argue, does not create the homogeneous successor states its proponents often assume will be created. Nor does secession reduce conflict, violence or minority oppression once successor states are established. Guarantees of minority protection in secessionist regions are likely to be illusory.'[76]

This does not mean that the Indian state will continue with its present policy of *status quo*. Today, a multi-ethnic society like India is moving on a razor's edge. The undemocratic and homogenizing tendencies of the ethnic movements are just a replication of state practices in India. Interestingly, if one analyses the propagandist literature of the NNC or the NSCN, it becomes clear that the grievances of the Nagas are not economic but socio-political.[77] It is a question of protecting their independent identity, which they have enjoyed throughout their history. Even the British preferred to keep them aloof and therefore they did not get an opportunity to become part of the Indian freedom struggle. On the eve of independence, the Nagas became highly apprehensive when they were sought to be assimilated into a pan-Indian identity over their own Naga identity. The Indianization process, reckless modernization with an exclusive focus on the bureaucratic form of governance, and the 'carrot and stick' policy created certain alienating conditions, which undermined the Naga village-based traditional economic-social system. This has created a profound sense of cynicism among the Nagas. Besides, they could never accept the massive human rights violations that began with the infamous Grouping System, and the Naga NGOs have always highlighted this issue as a major cause of alienation from the Indian state. The Indian state reacted by giving liberal financial grants as a means of tackling the issue. This has benefited a group of people—those in services, contractors, and businessmen. The liberal grants have also helped to sustain the insurgent groups in two ways. All state and central government officers posted in Nagaland have to pay about 10 per cent of their salary as tax to the NSCN. Secondly, it is alleged that a large chunk of the government money meant for rural development and welfare purposes goes to the rebels.

Politicians in the north-eastern region have developed a mutually beneficial relationship with the insurgents who are increasingly being utilized both by the central government and by the political parties in the states to meet their political aspirations. Every government in Nagaland since the state was formed has had some stake in the insurgency being continued.[78] The former chief minister of Nagaland, S.C. Jamir, is supposedly very close to the NSCN (Khaplang). For this reason he was kept out of the peace process. In Manipur, the governor, Lt. Gen. V.K. Nayar (Retd.) accused the then chief minister of having a close relationship with the NSCN (I-M).[79] Another important reason why the political elites in the north-east want the insurgency to continue at a manageable level is that it helps the resource-crunched north-eastern states to ask for money from the centre.[80]

The time has come for a solution to the Naga issue. The negotiation process has already continued for more than eight years, from 1997 onward. Instead of playing tactical games like buying time, the centre should address the real issue of Naga identity. The government, in order to find an amicable solution, must address the basic issues such as land, territoriality, cultural autonomy, and the political freedom of the Naga people. But so far there has been no substantial progress on these issues. The Government of India must resist utilizing the insurgent groups for its narrow political gain.

Judging from recent activities it becomes clear that the NSCN and the Naga groups are ready for some sort of regional autonomy which will allow them to exercise self-rule. The most perplexing question left then is the issue of Greater Nagaland, which has already led to considerable bloodshed in the region. This is a very sensitive issue not only for the Nagas but also for other ethnic groups, particularly in Manipur and Assam. In such cases, where the territory of other regions is claimed, the state cannot adopt a tribal-to-tribal approach. If the government imposes a decision by entering into an agreement with the NSCN, it will cause ethnic clashes in other parts of the north-east. Doing nothing, or simply buying time would be playing with fire.

Because how the Government of India settles the Nagaland issue has a considerable bearing on other secessionist movements in Kashmir, Tripura, Assam, and Manipur.

One very remarkable aspect of the ethnic conflict in NE India is the growth of vibrant civil society organizations in Nagaland and Manipur. Some of the organizations that have helped to practically stop inter-ethnic fights in the midst of the ceasefire beyond Nagaland in 2001, are the Naga Hoho, the Naga-Mothers Association, Meira Paibi, Council of Baptist Churches, the Naga Peoples Movement for Human Rights and the Naga Students Federation. In the midst of the 2001 ethnic riots, these organizations reached out to every corner of Assam and Manipur by building alliances with their counterparts, such as the Assam Sahitya Sabha in Assam and the Naga Women's Union of Manipur, and prevented killing and looting. However, things are not that rosy as far as the role of civil society movements are concerned. The close alliance of these organizations with the insurgent groups is well known. Unfortunately, these organizations too are reiterating the same stand as the NSCN so far as the attainment of Greater Nagaland is concerned.[81]

In such a situation, instead of imposing a decision unilaterally by coming into some kind of agreement with the NSCN, the Government of India needs to initiate a dialogue among the affected communities of the region. Issues like claiming the territories of other states or communities must be included in such a dialogue. A solution may not be found overnight, but a dialogue will help in understanding each other's minds. In conflict resolution literature, this process is known as the informal problem-solving approach, or workshops, where a third party assists conflicting parties to find solutions to their problems. The philosophy of these workshops is not to force the parties to accept a settlement, but to provide an informal atmosphere where the parties can exchange their perspectives and conceive a solution that satisfies the needs of those involved in the conflict.[82] The primary objective is to build channels of communication that enable the parties to learn more about each other. This process, in other words, transforms the negative stereotypes and images constructed during the development of the conflict. Dialogue is the basis for the resolution of social conflicts, as communication between parties can heighten mutual understanding, leading the parties to create new social structures and institutions to resolve conflict.[83] Here the opinion of John Burton, a pioneer scholar in the studies of conflict resolution, is very pertinent. He says that such a problem-solving process '[a]lso enables the parties, especially the parties which perceive themselves to be the more powerful, to make an accurate costing of the consequences of pursuing existing policies. Both those who might seek change and those who might seek to resist change are able to perceive directly the motives, concerns, dedication and needs of the other side. This costing is an important first step in arriving at [an] agreement when parties are considering structural change.'[84]

An agreement, which would essentially come from the civil society, would make an everlasting impact on the conflict-prone areas of north-eastern India. Such conflicting rights and claims are confined not only to Nagaland, but exist also in other areas such as Assam and Tripura.[85]

## CONCLUSION

Nagaland provides a peculiar challenge to the process of nation-state building in India. Unlike other ethnic conflicts in South Asia, where issues of economic underdevelopment, exploitation of resources by the centre, protection of indigenous identity, systematic discrimination, etc., form the basic source of strength for the ethnic movements,[86] in Nagaland the grievances are completely different. The Nagas never argued they were exploited or that regional disparity provoked them to take up arms as happened in the neighbouring north-eastern states of India. It was all about realizing an independent homeland where the 'Naga way of life' would be protected. Here historical and cultural factors were used to play a dominating role. Horowitz's comment is very pertinent in this regard: 'the psychological sources of conflict don't lend themselves to modification through material benefits that is so often the stuff of modern policy making. For similar reasons, symbolic demands seem to be less compromisable than claims that can be quantified.'[87]

At the time of independence, the Nagas were not psychologically prepared to be a part of India but the state understood this to be an act of defiance. By the time the Indian government had created the state of Nagaland and provided sufficient protection for the Nagas, much damage had already been done. Under the existing arrangement, the Naga way of life is protected by the Constitution of India, which no other community in the region has been able to secure.[88] The Government of India, however, must repeal repressive acts like the Armed Forces (Special Powers) Act and the Disturbed Areas Act which have resulted in considerable human rights violations in the region. Here the observation of Udayon Mishra is noteworthy: 'Above everything else, certain set of attitudes regarding the Nagas which developed during the colonial period and were nourished, consciously or otherwise, after independence, must be replaced with feelings of equal trust and mutual respect.'[89]

In order to have an effective presence in its periphery, the Indian state needs to take the present negotiation process with the rebels to its logical conclusion. A continuation of the policy of intentional dithering and calculated procrastinations will not only aggravate the already vexed Naga issue but also adversely affect other insurgency movements in Assam, Manipur, Tripura, Meghalaya, and Kashmir. In addition, the nation state needs to redefine itself beyond its territories. A transnational approach is required in states like Nagaland, which can think beyond the borders with its tribes across India. Many scholars have advocated a non-territorial solution to the Naga issue which would strengthen the 'Naga way of life' without affecting the territories of other states. Thus B.G. Verghese recommends the formation of a Naga National Council which would give Nagas outside Nagaland a say in cultural matters.[90] Noted anthropologist and adviser to several prime ministers of India, B.K. Roy Burman, suggested a model on the lines of the Saami Council which is recognized as the official representative of the Saami people living in Sweden, Finland, and Norway. The council has a say in the socio-economic and cultural affairs of the Saami people living in these countries.[91] Professor Sanjib Barua also proposes the creation of transnational institutions involving the Naga tribes of Myanmar and India.[92] The Naga leaders also need to look at the issue realistically. The Naga people mustn't fall into the alienating logic of the nation state with its dogmatic emphasis on a homogenized territory which is exclusive and non-accommodative. Now it is the turn of the Indian nation state to show its elasticity—will it stick to the old-fashioned national security approach or will it treat one of the world's most protracted and tragic armed conflicts with a 'significant shifting of gears',[93] and imagination?

## NOTES

1. For details see, Navnita Chadha Behera, *State, Identity and Violence: Jammu, Kashmir and Ladakh* (New Delhi: Manohar, 2000), pp. 10-13.
2. Rajni Kothari, the most well-known political scientist from India, believed in such a democratic modernization process, although in the 1970s Kothari subsequently changed his opinion. For details see, *Politics in India* (New Delhi: Orient Longman, 1970), Introduction.
3. Ashis Nandy, 'Nation, State and Self-Hatred', *Himal South Asia*, July 1996, p. 17.
4. Ranajit Guha (ed.), *Subaltern Studies: Writings on South Asian History and Society,* vol. 1 (New Delhi: Oxford University Press, 1982), p. 1 and 'Introduction', in *A Subaltern Studies Reader 1986-1995,* Ranajit Guha (ed.) (New Delhi: Oxford University Press, 1998), pp. xiv-xv.
5. Ponna Wignaraja (ed.), *New Social Movements in the South: Empowering the People* (New Delhi: Vistaar, 1993).
6. Behera, *State, Identity and Violence*, p. 12.
7. Ibid., p. 13.
8. Wignaraja, *New Social Movements in the South*, p. 7.
9. Some of the major problems that the Indian state faced in 1947 were the Partition, Pakistan's attack in Kashmir, integration of the princely states, and declaration of independence by the Nagas in NE India. All these developments led to the creation of a strong centre. For details, see the *Constituent Assembly Debates,* vol. IX, 1005.
10. Some of the articles that are important in this regard are Articles 1, 352, 356 and so on. See Durga Das Basu, *Shorter Constitution of India* (New Delhi: Prentice-Hall of India, 1988).
11. Imtiaz Ahmed, 'A Post-Nationalist South Asia', *Himal South Asia*, July 1996, p. 10.
12. Ibid., p. 11.
13. The whole region is connected with the rest of the county by a tenuous 22-km land corridor through Siliguri in the eastern state of West Bengal—a link that has come to be referred to as the 'chicken's neck'. Comprising only 8 per cent of the country's geographical area, the north-east is home to a total of 39,035,582 people (2001 census),

which represents 3.80 per cent of the country's population. The entire region can be divided into two parts—hills and plains. The majority of those living in the plains are Hindus and Muslims while the Hill tribes inhabiting the states of Meghalaya, Mizoram, and Nagaland are mostly Christians. The most populous part of the region is the Brahmaputra valley in Assam, which constitutes 22 per cent of the total population.

14. Naga itself is a generic term for a cluster of 32 tribes, 5 of them in Burma and the remainder scattered within Nagaland (16), Manipur (7), Arunachal (3) and Assam. For details see, B.G. Verghese, *India's North-East Resurgent* (New Delhi: Konarak Publishers, 1996), p. 83.

15. Originally Nagaland was a part of Assam. The Government of India created the state of Nagaland by the 13th Amendment to the Constitution (Act No. 73 of 1962) comprising three districts. The states of Mizoram and Meghalaya were also a part of Assam, which were later on carved out to satisfy growing ethnic demands.

16. Udayan Mishra, *The Periphery Strikes Back—Challenges to the Nation-State* (Shimla: Indian Institute of Advanced Studies, 2000), p. 15.

17. Certainly the missionaries played a very important role in the socio-economic development of these regions which had produced a group of elite people who later on became critical of the Indian state. However, there are no reliable reports available to suggest that the missionaries were responsible for such anti-Indian feelings.

18. Nagamese (patois Assamese) is the *lingua franca* of the Naga tribes. English is also widely spoken in the urban areas.

19. For details see, Udayan Mishra, 'The Naga National Question', *Economic and Political Weekly*, Bombay, 18 April 1978.

20. A term used by Horowitz. See, Donald Horowitz, *Ethnic Groups in Conflict* (UC Berkeley, 1985), pp. 41, 52.

21. Nagaland is governed by inner line regulations, which make it mandatory for Non-Nagas to secure entry permits into the state. There are restrictions on the non-Nagas acquiring landed property or to carry on business as in other parts of the country.

22. Nagaland is a special category state receiving 90 per cent grants and 10 per cent loans from the centre. However, the majority of the funds were misappropriated as the insurgent groups claimed tax and donations from every businessman and government official. On many occasions a heavy proportion of the sectoral amount earmarked for social welfare and other departments was siphoned off by corrupt bureaucrats or extorted by insurgents. The central government was fully aware of the situation but wanted to keep at least a few Naga elites satisfied.

23. It can be mentioned that by self-determination the Naga groups mean

secession and constitution of a separate independent state. Regarding the views of the Naga civil society groups on the issue of Naga independence see, http://www.satp.org/satporgtp/countries/india/states/nagaland/index.html

24. This extremely fierce character of the Nagas has been described by various adjectives. In neighbouring areas the term 'Naga' means something very extreme. For example, if the edge of a knife is very sharp, it is referred to as 'Naga da' (Naga knife)', or if a lemon is too sour, it is referred to as 'Naga tenga' (Naga lemon), and so on. The image of a Naga man is someone who is naked (except for the genitals), with sharp weapons and ever ready to attack. These are some of the stereotypes associated with the Naga tribes.

25. Lakshmi Devi, *Ahom-Tribal Relation* (Gauhati, 1968), p. 21.

26. Mishra, 'The Naga National Question', in *North-East India* (New Delhi: Omsons, 1988), pp. 3, 4.

27. Ibid., p. 6.

28. The Naga Club, the first of its kind in the Naga Hills, was formed in 1918. It was the first effort for an organized Naga opinion.

29. M. Alemchiba, *A Brief Historical Account of Nagaland* (Kohima: Naga Institute of Culture, 1970), pp. 162-4.

30. Ibid., p. 163.

31. Udayan Mishra, *The Periphery Strikes Back*, p. 30.

32. Urmila Phadnis, *Ethnicity and Nation-Building in South Asia* (Delhi, London: Sage Publication, 1989), p. 14.

33. In December 1946, the NNC declared: 'the NNC stands for the unification of all the Naga tribes and their freedom. . . . We shall enjoy Home-rule in our country, but on broader issues be connected with India. We must fight for it , we must get it; keep on watching.' Yusoso Yuno, *The Rising Nagas* (New Delhi, 1974), pp. 166-8.

34. See Udayan Mishra, *The Periphery Strikes Back,* p. 31.

35. Zapu Phizo, an Angami Naga was the undisputed leader of the NNC. A former soldier of the INA of Subhas Chandra Bose, he was elected president of the NNC in 1949. He lived in England in self-imposed exile until his death.

36. B.G. Verghese, *India's North-East Resurgent*, p. 87. Also see Yuno, *The Rising Nagas*, p. 182.

37. Article 9 said: 'The Governor of Assam, as the agent of the Government of [the] Indian Union, will have a special responsibility for a period of ten years to ensure the due observance of the Agreement. At the end of this period, the NNC will be asked whether they require the above agreement to be extended for a further period or a new agreement regarding the future of the Naga people is arrived at.'

38. Keeping in view the special needs of the tribal population and their identities the 6th Schedule of the Constitution was added under which

nine district councils were created. For details see, Partha Ghosh, *Ethnic Conflict and Conflict Management: The Indian Case* (Sri Lanka: ICES, 1996), pp. 25-6.

39. Selected works, vol. l, 1984, p. 42, referred to in Udayan Mishra's *The Periphery Strikes Back*, p. 35.

40. Bordoloi, a great freedom fighter against British colonialism and the main architect of the 6th Schedule of the Constitution, was the first chief minister of Assam. Chaliha who was the third chief minister of Assam had a deep understanding of the Naga problem. He was one of the members of the peace committee of 1964.

41. Udayan Mishra, *The Periphery Strikes Back*, p. 35.

42. Rajat Ganguly, 'Introduction: The Challenge of Ethnic Insurgency and Secession in South and South-East Asia', in Ian Macduff and Rajat Ganguly (ed.), *Ethnic Insurgency and Secession in South and South-East Asia* (New Delhi, London: Sage Publication, 2003), pp. 16-17.

43. Article 371A(1) of the Constitution reads, 'Notwithstanding anything in this constitution—(a) no act of parliament in respect of (i) religious or social practices of the Nagas, (ii) Naga customary law and procedure, (iii) administration of civil and criminal justice involving decisions according to Naga customary law, (iv) ownership and transfer of land and its resources, shall apply to the state of Nagaland unless the Legislative Assembly of Nagaland by a resolution so decides'. It came into effect on 1 December 1963.

44. Jayaprakash Narayan, popularly known as JP, was a Gandhian. He launched a totally non-violent revolution in the 1970s to wipe out corruption and other malpractices in the northern states of India. B.P. Chaliha was the third chief minister of Assam and Michael Scott worked in South Africa against apartheid.

45. Federal Government of Nagaland is the name of the rebel government.

46. Alemchiba, *A Brief Historical Account of Nagaland*, pp. 210-11.

47. Isak Swu and Th. Muivah, *Manifesto of the National Council of Nagaland* (Kohima, 2nd edn., 1982), pp. 37-9.

48. Ibid., pp. 36-8.

49. Verghese, *India's North East Resurgent*, p. 96.

50. The Kuki, a hill tribe, belong to the larger Chin group of Burma. They are scattered in the states of Assam, Manipur, and Nagaland. The Kukis too demand 'Kukiland' comprising the territories of Nagaland and Manipur. Nagas consider the Kukis to be outsiders from Burma who want to capture Naga inhabited areas. Moreh—a border point between India and Burma, where there is a large dominance of the Kukis—is the nodal point for smuggled goods. Every local insurgent group wants to control the region. This also leads to a Kuki-Naga fight for supremacy. This was quite evident when the author visited the areas.

51. For an account of these groups and their activities, see http://www.satp.org; Also M.S. Prabhakar, 'States of Insurgency', *Frontline* (Chennai, 11 February 1994), p. 28.

52. Navnita Chadha Behera, *State, People and Security: The South Asian Context* (New Delhi: Har-Anand Publications, 2002), p. 26.

53. See Nani Gopal Mahanta, 'Assam—Politics of Peace Making', *EPW,* January, 2005, p. 25.

54. Tatar Hoho was made up of representatives of various tribes. See Udayan Mishra's *The Periphery Strikes Back,* p. 56.

55. In the states of Nagaland and Manipur where Nagas and Kukis are spread out, a total of 5314 people have been killed in the last ten years. For details see, http://www.satp.org

56. It is said that the Kukis were settled in the Naga inhabited areas by the Britishers to defeat the Nagas. For details see K.C. Chaudhury, 'The Genesis of Naga-Kuki Feuds', *The Statesman,* 1994.

57. H.K. Borpujari, *North-East India: Problems, Policies and Prospects* (Delhi: Spectrum Publication, 1998), p. 109.

58. For the Nagalim map and territorial claim of the NSCN, see the official website of NSCN, http://www.nscnonline.org

59. On the origin of the Meiteis, Verghese writes: 'The Meiteis are probably of Tibeto-Burman rather than of Mon-Khmer origin . . . ', B.G. Verghese, *India's North East Resurgent,* p. 113. However in the eighteenth century, Vaishnava Hinduism became highly popular and the Meiteis embraced Hinduism. On account of the present conflict and in order to gain more government concessions (as they are not Hill Tribes), some of the Meiteis are advocating a return to their original customs and religion—what they call 'Senamahi'.

60. The Manipur Assembly adopted a resolution on 6 May 1995 aimed at protecting their territorial integrity and rejected the concept of Greater Nagaland. This resolution has been ratified several times. It shows how concerned the representatives are about Greater Nagaland.

61. The Nagas are also claiming some areas of Assam. These include some portions of Sibsagar district (Amguri and Sonari), Golaghat district and Karbi Anglong Hills. On various occasions the Nagas have tried to capture territories of Assam. In one such incident twenty Assamese were killed in Merapani in 1985.

62. This was disclosed by an officer of the Intelligence Bureau (IB) posted in the north-east, during a private conversation in Guwahati. He said that as a result of the clashes the NSCN (I-M) had lost its patronizing role among the insurgent groups of the north-east.

63. However, there is no declaration on the part of the NSCN that they have abandoned the demand. Nevertheless the interlocutor on behalf of the Government of India has made announcements that the issue of independence is no longer the stumbling block. In addition, NSCN

leaders in self-exile in Bangkok, Thailand, visited India for talks with the prime minister about their Indian passports.

64. Udayan Mishra, 'Naga Peace Talks; p. 596.

65. Donald L. Horowitz, 'A Right to Secede?' in Stephen Macedo and Allen Buchanan (eds.), *Secession and Self-Determination* (New York: New York University Press, 2003), pp. 55-6.

66. Some of these groups are, United Liberation Front of Assam (ULFA), National Democratic Front of Bodoland (NDFB) in Assam, United National Liberation Front of Manipur (UNLF) , PREPAK in Manipur, National Volunteer Force (TVF) of Tripura, etc., For details see— http://www.satp.org

67. There are over 225 communities in NE India and over 150 spoken languages. For details see B.G. Verghese, *India's North East Resurgent,* pp. 2-3.

68. On a visit to Kohima in January 2004, a leader of the NSF told the author that such an order was required as people who have no interest in tribal life project a very negative image about the Nagas.

69. M.S. Prabhakar, 'Objects of History', *Frontline,* 26 September 2003, p. 42.

70. In the absence of any meaningful discussion, the right to self-determination for all the ethnic groups in India or South Asia invariably means the right to secede.

71. One commentator raised the question of why this figure could not be a hundred per cent instead of 99.9 per cent. Sanjay Duara, 'Nagas' Claim for Self-Determination', *Assam Tribune,* 20 March 1984.

72. For example, the official website of the NSCN declares: 'HISTORICAL BASIS FOR NAGAS CLAIM TO THE RIGHT TO SELF-DETERMINATION—Based on their inalienable historical rights, Naga people's stand on the right to self-determination and sovereignty is not of recent origin. . . . On 16 May 1951 the plebiscite began in Kohima and 99.9% of the Naga populace voted in favor of remaining independent...' see, http://www.nscnonline.org/webpage/home.htm

73. Mishra, 'Naga Peace Talks' in *Economic and Political Weekly,* 15 February 2003.

74. Michael Scott 'Bearings on the Future of Nagaland', as quoted in Udayan Mishra, 'Naga Peace Talks'.

75. In India, the Prevention of Terrorism Act (POTA) was passed to meet the growing threat of terrorism.

76. Horowitz, 'A Right to Secede'? p. 50.

77. For example, a look at the NSCN website makes it clear that they don't talk about economic exploitation against the Indian state— their main argument is that the Nagas are different.

78. Udayan Mishra, *The Periphery Strikes Back,* p. 55.

79. Verghese, *India's North East Resurgent,* p. 104.

80. The main argument of the politicians is that most of the money is being spent on law and order and hence the centre should pay special attention to these terrorist-affected states.

81. The author had a long interview with the president of Naga Hoho (the highest tribal assembly), M. Vero, on 10 June 2003. Vero said that what they are looking for is an honourable settlement of the vexed issue. He, however, made it clear that the integration of Naga inhabited areas is a very emotive issue for the Nagas.

82. Carlos L. Yordan, 'Instituting Problem-Solving Processes as a Means of Constructive Social Change', *Online Journal of Peace and Conflict Resolution*, November 1998, no. 1.4.

83. Ibid.

84. John Burton, *Violence Explained* (Manchester and New York: Manchester University Press, 1997), p. 45.

85. In Assam, the government has come to an agreement with one faction of the Bodos and granted them a Bodoland Territorial Council. The majority of non-Bodos, who constitute about 60 per cent of the total population, are now up in arms against this decision.

86. Some such movements are related to the Chakma issue in CHT in Bangladesh, the LTTE demand in Sri Lanka, the fear of losing identity in Assam and Tripura and Manipur in India, ethnic conflict in Sindh in Pakistan, etc.

87. Donald L. Horowitz, *Ethnic Groups in Conflict* (Berkeley: University of California Press, 2000), p. 566.

88. These provisions were created by the Constitution Amendment Act of 1962. Article 371A deals with the special protection of the Nagas in relation to employment, land, prevalence of Naga customary law, etc.

89. Udayan Mishra, *The Periphery Strikes Back*, p. 162.

90. Cited in Sanjay Hazarika, 'Of the Nagas, Regionalism and Power', *The Statesman*, New Delhi.

91. See www.saamicouncil.org

92. See Sanjib Barua, *Durable Disorder—Understanding the Politics of North-East India* (New Delhi: Oxford University Press, 2004), p. 119.

93. Ibid., 119.

# CHAPTER 11

# Communalism as a Political Weapon in India

## B.V. Muralidhar

## I. SECULARISM AND NATION-BUILDING IN INDIA

Secularism is the backbone of the Indian Constitution. The Constitution writers deliberately included secularism because India is a land of many religions. From the days of British rule there have been occasional communal conflicts between Hindus and Muslims and Hindus and Christians. They have become a regular feature of late. The differences between the Indian National Congress and the Muslim League during the independence struggle sparked communal tensions which were exploited by the British. The partition of the subcontinent in 1947 is the result of the hatred between these two communities. The purpose of this chapter is to trace the roots of this problem. It is an enquiry into secularism in post-independent India against the backdrop of the Gujarat riots of 2002.

### 1. SECULARISM AS CONSTITUTIONAL PRINCIPLE

In the West, the term secularism was coined by Holyoke in 1849. To India and Nehru it meant 'granting of equal status to all religions'.[1] Secularism involves a whole way of life—an enlightened, rational view of society. It demands that not only should there be tolerance between various communities but there should also be a close and active interaction among them.[2] The main concern of the leadership during the independence struggle was to build an integrated nation. India being an ethno-cultural mosaic provides scope for variety and diversity. At the dawn of independence, religion became a formidable force and led to partition after considerable bloodshed and painful migration on both sides of the border.

After independence, the fact remained that India still had the second largest Muslim population in the world next only to Indonesia.[3] Leaders like Mahatma Gandhi, Jawaharlal Nehru, Moulana Azad, and others tried their best to preserve the unity of India. This was partly because of their training in the West and partly due to their non-religious character which was against the domination of religion in politics. Nehru wished to have a 'unity of mind and heart, which breaks down the barriers raised in the name of religion'.[4] This brand of secularism was seen as a radical form. The Indian model of nation-building should be viewed against the background of a highly diverse society with a long history of disunity.

Though the Nehruvian model of secularism was put into practice, there were threats to this concept even during his tenure as prime minister of India. The painful memories of partition and the ever-present problem of Kashmir since independence, in addition to communal tensions tested the applicability of this model. But as Rajni Kothari (1977) observes, certain elements in the nation-building process prevented any major danger to this concept during the first decade of India's independence.[5]

## 2. GROWTH OF SECULARISM

Indian secularism has been buttressed by its people's fascination with non-violence and aversion to violence in the course of its enquiry into the nature of life, as manifested till date in its vegetarianism. It started with Buddhism and Jainism, and though it was also extolled by the Upanishads (ancient scriptures), it was seldom followed because of myriad other competing values. Buddha was the embodiment of non-violence and later Mahavira (founder of the Jain religion) treated non-violence as an absolute and supreme virtue. Buddha's teachings and message were carried across the world by Emperor Ashoka (after the Kalinga war) and by Buddhist monks who spread them to Tibet, China, South-East Asia, and Japan.[6]

The tragedy, and bane, of India has been that, after Ashoka, the logic of non-violence was not carried to politics or statecraft. It was left to Mahatma Gandhi to link non-violence with the country's political culture and social change. He became the greatest revolutionary of his time and addressed the crucial importance of the purity of both ends and means in attempting social change.

Gandhi adhered to Jainism for its principles of non-violence and universal tolerance. He was greatly impressed by Buddha and Christ for their revolutionary nature which sought to change the old, rotten traditions. He thus observed, 'Jesus and Buddha were capable of intensely direct action. Christ defied the might of a whole empire and Gautama brought down on his knees an arrogant priesthood'.[7] The same attitude was carried into the independence struggle by Gandhi and other leaders of the Indian National Congress.

Ever since India's independence, the adult franchise extended to the millions of people slowly forcing castes and communities to realign. The first prime minister, Jawaharlal Nehru, adopted various methods to foster national unity. He suppressed separatist and secessionist tendencies besides regional and communal fanaticism. Due to his efforts these latter elements were made to accept a secular framework through modification of their respective stands. The Congress party was the one that stood by the Muslims. Mrs Indira Gandhi who came to power after the split of the Congress party in 1968, placed a great deal of emphasis on secularism and socialism, which continued till the 'Emergency period'.[8]

## 3. THREATS TO SECULARISM

The qualitative change in the thinking of Muslims against the Congress began after the 1977 general elections as the latter started to adopt a policy of 'soft Hinduism'. Such a step pushed parties like the Bharatiya Janata Party (BJP) to the other extreme, the hard 'Hindutva' line, which naturally did a great deal of damage to the secular polity.[9] The progenitor of the concept of 'Hindutva' was V.D. Savarkar, who implied that a Hindu alone and exclusively is a full-fledged Indian (quoted in his work, *Who is a Hindu?*), thus also implying that Muslims and other religious minorities were inferior and not complete Indians. The emergence of Hindu fundamentalism naturally stimulated other forces which eventually weakened the nation-building process. Besides the

Hindu-Muslim problem, the Sikh issue in Punjab also became a focal point.

The role of local issues or micro-level factors have to be taken into account to understand the pattern of communal politics in India in the recent past. Asghar Ali Engineer, a noted columnist, argued that changing socio-economic factors played a crucial role in the communally sensitive areas such as slow economic growth leading to large-scale unemployment and poverty. They allowed the ruling classes in India to easily convert the economic problems into caste and communal problems.[10] Though the word 'secular' was incorporated into the Constitution through the 42nd Amendment in 1976, the handling of this sensitive concept produced negative results.

The social transformation that took place during Nehru's prime ministership gave birth to a spirit of nationalism and identity as Indians. A sense of belongingness, though not cultural but secular emerged in the years after independence. It is this feeling that was rudely shaken in the communal frenzy since the 1980s. The communal riots in Meerut, Aligarh, Moradabad, Jamshedpur, Benares, Bhiwandi, the old city of Hyderabad, Coimbatore, to name a few, made the common man loose faith in the practicality of secularism in the Indian context.

It is unfortunate that while paying lip service to secularism, the political elite made all attempts to exploit religion. The majority political parties made compromises with the fundamentalist zealots for the sake of power and political benefit. Another trend that has emerged in the recent past indicates that the government itself sometimes succumbs to the communal pressures. This politicizes the religious identity and in turn gives a legitimate role to communal organizations as real representatives of different religious communities.[11] Thus the Hindutva concept long submerged in the body politic surfaced again. Its proponents began to question the very secular spirit of the Constitution. Gradually, they became a major challenge to the secular fabric of the country. To achieve their narrow political goals, places of worship became a battlefield to gain the support of what was believed to be the 'Hindu vote bank'. Post-Ayodhya developments are particularly revealing: The failure of the ruling class to preserve the principles of secularism in the face of communal pressures, the emergence and later submergence of fundamentalist elements on both sides and the realignment of forces against such communal flare-ups.[12]

The incidence of poverty and the rate of illiteracy are very high in India. They are the pillars through which the journey of communal riots starts. Those affected cannot understand the 'ifs' and 'buts' of religious conservatism. It is easy for the political elite to fool the public and achieve their goal of mobilizing vote banks through the communal card, if people are poor and illiterate. They are the soft targets of politicians who use them for their selfish political ends.[13] This is very much in evidence in any incident of communal violence. It is once again the poor who are the prime targets and pay dearly with their lives; during riots as the post-Babri Masjid demolition, the Bombay riots, and even worse, Gujarat's Godhra carnage testify.

## II. COMMUNAL VIOLENCE

### 1. REASONS AND EXPLANATIONS FOR COMMUNAL VIOLENCE

Why is there communal violence in India? Steven Wilkinson, in his seminal 'Putting Gujarat in Perspective',[14] deconstructs the entire debate on state complicity by delineating a wider shift in Indian politics. The state government's delay in calling in the army established beyond doubt that the anti-minority pogrom was being carried out with the involvement of not only the politicians but the state machinery as well.

As in most riots in the country before and after independence, the minorities suffered disproportionately in Gujarat from 27 February 2002 to the beginning of April 2002. The Minorities Commission's figures on the communal riots that took place between 1985 and 1987 stand as a testimony that in almost every bout of communal violence, the minorities are butchered. Given the fact that the state governments are responsible for law and order in India, the question why some state governments are successful in controlling riot situations and prevent them from occurring while others are not is not only relevant but also vexing.

Wilkinson argues that ethnic riots[15] are far from being spontaneous eruptions of anger. Instead they are often planned by politicians for a clear electoral purpose. Subsequently, it then follows that these very politicians will also prevent riots if and when it is in their interest to do so. These violent conflagrations are therefore caused by political elites who play on existing communal tensions to advance a political agenda.[16]

Instrumental political explanations for violence have been labelled 'unsatisfactory' not only by Wilkinson but also by other theorists. The Duke University professor lends credence to his criticism of instrumental explanations by invoking the actions of certain state governments. The first point of refutation that he makes is that scholars who look at political elites and their reasons for inciting violence offer little insight into why some politicians tend to do exactly the opposite and use their political capital and control of the state to prevent ethnic conflict. The second major problem identified by Wilkinson with many political explanations for ethnic violence, is that they fail to account for *the variation in patterns of violence* within states.

In order to clear any confusion arising out of the criticism made against the existing theories, Wilkinson posits three 'possible' explanations for the differences in state performance, which will be elaborated on in the course of this chapter.[17] First, decades of corruption, criminalization, politicization, and a general lack of state capacity have left Indian state governments too weak to prevent riots. Second, Indian state governments are unable or unwilling to protect minorities because they systematically underrepresent them within their governments, police forces and local administrations. Lastly, and most importantly, the degree of party competition affects the value governments place on attracting 'Muslim swing voters'. It influences the actions of the government, whether or not it will order the respective administrations to protect the minorities.

Since Wilkinson primarily deals with the actions of the state in fomenting or preventing ethnic violence between Hindus and Muslims, it is imperative to take a detailed look at the arguments that he posits in this regard. He focuses on state- and town-level electoral incentives which remain important even if we assume various other factors, socio-economic or otherwise, to be constant and controlled.

At the local level, the politicians would try to ensure that the identity that favours their party is the one that is most salient in the minds of a majority of the voters. Those parties that represent elites within ethnic groups will invariably use polarizing anti-minority events in order to encourage the members of their ethnic category to identify with their party and the 'majority' identity.

The most effective method, according to Wilkinson, for elite-dominated ethnic parties to mobilize those target voters who are at risk of voting for the main rival parties will be to use 'ethnic wedge issues'. This is summarily accomplished by highlighting the 'Muslim threat', especially in urban areas where the party hopes to win over the pivotal Hindu voters.

The form of anti-minority mobilization taken recourse to depends on both the identity that the party wants to make salient and also the fact that the Indian state, similar to other states, privileges some form of public ritual or procession which culminates in immense mobilization. In fact, riots occurred because of, or in the wake of, religious processions in the late eighteenth and early nineteenth centuries. It has also been noted that processions often degenerate into rioting as a result of manipulation by leaders who wish to bring about some form of mobilization in their favour.[18]

Defensive counter-mobilization by the minorities is portrayed as 'anti-national' and the myth of the 'foreign hand' is often invoked. When large crowds face each other, the threat of the situation deteriorating increases, which is then construed to be the handiwork of the Muslims alone. Conditions such as these produce 'community consciousness', which translates into a wave for or against the party, further leads to a swing that brings either rewards or brickbats. Wilkinson argues that to win an election it is not necessary to appeal to each and every voter but to the pivotal swing voters who generally are those undecided voters who fear the consequences of not taking a defensive stand against the members of the other community.

Statistical evidence suggests that proximity of an election sharply increases the likelihood of a riot. Factors such as economic competition, Muslim population, and percentage of refugees from Pakistan are not numerically significant in explaining the occurrence of a Hindu-Muslim riot even though computations show that as the Hindu-Muslim balance of a town reaches 50-50, the possibility of a riot goes up a few notches.

Three kinds of situations may develop which prove that, as electoral competition increases, the level of riots goes down. First, the existence of three or more parties provides a security blanket to the minorities as the importance of swing votes increases provided the majoritarian party is not trying to attract the fringe Hindu votes. A bipolar state party system creates a potentially dangerous situation for the minorities, especially when the majoritarian party, which owns the anti-minority issues, tries to foment violence.

The third situation can be exemplified by Gujarat and the events that unfolded in the state in the year 2002. Disaster awaits the minority community when the anti-minority, majoritarian party is in power. Such an anti-minority government will prevent violence only when the destruction threatens to wean away the loyal voters. Any potential advantage to the government will not be sacrificed in order to protect the minorities.

Over the years there has been an upswing in the number of elections that are preceded by communal killings, especially since the Hindu nationalist BJP gained political prominence. If the L.K. Advani-led *rath yatra* (chariot procession) that traversed most parts of the country left a trail of blood in its wake, the mammoth saffron wave that swept India in election after election proves beyond doubt that Hindu-Muslim riots increase the likelihood of the BJP improving its electoral performance.

The forgoing argument refutes the claim made by Ashutosh Varshney in his work on ethnic violence in which he almost absolves politicians, denying the strategic roles played by them in fomenting violence, and of the *Sangh Parivar,* which has been associated with most post–independence Hindu-Muslim conflicts. He stresses by contrast the existence or absence of civic ties between members of the two communities as the major factor that leads either to violence or to peace.[19]

Electoral incentives are the prime movers of an ethnic riot. Wilkinson, however, further investigates the reaction of a state government and its administrative machinery to communal violence, whether in controlling the conflagration or letting the fires burn. The two major indices that are used for this purpose are state autonomy[20] and state capacity.[21]

Wilkinson's central argument is that weakness does not account for state-level differences in the amount of Hindu-Muslim violence. He finds that the relationship between state autonomy (the lack of political interference or otherwise) and state capacity is inversely proportional to variations in the occurrence of Hindu-Muslim riots. States that are said to be the lowest on the autonomy and capacity barometer have done remarkably well in preventing riots. Even the weakest state governments, like Bihar and Uttar Pradesh, still seem to possess the minimal state capacity necessary to prevent Hindu-Muslim riots if this is prioritized by the state's political leaders.

The mere fact that there are sharp state-level variations in the occurrence as well as the prevention and control of riots suggests that the problem is not so much that of government leaders telling state officials whether to protect or not to protect minorities. Certain specific aspects, however, are linked to state capacity and poor performance in preventing riots.

The financial weakness of some state governments can be a cause for concern. Interestingly enough, the Gujarat state government was hardly cash-strapped when the pogrom took place in the state. Secondly, the police and judicial systems in many states are understaffed and overloaded, which reduces the perceived risk rioters face of arrest, prosecution, and conviction.

Punitive transfers also have an independent negative effect on riot-preparedness, because frequent transfers reduce officers' knowledge about their districts, the potential trouble spots and the one best way to prevent a riot.

Political interference with state autonomy is alleged to increase Hindu-Muslim violence in different ways. Instructions from the political bosses to either drop or go slow in investigating cases of mob brutality and murder or of political retribution by certain influential members of the citizenry; that they delay taking stern action, especially against groups that enjoy state protection, are the common ways in which state autonomy is eroded and in some cases demolished.

Obviously enough the central thrust of the work done by
Steven Wilkinson traces the linkages between party competition
and ethnic violence but at the same time he finds that high levels
of electoral competition can reduce as well as precipitate ethnic
violence. Both situations can be reproduced in equation form in
the following manner:

$$\left.\begin{array}{l} \textit{Party competition } (\uparrow) + \\ \textit{Muslim swing votes } (\uparrow) \end{array}\right\} = \text{Levels of violence } (\downarrow)$$

$$\left.\begin{array}{l} \textit{Party competition } (\downarrow) + \\ \textit{Muslim swing votes } (\downarrow) \end{array}\right\} = \text{Levels of violence } (\uparrow)$$

## 2. Differences in the Occurrence of Violence

That the existence or otherwise of civic ties between Hindus and
Muslims at the town level is the primary cause of conflict or the
lack of it between the two is Ashutosh Varshney's central assertion
in his recent work on the subject.[22] Where such networks of
civic engagement exist, tensions and conflicts are regulated and
managed; where they are missing, communal identities lead to
endemic and ghastly violence.

These networks can be broken down into *associational* forms[23]
and *everyday* forms[24] of engagement. Both forms of civic engagement—if intercommunal—promote peace. The capacity, however, of the associational forms to withstand national-level
exogenous shocks is substantially higher.

Varshney argues that associational forms turn out to be sturdier
in the face of politicians trying to foment communal trouble.
Vigorous associational life acts as a serious constraint on the
polarizing strategies of political elites. The mechanisms that
connect civil society (non-state domain) and ethnic conflict can
be broadly classified into two categories.[25]

By promoting communication between members of different
religious communities, civic networks often make neighbourhood
peace possible. People come together routinely to form temporary
organizations in the face of tensions. These can be highly effective
and are known as 'peace committees'. Such organized bodies

are difficult in those urban concentrations where civic engagement between Hindus and Muslims does not exist.

The second mechanism describes why associational forms of engagement are sturdier than everyday forms in dealing with ethnic and communal tensions. Vibrant organizations serving the economic, cultural and social needs of the two communities can promote communal peace, which can be solidly expressed. Varshney, however, presents a profound paradox. Everyday engagement is so complete at the village level in India that associational forms of engagement are few and far between. Yet rural India has experienced fewer riots since independence. In contrast, though associational life flourishes in the cities, even petty rumours can cause deadly bouts of communal violence.

The argument fails to stand its ground once the 'anonymity' argument is put forward. Cities tend to be less interconnected and more anonymous. Size can reduce the extent and effectiveness of everyday interactions. This explanation leads us to the two other major findings by Varshney. First, the share of villages in communal rioting is remarkably small. Hindu-Muslim violence is primarily an urban phenomenon. The violence in Gujarat can be termed unique in several ways including the occurrence of large-scale communal violence in the rural areas.

The second argument Varshney makes as far as town-level variation is concerned is a little more problematic than the first one. He differentiates between 'riot-prone cities' and others; he identifies eight cities—Ahmedabad, Mumbai, Aligarh, Hyderabad, Meerut, Baroda, Kolkata and Delhi—as being particularly high on the riot scale. Eighty-two per cent of the urban population, therefore, is not riot-prone.

India's Hindu-Muslim violence, therefore, is city specific. State-and national-level politics provides the context within which the local mechanisms linked with violence are activated. Cities are also the sites for large-scale civic engagement, which constrains local politicians in their strategic behaviour. Riot-prone cities lack such forms of engagement which leads to the political elites taking advantage of the volatility of the situation.

In peaceful cities, an institutionalized peace system exists where organizations are communally integrated. These civic organizations, for all practical purposes, become the ears and arms of the local administration. It then follows that, if the civic edifice is inter-ethnic and associational, it can cope with 'ethnic earth-quakes' such as partition or desecration of a holy place. If the form of civic engagement is intra-ethnic in everyday life, earth-quakes of smaller intensity can bring the edifice down.[26]

Varshney thus states that a multi-ethnic society with few inter-connections across ethnic boundaries is very vulnerable to ethnic disorders and violence. In Hyderabad city, for instance, most Hindus and Muslims do not meet in a civic setting where mutual relations can be formed. Lacking these networks, even competent police officers and administrators watch helplessly as a riot unfolds.

The emphasis on civic engagement as the mechanism that either foments or controls communal violence tends to displace the focus from the role played by the Hindu nationalist *Sangh Parivar* in engineering riots and pogroms since independence. Paul Brass is critical of Varshney's 'blame displacing' theorization and the fact that he identifies the Gujarat violence as the first of its kind in India.

## 3. THE PRODUCTION OF COMMUNAL RIOTS

'Most of his work gives a clean chit to the *Sangh Parivar*,' com-mented Paul Brass in the course of a lecture. Varshney, according to the celebrated theorist, refuses to recognize that many riots in the post-independence period have been outright pogroms. He indulges in a kind of 'apologetics' as to the *Sangh Parivar*.

The phrase 'ethnic earthquake' is, in the words of Professor Brass, a myth suggesting spontaneous outbreaks of communal violence. What is not a myth however is that communal riots are 'organized' and 'produced' by a network of known persons in the city or town. Most of these known persons are members of the *Sangh Parivar* who are devoted to the cult of violence for the protection of Hinduism.

Despite the fact that there are 'waves' or 'chains' in the occurrence patterns of communal rioting, there has been no notable period when such violence has been absent. Paul Brass develops and demonstrates the argument as to why communal tensions are maintained, accompanied from time to time by lethal rioting, and how it is essential for the development of militant Hindu nationalism and for other organizations and individuals.[27] Communal riots are endemic in India. The phenomenon of certain sites that are prone to violence or otherwise, entering and disappearing from the list of riot-hit cities, is therefore, somewhat flummoxing. While investigating the spatial variation in the incidence of Hindu-Muslim riots, Brass classifies the various aspects in categories of persistence/differential incidence/timing, classification/meaning and power.

The struggle over meaning, explanations and power relations requires attention to a communal discourse that has entrenched itself rather deeply in the body politic of the country. Brass uses the term 'hegemonic' to explain the communal discourse that pervades Indian politics. This discourse, fiercely Hindu nationalistic, has been successful in corrupting history as well as memory.

He identifies three elements inherent in the spread of this hegemonic communal discourse. Historization leads to the distortion of history and the division into periods where Muslims are seen as conquerors. The fundamental antagonism is overemphasized. The aspect of memorialization includes greater attention given to the dead heroes of one particular faith. The dramatizing and exaggerating nuances used to glorify what the *Sangh Parivar* calls 'the struggle for the birthplace of Lord Rama', is essential to memorialization.

Evidence exists to show that memorialization leads to the demonization of the 'other'. The Muslims, the 'others' in the Indian case, are portrayed in literature, cinema, and other forms of human expression as 'racially different inferior beings who invaded our country and cultural space'. Muslims are seen as violent and a danger to Hindu women. Myths, lending credence to this process of demonization, are taken recourse to in the form of the spoken as well as the written word.

Some utterly preposterous myths that have made their presence felt in the last two decades or so are that the reason for the higher rates of population growth among the Muslims is because they are trying to take over power both at the local and at the national level, and that most of them are 'Pakistani agents'.

Another feature of the communal discourse is 'body symbolism'. Muslim rule is portrayed as 'slavery' of the Hindus. The politics of body symbolism depicts the Partition in visceral terms, i.e. tearing apart of the Hindu body. The Muslims thus are dangerous to the Hindu body and need to be removed before the danger can actually present itself. This explains why most post-independence riots have been outright pogroms against the Muslims.

Paul Brass delineates three phases in the production process of riots. He compares a riot to a 'staged drama'. Dipankar Gupta uses the term 'picnic rioting' to describe the manner in which Hindu mobs actually celebrate the killing of Muslims. The Gujarat riots exemplified the herding of saffron-clad mobs into trucks and the subsequent journey into specially marked colonies of Muslim concentration.

The first phase, therefore, is one of preparation (*rehearsal*) in which tensions are kept alive. Killing a cow and kidnapping of a Hindu girl are the common methods. The next phase is one of activation (*enactment*). The political circumstance must be right for a riot to be precipitated. The pre-election period could be such an occasion. The last phase of riot production is explanation or interpretation where blame displacement comes into play. Professor Brass further argues that there exists a division of labour in the production of riots. Riot systems are institutionalized. Specific roles are assigned, like that of scouts or informants, rumour mongers, and propagandists.

Vernacular journalists enact their part admirably by printing wild and inciting stories. The recruiters are those who collect people to form mobs. The role of the politicians have already been documented earlier in the chapter. Special duties are assigned to people, Brass calls, 'fire tenders', who go around scouting for rumours which could help in fomenting a riot. These men invariably are members of either the Vishwa Hindu Parishad (VHP) or the Bajrang Dal. 'Conversion specialists' ultimately decide whether to begin a riot or not.

Causal questions about the spatial spread of riots are of utmost importance. Why exactly are they produced in certain cities or towns and why not in others? Steven Wilkinson's answer to this question has already been looked at. Brass asserts that the contexts are primarily political as mass mobilizations usually precede elections.

A sizeable number of Muslims in a particular town or city are essential for the production of riots. The demise of the Congress system has created a space that is normally filled by another political formation, which also benefits from riots and their production. The BJP has emerged as such a formation that benefits disproportionally through riots. The Gujarat situation is self-evident in this regard.

Brass and Wilkinson agree therefore that riots and electoral politics are closely connected to each other. They proclaim in their respective works that there exists an absence of political will to control riots and this cuts across political parties. Both further argue that the *Sangh Parivar* has been the primary source of most communal conflict in the country since independence.

Sociologists have a penchant for examining social conflict and Imtiaz Ahmad is no different in his approach. He, being one of the first scholars to propound the socio-economic theories for communal conflict, views the Hindu-Muslim conflict as an extension of the wider social conflict that includes inter- as well as intra-communal riots, caste violence and other forms of sectional upheavals. The emphasis placed on Hindu-Muslim conflict in case of social and communal violence comes but naturally considering the huge impact the various riots between the two communities have had on the Indian polity and society.[28]

Ahmad argues that economic prosperity of the Muslims is a factor that precipitates endemic anger on the part of the Hindus who fear being swamped, both socially and economically, by the *nouveaux riches* Muslims. This antagonism results in riots which spread to other parts of the state. An argument that has been advanced by numerous scholars following Imtiaz Ahmad, it brings into focus the social contradictions that have given rise to many communal conflagrations in the past and are likely to do so in future.

The ghosts of Gujarat cannot be invoked here as the violence there was 'produced' by the government of the day. The tensions that prevail in the rural plains of the north-western state are somewhat akin to the argument made by Ahmad. Frequent riots in the diamond city of Surat prove his point beyond any doubt.

The democratic process, therefore, is responsible for communal conflict and the lack of it. This does not mean that democracy has to be blamed. It was introduced after much thought and discussion when the Constitution was drafted. The problem is with certain political organizations, parties, leaders who are exploiting the weaknesses in the system to their own advantage. Thus the system is weakened. The scholars discussed earlier have advanced conclusive arguments that the electoral system that gets institutionalized over time determines the frequency of communal riots. Further, the arguments made earlier prove that riots are produced by specialists who could be politicians or members of the majoritarian formation.

## III. THE GUJARAT RIOTS OF 2002

### 1. BACKGROUND TO THE GODHRA CARNAGE

It is against this background that the Godhra carnage has to be studied. If communal politics began to dominate the political system in the 1990s, another malaise which afflicted the body politic from the beginning was corruption. It has transformed the entire nature of Indian politics into a more visceral politics based on caste, and a communal agenda. It was the result of a policy change by the central government led by V.P. Singh to implement the Mandal Commission's findings. The decision to reserve jobs for the Other Backward Castes, excluding caste Hindus, led to a great upheaval in the country particularly among the youth. The BJP, which was waiting for an opportunity to garner the Hindu votes, decided to meet the Mandal challenge with 'Kamandal'.[29] The party, which was a coalition partner, withdrew support of the government on this issue. It also successfully mounted a national campaign to build a Ram temple at the site of the Babri Masjid in Ayodhya. The BJP forcefully argued that the mosque had been built on the site of a temple that had been pulled down for the purpose.

In the early 1980s, the BJP in order to consolidate its position began to question the Nehruvian concept of secularism and attacked it as 'pseudo–secularism'. It started a strong propaganda saying that it was a sham and was meant only to create a Muslim vote bank. It also demanded a 'Common Civil Code' (at present the Muslim Personal Law allows a Muslim to have four wives, whereas under the Hindu Code Bill of 1956 Hindus can have only one). This demand was further aggravated by the agitation launched by Muslims against the judgement in the Shah Bano case.[30] The Muslim leadership in the country construed the Supreme Court's verdict as interference in the *Shari'at* law, which is divine and cannot be changed. Without realizing the long-term consequences, they launched a very aggressive movement forcing the then Rajiv Gandhi government to change the law for Muslims. When the Muslim Women's Rights on Divorce Act was passed which makes section 125 of the CrPC inapplicable to Muslims,[31] Rajiv Gandhi, as a balancing act, had the doors of the Babri Masjid in Ayodhya opened, where the idol of Ram Lalla has remained sealed under court orders since 1949.

Rajiv Gandhi's step unleashed another controversy which was exploited to the hilt by the BJP. In order to expand its political base in rural areas, which until then was confined to urban upper-caste Hindus, it decided to vigorously pursue the 'Hindutva' policy. It launched an aggressive movement for the construction of a Ram temple in Ayodhya by taking the Ram-janmabhoomi movement into rural India. The BJP propaganda easily caught on and began to pay rich political dividends. In the 1989 general elections, V.P. Singh made seat adjustments with the BJP to prevent the Congress party from coming to power. The Ramjanmabhoomi movement and the *'rath yatra'* across the country by L.K. Advani helped the BJP to win eighty-eight seats (against the 2 seats it had won in the 1984 elections). On the other hand, as a result of the *rath yatra* nearly 300 riots took place all over India.

## 2. BABRI DEMOLITION AND ITS AFTERMATH

The V.P. Singh government could not complete its term and this led to mid-term elections in the country. During an election campaign in Sri Perumbadur, Rajiv Gandhi, the former prime minister, was assassinated. The elections returned the Congress party to power with P.V. Narasimha Rao as the prime minister.

Keeping up the pressure on Rao's government, the BJP and its other constituents like the *Sangh Parivar*, the Rashtriya Swayam-sevak Sangh (RSS), the VHP and the Bajrang Dal (BD) decided to construct the Ram temple at the very site where Babri Masjid stood. As a response to the call given by them to their supporters and party workers, to enter Ayodhya, thousands of 'kar sevaks' from all over the country came to the city despite prohibitory orders. The Uttar Pradesh government sensing trouble asked the centre for full police assistance. The response of P.V. Narasimha Rao's government was not encouraging. Ultimately, taking advantage of the dilemma of both state and central governments, the Kar Sevaks demolished the Babri Masjid on 6 December 1992, an act which shocked the nation. This was followed by communal riots in Mumbai, Surat, Ahmedabad, Kanpur, Bhopal, Delhi, and several other places. The impact of the demolition could be felt even outside India, in neighbouring countries where Hindus were attacked. Mumbai witnessed one of the worst riots in post-independent India.[32] It was a black day in the history of the nation.

Though there was a lull in the communal violence after the post-Babri Masjid riots, Gujarat remained hypersensitive through-out. On every festive occasion of either Hindus or Muslims, riots broke out claiming a few lives. After coming to power in the Mumbai state elections with the Shiv Sena as its ally, the BJP was planning carefully to seize power in Gujarat also. In the following assembly elections it won a majority and Narendra Modi, the hard core RSS 'pracharak', was appointed chief minister of Gujarat. From then on, the VHP and BD became increasingly militant and started attacking both Muslims and Christians under one pretext or the other. They claimed that Christian missionaries were bent upon converting low caste Hindus to Christianity. The Gujarat riots, therefore, must be seen against this backdrop. The Godhra carnage did not occur sud-denly and simply in reaction to what happened on 27 February 2002. The liberal funds from Gujarat non-resident Indians (NRI) to the VHP, the defeat of the BJP in assembly elections in Uttar Pradesh and Punjab, the scandals surrounding the Gujarat earthquake relief fund of January 2001 were some of the hard reasons that caused the state and central governments to polarize Hindus and Muslims and consolidate the Hindutva forces. According to different mass media and press reports, the action was well planned and executed with finesse (see Engineer 2003).[33] It all started when a group of Muslims, in a fit of rage after a heated argument with 'kar sevaks' who where returning from Ayodhya, allegedly set fire to coach no. 6 of the Sabarmati Express in which the latter were travelling. Fifty-six passengers were roasted alive, forty-three sustained injuries. The state government ordered an inquiry. Even before the investigations into the reasons for the incident could be completed, the Gujarat government jumped to the conclusion that Muslim militants, at the instance of the Inter Services Intelligence of Pakistan (ISI), had planned it well in advance. The next day, the VHP announced a Gujarat 'bandh', and the government assured the police that it would be peaceful. On the contrary, violence broke out on a large scale and by the end of the day more than 100 persons had been done to death. Chief minister Modi's justification was that the violence subsequent to the Godhra incident was in keeping with Newton's law of action and reaction.

The violence continued unabated for more than sixty days with only one section of the population becoming the prime target. The whole police force, with some honourable exceptions, was communalized or abdicted its duty. The administrative apparatus was no different. People were burnt alive, women raped in front of their own children and family, infants were done to death before their mothers. By the time the state government, under severe criticism both inside and outside the country, realized its blunder, more than 2,000 people had been killed.

## 3. SPECIAL FEATURES OF THE GUJARAT RIOTS

1. The Gujarat violence was not a pure Hindu-Muslim riot. It was a carnage meticulously planned and organized against one community.
2. Never in any of the communal riots of the past was there such a furious outburst of violence against one community.

3. There was complete police inaction or complicity throughout.
4. The participation of cabinet ministers in leading the mobs
   against the Muslims and threatening the police if they
   booked cases is a disturbing trend.
5. For the first time foreign nationals were killed, even though
   they showed their passports for identification. They were
   attacked deliberately just because they were Muslim.
6. A first for the country was that some members of the
   European Union sent their investigating teams and submitted demarches to the Union government for failing to
   save the lives of innocent people.

On the other hand, despite condemnation, the state government
defended the killings. This is evident from the fact that not a
single accused person in the Gujarat communal carnage of
February-April 2002 has been punished so far. In all, eighty-
eight persons from the police and bureaucracy stand indicted,
including some leading officials. Also, 730 people, many of them
from the *Sangh Parivar*, have been named and identified as
perpetrators of mass crimes by witnesses, victims and NGOs.
The case is now in the Supreme Court which was highly critical
not only of the state government but even of the High Court for
the way they handled this sensitive case.

The National Human Rights Commission (NHRC) and several
public interest litigations filed in the courts have appealed that
the riot cases be handed over to a body which is not under the
control of Chief Minister Narendra Modi and his administration.
The state government has consistently refused to recommend a
CBI investigation. 'I told NHRC to recommend a CBI enquiry
from the very start,' reminds Amubhai Rawani, former chief
judge of the Rajasthan High Court. In 2003, the NHRC also
asked the Supreme Court to intervene and initiate a CBI enquiry.

Several cases have also been stayed. This has halted the process
of punishing the perpetrators of hate. Out of a total of 4,256
first information reports (FIRs) filed, the police summarily
dismissed 2,108 on the grounds that none of the accused were
found. This means that in as many as 49.75 per cent of the
cases, no legal action was taken. In 2,130 cases charge-sheets
were filed by the police.[34]

## 4. GOVERNMENT RESPONSE TO THE CARNAGE

Both state and central governments took their time to react to the worst carnage ever in the history of independent India. When the state government turned a blind eye to the happenings, the centre should have acted more firmly. The then prime minister not only failed to control the situation but also lost credibility by making totally contradictory statements. He visited Ahmedabad more than a month after the carnage. While visiting a refugee camp he asked, 'what face shall I show to the world?' He further stated that the Gujarat events were a blot on India which had so far enjoyed respect and prestige in the comity of nations because of the way in which a hundred crore people of diverse religions, cultures and ethnic groups lived together happily, shared their grief and joys, but never forgot the message of peace and brotherhood. He felt the happenings in Gujarat were not only heart-rending but most inhuman and horrible and advised Narendra Modi to follow *Raj dharma* (ruler's duty towards the subjects).[35]

At the meeting of the National Executive of the BJP, the prime minister made a complete turnaround and accused Islam and Muslims of militancy and conflict. He almost echoed Narendra Modi's line on Gujarat. Thus Vajpayee proved to be as much an RSS 'pracharak' as Modi himself. The BJP, which had promised a 'riot-free India' in its election manifesto, was unfortunately doing quite the opposite. Vajpayee's statements clearly show that the BJP fully approved Narendra Modi's policies for tackling the communal situation in Gujarat. The party would like many more 'Gujarats' to happen in order to establish '*Hindu Rashtra*'.[36]

It is not the intention of this author to beatify one and demonize another section of Indians. To externalize the enemy is a common human failing, to which Indians are not averse. Because of its subcontinental size and great diversity of race, religion and social status, the enemy is often externalized within the country's borders and not without.

The people of India are not gullible and have traditionally seen through and rejected false images. And the secular Indian from all religions has condemned the Godhra train incident and the subsequent massacre of the innocent which would put even a dictator to shame. The fires are out. The smoke has settled. But the carnage still haunts one community very much. They feel persecuted and have lost faith in the administration. The culprits are still at large. For the living dead, justice is the only hope. The guilty—to whichever community he may belong— must be punished. Non-governmental organizations (NGOs) are making every effort to bring Hindus and Muslims closer together in Godhra. Both the communities are meeting frequently thanks to innovative programmes conducted by these NGOs. Hindus and Muslims badly needed space to meet each other, which the NGOs are providing. Their efforts should be appreciated and encouraged.

The photograph published in many dailies during the Gujarat turmoil, of a 'Muslim pleading with the rampaging mob with folded hands to spare him', is still fresh in the memory of every Indian. This is not what the founding fathers of the Indian constitution wanted for the country.

## CONCLUSION

From the foregoing evaluations, it is observed that the basic diversity of the Indian society is profound and has been a rigidly structured one. Hence the founding fathers of India consciously chose secularism as the best model to suit the Indian polity with its variety and diversity. Nehru's charismatic appeal, his long innings in the power structure, and his handling of it helped in the management of divisive forces against secularism and nation-building. Adult franchise and the subsequent realignment of forces in independent India were accommodated in the body politic without disturbing the elements of national integration. The voting pattern of the minorities indicated that they voted for the national parties, especially the Congress, to secure peace and protection. The emergency period under Mrs Gandhi was a watershed and the various developments since this period show a steady deterioration in communal relationships. Consequently, the effective management of divisive forces against national integration became difficult. In a competitive environment the ruling elites instead of strengthening the secular options tend to use religion as a vehicle to promote their narrow economic and political goals. A careful analysis of communal conflicts indicate that though they are mostly influenced by economic factors, the ruling elites in India can convert them into communal problems. Such diversion has ultimately affected the process of national integration and led to the emergence of Hindu fundamentalism. Fundamentalism in any form is dangerous to secularism. The average Indian voter, after this crisis, clearly warned against playing too much the communal card. The emergence of secular and moderate elements on both sides of the majority and minority communities, the verdicts of the ever vigilant Supreme Court in favour of secular options, and the vigilance of the Chief Election Commissioner against communal elements in popular elections raises the hope that secularism will survive in the Indian context so that it can strengthen the elements of national integration despite all challenges.

## NOTES

1. Mridula S. Ghule, 'Nehru and Secularism', *Third Concept*, vol. 4 (46), December 1990.
2. Satish K. Singh, 'Crackdown on Secularism', *Third Concept*, vol. 4 (46), December 1990.
3. K. Mohanasundaram, 'Secularism and Nation-Building—The Indian Experience', *Third Concept*, vol. 13, October–November 1999.
4. Ravinder Kumar, 'Secular Culture of India', in Rasheeduddin Khan (ed.), *Composite Culture of India and National Integration* (New Delhi: Allied Publishers, 1987).
5. Rajni Kothari, 'Nation Building and Political Government', in S.C. Dube (ed.), *India since Independence* (New Delhi: Vikas, 1977).
6. S.S. Sharan, 'Saga of Indian Secularism and the New Crisis', *Mainstream*, 27 December 2003.
7. Rakesh Raman Jha, 'Communal Harmony: A Gandhian Perspective', *Third Concept*, vol. 14, November 2000.
8. K. Mohanasundaram, n. 3.
9. Ashgar Ali Engineer, 'Muslim Vote in Maharashtra', *The Hindu*, 19 January 1995.
10. Ibid., 'Communal Riots and Causes—III', *The Hindu*, 15 February 1995.
11. Ajay Kumar Singh, 'Concept and Practice of Secularism in India', *Third Concept*, vol. (3)25, December 2003.
12. K. Mohanasundaram, n. 3.

13. Purnima Singh, 'Gujarat—Tribute to Gandhi's Principle of Non-Violence?', *Third Concept*, vol. 16, May 2002.
14. Steven Wilkinson, 'Putting Gujarat in Perspective', *Economic and Political Weekly*, 27 April, 2002.
15. Wilkinson uses the term 'ethnic' in the broader sense to describe Hindu-Muslim riots in India. Horowitz argues that all conflicts based on ascriptive identities—race, language, religion, tribe or caste—can be called 'ethnic'. The term 'ethnic cleansing' has also been used to describe the atrocities in Gujarat.
16. Steven Wilkinson, *Forthcoming*.
17. Wilkinson, n. 14.
18. Christopher Jaffrelot, 'The Politics of Processions and Hindu-Muslim Riots', in Atul Kohli & Amrita Basu (eds.), *Community Conflicts in India* (OUP, 2001).
19. Ashutosh Varshney, *Ethnic Conflict and Civic Life: Hindus and Muslims in India* (Yale University Press, 2002).
20. 'State autonomy' signifies the power of the administration to take independent action.
21. 'State capacity' includes the fiscal disposition, judicial capacity and rate of transfers within the state.
22. Varshney, n. 19.
23. Some examples are: business associations, professional organizations, film clubs, sports clubs, trade unions, etc.
24. Some examples are: Hindu and Muslim families visiting each other, eating together, joint participation in festivals, etc.
25. Varshney, n. 19.
26. Ibid.
27. Paul Brass, *The Production of Hindu–Muslim Violence in Contemporary India* (University of Washington Press, 2003).
28. Imtiaz Ahmed, *Original Manuscripts*.
29. S.S. Sharan, n. 6.
30. The case is infamous in India and has generated political controversy in the country. Shah Bano, a 62-year-old Muslim woman and mother of five children, was divorced by her husband in 1978. Muslim personal law (different for Christianity, and Hinduism) allows the husband to divorce his wife without her consent. He has just to speak the word 'Talaaq' three times before witnesses for a valid divorce. Shah Bano asked for maintenance from her husband to support herself and her children. She approached the Supreme Court which took eight years to take up the case. The Supreme Court invoked Article 125, stating that applied to everyone regardless of caste, creed, or religion, and ruled that Shah Bano be given the maintenance amount.
31. Article 125 Criminal Procedure Code (CrPC) 1973, deals with the

right to maintenance. It imposes a legal obligation on the husband to maintain his wife, provide shelter to her and their children, and give a monthly allowance not exceeding Rs. 500 (US $15). It has now been raised to Rs. 3,000 (US $65) per month. This is not applicable to Muslim women according to their personal law.

32. Ashgar Ali Engineer (ed.), *The Gujarat Carnage* (New Delhi: Orient Longman, 2003).
33. Ibid.
34. Batuk Vora, 'Gagged Elsewhere', in *Tehelka Special Report*, 6 March 2004.
35. Engineer, n. 32.
36. Ibid.
37. For further reference see Roshini Sengupta, 'Communal Violence in India: Perspectives on the Causative Factors', paper presented at the 18th EAMAS Conference held at Lund, Sweden, July 2004.

# CHAPTER 12

# Political Economy of Communalism: A Response from the Left

*Dipak Malik*

The modernizers, the Left, and other fringe movements working on the agenda of progressive transformation face two major stumbling blocks, the religious-communal divide and the perennial Hindu caste, an archaic, hierarchical system complete with relationships of master and semi-slave bordering on the non-racial social-apartheid system, systemically preventing construction of a national and socially democratized society in the large canvas of Indian history. They have caused many a convulsion in Indian history. Modern nation-building, modern class formation, even the pace of bourgeois development as against a massive wall of feudalism, remain either muted or somewhat unfinished. There is the other side of the story too, of the massive plunder of this subcontinent by colonialism. It has been described by many but the graphic description and prognosis by Karl Marx and Frederick Engels remain a significant contribution to the decolonization discourse of degeneration and regeneration.[1] This lineage trickles down and continues in the works of R.P. Dutt, M.N. Roy, A.R. Desai, and a score of Soviet scholars. Marx built up a prognosis of impending political changes in more substantial terms in his later essays.

## I. COMMUNALISM AND COLONIALISM

The two major stumbling blocks that created a distinctive history as well as specific historical trajectory are the sociology and politics of communalism[2] and the sociology of the caste system[3] and political economy of caste.[4] We will mainly try to track down the former, which unfolds as a fairly comprehensive process in the Indian polity.

The question of the caste-class dichotomy received much attention in the sociological discourse in the 1960s and 1970s, but it is no longer in focus. Subaltern historians have been raising these questions lately, but their critique, though it points out an unexplored region of resistance by the marginalized people, is unable to explain the comprehensive picture of a political struggle emerging in an anti-colonial context. The subalterns of course have tried to see the subaltern resurgence as completely un-contaminated by the mainstream national struggle. This distinction line naturally raises substantial questions[5] which need further exploration.

Communalism has a class angle too, but that angle may not be the dominant structure in the making of communalism. Of course there are some instances like the emergence of communalism in Bengal in pre-partition days, where the class role had a big presence. In a contemporary situation, communalism serves as a diversionary tactic, to move attention away from main economic issues that adversely affect people in day-to-day life. It is not always deliberately offered as an option by communally-oriented parties but it is a kind of fringe benefit which a communal party can reap as it can always avoid the uncomfortable questions relating to the difficult issues of poverty, widespread inequality, and unemployment. In the pre-British days there were several instances of orthodox zealots in the ruling circle affecting the management of the state, but the common people and subjects at large were neither affected nor as a desperate response did they resort to the collective dynamics of communalism. If communalism is taken as an exclusive artefact of colonialism, then the class dynamics becomes secondary. Though once communal consciousness arrived on the stage, it was the modern middle class with English education that became the major actor in this game. A new denominational identity as well as demographic profile was arrived at as a result of the first British census operation in 1872.[6] The one definite effect of the census was that it divided the Indian society into a number of religious groups amongst whom the Hindus had the overwhelming majority. The Muslims overnight were turned into a minority group. Thus this census, though very innocuously designed to facilitate the colonial administration on a day-to-day basis, brought about the most irreconcilable schism. Similar tendencies are again visible in the post-independence period when the language newspapers and non-national dailies flaunt caste statistics in a large number of constituencies and emphasize the big role of caste in the elections. This is ultimately being converted into the material reality of caste vote banks and has finally resulted in strengthening caste factors, thus bringing an element of primordiality as a *fait accompli* in the elections almost all over India except in a few areas of metropolitan Delhi, metropolitan Mumbai and the state of West Bengal, where elections are still run on an ideological political rather than a caste vote-bank platform.

The Indian middle class, which pioneered the process of modernization as well as modern Indian nationalism, was equally present in the denomination centred polity. It was not the marginalized subaltern or the illiterate peasant masses that brought forth the new denominational identity. Actually this newly emerging anglicized middle class was to replace the so-called natural leaders of the people, the feudal lords, old aristocracy, and the native princes. The British colonial polity in India was looking for an ally after 1857, and they found it in the troubled waters of an empire-in-making: it was the old feudatory from the late Mughal era that was now being co-opted in the machinery of colonialism's management, particularly in revenue collection. But the metropolitan centres, the port cities founded by the British, were churning out a new middle class, which was to later become a pioneering class in the anti-colonial movement. Thus the Indian National Congress, which started its journey as an organ of the English educated intelligentsia, records about its Calcutta session in 1886 'The entire absence of old aristocracy, the so-called natural leaders of the people'. It also admitted that 'the ryots and cultivating classes' were insufficiently represented while petty moneylenders and shopkeepers were conspicuous by their absence, though the report claims that the higher commercial classes, the banking merchants, were fairly well represented. No

less than 455 of the 1,200 old delegates of the Allahabad Congress
(1888), for instance, were themselves lawyers, while there were
59 teachers and 73 journalists.[7]

The Hindu middle class increased by leaps and bounds and
received a modern education countrywide in 11 English colleges
and 40 English schools which were managed by the government
with another 92 schools run by Christian missionaries.[8] The
number of students went up fairly rapidly in 1887 to 2,98,000
and 5,05,000 in 1907, while the circulation of English language
newspapers climbed from 90,000 in 1888 to 276,000 in 1905.[9]

Similarly an anglicized Muslim elite had started taking shape
though its class character was less of a middle class and more
the remnants of the old governing aristocracy. As a matter of
fact the decline of the Muslim middle class started with the shift
from Persian to English as court language. The traditional
professionals who had command over Persian and Urdu were
rendered unemployed. The majority of such middle-level or lower-
middle level functionaries were Muslims, and soon the old feudal
section and colonial officials gathered and founded the Muslim
League. A deputation of Muslim leaders placed before Viceroy
Lord Minto in Shimla on 1 October 1906 a memorandum
originally drafted by Syed Hussian Bilgrami, in which they
prayed,

That [the] position accorded to the Muslim community in any kind of
representation direct or indirect and in all other ways affecting their
status and influence should be commensurate not merely with their
numerical strength but also their political importance and that in
estimating the latter, due weight should be given to the position they
occupied in India a little more than hundred years ago and of which
the traditions have naturally not faded from their mind.[10]

Thus in response to the emerging Hindu middle class, the Muslim elite launched a political party of Muslims on 30 December 1906. The initiative was taken by Nawab Salimulla of
Dacca and the Muslim League's first chosen president, Nawab
Viquar-al-Mulk. The Nawab of Dacca said in his speech that
such a body was necessary also to keep Muslims from being
submerged by an enormous majority of the other race.[11]

The middle-class formation can be observed in the number of
people employed in government positions where the salary was

less than Rs. 500, as the posts with salaries above Rs. 500 mostly went to Europeans. In 1867, out of 2,182 such posts, Europeans held 2,048, Hindus 99, and Muslims 35. But by 1912, out of 5,392 posts, the Europeans occupied 4,466 (82.8 per cent), Hindus 784 (14.5 per cent), and Muslims 142 (2.6 per cent). This was obviously a disproportionate growth track.[12]

Regarding middle-class intelligentsia formation the Muslims were obviously too small in number compared to the Hindus. In 1882, according to the Education Commission, there were 5,155 Hindus as compared to 57 Muslims holding a degree in arts.[13] It was this disproportionate growth of the middle-class intelligentsia that laid the ground for communal politics.

Sir Sayyed Ahmed Khan, the great social reformer in the Muslim community, and founder of Aligarh Muslim University, the first modern university in the whole *umma* (Muslim religious world system), right from Malaysia to Turkey, was very articulate about the numerical weakness of the Muslims. Hence he was against the democratic representation system as demanded by the Congress. In a speech delivered in the northern Indian town of Meerut on 14 March 1888, he told his audience that for the peace and for the progress of everything in India the English should remain for many years—in fact for ever—because it had been settled that the English government was necessary.

Sir Sayyed was a relentless campaigner against the Congress movement. He formed in 1888 the United Indian Patriotic Association which was supposed to be a body patronized by maharajas and nawabs and was to register its allegiance towards His Majesty's government. Sir Sayyed tried to bring Hindu and Muslim chieftains into this organization. The move though initially highly successful broke down with the Maharaja of Benares opting out to become the chief of the British Indian Association of the Oudh Taluqdars, a sort of Hindu version of empire loyalists. It was an attempt to organize the feudal class under one banner as against the middle-class dominated Congress. The latter was demanding democratic forms of representation which would have resulted in people's participation and would have ultimately snatched the privileges from the feudatories.

In Punjab, which was one of the two big Muslim-dominated

provinces, the state of class conflict was not that acute and articulated as in Bengal; but it offered a scene, or rather a rare example of a fine-tuned class organization of Muslim landlords of west Punjab, Sikh landlords of central Punjab and Hindu landlords of south Punjab (now Haryana and Himachal Pradesh) with the aim to protect them from the radical demands of tenants and Hindu moneylenders under the patronage of the Unionist Party. The result was that the Muslim League remained quite weak in Punjab till 1937. From 1937 to 1943 only, under the impact of the nationwide growth of communalism, the Muslims rallied to the Muslim League (Bipan Chandra, 1996: 83). Thus Punjab demonstrated a scene of class solidarity beyond communal lines for a fairly long time, particularly under the robust leadership of Sir Sikander Hayyat Khan who was to remain the leading figure as premier of Punjab for a long period. Another significant figure in this coalition was Sir Chhotu Ram, a Jat politician of considerable following who was a colleague of Sir Sikander.

## II. THEORY AND PRACTICE OF COMMUNALISM

### 1. THE SOCIOLOGY OF COMMUNALISM

The politics of communalism was based primarily on colonial promptings, the cultural distinctness of the two religious communities of Hindus and Muslims, and on the fear psychosis in the vast majority of Muslims of being overpowered by the Hindu majority once the democratic norm and form emerged. Above all, the very idea of Pakistan and Muslim separation was a product of the apprehensions of the proportionately small Muslim middle class and the old aristocracy and feudatories. The governing classes' urge to get back their powers in reality came out of a specific class aspiration. On the other hand, perennial cultural conflicts were no less responsible for the denominational politics. Thus it was with this ensemble of 'base and superstructure' dynamics under the hegemony of colonialism that the idea of communalism was born. The following diagram can explain the genesis of the sociology and politics of communalism:

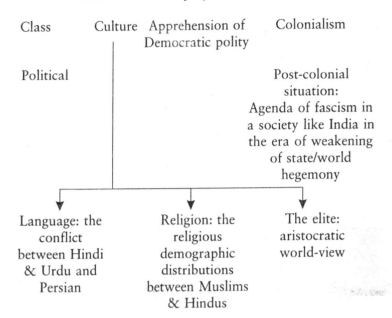

| Class | Culture | Apprehension of Democratic polity | Colonialism |
| --- | --- | --- | --- |
| Political | | | Post-colonial situation: Agenda of fascism in a society like India in the era of weakening of state/world hegemony |
| Language: the conflict between Hindi & Urdu and Persian | Religion: the religious demographic distributions between Muslims & Hindus | | The elite: aristocratic world-view |

## 2. CLASS RIVALRY AND POWER-SHARING CRISIS AS BIRTH-MARK

The roots of modern communalism go back to class rivalry in the early phase, when the Muslim elite realized that in a decolonized India they would be reduced to a subservient hapless minority. It was generated out of class rivalry between a numerically bigger Hindu middle class-cum-elite and a Muslim feudalistic elite class-cum-micro middle class. But then other aspects of class and culture also affected the multidimensional communal question.

Along with the raging debate about sharing the cake in a decolonized India, the cultural matrix inherited from the days of Bhakti and Sufi was also progressively dismantled. The heated debate about Hindi as the language of Hindus, a rejection of the mixed lingo of 'Hindustani', which was constituted out of the Sanskrit as well as the Persian lexicon, a rare example of a composite language so well built, was to create the cultural context of communalism. Sir George Grierson, an early English scholar of Hindi, noted that no separate language existed for those who recognized the need of the Hindus for a language of their own. The British thus initiated a new language—Sanskritized Hindi inculcated through the College of Fort William founded in 1800 in Calcutta. Hindustani and Urdu were supposed to be languages of 'foreign origin'.[13]

Sir Sayyed Ahmed Khan who was posted in Benares in those days, saw the Hinduization of Hindi and the systematic weeding out of Perso-Arabic elements from it. This was to have a deep impact on him and it made him wonder whether a composite culture of Hindus and Muslims was at all possible. Thus two composite languages, Hindustani and Urdu, which had developed in the vast Hindi heartland[14] of north India, took respectively separate paths; Hindi towards Sanskritic roots, Urdu towards Perso-Arabic roots. This brought the elements of communalization into culture, and the composite culture, that had been built over four hundred years in the pre-colonial period dissipated. The Hindi-Urdu conflict persists in the Hindi heartland and ignites communal passions even now. The Hindi heartland was witness to three major influences which communalized it. There was the early phase of rivalry between the Muslim aristocracy and emerging Hindu middle class and aristocracy. Since Delhi, and its surrounding area, was the seat of the great Mughals and Sultans for about 900 years this rivalry was bound to influence the feudals dispossessed in those parts. It was succeeded by the language conflict between Urdu and Hindi, followed in the post-independence era by the initiation of the movement for the restoration of Lord Rama's birthplace in Ayodhya by the *Sangh Parivar*. This was no simple communalism but a strategy for the takeover of the post-colonial state of India in order to install an indigenous fascist type state and society.

3. COMMUNALISM AND CLASS STRUGGLE
   IN COLONIAL DAYS: AN EXAMPLE

In Bengal, unlike UP, Bihar, MP, Rajasthan, Haryana, and Delhi, the Bengali language was shared by both Hindus and Muslims. After the short interval of the 1905 division of Bengal, the communalization process was based directly on the class question, between the overwhelming majority of the Bengali Muslim landless and poor peasantry *vis-à-vis* Hindu landlords, Hindu merchants as well as the Hindu-dominated colonial bureaucracy and the powerful and numerous Hindu middle class. The depression further deteriorated the paying capacity of the peasants. The most significant player of the class demands of the poor as well as middle peasantry in pre-partition Bengal was the Krishak Praja Party. It had proclaimed the abolition of *Zamindari* (landlordism) without compensation. Its manifesto called for land rent and revenue to be commuted and debts to be written off. In order to attract the rich middle peasantry (*Jotdars*) it demanded a permanent settlement, the reduction and capping of land rent, the abolition of other lessees as well as the establishment of Debt Settlement Boards. This caused consternation in the Hindu landlord class. The Congress party, in spite of its radicalization in the mid-1930s on an all India level, was in the grip of the conservative landlord lobby in Bengal though it had socialists like Subhas Chandra Bose in its ranks who ultimately landed in the lap of Fascist Germany and Tojo's Japan. Thus a scenario of class struggle and anti-feudal struggle against landlordism turned into communal strife as the majority of peasants and subjects were Muslim, while the majority of landlords were Hindus.[15]

Communal politics emerges out of spontaneous communal riots, which, right from the colonial days till today, are being enacted at different occasions starting from petty tiffs over a change in the fixed route permitted by the police for a particular religious procession to accidental attacks on temples and mosques, from cow slaughter during colonial days, to quarrels between neighbourhoods inhabited by two different religious groups, national communal calls for a boycott on a particular day, etc. But in contemporary India, communal riots have become well-planned and premeditated systematic moves by the BJP, the RSS and the VHP with a view to achieving their long-term objective of majoritarian communalism and goals of a Hindu Nation, which is actually a euphemism for an indigenous variety of fascism.

## III. COMMUNALISM AND POLITICS

### 1. THE RIGHT AND HINDU COMMUNALISM

The architecture of a Hindu communal polity is deeply associated with the emergence of the Rashtriya Swayamsevak Sangh (RSS or 'Association of National Volunteers') founded in 1925, as well as the rise of M.S. Golwalkar as the major theoretician of communal Hindutva. Golwalkar took a stand which disputed the Aryan migration theory. He maintained that Hindus came from nowhere, but are indigenous to the soil from time immemorial. This racial factor in his eyes is by far the most important ingredient of a discriminatory nationalism. By contrast the Muslims and other religious groups are of foreign origin and do not consider India as their holy land; their holy land being situated in Mecca and Jerusalem respectively. Golwalkar was greatly inspired by Hitler, so much so that in his main tract *We, or Our Nationhood Defined*, he eulogizes Hitler's ideology in these words.[16]

To keep up the purity of the race and its culture, Germany shocked the world by her purging the country of the Semitic race—the Jews. Race pride at its highest has been manifested here in Germany which has also shown how well-nigh impossible it is for races and cultures, having differences going to the root to be assimilated into one united whole, a good lesson for us in Hindustan to learn and profit by.[17]

Golwalkar very obviously pointing towards the exclusion of the Muslims in spite of 900 years of their presence finds his inspiration in the racial cleansing ideology.

Golwalkar, while outlining the agenda of the RSS wrote that the foreign races (read Muslims primarily, and Christians) in Hindustan must either adopt the Hindu culture and language, learn to respect and hold in reverence Hindu religion, entertain no ideas but those of glorification of the Hindu race and culture or may stay in the country wholly subordinated to the Hindu nation claiming nothing, deserving no privilege, far less any preferential treatment not even citizen's rights.[18]

In contemporary India, communalism is less a spontaneous affair than a packaged activity mostly by the Hindu majoritarian political combination of the BJP and its allied mass organizations, which clubbed together are called the '*Sangh Parivar*'. Thus the *Sangh Parivar* (Parivar means family) is a conglomerate of organizations with the RSS as its pivot. Apart from the BJP as the main political front there is a large number of mass organizations like the globally operating communal Hindu outfit Vishwa Hindu Parishad (VHP) or the Vidyarthi Parishad, an organization of Sangh oriented students. The *Sangh Parivar* defines as its goal the establishment of Hindu nationhood. It runs its politics, which may take many shapes, precisely with this aim. But most importantly, it is the agency of indigenous fascism. It is a much revised and revisionist version of European fascism between the two world wars with certain distinctive features. Thus the *Sangh Parivar* uses anti-Muslim tirades as a religious instrument of offence and discrimination rather than the racial instrument used by German Nazism. It is a fascist design, which uses the Muslim community as a scapegoat for establishing a strong dictatorship at the centre and in the state ultimately. It is not a product of a capitalist crisis only, it is rather an experiment with globalization, liberalization and privatization against the backdrop of a developing society of subcontinental size. Moreover, the period of European fascism was an era of strong nation states as opposed to the contemporary phase of weak and withering nation-states faced with the demands of the world capitalist market. It spreads its tentacles in a society which is still, by and large, semi-feudal and at places fully feudal. The cultural roots have their bases in this feudal social system, which remains quite intact in spite of bourgeois developments.

## 2. THE LEFT, MODERNIZERS AND THE QUESTION OF COMMUNALISM

The Left, and particularly the Marxist Left, has a historic responsibility in reconstructing nationalism in the post-colonial context. In its early phase of discourse, it primarily concentrated on class and class struggle calling for proletarian internationalism. The discourse on nationalism in the Left orbit was rather a derivative of class and class struggle. The demand for Pakistan by Muslim communal interests along with supportive gestures of British colonialism was read as the demand for 'self-determination' for a Muslim nationality. E.M.S. Namboodiripad, one of the most influential leaders of the CPI(M) till his death, described the mistake in the following words:

The essence of [the] mistake committed by the party was that, as opposed to the Marxist Leninist stand, the question of nationality should be dealt with not abstractly but as part of the class political questions (India's freedom struggle in this case). Equating the League demand for the division of India with the Congress opposition to it meant putting on par an avowedly pro-imperialist section of the bourgeoisie with its oppositional though compromising, rival in the same class—a stand which is clearly impermissible for Marxist–Leninist.[19]

Let us turn to the more important component of the Left narrative in the post-colonial period. As a matter of fact not only the Left but the eager modernizers like Nehru, who definitely charted a path of reconstruction of Indian society, polity, and economy, also believed that the pursuit of a modern developmental strategy would automatically erase the impact of communalism. Actually the Left was trapped in a mechanical application of the notion of base and superstructure. Communalism as a superstructure of its own would not disappear automatically. It has gained weight, and is actually an ensemble of both superstructure and base. This superstructural riddle has to be understood in the context of creating an 'alternative hegemony' where apart from the class forces, the non-class identity movements, movements for alternative cultures have to be taken into consideration.

In the early phase of the post-independence period, the rise of right reaction was noted at the 6th Congress of the Communist Party. The rise of the Jana Sangh, an earlier version of the BJP, was viewed with concern. This was the first major analysis of Hindu communalism in communist circles. This Congress is significant from the point of view of devising a strategy of nation-building where the communists do not merely pursue class tasks but combine them with national tasks. At this congress, Ajoy Ghosh, the then general secretary of the CPI, expanded the theory of unity and struggle while making common cause with the bourgeoisie[20] in combating the right reactionary forces, which still had not shown their true colours.

Perhaps one of the most unfortunate glossing over of the basic strategies by the Left was when, from 1967 to 1971, it willy-nilly submitted to the 'Non-Congressism platform' without distinguishing its independent position as a critical force. 'Non-Congressism' was a strategic bloc initiated by Ram Manohar Lohia, the socialist leader, to form a parliamentary alternative to Congress rule. This 'ensemble' included all non-Congress forces right from the Bharatiya Jana Sangh, and the Swatantra Party, the organ of the Indian monopoly, comprador bourgeoisie and native feudal kings—to the Left parties. This incongruous and directionless combination of the organized left, social democrats and a motely crowd of right-wingers, communalists, reactionaries of all kinds, could not survive, but would facilitate the route to the future Rashtra or nation. Madhu Limaye, a veteran socialist leader and theoretician, explained that the main distinction between parties related neither to their Leftism or Rightism nor to their adherence to democracy or totalitarianism, but was between those in the government and those who were 'out of it'. A state of permanent opposition or the prospect of being kept out of power produced frustration or a sense of desperation in Lohia as much as in the whole spectrum of right-wingers. Lohia wanted the opposition parties to join hands to achieve the urgent goal of throwing the Congress out of power without any radical break in the strategy of Nehruvian modernization. This non-ideological assembly of all non-Congress forces actually helped the right.[22]

This strategic alliance brought the Hindu communal outfit of the BJS (Bharatiya Jana Sangh, the earlier version of the BJP) into the mainstream of Indian politics. In several states non-Congress governments were formed and in the major state of the Hindi belt, UP, the Left joined the coalition government of a 'Non-Congress alliance' along with representatives of the BJS. It was not long before the party's grass-roots workers called a party plenum and asked their representative to leave the non-Congress outfit and sit in the opposition.

The Lohiaite exercise combining parliamentary opposition to

Congress with communal elements was repeated in 1977 when a Janata Party was created with the merger of all non-Congress bourgeois communal as well as *kulak* parties. The Marxist Left, however, kept itself out of this combination. In 1989, a short experiment was again tried when non-Congress forces combined to form a government this time with the BJP as a supportive party from the outside.

The fall of the National Front government was the beginning of the ascendancy of the '*Sangh Parivar*' ideology. In order to save its tottering government, the then prime minister, V.P. Singh, started to implement the Mandal Commissions' recommendations, regarding the reservation of jobs in government for 'Other Backward Castes' to correct the unequal structure of the Hindu caste system leading to exclusion in jobs, education, and governance. In reaction to the Mandal Commission, which had tried to ameliorate the anomalies built into the opportunity structure in the hierarchically built caste system, the *Sangh Parivar* developed a counter-strategy of communalization. It triggered the renewed ascendancy of Hindu fundamentalism and Hindu communalism. Thus, if in pre-partition days class had mattered in the construction of communalism, in the decade of the 1990s, caste and the return to the old hierarchical structure of Hindu society became somewhat a focal point in the Hindi heartland resulting in the use of a vigorous polity of communalism.

## IV. ORGANIZING HINDU FUNDAMENTALISM

### 1. THE BJP-RSS ORGANIZATION

Dr K.B. Hedgewar installed the RSS as a revivalist Hindu organization in Nagpur in 1925. Hedgewar was sent by the extremist Hindu Sabha leader, Moonje, a disciple of Bal Gangadhar Tilak, to Calcutta to study medicine. Instead of studying medicine, Hedgewar studied the structure of secret organizations like the Anushilan Samity.[23] The Bengali secret organizations against the British empire had a ritualized routine in which the worship of Goddess Kali, the guru-disciple system, strict discipline, and a top-down organization were cultivated.

These were largely emulated by the RSS. The aim of the organization was to build up a Hindu nation or Hindu *Rashtra*.[24] The concept was cultural and ethnic and not territorial. This is how the concept of cultural nationalism came into being in Sangh circles. Militantism, masculinity, patriarchy, and contempt for non-Hindus, particularly Muslims, defined the core culture of the RSS. It had its sympathizers all over including in the Congress Party, in eminent figures no less than Sardar Ballabh Bhai Patel, the deputy prime minister of India in the early years of freedom. The main builder and ideologue of the RSS, M.S. Golwalkar, was called Guruji (the teacher). Golwalkar was deeply influenced by 'German writers like Johann Kasper Bluntschli'.[25] Bluntschli has been referred to by D.V. Savarkar, the pioneering Hindu communal leader and president of the Hindu Mahasabha, and M.S. Aney, another tall Hindu leader. Savarkar wrote the preface to 'We, our nationhood defined', the canonical texts of the RSS.

After the assassination of Mahatma Gandhi the RSS was banned. The ban, however, was lifted with the help of Home Minister Patel even though the RSS did not budge an inch from its avowed aims. But for the sake of convenience and to avoid proscription, it declared itself a cultural organization which supposedly shunned politics. But immediately after his release from jail Golwalkar said that the RSS had not given up anything.[26]

After the lifting of the ban, the RSS decided to adopt the Jana Sangh, an outfit floated by S.P. Mookerjee, a prominent Bengali politician who was associated with the Hindu Mahasabha and who later was invited to join the first Cabinet of Nehru. This odd marriage did not last long, and Syama Prasad Mookerjee left the Congress government.

The RSS though nurturing some kind of apathy for the general stream of politicization in which it had no place, later decided to move into the arena of politics through a front organization in order to realize the programme of Hindu *Rashtra* or nation. So the newly formed Jana Sangh was entrusted to a young volunteer, Deen Dayal Upadhyaya, from the RSS for the purpose to build the organization. Upadhyaya was to emerge as the main ideologue of the Jana Sangh and the most important leader in the annals of the BJP's and the erstwhile Bharatiya Jana Sangh. As a matter of fact the NDA prime minister A.B. Vajpayee was one of the recruits trained by Upadhyaya. Indeed, Vajpayee credits Upadhyaya as being his as well as the BJ-BJP's ideological mentor. The relationship between the RSS and the then Jana Sangh and the contemporary BJP (as its respective political organ) was to remain at the level of a great and trusted teacher-disciple relationship, i.e. almost symbiotic. The world renouncing saffron activist, the disciple in the BJP, or the erstwhile Jana Sangh, enjoyed the patronage and disciplined training of the RSS. The relationship between the RSS and its party has been explained by M.S. Golwalkar: 'we aspire to become [the] radiating center of all the age old cherished ideals of our society'.[27]

The RSS in the meantime has changed into an organization which is ready to tolerate or experiment with other than stridently communal politics in its long-term pursuit of the transformation of society towards a Hindu nation or *Rashtra*. The RSS has at times toyed with the idea of other options for realizing its Hindu card. As a matter of fact, the anti-Sikh riots all over north India after the assassination of Mrs Gandhi provided an opportunity for the Sangh leadership to offer an olive branch to the Congress, as they interpreted the subsequent massive mandate for the return of a Rajiv Gandhi-led Congress to power as a sign of a vast Hindu consolidation not only against the Sikhs, but generally against all minorities. Recently some RSS leaders have found the somewhat middle of the road politics of the Vajpayee-led NDA government so alarming that they want the leadership to go to the younger lot which includes Sushma Swaraj, Narendra Modi, the chief minister of Gujarat, Uma Bharati, and Arun Jaitley. Ths RSS is also propping up 'Govindacharya' who is raising a movement combining opposition to globalization with the in-culcation of Hindutva as an experimental ground for the RSS.

## 2. A THREE-TIER SYSTEM

Amongst the political parties in the world, the BJP ultimately has a unique feature; it is at the minimum a three-tier political system. Justified by the RSS the three-tier system has three components:

The RSS
(Rashtriya Swayamsevak Sangh, National Volunteer organization)
(Secret; semi-military training; the goal of the creation of a non-democratic fascist regime under the euphemism of Hindu *Rashtra*, is seductive enough in a Hindu majority country)

The BJP (this is the new incarnation of the Jana Sangh. Formed in the 1980s, it means Indian People's Party, or Bharatiya Janata Party), it is till now the mainstream political mouthpiece of the RSS.

Even though the actor for the RSS in the parliamentary political field, it is publicly posturing as independent, with its true colours only occasionally revealed. Thus, Vajpayee, the former prime minister, after showing a presentable secular face in Washington declared in a separate meeting of RSS workers of North America that his basic loyalties were toward the RSS and would remain so. As a matter of fact, distancing from the RSS is done as a strategic move and some pseudo fire-fighting is permitted by the Sangh bosses to retain the liberal image of people like Vajpayee in a perfect Machiavellian-Chanakyan (an ancient Indian political scientist) fashion.

On the third level a whole range or family of mass organizations is found with allegiance to the RSS, which include the Swadeshi Jagaran Manch, the BMS, the VHP, the Bajrang Dal, the ABVP, the Yuva Morcha, and several other locally floated organizations. These add up to no less than seventy.

The following diagram can give an idea of the power matrix in the *Sangh Parivar* based on a network of organizations, that

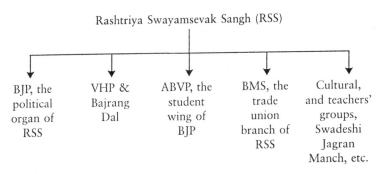

Rashtriya Swayamsevak Sangh (RSS)

| BJP, the political organ of RSS | VHP & Bajrang Dal | ABVP, the student wing of BJP | BMS, the trade union branch of RSS | Cultural, and teachers' groups, Swadeshi Jagran Manch, etc. |

have been floated under the direction of the RSS and which it continues to control by appointing its people to key positions in them.

The RSS has shown its brilliant side of running mass organizations and floating ever-new ones as needed as compared to the Left or middle-of the-road parties. It is rather ironical that the RSS has largely borrowed the idea of mass organizations from the Communist Left that had survived through these organizations at the time when the party was banned. But today the Left's mass organizations are in disarray. There is a need for rebuilding and for outreaching to different mass organizations which work on similar lines including even Gandhiite and progressive religious organizations that believe in a pluralistic society as opposed to unilinear majoritarian communal hegemony.

## 3. THE HYDRA-HEADED ORGANIZATION OF THE *SANGH PARIVAR*

Unlike other political organizations, which are democratic and open, the *Sangh Parivar* works in altogether different ways. The RSS appoints in affiliate organizations one organizing secretary who is the monitoring agent on behalf of the RSS and the main functionary of the organization in the final analysis. As a matter of fact, after Gandhi's assassination, it was realized that the RSS could not function any more in the political arena directly, and so the Jana Sangh was formed as the political wing.

This strategy of positioning an ideologically competent cadre in a mass organization is practised in communist organizations also. But the *Sangh Parivar* has excelled in the policy of influencing mass organization. The RSS constantly provides hardworking and politically well-briefed cadres to these outfits and keeps the controlling reins in its hand. It has further fine-tuned this system by launching feelers from time to time through one of its affiliates; if its feelers are not able to attract people's attention, then it may withdraw the move. As a matter of fact, the RSS has been able to install the most Machiavellian mass organizations. To the outside they pretend to be autonomous, and people believe in it, but in practice, the affiliates ultimately do what the RSS decides. The RSS's centripetal apparatus is able to keep control of the political process rather dexterously.

The second most important element in the *Sangh Parivar* machinery is connected to the three-tier political organization. The RSS lays the groundwork, cleans the swamps like advance scouts, and then invites the BJP to work in the area. At times, when the BJP as a political party faces decline, the RSS works as a cushion and its dedicated, industrious cadres are ready to carry on. In lean periods, additional RSS cadres are pumped into political organs like the Jana Sangh or BJP. The RSS is likened to an iceberg of which only one-tenth is visible, while the rest is under water. It has a large reservoir of low-key cadres who work in the political fields in the same way as minesweepers clear mine-infested areas for the arrival of the main column of the infantry. In this way, RSS cadres have been working for thirty years in tribal areas and their efforts have borne fruit. They have established primary schools particularly in north India. A network of about 50,000 such schools provides the RSS with the means of spreading its ideology in the villages and towns. There are many sections of the population, that are completely neglected by the mainstream educational drive: the RSS takes up work amongst them. A formidable organizational network in the Hindi heartland has been built up and now the RSS is moving to the southern states, right from Andhra Pradesh to Kerala, the old communist bastion.

The RSS can work successfully in the Left pocket borough state of Kerala, because it operates in an apolitical garb in such situations, so much so that people from different walks of life do not mind associating with it. Even Gandhi, who was assassinated by an extremist Hindu fundamentalist who was trained by the RSS, had some charitable words for the so-called constructive work of the RSS in its early phase.

The management of this organization, which keeps no record of membership, collects its resources once in a year through secret donations on the day of Goddess Durga's victory over the demon. It is a remarkably well-knit, large mass organization, which is expert in back-seat driving. Except for the communist parties whose influence is limited to the truncated state of West

Bengal, tiny Tripura, and a peripheral Kerala, the whole northern hinterland and now vast tracts of south India are no match for the RSS's arduous, hardworking, conspiratorial organization.

The hinterland politics dominated by sets of bourgeois or kulak-bourgeois parties depend either on caste mobilization or on strategic positioning on the communal, caste issues. They are not cadre-based parties, so the RSS has a walk-over in these areas. The quick development of BJP politics from the narrow confines of the urban petty bourgeoisie and stray feudal consti- tuencies in some rural enclaves into a mass party can be explained in terms of the RSS's silent work in different directions.

The Sangh Parivar with its different affiliates has developed a new communication strategy where it can speak differently through its different mass organizations and then gauge whether the real message that it wants to convey will be welcomed by the people or not. And then suddenly, one may find that all these differing faces start speaking in one voice. This is not *double-speak* so to say, but *multi-speak*. The *Sangh Parivar* with its strategy of mobilizing people has mastered the arts of deception, decoy, conspiracy, and rumour campaigns. Perhaps no other political party in the present world system, including the fascists of the past, can match it in this regard. Sometimes differences of opinion expressed in public are permitted to linger on as they may have some value in the future and maintain a level of confusion.

The Sangh Parivar roused the wielders of power as well as the mass media to a high pitch before the election of 2004. It was reminiscent of Goebbels', the way it sought to maim, buy and bulldoze the entire media, which a couple of months before the elections started predicting an overwhelming majority of seats for the BJP and its allies.[28] So did all opinion polls. The exit polls were no different. Everything was well managed. The BJP had succeeded in buying the national press and dominated the electronic media. It was an example of great deception and of how to turn lies into deceptive poll forecasting.

In the six years in government the BJP and the *Sangh Parivar* have managed to project former prime minister Atal Behari Vajpayee as a liberal among fundamentalist hawks. It was a typical image-building exercise, which has no basis in reality.

There is a perfect division of labour in the 'Sangh Parivar' and it is orchestrated with extreme dexterity. For instance, Vajpayee would play the liberal card and the VHP chief would play the hawkish card, but in the final reckoning both would converge at the point envisaged by RSS headquarters. Though there is a decline in the RSSs power to control the sprawling family, particularly the political organ, BJP, it has not yet lost its 'veto' nor is there any chance of doing it. Similarly during the Gujarat communal riots, Vajpayee played the 'liberal' by expressing his disapproval, though in a very moderate tone. He advised Chief Minister Modi to pursue 'The Raj Dharma', i.e. to run the government on constitutional lines and show a politically correct face. Modi did not pay heed to him. Neither the prime minister nor the BJP high command showed any inclination to stop the massacre of Muslims in Gujarat. There was a 180 degree turnaround when Vajpayee arrived at the BJP executive meeting in Goa to take stock of the Gujarat situation. Instead of criticizing Narendra Modi, the man responsible for the genocide, he launched a broadside against Muslims and gave a clean chit to the chief minister. So much for the so-called liberal image of Atal Behari Vajpayee.

Newspaper columnists and political analysts will take the stand which conforms with their own background and they have drawn a hypothetical, inflexible line between the hardliners and softliners. Caste affiliation also matters: the Brahmin penpushers particularly the Hindi language press, by and large, would be uncritical of Vajpayee. As to the English language press it would of course appreciate Vajpayee not for his caste tag but because he was the pro-globalization face in the Cabinet; after all this type of press is controlled by industrial and commercial houses who advocate globalization, privatization, and liberalization. An associate editor of a newspaper even argued that India did not gain by independence and should have remained in the ambit of the colonial market system. Similarly those who are in the communal camp would deliberately write columns and editorials explaining the helplessness of a liberal like Vajpayee in a hawkish party. As a matter of fact the liberal image of Vajpayee was a deliberate creation to help the *Sangh Parivar* to put together the coalition of non-BJP non-Parivar parties in order to come to power. Similarly the Parivar cultivates the hawkish image of some of its cadres to satisfy the appetite of communal Hindu opinion and voters. When in the 1990s the question of backward caste reservation was raised by the National Front Government led by Prime Minister V.P. Singh, 'The Organizer', an organ of the BJP, wrote that this was a move by secularists and the backward caste lobby to divide the Hindu community into upper and backward castes, that V.P. Singh threatened to achieve in one year what the British could not do in their 150 year long alien rule, namely to undo the great task of uniting Hindu society as it had been attempted from the days of Vivekananda, Dayananda Saraswati, Mahatma Gandhi and Dr. Hedgewar.[29]

In contrast to this editorial, the BJP as a political party could not condemn Singh's move as the backward castes constituted the bulk of the voting population. So the BJP leadership turned to its 'Hindu card' in order to subvert the move of bringing equality in Hindu society. Thus while its main publication kept the upper caste clientele of the BJP happy, the leadership, in order to not annoy the backward caste constituency, made a diversionary move.

When Vajpayee asked for the removal of Modi, the chief minister of Gujarat, blaming him for the party's 'rout' in the 2004 general elections, the newspapers carried the story, with the *Times of India* writing, 'Atal raised pitch to oust Modi'. BJP executive in Mumbai will decide fate of Gujarat Chief Minister'; The paper continued, the odds against the continuance of Modi lengthened considerably after the BJP patriarch publicly blamed the poll debacle on the party's failure to get rid of him in the aftermath of the communal conflagration.[30]

But on the same day the prominent Hindi daily *Hindustan* published a statement by the hawkish VHP leader, Praveen Togadia, which said that Atal was personally responsible for the defeat. The chief of RSS asked Vajpayee not to blame Modi for the defeat of the BJP. Venkaiah Naidu, the president of the BJP, followed the lead of the RSS boss and said that the Gujarat violence had not brought about the BJP's defeat. Pravin Togadia as well as the main figure in the Ramjanambhoomi (the birthplace of Ram) movement, Mahanta Nritya Gopal Dass, endorsed the

RSS boss's statement.[31] There was even a difference between Hindi newspapers and the English media. While the latter was out to promote Vajpayee as the lone liberal in the BJP, Hindi dailies gave inside news from RSS sources which were summarily dismissive of the *Times of India* story.

Ultimately, at the Mumbai meeting the 'Modi' issue did not come up at all; in fact, party President Naidu exhorted the BJP workers to get back to the politics of Hindutva. Advani said, 'ideological infidelity let us down'. Thus the whole issue of Modi's removal ended in a whimper. The media hype about conflict between the two lines, the hard line and the liberal line led by Vajpayee, had no connection with ground reality. The Mumbai conference did not even raise the Modi issue and, yet, Vajpayee was completely satisfied with the meeting where there was no dissenting voice whatsoever.

So the media's pet hypothesis about the hard line and the soft line gets exposed each time the moment of reckoning arrives. The final shot invariably, in spite of its declining dictating authority, belongs to the RSS, the pivotal organization of the *Sangh Parivar*. Yet this sort of road-show helps the BJP to prove to its home constituencies and abroad that its parliamentary leader is indeed a liberal. So in future, as and when opportunities arise, when some non-Sangh outfit wants to join the *Sangh Parivar*-led alliance, Atal can be safely trusted to speak their language and assure them of a veneer of political correctness.

As far as the alternative hegemony creating exercise is concerned, it started again in 2004 when a Congress government was formed with the Left as an outside critical supporter committed to the politics of unity and struggle as enunciated by Ajoy Ghosh in 1961. As a matter of fact for almost thirty-seven years, from 1967 to 2004, the Lohiaite strategy of building a 'non-Congress bloc' washed away the possibility of the formation of a progressive alternative government. By contrast, due to the uncritical attitude of the non-Congress political parties the 'politics of communalism and fascism' could acquire a space for itself. The Left has, by and large, positioned itself as a critical bystander. But since the Left's influence is limited to Bengal, Kerala, and the tiny state of Tripura, it has not been able to make much headway except since 1998 when a BJP government finally came to power at the centre.

The problem with the Left has been at times a spurt of Left sectarianism and at other times the inability to function outside its own safe bastion in India's vast hinterland where the forces of Hindu communalism dominate. The second weakness has been related to its inability to build a 'counter-hegemony' against the forces of communalism and fascism, a problem which is being corrected to a large extent since the BJP came to power in 1998.

## V. COMMUNALISM, MODERNIZATION AND THE LEFT

### 1. NATIONALISM AND MODERNIZERS

Nehru can rightly be called the architect of modern India: he was aware of the dangers of Hindu communalism. He was of the opinion that it had the potential of developing into a fascist polity, as it began to enjoy support of a majority. As a matter of fact, Nehru was the first Indian leader from among the ranks of progressive political parties, including those of the Left, who could clearly place 'communalism' as a basic source of fascism in India. Speaking at mass rallies in 1952, Nehru said that behind the façade of religion, vested interests, particularly the *zamindars* and the capitalists were fighting against the economic policies of the Congress. According to him, communalism was in fact 'the Indian version of fascism'. He was determined to avert the communalist threat to the country's unity. 'I will not allow India to be divided again. If there is trouble in any part of India, I will put it down with all my strength'. But as a pragmatic founding prime minister he had not yet seen the avalanche of the Hindu communal forces. The Congress party though a party of Indian nationalism, was a mixed bag, a united front of contemporary classes and interests.

Nehru was trying to experiment with the Indian version of Risorgimento and changes from above. The Nehruvian state was definitely a model in the world system of those days. The post-colonial state under the command of Nehru was quite fragile but could perform some strategic tasks of modern nation-building like introducing the Zamindari (Landlordism) Abolition Act of 1948. This was no mean achievement as it meant the dissolution of the artefact of a feudal system so assiduously woven by the British and their predecessors in the Mughal and Sultanate periods. It was a remarkably radical step; it changed the motion of the Indian polity, economy, and society from feudal-colonial to a non-feudal set-up. Of course, the semi-feudal vestiges of production relations and civil society still lingered on. The second step was planning, particularly when a strategy for indus-trialization was introduced. At the Avadi Congress (1955), Nehru charted the only possible path, the path of Indian social democracy. He declared the goal of the Congress party was to establish a 'socialistic pattern of society' through a number of instruments like enlargement of the public sector, development of small and cottage industries, land reform, establishment of co-operatives and finally to raise the public sector to commanding heights to overcome the vagaries of private capital. Thus intro-ducing a regulated mixed economy he tilted towards the poor and socialism. In fact, the resolution of the 60th Indian National Congress Session held in Avadi in 1955, proclaimed that 'Planning should take place with a view to the establishment of a socialist pattern of society where the principal means of production are under social ownership or control, production is progressively speeded up, where there is equitable distribution of the national wealth. Therefore the state will necessarily play a vital role in planning and development initially and operate large scale schemes providing services such as power, transport, etc., check and prevent evils of anarchic industrial development by the maintenance of strategic controls.'

Nehru's answer to the communal question, which he saw more as a stumbling block to the making of a modern mind and society, was the inculcation of a 'scientific temper'. Nehru believed that an increased pace of development would erase the problems and possibilities of communalism. But the riddle of communalism was not so unilinear; besides, post-independence communalism substantially developed against the backdrop of Partition. The irreconcilable differences between the Muslim League and the

Congress were a factor. The genesis of partition can be traced right from the Motilal Nehru Committee Report which came out with a rather unilinear formula of parliamentary democracy with adult franchise. This created for the Muslim League and other leaders the spectre of being reduced to a minority forever. This very unique problem could not be settled through straight-line formulas but needed innovative moves. It needed a person like Gandhi to mediate, someone who could combine the pre-modern compromises within modern institutions. The Motilal Nehru Committee along with Sir Tej Bahadur Sapru initially proposed the following formula which, if accepted, would have become a consensus point for Hindu-Muslim unity: 1. Immediate declaration of dominion status. 2. Joint electorates and 1/3rd reservation for Muslims in the National Assembly. 3. Muslim reservation in non-Muslim majority states according to per-centage of population. 4. Abolition of weightage system. 5. Adult franchise and direct elections. 6. Frontier, Baluch and Sind to be new states. 7. Secular state. 8. Centre to have residuary powers. 9. Declaration of fundamental rights. 10. Control and monitoring of native kingdoms.

Jawaharlal Nehru was opposed to the demand of dominion status and seat reservation for Muslims.

The Nehruvian path of modernization was an innovative strategy in the non-communist world system. It was somewhat akin to the 'non-capitalist path of progress' as enunciated by R.A. Ulyanovsky a major figure in modern Soviet-Indian studies.[32] Nehru himself was witness to the disintegration of his dreams in his lifetime, but his efforts at least merit an objective analysis.

## 2. THE RIDDLE OF COMMUNALISM AND MODERNIZATION

As a matter of fact, Nehru's strategy was definitely part of an Indian Risorgimento or change from above as enunciated by Antonio Gramsci, but it lacked the hegemony for realizing the goal.

When it comes to questions of hegemony, we can move a little further back. The Indian freedom struggle was a great exercise in 'hegemony formation' based on the idea of national independence. Perhaps the most perceptive and tallest leader of this whole process was Mahatma Gandhi who dominated the scene of the freedom struggle from the mid-1920s to 1948, though at the time of his assassination he had stopped wielding the moral influence, that he had commanded till 1944-5. Gandhi had built up a 'counter-hegemony'; his prescription was to build-up a state and society based on the precept of *Sarva Dharma Sambhava* (equality and equal treatment of all religious faiths by state and society). He was not a secularist in the Western sense; he was in fact an 'inclusivist'. As a matter of fact, an ancient agrarian country with such a long tradition could not be transformed immediately into a modern discerning society with a developed sense of scientific temper and secularism. In a pre-modern society, Gandhi had the knack of conceiving such political strategies, that would look quite antiquated yet were meant to lead towards 'incremental modernization'. In a vast agrarian country with very strong religious traditions, Gandhi's strategy of swaying the masses was perhaps more advanced than the slogan of instant secularization or the development of scientific temper. Scientific temper could develop in a section of the middle-class intelligentsia, which was, however, a microscopic minority. The working class of course goes through the trade union exercise hence some influence of secularism can be noted in its ranks, but an overwhelming section of the population remains outside. Thus Gandhi's idea of religious inclusivism, pluralism along with his critical treatment of untouchability, is an input of modernization in a pre-modern society.[33]

Gandhi attacked both the premises, which kept India under siege: the regime of differing and competing religions and the Hindu practice of untouchability. The nitty-gritty of social reform in an extremely conservative ancient society were taken up by him on a priority basis as he believed that freedom would be meaningless as long as the inhuman practices in Hindu society continued and Hindu-Muslim unity was not built-up. It is strange that even the Left held a hostile view about Gandhi's programme for fighting the worst possible exploitative system prevailing in the world. He insisted that the Left not ignore these questions. The noted socialist leader and ideologue, Acharya Narendra Dev, in preparation for the Congress Socialist Party's founding conference drew up a draft which he presented to Gandhi for his comments while soliciting his support for a socialist orientation of the Congress party. Gandhi read the draft and pointed out two glaring omissions: the removal of untouchability and communal unity. Though the founding father of the socialist movement had produced such a document a full three months after Gandhi had embarked on his anti-untouchability pro- gramme the young socialist horde was still blissfully unaware of the two most important roadblocks to a transition to any kind of modern system be it socialism or capitalism.[34] This also points to how doctrinaire and dogmatic were the Left leaders. The common theme of the Left's criticism was that Gandhi was diverting the anti-colonial struggle; some of the more dogmatic ones were parroting the sectarian suicidal opposition to Gandhi by the Comintern. The Left was of the opinion that these tasks would be settled by the Left with a magic wand once they came to power.

Gandhi's strategy was to build a modern civil society and create a cultural-political hegemony that assured the sustenance of a civilization, which included the nation and nation-state of India with a transformative-reformatory approach towards Indian society. The problem with the Left and the modernizers was that they presumed the existence of all the elements of a modern nation and accordingly entertained a mechanical notion of a Utopian leap. In this exercise Nehru was perhaps nearest to ground realities compared to others. The innovative use of the state was a landmark in the Nehruvian era. As a matter of fact the 'Nehruvian' foundation should have been the consensus point in modern India-building, but his formulations were attacked by the Left and the Right as well as the right in the Congress government and party.

The hegemony that was formed during the freedom struggle needed active but critical support, participation, and at times, opposition to elements of reaction. Instead, the ready-made protocol of opposition parliamentarianism attracted the Left. It was an easy option, but a suicidal one in the final analysis as the task at that time was to reconstruct the Indian nation dwelling on the minutest and sometimes very commonplace details rather than to work out a pompous parliamentary opposition. This seductive trap has been explained by Ajoy Ghosh, the last general secretary of the United CPI, very succinctly, though it was not understood in all its aspects, neither was it followed by his own party: 'Comrades may ask: what will be the relation of our party to the government? I am not in favour of the phrase 'Party of opposition' as defining this general character of our party because it is essentially a parliamentary concept. Ours will be a positive approach, a political battle on the basis of our alternative policies that strengthens our independence and our economy'.[35]

The post-colonial hegemony essentially relied on the politicization and mobilization of the masses. It was initiated by the Indian National Congress, Communists and others with Gandhi as prime mover. It came out against colonialism and in favour of an inclusive pluralistic state policy with regard to the multiplicity of religious groups, a deeper layer of democracy combining a modern parliamentary form with village grass-roots democracy (*Panchayat raj*). A second demand concerned a caring state for the poor together with the idea of near egalitarianism. They were strengthened by Nehru's visions of the post-colonial state, society and economy at the Avadi Congress. The *zamindari* abolition which preceded and the Industrial Policy of 1956 which followed symbolized the 'Indian path to the new social democracy which was not part of [the] cold war scenario'. This Gandhi-Nehru continuum is a very important element in the construction of the post-colonial people's hegemony aiming at a progressive caring state and society. Where does the Left stand in this scheme of things?

3. MOVE NOT TWO BUT MANY STEPS BACKWARDS

There was a lurking suspicion that the Left merely remained outside the ring, a bystander in the task of the Indian revolution. This has been loudly expressed by Ajoy Ghosh when he called his party's tag as a party of opposition being a cliché more relevant in the routine bourgeois tradition as practised in Western parliamentary chambers than in a decolonized nation trying to move out of the shell of feudalism and pre-modernism into independent nationhood. The Left did not sufficiently assess the historical message and depth of this statement by Ajoy Ghosh and remained a critical bystander at best. It is this accumulated history that has brought the contemporary situation to a crisis, where the Indian state and society stand thoroughly maimed and moth-eaten by the forces of majoritarian Hindu communalism. This is what history bestows upon the Marxist and non-Marxist Left to move not two but many steps backwards to address the very basic questions of communalism and a hierarchical caste system in order to rebuild the hegemony of civil society in a plural and democratized social space as the basis of the post-colonial construction. The hegemony formation for post-colonial society remained incomplete in the long struggle for freedom as the Left could not and did not participate in full force as a critical component in the modern nation-building exercise. Nor could modernizers of both hues, the Gandhian and the Nehruvian type carry the task forward as the essential hegemony was not constructed.

It must be noted, however, that the arena of the hegemony of the anti-colonial struggle, with Gandhi as a prime strategist and mover, got translated into a simple parliamentary majority once general elections started taking place from 1952 onwards. Thus the artefact of hegemony, which needed a new plural society, a new democratic conscience, a new and deeper concern for poverty eradication, underdevelopment, and egalitarianism, could not be installed. It resulted in the surreptitious entry of communal-fascist policies, which finally took to centre stage in 1999 when a *Sangh Parivar* government came to power at the centre.

The historic responsibility of reconstructing Indian nationalism now lies with the Left: if it is does not take it up and instead adopts an ostrich-like attitude history will not forgive it. The twin tasks before the Left is firstly to rebuild a new hegemony around an inclusive pluralist social policy with a long-term orientation towards an Indian variety of secularism in conjunction with a democratization of Hindu society replacing the hierarchical caste matrix with new social equality. There is secondly the need to build-up a new consensus for the revival of a self-reliant national economy moving towards the non-capitalist path of progress. This will be an alternative to the IMF-WB-MNC-dictated path of neoliberal economics which has been endorsed by both the BJP and its allies as well as the Congress party in its latest incarnation.

The election manifestos, editorials and resolutions of both the CPI and the CPM seem to reflect an awareness of the new responsibilities thrust on them. Thus the CPI Election Manifesto 2004 states:

The Party today is called upon to join forces with other left and secular forces to save our country from communal fascist offensives mounted by the BJP. This party's parent organization the RSS played no part in the freedom struggle. It is weaned on the philosophy of communal-fascism, whatever mask it wears. It came to power at the centre by rousing communal passions, and taking advantage of the sins of omission and commission of Congress rule, and the weakness of the Left.[36]

The CPI calls upon people to play their historic role by voting out the BJP and its allies, and electing left, secular and democratic candidates.

Increasing the representation of the CPI and Left parties is necessary as it is the Left that will be the driving force behind the secular coalition, and will ensure that the agreed common minimum programme is implemented in the interest of the country and our people.[37]

Similarly the Left is mobilizing people and putting up stiff resistance to the Congress party's preference for the beaten path of globalization, privatization and liberalization. In an editorial of *People's Democracy* of 12-18 July 2004 (organ of the Communist Party of India (Marxist), the major phalanx of the Marxist Left), the General Secretary Harkishan Singh Surjeet wrote that a retrograde economic policy can only benefit the BJP. 'The Left will try its best to ensure that no anti-people step is taken, as that would only go to benefit the communal BJP and its cohorts. But on this part, the Congress and the UPA too would do well to recollect that it was the retrograde economic policies that caused the defeat of the Rao government'[38] [a Congress government which had initiated the process of liberalization].

Even the third largest phalanx, which was considered a part of the ultra Maoist Left not so long ago, interpreted the verdict of 2004 with caution. 'This leaves the Left with a real challenge. The verdict of 2004 has given the Left ample scope to effectively intervene in national politics and the agenda for such an intervention has also been brought to the fore by the polls. If the Left can assert its independence and advance this agenda, the BJP can indeed be pushed back'.[39]

## NOTES

1. A series of articles on India written by Karl Marx in 1853 for the New York Daily Tribune became a pathfinder for many economic and general historians. Particularly essays like the Future Results of British Rule in India, written in London on Friday 22 July 1853 give a rare insight into history and the making of modern India. In this essay Marx says: 'The political unity of India, more consolidated, and extending further than it ever did under the Great Moguls', was the first condition of its regeneration. The unity imposed by the British sword, will now be strengthened and perpetuated by the electric telegraph. The free press, introduced for the first time into Asiatic society, and managed principally by the common offspring of Hindus and Europeans is a new and powerful agent of reconstruction. Similarly in 'The British Rule in India' (published in the New York Daily Tribune No. 3804 of 25 June 1853) he writes: 'All the civil wars, invasions, revolutions, conquests, famines strangely complex, rapid and destructive as the successive action in Hindustan may appear, did not go deeper than its surface. England has broken down the entire framework of Indian society without any symptoms of reconstitution yet appearing. This loss of his old world, with no gain of a new one, imparts a particular kind of melancholy to the present misery of the Hindu'.

2. History and Sociology of Communalism: Communalism is an ideology in which people belonging to a religious group treat the other as the non-malleable inflexible other. The common space like politics, economics, language and culture is also dichotomized. It treats 'the other' as a matter of complete exclusivity; it denies any possibility of inclusivism'.
   Historically communalism and distinct religious groups cohabiting with each other with their distinctness intact are two divergent historical artefacts in India. The peaceful co-existence, plural society integrating streams have been in existence in the vast subcontinent had learned to live in 'diversity'. The feudal structure had its own official religion but in spite of this association of state and religious clergy and institutions, it did not percolate the ideas of non-co-existence

and mutual hostility to the mass level. It was with the advent of British colonialism that communal identity was slowly built, and religious identity translated into mass community identity. Though it cannot necessarily be said that the colonial rulers deliberately pursued such a development, at a later period the policy of divide and rule did grip the colonial bureaucracy.

Therefore, communal politics as a mass politics of identity, resulting in the fragmentation first of the anti-colonial struggle, and later of subcontinental India, is rather a modern phenomenon.

3. Sociology of the Caste System: Caste is a category of power, status, entitlement, hierarchization within Hindu society. It was an ingenious means of the division of labour in a society moving from slavery to feudalism which was sustained through the concept of purity (pure and impure castes); it was also an instrument of the ruling section of society for maximizing surplus extraction in its favour. This is where it resembles the class system. The great leader and theoretician of the untouchable castes Dr Baba Saheb Ambedkar, considers caste as an enclosed class (*Baba Saheb Ambedkar, Writing & Speeches*, vol. I, Maharashtra Govt: Education Dept. 1989, p. 15).

Caste is a unilinear, closed hierarchical system, which forbids any kind of mobility in status, social mobility or even physical mobility. It became more and more rigid in the mid-Gupta period between the third to the sixth century BC.

Caste becomes the *sine qua non* of the Brahminic four-ladder system where four hierarchical categories are introduced: the Brahmins at the top, who were the priests, teachers as well as law-givers; Kshatriyas come second, who were entrusted with the maintenance and defence of statecraft and polity; Vaishyas, who were divided into a trading community and independent farmers followed next; and Shudras who were bound to serve the three categories above them in a sort of semi-slavery and social discrimination. Outside the above categories and literally treated as slaves were the untouchables who formed the bottom. That is how the Brahmanic system structured Hindu society, and how with some alteration it still continues. In practice it is like apartheid, particularly for the Shudras and the fifth category of untouchables. Based on discrimination great battles were fought in India's past religious history in an attempt to dismantle this semi–apartheid system. Jainism and Buddhism were great revolts against the caste system; similarly, in medieval India the Bhakti movement was also basically a revolt against the caste system and an alternative to the four-varna archaic scheme and the priesthood.

4. The subaltern had a parallel role. The line leadership of the national struggle has been given disproportionate attention and the subalterns have been ignored. Subalterns had different goals, they had their

autonomy and a separate *modus operandi* of movement. This is what Ranajit Guha concludes in his 5-volume subaltern's studies. Amalesh Tripathi, however, says that subaltern historians read too much into the autonomous role of the subaltern movement (Amalesh Tripathi, *Bharate Sangram Bharater Jatiya Congress (1885-1947)*, Ananda Publisher Private Limited, Calcutta, p. 22).

5. Peter van der Veer, *Religious Nationalism: Hindus and Muslims in India*, New Delhi: Oxford University Press, 2000, p. 25.
6. Sumit Sarkar, *Modern India (1885-1947)*, Macmillan India Ltd., 1984, p. 65.
7. Biman Biharⁱ Mazumdar, *Indian Political Association and Reform of Legislature (1818-1917)* Firma K.L. Mukhopadhyaya, Calcutta, 1965, p. 21.
8. Sumit Sarkar, *Modern India*, p. 65.
9. Majumdar, *Indian Political Association*, p. 241.
10. Ibid., p. 242.
11. Ibid., p. 220.
12. Ibid., p. 219.
13. Vasudha Dalmia, *The Nationalization of Hindu Traditions, Bhartendu Harishchandra and Nineteenth Century Banaras*, New Delhi: Oxford University Press, 2001, p. 149.
14. India is a multilingual country, but then vast tracts of north India speak Hindi and its dialects. This constitutes around 42 per cent of the population, i.e. about 420 million people speak Hindi. The other major languages are Marathi, Tamil, Bengali, Assamese, Oriya, Telugu, Kannada, Malayalam, etc.
15. Joya Chatterjee, *Bengal Divided: Hindu Communalism and Partition 1932–1947*, Cambridge University Press, 1996, pp. 75, 67.
16. Christophe Jaffrelot, *The Hindu Nationalist Movement and Indian Politics: 1925 to the 1990s*, Viking, 1996, p. 55.
17. Ibid., p. 55.
18. Ibid., p. 56.
19. E.M.S. Namboodiripad, *Reminiscences of an Indian Communist*, Delhi, 1987, p. 98.
20. Ibid.
21. Ajoy Kumar Ghosh; Articles and Speeches, Peoples Publishing House for Oriental Literature, Moscow, 1962, p. 242. 'Does it follow that a general united front with the Congress is possible today, that is, with the Congress as it is? No, our relations will inevitably be one of unity and struggle. The Congress is the organ of the national bourgeoisie as a whole including its right wing.'

This was in juxtaposition to Lohia's position, who wanted a parliamentary counting of all opposition heads right from Marxists to Fascists combined to dislodge Congress from power. Thus Lohia's proposition was a naked power capture exercise sans programme and ideology. It naturally paved the path for an indigenous brand of fascism to gain ground.

22. Jaffrelot, *The Hindu Nationalist Movement*, p. 181.

23. Ibid., p. 33.

24. In his last speech, made in 1940, he described the RSS as the Hindu Rashtra in miniature, ibid., p. 44.

25. The essence of people lies in civilization (Kultur). Besides this statement, Bluntschli differentiates the German view of the nation in the following sentence 'In Europe the word people implies nation of civilization, etymology is in favour of the German usage, for the word "natio" (from nasci) points to birth and race.' Ibid., p. 53.

26. Walter K. Anderson and Shidhar D. Dawle, *The Brotherhood in Saffron*, New Delhi: Vistaar Publication, p. 55.

27. Jaffrelot, *The Hindu Nationalist Movement*, p. 115.

28. *India Today*, 9 February 2004, p. 27.

29. Jaffrelot, *The Hindu Nationalist Movement*, p. 415.

30. *Times of India*, 14 June 2004.

31. *Hindustan*, 14 June 2004.

32. R.A. Ulyanovsky, *Socialism and Liberated Countries*, Moscow 1972.

33. Untouchability is a practice of extreme discrimination by the upper castes in Hindu society towards a population called Harijans (by Gandhi) and Dalits (oppressed) in the contemporary lexicon of post-colonial India. They were supposed to be untouchable, i.e. no upper caste Hindu would touch them, sit with them, eat with them or marry them. In the southern state of Tamil Nadu or erstwhile Madras Province, untouchables had to walk with a broom attached to their neck in order to clean the pavement as they passed by so that the upper caste men and women would not have to tread in their dirt. The Dalits had to move off the street to make way for upper caste men or women.

34. Baren Ray, Gandhiji's Campaign Against Untouchability (1932, 34) *Mainstream* of 1 October 1994.

35. Ghosh, Reminiscences, p. 248.

36. Communist Party of India, Election Manifesto 2004, New Delhi, p. 1.

37. Ibid., p. 5.

38. People's Democracy—Weekly organ of the Communist Party of India Marxist, 12-18 July 2004, p. 14.

39. *Liberation*—central organ of the CPI (ML) – vol. 2, June 2004, p. 3.

# CHAPTER 13

# 'Training of a Nation':
# The Gandhian Vision and Indian Politics

*Hiroichi Yamaguchi*

## INTRODUCTION

When M.K. Gandhi was preparing for the Quit India movement, the last and greatest struggle he was going to lead, he talked of the twenty-two years of 'the training of a nation by him for the development of non-violent strength'.[1] This was on 18 June 1942. 'Twenty-two years' apparently means from 1920, the year of his first mass movement, to 1942. In this chapter, it is intended to help determine how the 'training of a nation' has been continued after his demise.

In his time, the aim of 'the development of non-violent strength' was primarily the attainment of independence. But afterwards the aim should be restated as the solution of the wide disparities existing in the country and the upliftment of the underprivileged, as will be clear in this chapter. We will first, by way of an introduction, look at Gandhi's place in modern Indian and the broader Asian history, and move on to discuss Vinoba Bhave as successor to Gandhi's 'training of a nation' effort. We will then identify the salient features of the 14th Lok Sabha Elections held in April and May 2004, first from the point of view of socio-economic disparities, and then of communal and caste tensions. This is necessary to highlight the crucial importance of the employment problem in India today, which will bring us to the examination of the National Employment Guarantee Scheme as a possible means of extending this training to our time.

## I. INDEPENDENT INDIA AND GANDHI

Both inside India and outside, the usual question mark over Gandhi is how much longer will his name be remembered. There are many who say that he will be forgotton because his ideas are out of date. As recently as July 2004, one of the foremost Indian sociologists, Dipankar Gupta, is reported to have told an American newspaper that Gandhi's idea was 'a backward Utopia', and 'Gandhi believed that Indians could have lived without the desire for progress'.[2] Earlier in the year, the Indian National Congress, the very party Gandhi helped become a mass-based party, refused an application by one of his great-grandsons to stand from Porbandar, Gandhi's birthplace, while selecting the candidates for the 14th General Elections. From Porbandar itself voices were heard that in today's world, which recognizes only power, his ideas are useless.[3] As a matter of fact the Congress was defeated in Porbander at the hands of the Bharatiya Janata Party (BJP).

As to the question of Gandhi's ideas being outmoded, this author has a different view. First, we will look at him in the context of India's internal politics.

### 1. GANDHI AND INTERNAL POLITICS IN INDEPENDENT INDIA

During the half century of independent India, two great political upheavals have taken place. The first was the Jayaprakash Narayan (JP) movement started in 1974, the declaration of an Emergency by the then Prime Minister Indira Gandhi in 1975, and the first electoral defeat of the Congress in the 1977 General Elections. These happened at the halfway point of the post-independence half century. The second was the defeat of the National Democratic Alliance (NDA) government centred around the BJP, and the coming into being of the government of the United Progressive Alliance (UPA) led by the Congress, as the consequence of the 14th Lok Sabha Elections.

Have these two events, or series of events, got something to do with the name of Gandhi? It was apparently so on the first occasion. JP and his wife, or his father-in-law to begin with, were known to be close to Gandhi. (There is an important question of whether JP was a Gandhian. But let us put it aside here.) JP, in spite of his ill health, tried hard to end the Emergency and revive democracy. Besides, such leaders as Acharya Kripalani and Morarji Desai, also close to Gandhi, played an important part in the defeat of the Congress.

What about the second occasion? As has been suggested in the foregoing the Congress did not fight the elections under Gandhi's banner. Look at the Common Minimum Programme (CMP) published by the new government on 27 May 2004, however. It has as its 'six basic principles of governance': (1) social harmony, (2) 7-8 per cent growth in a manner to create employment, (3) attention to farmers, farm labour, workers, especially in the unorganized sectors, (4) empowerment of women, (5) equal opportunities for Scheduled Castes, Scheduled Tribes, and Other Backward Classes particularly in education and employment, and (6) releasing the creative energies of the people. Thus the CMP is broadly oriented towards the underprivileged, and as such reminds us of the name of Gandhi, even if it is not mentioned. But there is no attempt to arouse awareness of these problems among the common people, whether under Gandhi's name or otherwise. We will come back to the CMP later, particularly to the crucial part concerning the employment policy.

Thus Gandhi's name was recalled, one way or another, on both occasions of the two great political changes in independent India. In this sense it is not likely that his name will be easily forgotton. Also in this writer's view it is not correct to say that Gandhi denied progress. He clearly recognized that India was poor, but he did not accept poverty at all. On the contrary, he tried to improve conditions by advising people to raise their standard of living, even in his ashram itself. Second, it would also be possible to discuss Gandhi in the context of the wider Asian history.

## 2. GANDHI AND POST-COLONIAL ASIAN HISTORY

It is possible to mark several epochs in the modern history of Asia after the Second World War to the present time. The first was the period of decolonization, or of achieving independence. It extends roughly to the mid-1950s, characterized by the armistice in the Korean War, the Geneva Conference ending the first Indo-Chinese (against the French) war, and the Afro-Asian Conference at Bandung. Gandhi's contribution towards the independence of India, and through it towards the freedom of other Asian or African countries, cannot be in doubt.

The second period was that of the Cold War, which continued till the end of the 1980s. Gandhi of course was not alive during this period. His ideas of peace and non-violence, however, were disseminated extensively mainly through the foreign policy of Jawaharlal Nehru. This was exactly what Gandhi had expected of Nehru as his political heir. It is to be remembered that India at that time had a relatively small military, until she got into trouble with China in 1962. Nehru's achievement was possible in spite of, or rather because of, India not being strong militarily.

The third and the present period after the Cold War is one where the easing of tensions and alleviation of poverty have surfaced as the major tasks before humanity. To say so goes counter to the perception that the international community shｕ ｌd come together to cope with international terrorism, which might attack anywhere anytime. The said perception leads to, and is the product of, a vicious circle where a unilateral and pre-emptive attack would create a hostile atmosphere, and even provoke a counter-attack. It is the task of the international community to aim at democratization, de-militarization, and poverty alleviation so that terrorism would have no ground to stand on. Gandhi's thoughts still have a lot to offer both for the achievement of peace and for solving poverty.

If seen in this manner, it would not be an exaggeration to say that Gandhi is an example whose ideas have withstood the test of time through the different phases of modern Asian history. It would be difficult to find similar leaders in other Asian countries. One such could possibly be Ho Chi-Minh. At first sight he seems to be at the opposite of Gandhi as he resorted to violence in many phases of his life. Probably it would be possible to say that he was forced to do so. But this is not the place to discuss Ho. Our task here would be to pick up Gandhi's work and see if it has been continued in independent India.

## II. VINOBA BHAVE AS SUCCESSOR TO
## GANDHI AND HIS WORK

### 1. GANDHI AND VINOBA

Let us come back to Gandhi's 'training of a nation'. Gandhi himself took every care to see that his thoughts in this regard would be implemented. His 'retirement' from active politics in the latter half of the 1920s, and again in the latter half of the 1930s, was to him necessary to propagate his ideas and bring up the cadre of people.

He was not satisfied with the results of his training himself. Again, shortly before the Quit India movement he said in effect that the training was still not enough, and he could not expect the masses to completely adhere to 'ahimsa in thought, word and deed' in this coming struggle as in the previous ones, and he would be content with their ahimsa 'in word and deed' alone.[4] Still, by that time he had a sufficient number of cadres to depend upon, to whom he was regularly issuing directions through the *Harijan*, a weekly in several different languages, and through meetings held mainly at Sevagram. He wrote many letters and gave a number of interviews to both Indian and foreign journalists. This was remarkable since a large part of the media was in the hands of the British and he was not in a position to call an official press conference. On this basis he was able to appeal to the British, American, Chinese and Japanese people. The 'training of a nation' was thus a very complex and many-sided process. Since the coming struggle would be on a scale much larger than before, it provided a better occasion for Gandhi to do the necessary training.

It would now be in order to ask how this training has been done after the death of Gandhi. Who has taken over his work? If, as we have just seen, the second political upheaval in independent India was not such an occasion, at least not yet, how was the first one, the JP movement?

It is difficult to say that it was a vehicle of such a nationwide attempt. It may have been at the heart of the initiator of the movement at the beginning. But very soon the movement was snatched away by the communal forces, except in JP's home state of Bihar.[5] It may have been turned into their own training ground.

Thus we may say that neither of the two great political changes became an occasion for the training of a nation in the Gandhian sense.

Who then was in charge of it after Gandhi's death? The one person most people would point to is Vinoba Bhave (1895-1982). Let us turn our attention to the relevant part of his life and work. Vinoba belonged to the next generation after Gandhi as he was born twenty-six years later, and survived him by thirty-five years. Unlike Gandhi, Vinoba never played a part in active politics. But he was with Gandhi for a very long time, even longer than almost any of the Congress Old Guard brought up by Gandhi for political activities, as he joined him in 1916 at his very first ashram in India, the Kocharab Ashram in Ahmedabad. It was still very early in Vinoba's life, and presumably because of this he said Gujarat was his second birthplace although Maharashtra was his home state.

Vinoba came to Wardha and settled there in 1921, more than ten years before Gandhi. He began to live in a Dalit settlement in 1932, before Gandhi's arrival in Sevagram. He moved to his own ashram at a nearby place called Paunar in 1938 and built Brahma Vidya Mandir there in 1959, where he lived till the end of his life. The Mandir is still very active, with the 'Vinoba Niwas' preserved there. Vinoba became known nationwide as he was the first Satyagrahi nominated by Gandhi in his Individual Satyagraha in 1940, prior to the Quit India. It was from his ashram at Paunar that Vinoba started his satyagraha.

When Gandhian constructive workers met at Sevagram in March 1948, shortly after Gandhi's death, to chalk out an immediate programme, Vinoba was unanimously nominated as their representative. Gandhi had long before nominated Jawaharlal Nehru as his heir, but it was as an heir in the political field, as one who would represent an independent India politically, as its prime minister. For those areas of action that were dear to his heart, he had not done likewise. But Vinoba at that time was the only person who could co-ordinate those areas.

It seems it was at this time that the workers also decided to have two organizations among themselves. One would be the

Sarvo-Sewak Sangh, organized by those workers occupying key positions in the constructive work. It would have a membership system, and the members would be called Lok Sewaks. The other would be a somewhat looser organization, open to anyone, and would be called the Sarvodaya Samaj. The workers, by and large, would keep themselves aloof from politics. This was in accordance with Gandhi's advice that 'constructive workers should not take part in politics. If they take interest in both, they will be able to do justice to neither'.[6] Rajindar Sachar writes, however, that in the recent elections the defeat of the NDA was also brought about 'by the Sarvodites/Gandhiites and other NGOs', who usually kept away from politics but worked hard for the purpose of 'Defeat BJP' this time.[7]

## 2. VINOBA'S WRITINGS AND HIS BHOODAN MOVEMENT

We will now look at the written works of Vinoba. They are available in the recently completed twenty-one-volume *Vinoba Sahitya*.[8] Roughly, the first half are works on philosophy, and here is probably one important difference between Gandhi, who wrote hardly any important philosophical work except a book on the Gita, and Vinoba. Vinoba was a devoted follower of Gandhi, but this went as far as he was convinced of Gandhi's worth, and it would be safe to call him a thinker who was relatively independent of Gandhi.

As against this, the volumes in the second half are on a wide variety of subjects. According to the editor, Gautam Bajaj, not all of Vinoba's writings are included, as in the case of Gandhi. In fact, only about a quarter of them are there. Vinoba himself was not enthusiastic about preserving his writings and destroyed a lot of it himself. He testified to this lack of interest in his letter to Pyarelal in 1959, contained in volume 13.

There is a short essay titled 'Gandhiji' in volume 20, in which Vinoba says, in effect, that Gandhi is a successor to Buddha, Mahavir and Shankar. This is interesting, as Vinoba thus seemed to think that Gandhi stood in the orthodox stream of India's intellectual history. There are researchers on Gandhi who do not seem to agree. A political theorist, Ronald J. Terchek, for example, quotes from Bhikhu Parekh's work that Gandhi 'remained a marginal man all his life'.[9] He also says in the concluding chapter of his book that 'Gandhi's walk into the twenty-first century, then, may be a lonely one'.[10] These quotations do not necessarily refer to Gandhi in the Indian context alone, particularly not the latter one. Still, Vinoba's view on Gandhi's place could be understood to be contrary to them. It is as if the philosopher in Vinoba lends authority to Gandhi's place in history.

Let us be more specific and look at what is there in the *Vinoba Sahitya* on his Bhoodan (land donation) movement, not only because this is an area of activity where Vinoba's reputation as Gandhi's successor has been established, but also it is of particular interest from the point of 'the training of a nation'.

There are in the *Vinoba Sahitya* seventy-three letters, written from 1951 to 1966, and also several articles concerned with the Movement, and a chronology of the *padyatra*. It is the last-mentioned that particularly invites our attention (in volume 20). It records the places he visited, and the distance in mileage that he walked everyday since he started the *yatra* on 8 March 1951. The chronology shows that, except for the period from October 1959 to November 1960, when he was not in good health, Vinoba constantly kept walking, obviously talking to people and inviting them to donate their land, covering almost the entire country from March 1951 to the end of 1967. There are still many at his ashram at Paunar, or elsewhere at Wardha, who walked at least some parts of the yatra with him. This writer has learnt from them, for example, that he walked very fast, as Gandhi himself did. There seems to have been a core of Vinoba's disciples consisting of five to seven people always by his side.

He did not wind up his yatra altogether in 1967, and went on the 'motor-yatra' in 1968 and 1969. But its record is not in the chronology, presumably because the editor judged that it was somewhat different in nature. One may say, therefore, that he was in his mid-fifties at the beginning of his *yatra* and in his early seventies at its end. He returned to his ashram in 1970 to resume his own work. It is possible to say that Vinoba retired then, if you look at his life from the point of view of the life of Gandhi, who had never thought of retiring from his practical work. One may say that he could do so because unlike Gandhi he was a scholar. But he walked for nearly seventeen years, or sixteen if you exclude the time of his illness. This was something unprecedented, even Gandhi had never done it. We may say that this was the greatest attempt at 'the training of a nation' after the death of Gandhi till today.

### 3. GHAFFAR KHAN AND VINOBA

Before considering the meaning of Vinoba's *padyatra*, let us digress a little here, and look at some aspects of the life of another Gandhian, who was older than Vinoba by some five years but survived him by several years. This will help us to understand the role of Vinoba at the time of his *yatra*. He is Abdul Ghaffar Khan, the 'Frontier Gandhi'. The following passages are based on a recent biographical study of him by Rajmohan Gandhi.[11]

He became so dear to Gandhi that the latter said he was the only one among the Congress leaders, besides Gandhi himself, who had accepted non-violence as a creed.[12] But his hope at the time of Partition of having a third alternative of getting the Pakhtuns, or the North West Frontier Province (NWFP) in which the Pakhtuns were in the majority, independent, or at least self-governing in Pakistan, was dashed by all the three parties concerned in the decision-making process, the British, the Congress, and the Muslim League. Even though he and his followers pledged loyalty to Pakistan, they were maltreated by the government for a very long time. Ghaffar Khan was put behind prison bars for as long as fifteen out of seventeen years since Partition, to 1964 when he was allowed to leave Pakistan for treatment of illness.

His life changed dramatically when he arrived in Afghanistan in 1964, ignoring the ban imposed by the Pakistan government. From then on, based in that country until his death in 1988, he resumed contact with his old friends in India, Vinoba included. He also visited India several times, starting with his visit on the occasion of Gandhi's birth centenary in 1969.

Vinoba wrote to him in 1965, presumably during his *padyatra*, saying that 'in our freedom fight a great injustice had been done to you and you have been practically let down by your friends'.

Ghaffar Khan replied that 'I was deeply touched by your affectionate letter . . . to a person who is fighting a losing battle not only with his adversaries but with his own rank and file who have become so desperately disgusted with the tyrannical government of Pakistan. They are losing confidence in the creed of non-violence. . . . Their argument is that with the Britishers non-violence could have its efficacy, but not with Pakistanis. . . . My comrades in India who are now in government cannot realize my difficulties. . . . I am now a man of a different world to them . . . I do not know what their conscience says.'[13]

From this alone we might conclude that the Partition was a great human tragedy, also a great mistake, engineered mainly by the British and the elite Muslim Leaguers. One is reminded of Gandhi here, who repeatedly demanded that the British should quit first and leave the decision concerning the division of India to the Indians. More relevant for the purpose here is that in Ghaffar Khan's view, 'In India Gandhism is dead. Gandhi is completely forgotten'.[14] In fact, when he was visiting India in 1969, communal riots broke out in many cities in India, including Gandhi's own, Ahmedabad, and the shocked Ghaffar Khan fasted for three days in Delhi praying for peace.

The above view on the condition of Gandhism in independent India, given by such a seasoned politician and satyagrahi as Ghaffar Khan, may well have been a testimony to the fact that Vinoba's *padyatra* was very much a solitary effort, aimed at social reform in a non-violent manner.

### 4. VINOBA'S *PADYATRA* AND GANDHI'S CONCEPT OF TRUSTEESHIP

Let us return to the *padyatra* and consider what it has meant to the Indian society. The first Bhoodan was made on 18 April 1951, after forty days from the beginning of the movement. It is interesting that this was made in the present-day Andhra Pradesh where an armed struggle known as the Telengana movement was taking place. It is not clear to this writer how much Vinoba viewed his move as a land reform measure to counter a move for more drastic socio-economic revolution. It is not clear either how much land was donated altogether, how much of it was cultivable, and how much was actually distributed to marginal or landless peasants. It seems most of the land donated was in Bihar, and the Movement did not produce the desired effect elsewhere.

Does it mean that Vinoba's seventeen-year-long effort was largely wasted? Not necessarily. It may be presumed that for Vinoba the yatra was in itself the continuation of Gandhi's 'training of a nation'. It also shows how enormously difficult it is to attempt a land redistribution without a serious backing by the government. Even Gandhi did not try to do it. Gandhi mostly contented himself with pleading with landlords, capitalists, and princes to be trustees of their properties and power. He said the concept of trusteeship would be a gift by India to the world. He went on to say that he was an enemy of none of these three; he wanted to make friends of all of them, they would then change their minds and would serve the people, and in a new India everybody would find his place.

However, even in Gandhi's view the idea was slow in taking root among these three categories of people. Asked on the day before his assassination if he knew any example of a capitalist who had reached his ideal of trusteeship, he replied that some were 'striving' in that direction.[15] Similarly, he had said several years before that only Jamnalal Bajaj 'came near' his idea of a trustee among the businessmen of India.[16]

A rare moment in Gandhi's life came when he was staying in Noakhali, in the then eastern part of Bengal, to work for communal peace, from early November 1946 to early March 1947. Not far from where he was staying the Tebhaga movement was going on, demanding a reduction in the intake of the landlords from the tenants from one-half to one-third of the harvest. Gandhi gave the peasants his blessings as requested, saying that 'all good movements' had it.[17] This was rare because Gandhi usually kept aloof from such movements for re-distribution of property or produce. In his view agricultural produce should belong to the cultivators, and it is wrong to privately own land. He, however, also said that this should not be achieved through 'the use of compulsion or violence',[18] and if land was to be appropriated from landlords, it should be done on the basis of compensation.[19]

It may be assumed that Vinoba saw the ongoing armed struggle in Telengana, and sensing the possibilities of impending uprisings elsewhere, decided that the solution of the land question was of paramount importance in independent India. This led him to make an attempt to put the Gandhian concept of trusteeship into practice as a counter-measure. Also, he stuck to the Gandhian principle of not resorting to 'the use of compulsion and violence'. He finally failed. His failure was a failure of the ideal of trusteeship.

Does this mean that Gandhi was satisfied with simply formulating the idea of trusteeship, though he had hardly survived the independence of the country? It would be less than fair to him to say so. There are signs that he would move one step forward to face the sharp disparities existing in the country once India achieved freedom, even though he would be constrained by the above principles enunciated by himself. Shortly before independence, for example, he said that once independence was achieved, India would have to take on the question of 'providing everyone at least with a square meal, enough clothing to cover himself and a house to live in'.[20] On 18 July 1947, almost on the eve of independence, he again said that the time had come to face the task of 'feeding and clothing the ill-fed and ill-clad millions'.[21]

On a slightly different plane, Gandhi drafted a new Congress Constitution for an independent India, and completed it on the last day of his life. It said, as is well known, that the Congress would be transformed into a Lok Sewak Sangh, an organization to serve the people, especially in the rural areas. If he were alive today he would have defended his draft to the utmost of his ability. Behind this draft was his formula for village self-government. The village would be 'a complete republic', self-supporting in foodstuff and cotton, equipped with recreational facilities and playgrounds, where clean drinking water would be provided, compulsory education would be assured, there would be no castes, security would be maintained by the villagers themselves by rotation, and a panchayat would be elected every year which would have legislative, judiciary and executive powers.[22] Certainly a lot of backward-looking Utopianism here!

In reality, however, towards the end of his life Gandhi was preoccupied with the communal riots taking place everywhere and had hardly any time left for his own programmes outlined above. This is where Vinoba came in, although there was an interval of three years after Gandhi's death. Vinoba moved Gandhi's attempt forward, and came up against the most difficult task while sticking to the principle of non-violence. It is little wonder, then, that by and large it got stuck, and failed to bring about an upheaval. The Mandal Report was a testimony to the glaring disparities that still existed as of December 1980, when Vinoba was still alive. After recommending reservations for the Other Backward Classes (OBC), it said that without a drastic land reform there would be no real solution of those disparities. Many parts of the report have been respected, but not this part, and the matter has remained at that to this day.

Within a few years of Vinoba returning to his ashram, the JP movement got underway. Vinoba was against the Gandhian workers taking part in it, although it is true that JP helped Vinoba in the earlier phases of the Bhoodan. It was presumably because he wanted to be true to the advice of Gandhi, as mentioned earlier. When Vinoba passed away in late 1982, there was nobody capable of coordinating the constructive work this time. Conscious of this or not, he is reported to have said that it was the birds flying in the sky that would succeed him.[23]

Would it then be justified to conclude that 'the training of a nation', started by Gandhi in 1920 and taken up by Vinoba after his death, came to an end when Vinoba terminated his *padyatra*? Before answering this question let us go through the results of the recent Lok Sabha elections.

### III. THE GREAT POLITICAL UPHEAVAL OF 2004— A NEW LEASE OF LIFE FOR GANDHI'S VISION?

#### 1. THE DEFEAT OF 'INDIA SHINING' IN THE ELECTION OF 2004

The NDA government advanced the date of the elections by about six months, for the reason that the growth rate had gone up, as there was a good monsoon in many parts of the country after some years of drought, and that in three out of four states where state Assembly elections had been held earlier, the NDA had recorded a landslide victory. Their calculation went wrong, and A.B. Vajpayee tendered his resignation as prime minister the day the results came in. After some negotiations, the president nominated Manmohan Singh as prime minister, and the Cabinet was sworn in on 22 May 2004.

The difference in the number of seats between the Congress, the main government party, and the BJP, the main opposition party, was only a single digit, but the gap between the UPA and the NDA amounted to more than fifty, and the former was assured of the support of the four Left parties.

Did the Congress win the elections? Yes, as a whole, but not equally across the country. In many populous states starting from Madhya Pradesh, Karnataka and Rajasthan, it was the BJP which won by a large majority. The Congress lost in many states, particularly in Karnataka where it lost to the BJP, and in Kerala, where it had fielded seventeen candidates, all of whom were defeated at the hands of the Left, for the first time in Kerala's electoral history. If seen somewhat differently, the Congress increased its seats by only twenty-nine, which was more than matched by the increase of thirty-three registered by its UPA allies. It was the RJD-Rashtriya Janata Dal (National People's Party) and its allies in Bihar which registered the greatest increase of eighteen seats. Similarly the BJP's loss of thirty-eight was more than matched by the loss of the forty-nine recorded by its NDA allies.

Where then did the Congress increase its seats? By far the largest increase was in Andhra Pradesh, where formerly seven seats had been held by the BJP, twenty-nine by the Telugu Desam Party (TDP), a regional party allied to it, and only five by the Congress. But this time the BJP was reduced to zero, the TDP to five, but the Congress swelled to twenty-nine, its new local ally, the TRS getting five. In the Assembly elections held simultaneously in that state also, the TDP met a crushing defeat and its chief minister resigned instantly. He had become famous by holding TV conferences with his district officers, and by making the state capital a great cyber city. But it would be relevant to attribute his defeat to the conditions in the countryside where there had been a poor harvest due to the failure of rains and the falling water table, and to a large number of peasants, reported to be more than 3,000 in the past seven years, who had committed suicide because of their inability to repay the heavy loans they had taken from moneylenders.

The poor-rich disparity is often connected with social hierarchy. In Nellore District in the state of Andhra Pradesh, it was reported that the Dalits, who comprise 25 per cent of the population, are still not allowed access to the same wells as other villagers, or wear sandals or ride bicycles in other castes' residential areas, or drink tea from the same steel tumbler at the teashop. Their children are not allowed to sit in school in the same classroom with other caste children or play cricket with them. Local politics is in the hands of dominant castes like the Naidus, Reddys, Kammas, and Kapus, who are affiliated with in the BJP or TDP. Dalits have to put up with all this because they are daily labourers to other castes. The same situation prevails in the whole of the Rayalseema districts including Nellore. And Nellore happens to be the former birthplace of the former BJP president, who was telling the country that 'India was Shining', which became the party's, electoral slogan.

But in the Nellore Lok Sabha constituency (SC), the BJP was defeated by the Congress, showing that the Dalits or perhaps the people at large were in a mood to revolt. The suicides of the peasants continued in the state even after the election results were in. The common factor was debt. An agro-economist C.H. Hanumantha Rao, himself from Andhra, said that most of these peasants were small or marginal farmers and tenants who had no one but moneylenders to borrow from, at exorbitant interest rates because they were not in a position to take loans from banks or cooperatives. The way to save them would be to strengthen rural infrastructure by public investment in the long run, and to expand institutional credit in the short.[24]

After discussing the suicides in Andhra Pradesh at some length, P. Sainath concludes that 'Almost every sector of Indian democracy failed the AP farmer; the government and the political class; the tame intellectuals and planners. The human rights groups and a once-activist judiciary. And the media . . .'.[25]

Similar stories were also reported from other states. The same

Sainath writes that 'distress migrations' have increased since the early 1990s, and 'exploded since the late 1990s, with the collapse of rural employment . . . '.[26] It was reported in a news magazine that the number of people below the poverty line (BPL) is allotted to each state by the Central government. The current total is 48.8 million families, which roughly corresponds to the number of those whose monthly income is below Rs. 350. The process will exclude 50 million families. The BPL people will thus add up to around 40 per cent of the population.[27] Another source says that those living on $1 or below constitute 34.7 per cent,[28] a roughly corresponding figure. At the other extreme we see, for example, a matrimonial advertisement by a twenty-seven-year-old who states that he is a software professional, a BA from an IIT, and his annual income is Rs. 1.1 million. Poverty is obviously no longer talked about.

Did the city dwellers support the NDA, then, as opposed to the rural people? Take the four metropolitan cities of India, and we find that apart from Chennai, where the opposition DMK was confirmed in all the three seats there, the BJP and its allies lost seats to the Congress or the Left in Mumbai, Kolkata, and Delhi. The total population increased at 2 per cent a year from 1991 to 2001. But the increase of the urban population was at 3 per cent, the metropolitan population at 4 per cent, and the slum dwellers at 5 per cent. It is the result of all this that the NDA has lost in the cities as well, in spite of the 'India Shining' slogan, or, as some say, because of it. In other words because of growing disparities. This has been the first and foremost characteristic of the General Elections of 2004.

In view of the social disabilities mentioned above, what Yogendra Yadav writes concerning the electoral results is suggestive. According to him, there has been an expansion of 'the democratic space' in progress for more than a decade at the hands of the 'Dalits, Adivasis, women, poor'. It is because the Mandal Report (of the second Backward Classes Commission, submitted in 1980 and put into effect in 1989 and afterwards) has produced a series of effects beyond the OBCs, its main targets, and especially in north India, where they are numerically strong.[29] Apparently all those social categories mentioned here are, by and large, outside that part of India that was shining.

## 2. THE ROLE OF ANTI-COMMUNALISM AND OTHER BACKWARD CLASSES

The second characteristic of the last general elections was the upsurge of anti-communalism. To look into this aspect we will take the example of Gujarat state, where a terrible persecution of Muslims took place in the wake of the even now mysterious burning of the Sabarmati Express on 27 February 2002. In the elections the BJP got fourteen out of twenty-six seats in the state, and the Congress twelve. True, the Congress did not win, but they increased their seats by ten while the forecast for them had been around only two.

One remarkable element in the Congress gain was that all the three ST constituencies, where the tribals concentrate, voted for it. They had been under the influence of the *Sangh Parivar*, organizations centred around the Rashtriya Swayamsevak Sangh (RSS) aiming at Hindutva or a society in which Hinduism in their own simplified and uniform version would hold sway. Many tribals had joined the attack on the Muslims, hand in hand with caste Hindus and, Dalits in the 2002 riots, but they were said to be frustrated by the 'India Shining' and Hindutva platforms, neither of which had brought them any substantial gain.

How did the Muslims in the state, said to be about 9 per cent of the population, vote? They were described by the *Sangh Parivar* as terrorists, which would have fitted very well with the predominant image of Muslim fundamentalists after 11 September 2001, and also with the popular image of Pakistan, which had backed the Mujahedeen and the Taliban in Afghanistan, the latter embracing the Al-Qaida from a certain point in time onward, and therefore with the American global policy as well. The fact of the matter is that no Indian Muslim has been identified as a Mujahedeen fighting in Afghanistan or elsewhere. But it worked very well at the Assembly elections in that state late in 2002, particularly as there was a shoot-out at an important Hindu temple in Ahmedabad.

As against this it seems the Congress saw fit to avoid a head-on clash with the Parivar in the state. The Congress fielded candidates in all the twenty-six constituencies. But judging from their names none of them was a Muslim. Apparently the Congress again adopted the stand of 'soft Hindutva', as it did at the time of the Assembly elections. Still, in the absence of any alternative, it is clear the Muslims voted for the Congress. This, together with a sense of danger aroused among the majority Hindus by a continued critical communal situation in the state, must have brought about the ten 'additional' seats to the Congress.

Neither in Gujarat nor elsewhere have the Muslims today political parties of their own as they did at the time of the Partition. For whom did they vote? For one thing, they voted for the Left with the Communist Party of India (Marxist) as its axis. In Kerala, one of their strongholds, the CPM fielded thirteen candidates of whom three were Muslims. In West Bengal, the other stronghold, out of the thirty-three CPM candidates six were Muslims. In these two states the Left was a great recipient of the Muslim votes.

What about the Congress? Let us look at Uttar Pradesh (UP), the most populous state, to which the Nehru-Gandhi family belongs. The Congress obtained only nine out of the total eighty seats here, the same as on the previous occasion. The nine include Sonia Gandhi, the president of the party, and her son. At the same time the BJP's seats decreased from fourteen to eleven, the biggest loss for the party state-wise.

Who won in UP? It was the SP [Samajwadi (Socialist) Party], which won thirty-four seats, and the BSP [Bahujan (masses) Samaj Party], with nineteen. The advance made by these regional parties, together with that by the RJD and its allies, are the hidden elements behind the defeat of the NDA and the victory of the Congress. Their advance is the third characteristic of the elections, and the increase of the Leftists' seats, mainly in Kerala and West Bengal, the fourth. All the four are closely related.

In UP, all the four major parties had an eye on the Muslim votes. Originally the SP was based on the OBCs, particularly the Yadavs, and the BSP on the Dalits. But this time both of them had four Muslims each among their successful candidates. The BSP had as many as five Yadavs among its new MPs as well. The BJP and the Congress, on the other hand, had no successful Muslims. The Muslims are said to have left the Congress after the demolition of the mosque at Ayodhya in 1992. Incidentally, out of the seventeen who were elected from the SC constituencies in UP, seven belonged to the SP, five to the BSP, three to the BJP, and only one to the Congress (there are no ST constituencies in UP).

It is said that India entered the age of regional parties and coalition governments in the mid-1990s when the first United Front government came into being. The combined voting rate of the regional parties shot up from 19 per cent to 36 per cent at the 12th General Elections in 1998, and has been maintained at that level until now. Correspondingly the combined votes for the two major parties, the Congress and the BJP, has, if anything, gone down from the previous 52 per cent to 49 per cent.[30] The Congress for the first time has opted for a coalition government. Is India on the way to fragmentation?

When the Mandal Report was published, many people in India, some notable scholars among them, warned that its adoption would bring about a further fragmentation of the Indian society (B.P. Mandal, the chairman of the commission, was himself a Yadav from Bihar). Their warning was well-reasoned, and one may say that it was testified to by the upsurge of those parties based on, or having an eye on, the OBCs in the all-important Hindi-speaking large states as mentioned earlier. If, however, the report has led to the expansion of the 'democratic space', and has thus contributed to the great political upheaval of May 2004, it must be said that the warning has, by and large, gone astray. As Pai Panandiker said, the Indian democracy has been able to 'hold together' the diverse elements of the country.[31] Moreover, the electoral debacle of the BJP, which has been trying to divide the people along religious lines, means that the factor of fragmentation has receded to that extent. Indeed the elections meant virtually the first, and historic, defeat for the BJP.

Closely related to the fragmentation issue is that of whether the multi-party system and the coalition governments are able to adjust to the centre-state relations as stipulated in the Constitution. It is true that the federal system has been badly affected in the past, particularly during the Emergency. In the recent past also the leadership of both the major parties has in fact nominated the chief ministers for the states under their rule. It remains to be seen whether the Congress, which has accepted the role of regional parties and has opted for a coalition government for the first time, will adapt itself to the federal system.

### 3. Employment Guarantee Scheme: A Vehicle for the Training of a Nation?

Where do the election results come into the picture of the 'training of a nation'?

We have suggested that the Common Minimum Programme (CMP) of the new government was a response to the electorate at large which had demonstrated an increasing awareness and had the courage to overthrow the incumbent NDA government. As to the awareness of the common people of India, a sample of testimonies by keen observers during the election campaign may be cited: 'people will begin to ask more questions . . . and the questions keep getting sharper' (T.N. Seshan), or; people will not vote according to their 'inherited loyalties' (Prem Shankar Jha), or; 'politics has always divided people along traditional lines of caste and ethnicity, but this time, there's been a strong divide between rich and poor' (Prem Shankar Jha); or, the 'ordinary, humble Indians' called the 'common man' wants 'a decent standard of living' and points to 'open drains, unbuilt roads, irregular supplies of electricity and water'(Tavleen Singh). The awareness had grown in the psychology of the voters by the sharp disparities, the 'India Shining' slogan, by communalism, and the numerous other signs of our times. The people are thus expecting to be satisfied, to be fed and clad, to be given 'the training of a nation' in one way or another. It would be at its own risk for the new government to ignore all this. It would then boomerang on them. What would be the governments answer to this awareness, to this expectation?

If we look at the CMP closely, we will see that a very important, even crucial part of it under the present circumstances of widespread unemployment and semi-starvation is its employment policy. It says that one person each from a needy family both in rural and in urban areas would be employed at the minimum wage for at least 100 days a year in 'asset-creating public works', and in the meantime a food-for-work programme would be put into place. Gandhi would have proceeded somewhat differently by inserting *khadi* and other village industries as the means of creating employment. This is the first time an employment policy has been enunciated on such an extensive scale, and the first time an employment policy has been related to the building of infrastructure. Could this be the basis of a new 'training of a nation'? It could, but not by itself as long as it remains on paper, and as long as people are not mobilized.

On 9 September 2004, a full meeting of the Planning Commission with the prime minister present, decided to spend Rs. 2,020 crore on the food-for-work programme for 150 of about 600 districts across the country considered to be most backward.[32] The sum was said to be 'grossly inadequate', and the entire Employment Guarantee Scheme was said to need Rs. 20,000 to 40,000 crore.[33] The prime minister officially launched the National Food-For-Work Programme (NFFWP) from a village in Ranga Reddy District in Andhra Pradesh on 14 November, Jawaharlal Nehru's birthday, also celebrated as Children's Day in India, and stressed the importance of such works as water conservation, drought-proofing, land development, and road connectivity.[34] It may be recalled that about a month after being sworn in, the prime minister visited the families of those farmers who had committed suicide in Andhra Pradesh, his first trip outside Delhi, and announced some relief measures.

This was the food-for-work programme. On the larger issue of employment guarantee, the National Rural Employment Guarantee Bill was presented before the parliament on 21 December 2004. On this Bill Jean Dreze wrote that 'the twin principles of universality and self-selection have been seriously compromised by the augmentation of "the states" discretionary powers'.[35]

Gandhi, if he were alive, would have risen to the occasion and said that the aim of his lifelong struggle was after all to see that the people would become independent of the government, or, to use a current phrase, be empowered.[36] A national employment guarantee scheme could be utilized for this purpose. It could very well be developed into the next stage of 'the training of a nation' by covering the entire country and encouraging people to come forward with their ideas, problems, and solutions, as it is so vital an issue to the vast masses. That would be the way to extend the works of Gandhi and Vinoba. Otherwise the second great political upheaval in independent India would largely have lost its meaning, and, we would have to finally conclude that 'the training of a nation' was over when Vinoba's *padyatra* ended in 1970.

## NOTES

1. Government of India, *Collected Works of Mahatma Gandhi* (hereafter CWMG), vol. 76, no. 271 (New Delhi).
2. *Christian Science Monitor*, 27 July 2004.
3. *BBC News Online*, 8 April 2004.
4. *CWMG*, vol. 76, no. 374.
5. Bipan Chandra, *In the Name of Democracy—JP Movement and the Emergency* (New Delhi: Penguin, 2003).
6. *CWMG*, vol. 88, no. 365.
7. Rajindar Sachar, *The Hindu*, 27 May 2004.
8. Goutam Bajaj (ed.), *Vinoba Sahitya*, 21 volumes (Wardha: Parandham Prakashan/Laximinarayan Devasthan, 1993-2002).
9. Ronald J. Terchek, *Gandhi—Struggle for Autonomy* (New Delhi: Vistaar, 2000), p. 16 (n. 17).
10. Ibid., p. 234.
11. Rajmohan Gandhi, *Ghaffar Khan—Non-violent Badshah of the Pakhtuns* (New Delhi: Penguin/Viking, 2004).
12. *CWMG*, vol. 88, no. 367.
13. Gandhi, *Ghaffar Khan*, pp. 237-8.
14. Ibid., p. 250.
15. *CWMG*, vol. 90, no. 477.
16. Ibid., vol. 76, no. 11.
17. Ibid., vol. 86, no. 511.
18. Ibid., no. 543.
19. Ibid., no. 596.
20. *CWMG*, vol. 87, no. 205.
21. Ibid., vol. 88, no. 382.
22. *CWMG*, vol. 76, no. 350.
23. On Vinoba's life and conversations after his 'retirement', see *Maitri*, vol. 35, nos. 10, 11 and 12, 1998; vol. 36, nos. 3 and 4; 1999; vol. 37, nos. 10 and 11, 2000; vol. 40, no. 11, 2003; vol. 41, no. 11, 2004. Those six issues are special numbers on Vinoba Sannidhi, covering 1974 to 1980. Courtesy: Kusum, the editor.
24. C.H. Hanumantha Rao, *The Hindu*, 11 June 2004.
25. P. Sainath, *The Hindu*, 22 June 2004.
26. Ibid., *The Hindu*, 15 March 2004.

27. *Outlook*, 14 June 2004.
28. Tavleen Singh, *Indian Express*, 13 July 2003.
29. Yogendra Yadav, *The Hindu*, 21 May 2004.
30. *The Hindu*, 21 May 2004.
31. V.A. Pai Panandiker, *Indian Express*, 25 May 2004.
32. *The Hindu*, 10 September 2004.
33. Ibid., Editorial, 'Going Back on a Big Promise', 13 September 2004.
34. *The Hindu*, 15 November 2004.
35. Jean Dreze, *The Hindu*, 31 December 2004.
36. For example, *CWMG*, vol. 89, nos. 346ff., where Gandhi repeatedly pleads for decontrol of some commodities, and says that it would make people less dependent on the government and able to broaden their view. Or, vol. 90, no. 461, where he talks of building a society that does not depend on a strong and centralized government. This writer is doubtful whether Gandhi would have been happy with the current term 'empowerment'. Probably it is somewhat different from his idea of making the people and the society independent of the government. Here it may be worth revisiting the subtitle of Terchek's book quoted above, *Struggle for Autonomy*.

# Index

capitalism and social
configuration 23-5
class structure and interest
articulation 25-7
communal riots *see* conflict/riots/
violence; *see also*
communalism
communalism 56; **and
colonialism**: 363-6; Aligarh
Muslim University 367;
anglicized Muslim elite 366;
British Indian Association of
the Oudh Taluqdars 367;
caste-class dichotomy 364;
Education Commission 367;
first British census 364-5; in
Bengal 364; Indian middle
class 365; Indian National
Congress 365; Muslim League
366, 368; Nawab Viquar-al-
Mulk 366; Sir Chhotu Ram
368; Sir Sayyed Ahmed Khan
367; Sir Sikander Hayyat
Khan 368; Syed Hussian
Bilgrami 366; United Indian
Patriotic Association 367;
**sociology of:** 368-9; class
rivalry and power sharing
369-70; and class struggle in
colonial days 370-1; and
politics 372-6; Right and
Hindu 372-3; Left,
modernizers and question of
373-6; modernization and
Left 386-94; Nationalism and
modernizers 386-8; and
modernization 388-91; Sir Tej
Bahadur Sapru's formula for
Hindu–Muslim unity 388
Communist Party of India
(Marxist) 416
conflict/riots/violence, *see also*
Gujarat, communal riots;
caste violence 56; class

struggles 55-6; differences in
346-8; ethnic/religious groups
54; ethno-national political
violence 55; factors of 343-4;
gang wars 55; Huntington on
68; inter-ethnic struggle 55;
internal 76; management of
59-60; in Meerut 340;
monopoly of 29; pogroms 56;
reasons for 341-8; regional
47-51; riot-prone cities 347;
sectarian clashes 54-55; social
banditry 56; structures of 57-
62; transformation 65-71;
types of 56-7; typology of 54-
7; vernacular journalists and
350
Congress, Common Minimum
Programme 401, 418;
Emergency 417, Employment
guarantee scheme 418; food-
for-work programme 418-19;
Manmohan Singh 412; and
soft Hindutva 416

decolonization 32
democracy *vs* democratization 27-
9

East Pakistan *see* Bangladesh
ethno-sub-nationalist movements
303

federalism 21

Gandhi, Indira, assassination of
53, 60; Sikh massacre 57, 60
Gandhi, Mahatma, Ahimsa 403;
Bhikhu Parekh on 405-6; his
Congress Constitution 410;
Dipankar Gupta on 400;
*Harijan* 403; independent
India and 400; Indo-Chinese
war 402; and internal politics